The Integrated Self

THE
INTEGRATED
SELF

AUGUSTINE,
THE BIBLE,
AND
ANCIENT
THOUGHT

BRIAN STOCK

PENN

UNIVERSITY OF PENNSYLVANIA PRESS

PHILADELPHIA

A volume in the Haney Foundation Series, established in 1961
with the generous support of Dr. John Louis Haney.

Published by
University of Pennsylvania Press
Philadelphia, Pennsylvania 19104-4112
www.upenn.edu/pennpress

Printed in the United States of America on acid-free paper
1 3 5 7 9 10 8 6 4 2

Library of Congress Cataloging-in-Publication Data
ISBN 978-0-8122-4871-5

to
Giles Constable
and in memory of
Olivia Remie Constable

CONTENTS

Introduction

The major theme of the essays in this collection is the configuration of the self in Augustine of Hippo.

Augustine's concept of the self is traditionally understood to be a product of rhetorical and philosophical influences, as well as his personal manner of approaching questions of identity through autobiography. Throughout the book I speak of this way of conceiving the self as "integrated." In adopting this term I have in mind Augustine's use of different disciplines in giving form to his notion of the self, as well as one salient feature of his thinking. This consists in replacing a dualistic view of the self, which he took over from Platonic and Neoplatonic sources, with a view that is largely inspired by the Bible, in which mind and body are given roughly equal roles in the self's makeup.

In Chapters 2 and 3 I draw attention to a second feature of Augustine's thinking about the self. This is its pragmatic nature. Nowhere in his writings do we come upon a purely conceptual scheme for the self's configuration. His attitude to questions involving the self, personal identity, or the notion of the individual is on the whole practical rather than theoretical, and even when theoretical, for example in speaking of will, memory, and time, he is strongly influenced by his personal experience. This is particularly true of his statements on the self in the *Confessions*, where many of his important insights on the subject are found.

In approaching the self in this manner, Augustine made frequent use of a pair of literary strategies, neither of which was his invention. One of these was the Socratic method of self-examination, which is utilized extensively in his early writings and the *Confessions*. This is often found in the form of an interior dialogue, that is, as a conversation that takes place entirely within his own thoughts. The other literary technique that he repeatedly employed was sacred reading (*lectio divina*), which originated in Jewish and Christian devotions and had become a regular feature of monastic life in his time. This type

of reading was an ascetic exercise involving both mind and body in which it
was difficult for practitioners to think about themselves in anything but an
integrated fashion.

Although Augustine's combining of these methods was unusual in his
time, he was not the first thinker to entertain the possibility of a holistic self.
He was preceded by statements of comparable views in both philosophy and
medicine. In philosophy, this thinking had already arisen in Epicureanism
and Stoicism, in which, as Christopher Gill has demonstrated, an effort
had been made during the Hellenistic period to formulate questions concerning the self in terms of "psychophysical and psychological wholes or
units."[1] Another source was the anatomical and physiological studies of
Galen, Herophilus, and Erasistratus, in which, Heinrich von Staden notes, "the
discovery of the nerves entailed the first significant erosion of the vast territory ruled by the soul in Platonic and Aristotelian philosophy, an erosion accompanied by the expansion of the rule of 'nature,' visible not only in medicine
but also in philosophy."[2] Among late ancient thinkers, it is Augustine who offers the most consistent and influential thinking about the self in terms of an
interrelationship between mind and body. Also, in his early dialogues and the
Confessions, he presents the period's finest Christian response to the enduring
influence of Socrates,[3] through whom, Gill has observed, "philosophy was
presented as a basis, and in some sense an authoritative one, for setting ethical
norms by which people in general—and not just philosophers—should frame
their lives."[4]

However, Augustine arrived at this position by means of an intellectual
route that did not have as its point of departure Epicurean/Stoic naturalism,
Greco-Roman medical investigations, or Hellenistic adaptations of the
Socratic elenchus, that is, the method of elucidating truth by means of
cross-examination.[5] His chief source of thinking was derived from the Bible,
which he considered the repository of the most ancient and authoritative body
of writing on the self.[6]

The evolution of his ideas on the subject can be dated with reasonable
certitude. Down to the winter of 385–386, when he was residing in a borrowed
villa at Cassiciacum, along with friends, relatives, and junior associates, his
reflections on the self were based almost exclusively on a group of eclectic readings in the field of philosophy, in particular on the *libri Platonicorum*. These
"Platonic books," as he calls them, had been presented to him by the rhetorician Marius Victorinus, and are thought to have contained Platonic and/or
Neoplatonic texts, mostly, it is assumed, translated from Greek.[7] After his

conversion at Easter 386, and for the remainder of his lengthy career, his quotations from philosophical texts serve a different purpose in his writings, both in his thinking about the self and on other problematical matters in ancient thought. This consists in supporting arguments arrived at through the teachings of the Bible.

In sum, before baptism, Augustine's thinking on the self is philosophical in orientation, whereas afterward it is theological, or, one might suggest, exegetical, since philosophy is employed as a way of revealing the inner meaning of statements made in the opaque language of scripture. And it is from the Bible, which Augustine frequently opposes to philosophy, that his mature philosophy of the self is constructed. He is reluctant to abandon philosophical methods, especially those with Socratic origins, but the issues he takes up are invariably Christian in conception and sometimes Jewish in their roots. He uses philosophy to analyze the functions of the soul, from which his thinking on the self is derived. But he is convinced that the origin of the soul takes place through its creation in God's "image and likeness" (Gen. 1:26). Much of his discussion of the self is based on another biblical theme, namely the assumption that mortals are created with freedom of will. In his final consolidation of his views, it is this thinking that he chiefly wishes to integrate into his notion of the self.

In the *Confessions*, Augustine likewise provides literature with an enduring portrait of a divided self, in which flesh is constantly at war against spirit. However, it is against the backdrop of the soul's essential permanence, which is founded in biblical doctrines, that the drama of the conflictual self is played out in the autobiography. In books 1 to 9, Augustine's life history is presented to the reader dramatically, rhetorically, and as a deliberately staged narrative. But the dispersed or fragmented state of mind that is so vividly portrayed in this story should not be mistaken for the bishop of Hippo's conception of human identity, which is ultimately based on theological considerations. On this subject he is categorical: as the soul participates in the eternity of God, so the self participates in the eternity of the soul.

The divided self is the configuration of the self that has to be discarded like an old and worn garment, as St. Paul said, so that a new self can take its place (Eph. 4:22). There are many such dualisms in Augustine's thought, and they are all framed around the opposition of time and eternity: these include appearance and reality, flesh and spirit, evil and good, and of course human and divine. It is important to distinguish between such two-sided thinking in his writings and the principle of integration that underpins his fundamental theological doctrines, those, for example, dealing with sin, grace, redemption, or the resurrection, in which there can be no meaningful separation between mind or soul and body. It is in this aspect of his reflections on the self that Augustine abandons dualistic thinking and moves most clearly in a direction that differs from his ancient predecessors in the field, in particular Plato and Aristotle.

In the final analysis, his view of the self is based on biblical history. Philosophical discussions of the soul, despite numerous insights, have to be viewed in the context of the events recounted in the Bible, which, to his mind, are documented truths. It is in relation to a factual record of human origins and development, therefore, that we must view both his philosophical and psychological notions of a divided self. In his view, the isolated and unattended self is in continual conflict with itself, as Pascal was later to observe, because of an inherent flaw in its historical legacy, which in time can, and, it is hoped, will be overcome. The fault in the self's structure arose from the disobedience of Adam and Eve in the Garden of Eden, which introduced to mortals a type of self-knowledge that was hitherto unknown, inasmuch as it was concerned with the ineradicable potential for good and evil that is lodged in us all.

In the light of this situation, the study of the self cannot be carried on as a purely rational inquiry, as it is in schools of philosophy, but has to be taken up by means of a combination of philosophy, theology, and history. This is the larger context of Augustine's thinking about the self, and arises in his writings on the subject at a personal level, in the *Confessions*, as well as within his conception of the playing out of history itself. It is this process that he has in mind at the beginning of book 11 of *The City of God*, where he refers to the way in which the earthly and heavenly cities are "interwoven in this present transitory world, and, so to speak, intermingled with one another": *in hoc interim saeculo perplexas quodam modo diximus inuicemque permixtas.*[8]

This is an unalterable state of affairs, which, needless to say, has ethical implications. Augustine is convinced that there are essentially two pathways open to mortals for the improvement of the self, and both depend on faith. One leads upward through mysticism, by which we can temporarily achieve unity with the deity, as took place, in his view, in his final conversation with his mother, Monica, preceding her death at Ostia in 387.[9] The other lies through a coherent program of reform and redirection for the self in this world, which can prepare the way for salvation, even though it cannot offer a guarantee, by helping us to lead virtuous lives. The method advocated by Augustine for achieving this goal consists in a set of mental and spiritual exercises in which asceticism, in the ancient sense of a "training" (*askesis*), is identified with the patient, meditative study of the Bible. This is an important dimension of what he understands by a "Christian philosophy."

In these studies I am chiefly concerned with the second of these approaches to the self. My aim is to show that Western thinking on the topic of the self cannot be said to have arisen through a series of purely conceptual advances, as suggested in an influential study by Charles Taylor and other analytical explorations of the theme,[10] but from a combination of theory and practice in which, in its late ancient stages at least, practice appears to have played a very large part. The chapters of the book are designed as a set of essays that deal with different dimensions of this way of approaching the self. In Chapter 1, I am concerned with the principles of late ancient sacred reading as they are outlined in the writings of two acknowledged founders of this discipline, John Cassian and Benedict of Nursia. In Chapter 2, I suggest that Augustine's notion of the self is a combination of elements taken from this discipline as well as from his thinking about the creative imagination. Chapter 3 turns to a dimension of the late ancient revival of the Socratic elenchus: this consists in the use of inner dialogue for seeking self-knowledge and ethical guidelines for life. Chapters 4 and 5, continuing the discussion of related themes, deal respectively with the relationship between soul and self in two early works of Augustine and with his reinterpretation of the Platonic notion of reminiscence as a type of literary memory. In Chapter 6, by way of conclusion, I move forward in time to a contemporary topic which has links with late ancient and medieval ideas about mind and body. This is the use of meditative and contemplative techniques in alternative medicine, which, I propose, are the outgrowth of both Christian and non-Christian traditions.

* * *

In the background of these studies, and serving as their foundation, is the considerable amount of research that has been done by scholars over the past two generations, in which it has been shown that the centuries between the birth of Cicero in 106 B.C. and the death of Augustine in 430 A.D. constitute a period of growth in reflection on the elusive entity that we call the self.[11]

Among Hellenistic thinkers who took an interest in the practical as well as theoretical aspects of the subject were Seneca and Plutarch; later contributions were made by Epictetus, Marcus Aurelius, Plotinus, Augustine, and Boethius. The Western conception of the self was highly influenced by Augustine and Boethius down to the eleventh and twelfth centuries, when new directions in thinking on the nature of the person and the problem of individuality arose from within European thought, for example in Peter Abelard, Bernard of Clairvaux, and a variety of authors writing in Old French.[12] It is during this period as well that one sees the first significant modification of the biblical model of the self under the influence of a new type of naturalism based on empirical observations in such writers as Bernardus Silvestris, Thierry of Chartres, and William of Conches.

Late in the century and continuing into the thirteenth, the intellectual landscape for discussions of the self was altered by the reception of the full corpus of Aristotle's writings from Greek and Arabic sources. However, even after the assimilation and transformation of his teachings on the nature of the soul by thinkers such as Aquinas, Albert the Great, Duns Scotus, and William of Ockham, Augustine continued to exert a powerful attraction on both the literary and philosophical notions of the self. His distinctive use of the dialogue as a vehicle of self-exploration reappeared in a literary context in Dante and Petrarch, while his views on the philosophical dimensions of self-hood were taken up by a diverse group of writers at the end of the Middle Ages and during the Renaissance, including Bonaventure, Ficino, and Montaigne. In Descartes's *Meditations*, begun in 1639, the Augustinian proof of the self's existence was transformed into an iconic formula of both popular and learned thinking on the subject, namely "Cogito ergo sum." In John Locke, who died in 1704, the notion of the soul was definitively abandoned, and philosophical writing on the subject was subsequently concerned only with the self. The dialogic conception of the self was rethought by Rousseau.

In view of the length and complexity of Augustine's influence on these developments, it is tempting to argue that, along with Plato, Aristotle, and possibly Plotinus, he can legitimately be considered one of the founding figures in Western thinking on the self. As the classical age comes to an end, there is no work of literature or philosophy that so dramatically focuses on the nature, internal conflict, and ethical parameters of the self as the *Confessions*. However, problems arise when we try to situate Augustine's thinking on the self within the curriculum of ancient disciplines dealing with aspects of the topic, since, unlike Platonists, Aristotelians, Epicureans, and Stoics, his reflections were not expressed uniquely within a conceptual tradition but through a flexible combination of philosophy, theology, and literature. Also, in the literary dimension of his writings on the theme, he is heir to expressions of selfhood in ancient drama and epic that have their origin in the deliberative speeches in Homer.[13]

If an attempt is made to grasp his thinking on the self as a whole, therefore, and to give a specific meaning to the term "integrated" in discussing its parameters, it must be done through more than one discipline in the late ancient curriculum. This is a daunting task, and is made more difficult by another aspect of Augustine's configuration of the self, namely the manner in which his thinking incorporates a union of philosophy and rhetoric. By the time he wrote the *Confessions*, between 397 and 400 A.D., the venerable dispute between these disciplines had been settled in favor of a compromise. The argument against the unprincipled use of the persuasive arts that is found, for example, in Plato's *Gorgias*, was largely accepted, but an answer had been framed in which it was proposed that philosophy and rhetoric could work together in a mutually beneficial manner in the creation of an ethical outlook, as they do in Cicero. By Augustine's time it was no longer thought that a hard-and-fast division between the two disciplines was possible or even desirable among pagans or Christians.

The reassessment of the relationship between philosophy and rhetoric was accompanied by changes in the way these and other disciplines were taught. This consisted in the use of doxographies or handbooks, in which the essentials of the respective doctrines could be communicated in a classroom setting. In the Hellenistic period and in late antiquity, training in philosophy began to take place regularly in such institutions, in which instruction consisted in the close reading and interpretation of the canonical writings in the major schools. Students acquired their knowledge of doctrines by attending lectures and by studying the edited writings of prominent figures such as Plato, Aristotle, Zeno, and Epicurus. Something similar occurred in the teaching of rhetoric, although the transition took place later, when the field was no longer confined to instruction in oratory, as it is, for example, in Cicero's *Orator*, or to pleading in the courts, as in Quintilian's *Institutio Oratoria*, but had begun to accommodate other genres of persuasive discourse, many of them existing in both oral and written forms. As E. R. Curtius noted, from the third and fourth centuries, this broadening of the field was acknowledged in teaching manuals, for example in the writings of Cassiodorus and Isidore of Seville.[14] One of the inevitable by-products of these developments in the teaching of philosophy and rhetoric was that the notion of the self, to the degree that it arose in these disciplines, became more or less interdependent with the norms of a reading culture. Thinking about the self was carried on in a continual dialogue with texts, physical or mental, and it was in the manner of this engagement that the notion of the self was conceptualized, as it is, for instance, in books 1 to 9 of the *Confessions*.

During the period of these changes Roman education had been gradually extended into regions in which the dominant spoken languages were other than Latin. As a consequence, types of discourse that were designed in the republican and early imperial periods to be heard by groups of people familiar with Latin were received and thought about by a variety of communities whose access to this material was chiefly by means of reading and writing. Like changes in teaching methods, this linguistic development was favorable to the expansion of reading.[15] While it was possible to speak to many people at once, let us say in a lecture or sermon, a written text could only be read by a single person (or, if read collectively, by individuals reading alone within a group and sharing the same text, as in a monastic community). The inevitable consequence was to personalize and, even, in a limited sense, to individualize thinking about the self, at least in the context of such exercises, to the point at which the self became identified with the notion of a reading subject.

Augustine reflects this change at two levels. As a student of rhetoric, he takes a speaker's approach to the Latin language, for example, in book 4 of *On Christian Doctrine*, in which the topic is the composition of sermons; here, as Erich Auerbach pointed out, it is verbal rhythms and cadences that occupy his attention, as well as ancient canons of style, which are transcended in his notion of *sermo humilis*.[16] Later, however, in his commentaries and systematic theological treatises, he is almost always writing for potential readers rather than for an audience that he is personally addressing, as in his voluminous and instructive correspondence. In these works we can still hear his distinctive speaking voice, whose style and phrasing are like those of no other writer in Latin antiquity; nonetheless, we are aware that the conventions with which he is working are largely textual.

His achievement appears all the more remarkable if we take into consideration that he was unacquainted with many of the earlier philosophical writings on self-direction by means of reading that were composed by non-Christian writers.[17] The major impediment to his acquisition of this knowledge has generally been ascribed to his inadequate understanding of Greek. His knowledge of the language certainly improved over his lifetime but never reached anything like his competence in Latin. In his commentaries on the Bible he occasionally compares Greek and Latin texts and makes observations of limited philological interest, as Jerome observed in an engaged correspondence.[18] But his knowledge of Greek poetry was weak, and early in his career he was obliged to read most of the Greek philosophy to which he had access in Latin translation.[19] He had little or no understanding of the theology of the Greek church, in which many elements of Hellenism were preserved, for example, in the writings of Clement of Alexandria and Gregory of Nyssa. If we can trust his recollections, the Greek he acquired at school had to be drummed into him. He contrasts his pleasure at reading Virgil in a language he immediately understood with his difficulty in reading Homer (and suggests that Greek-speaking youngsters must have the same difficulty with Virgil). He sees the main problem arising from the fact that he learned Greek as a written language, through books, whereas he acquired Latin from infancy, *non a docentibus sed a loquentibus* (not from teachers but from speakers).[20]

As an alternative to this interpretation (which, in my view, relies heavily on what Augustine wants us to think about his early education), it is worth pointing out that he was likewise unacquainted with the central figure in the Latin tradition of teaching ethics through reading. This was Seneca,[21] who spends a good deal of time in the *Moral Epistles* drawing the attention of his protégé, Lucilius, to the value of instructive books.[22] His advice consists in gems of pedagogy and common sense, especially in the early letters, along with studied reflections on Stoic writings, which are fleshed out as the correspondence proceeds. Scattered about in the letters is a series of pointers on how to read seriously, with depth and meaning; we assume that these reflect not only Seneca's views but those of other teachers of philosophy in his time.

The image of the letter writer is thus united with that of the author of philosophical dialogues in the evolution of the Hellenistic methods used for ethical instruction.[23] Lucilius is advised not to take up many books but to concentrate on a few well-chosen classics; these are to be read, reread, and thought about, until their message is securely in his mind (*in animo fideliter sedeat*, 2.1). Through this he is to learn the value of focused attention, which, in Seneca's view, is a necessary step toward dispossessing oneself of negative or unwanted emotion. During periods of study he should eliminate from his field of perception anything that does not enhance his perusal of his chosen texts (5.1; 8.1–2). This amounts to a type of directed meditation, with reading as its catalyst, which is in harmony with the detached and passionless attitude he is encouraging in his student. Guided by this method, he claims, Lucilius will be able to withdraw from the crowded and confused world around him and enter into the realm of his true self (7.8; cf. 9.16–17).

In Seneca, this discipline of reading and meditation is encouraged as a part of the Stoic way of life, as it is, in a Platonic setting, in Plutarch, who talks about reading in a broader context in a pair of propaedeutic treatises which are devoted, respectively, to *How the Young Man Should Study Poetry* and *On Listening to Lectures*. David Konstan observes that in the first of these works, "Plutarch's model for reading, or for listening to recitations" is a form of inner dialogue, that is, "to talk back to the text, to interrogate it, to expose its inconsistencies and fallacies."[24] This advice is an attempt to undermine the confidence of young readers in poetry in the hope that they will develop a higher regard for philosophy, as does Augustine in books 1 and 3 of the *Confessions*. In *On Listening to Lectures*, the guidance is more extensive, since the beneficiary of this work, a certain well-born Nicander, has acquired the *toga virilis* and already attends lectures on philosophical topics. By this stage of his education, Plutarch assumes, philosophy has replaced the study of literature as the major focus of his thinking on ethical issues.

However, when listening to a lecture on a serious topic, the untrained ear is apt to be misled, since, by means of hearing alone, we are susceptible to appeals to emotion as well as reason (c. 2). How one listens to such a speech, therefore, and thinks about it afterward, can be included among the training exercises that are envisaged for a life in philosophy. Because the lectures in question are assumed to be read from prepared texts, we can conclude that the type of study recommended by Plutarch does not differ from the informed and directed reading that constitutes Seneca's advice to Lucilius. In both cases the text is conceived as being communicated to a single person, and opinions on its value are generated from within.

However, Plutarch goes a step further than Seneca in suggesting that this component of Nicander's training may require a theoretical foundation. This is necessary because a person who attends a lecture experiences an instructive text in an isolated fashion and lacks the spiritual guidance that normally accompanies the late Hellenistic introduction to the philosophical life.[25] The hearer has to rely chiefly, although not perhaps exclusively, on himself for understanding the lessons that are to be drawn from the talk. In Plutarch's view, the difficulties of such a task are many, especially for a beginner. The safest policy is for him to remain silent (c. 4), and, while listening to what is being said, to pay attention to the content of the text as well as to his own state of mind, as the lecture proceeds. Above all he is to be circumspect in his deliberations. If, for instance, the speaker displays an inappropriate level of emotion (let us say envy of another person that goes beyond what is necessary in the context), he has to be aware that his attention may be distracted from the otherwise useful content of the speech. He may wish to intervene at this point and criticize the speaker for his exaggeration. But he should resist this impulse, since it is more important for him to pass judgment on what is being said (c. 5). If valid points are made, the techniques of argumentation should be noted, so that they can be imitated, but if the speaker displays weaknesses in thought or expression, consideration must be given as to how these can be avoided.

In chapter 6 of the treatise, Plutarch goes beyond this advice and offers the potential listener some specific instructions which take the form of a mental exercise. This anticipates the use of such configurations by a number of Greek and Latin authors in the Platonic tradition, including Augustine, who are interested in the contemplative practices associated with the disciplines they study.[26] In cases in which Nicander perceives that the speaker in question has committed errors in speech or in behavior, he should first transfer his scrutiny of the situation, as noted, from the speaker to himself and ask himself whether he might not in similar circumstances be susceptible to the same sorts of mistakes. For, in Plutarch's view of interpretive situations, the chief philosophical reason for drawing attention to the type of faults that occur in the speaker's words is to find a way of correcting them, either in others or in ourselves, so that they will not occur again. When we look into someone's eyes, he notes, we frequently see what is reflected in our own; in a similar way, we can arrive at a mental picture of how we must sound when we speak in public by listening to the speeches of others, utilizing a type of *phantasia* (mental impression).

Plutarch then advises the listener to compare the words that have been spoken with the words that he himself might utilize in the same circumstances. Once the lecture is finished and, with the audience dispersed, he finds himself alone, he should concentrate his thoughts on the topics that in his view were inadequately dealt with. Then he should give a silent speech to himself in which he improves on what he heard, adding what the speaker has left out and putting the talk in a better form. He may even address the central theme in a new way. This, Plutarch observes (perhaps not altogether accurately), is what Plato did after hearing the discourse of Lysias, which is recorded in the *Phaedrus* and forms the basis for the subsequent dialogue. It would have been easy, he proposes, for a thinker with Plato's talents to limit himself to his objections to what Lysias had allegedly said, since he had the very words before him; however, it was a more rewarding task for him to reconstruct the speech from the beginning, according to his own arguments.[27] In short, the point is not just to find areas of disagreement, but, by inventing an inner speech of one's own, to offer oneself a model of philosophical behavior.

Plutarch and Seneca are concerned with self-transformation that is based on another person's words or writings, and in this respect they are predecessors of Augustine. In the *Moral Epistles*, Seneca is talking about books that he and Lucilius have read and about the conversations that they have had about these books, either within themselves, individually, or with each other. The latter have taken place when they have met to discuss philosophical questions or when they have exchanged their views in letters. Plutarch is using as his frame of reference the more limited occasion of a single person who is listening to a public speech, either to a spontaneous discourse, or, as in the example of the *Phaedrus*, to one that is read from a previously prepared text. In the *Moral Epistles*, the dialogue in question takes place individually in the minds of Seneca and Lucilius, when they meet or correspond; in *On Listening to Lectures*, it arises in the mind of the putative listener to the speech, presumably during the performance as well as afterward. Just as Seneca suggests to Lucilius a type of reading, accompanied by inner conversation, in which he has himself engaged,[28] Plutarch proposes a type of dialogue to Nicander, which, one suspects, is a product of his own experience of listening to lectures in philosophy, in which there have possibly been disappointments. In Seneca, the interpretation of a reading is supposed to lead to the improvement of a life, whereas in Plutarch, that comes only after the improvement of the discourse that one has heard or read. The one consists in applying the lessons of a text, the other in its recomposition.

Seneca tells Lucilius that this is how he regularly communes with himself (*mecum . . . loquor*) on matters of intellectual and moral concern, and how, through the written product of these internal conversations, he intends to speak to future generations (*cum posteris*, 8.6). In a similar manner, Plutarch invites Nicander to mull over what he has heard in lectures on philosophy and to recreate what he has heard within his thoughts afterward. Both are giving advice to individuals who presumably wish to take up a philosophical life, and each makes use of variants of the same literary form. This is the inner dialogue, discussed in Chapter 3, which became popular in late antiquity and was utilized by both Augustine and Boethius, as much later by Dante, who claims their dual patronage for the literary form of *The Divine Comedy*.[29] In Seneca, Plutarch, Epictetus, and Marcus Aurelius, who are unknown to Augustine but point the way to his use of such inner conversations, there is a progressive firming up of the connection between the literary form of this type of dialogue, with its emphasis on the articulation of inner thoughts and motivations, and the notion of the self, from which issue the voices in the conversation.

The rise of inner dialogue in late antiquity was accompanied by another technique for getting at questions of selfhood, which is taken up in Chapter 5 of this book: this is narrative. Seneca and Plutarch both use stories to illustrate the type of life in which the inexorable passage of time is challenged by timeless philosophical values. Richard Sorabji notes that, when "writing about tranquility, Plutarch says that we need to use our memories to weave our life into a unified whole" and it is "a version of the same advice" that is frequently advocated by Seneca.[30] The tradition of this type of thinking goes back at least to Epicurus, who claimed to gain tranquility on his painful deathbed by recalling, not his life as a whole, but the moments of his philosophical discoveries.[31] Seneca likewise returns to narrative in passages that are often quoted by his later admirers. "Life is divided into three periods," he notes, "that which was, that which is, and that which will be. Of these the present is brief, the future doubtful, and only the past certain," since it cannot be changed.[32] Nothing that we see or touch can truly be said to among the things that exist (*quae esse*):

> For they are in a state of flux, constantly diminishing or increasing. None of us is the same man in old age as he was in youth; nor the same on the morrow as on the day preceding. Our bodies are hurried along like flowing waters; of the things that we see, nothing is fixed. Even I myself, as I comment on this change, am changed myself. This is what Heraclitus says: "We go down twice into the same river, and yet into a different river." For the stream keeps the same name, but the water has already flowed past.[33]

He advises Lucilius to "keep on as you have begun, and make haste, as much as you can, so that you will enjoy a lengthier period in which your mind is improved and set at peace."[34] For the time at our disposal must be put to good use:

> Take up today's task, and you will not need to depend so much on tomorrow's. While we are putting things off, life passes us by. All things are foreign to us: nothing is ours for sure except time (*Omnia aliena sunt, tempus tantum nostrum est*).[35]

Our thoughts should be focused on the end:

> I would put it this way: from the moment you were born, this is the
> direction in which you have been led. We have to turn this over in
> our minds . . . if we want to approach our final hour in a calm state
> of mind.[36]

In both Plutarch and Seneca it is the stringing together of the memories
of otherwise dissociated events that provides the background for creating a
meaning for a life. Plutarch, anticipating Montaigne, suggests that this process takes place in the "store-rooms in our souls, where we find lasting tranquility (*euthumia*)."[37] Augustine likewise considers the rehearsing of narrative
as a "spiritual exercise," whose purpose lies beyond the streams of words and
time and leads by means of memory from the meaning of the text to the eternal message of God.[38] However, in other respects his approach to narrative,
like his sense of more general historical connections, represents a break with
this type of ancient thinking.[39] For he is convinced that stories are not just
illustrations of moral principles but, in their inner logic, one of the basic features of human thinking.[40]

This approach to narrative is an advantage in two senses. One consists in
a personal understanding of the narratives of our lives, by which we understand
ourselves; the other is more general, suggesting that it is by means of narrative
that we come to realize that our will, which is the self's source, differs from
that of God. In an important aside in letter 80, Augustine remarks that our
knowledge of the divine will "does not come about through a voice from
heaven, the words of a prophet, the revelation of a dream, or the type of mental
elevation that is called ecstasy, but through events themselves, as they take
place and call us to something other than what we had planned."[41] The interpretation of narrative, therefore, is both an intellectual activity, which gets at
the different levels of meaning of a story (later authors will classify these as
moral, anagogical, or allegorical) and also a tool for revealing to us what we
cannot anticipate, either through God's decisions for us or, more generally,
through the inherited layers of historical experience that each of us possesses
unconsciously through our participation in a religion, ethnic community, or
stage of civilization. This is another theme that links the story in the *Confessions*
with the historical developments outlined in *The City of God*.

In view of his awakening to these dimensions of experience, it is not surprising that Augustine gradually abandoned the use of nonnarrative thinking

as a means of working out the kind of ethical life that is evoked in the writings of figures such as Seneca and Plutarch. He framed his approach to narrative within a consistent philosophy of language and memory, arguing that a narrative consists in words united in a grammatical arrangement of sentences, paragraphs, and larger units, which are understood as they are recalled.[42] He distinguished within this linguistic framework between episodic and semantic memory, that is, between the memory of experiences and specific events, which he was the first to place in an autobiographical context, and the more structured record of facts, meanings, and concepts, which, possibly anticipating contemporary neuroscience, he saw as being supported by the spatial and temporal context of episodic memory; this topic is examined through the example of *anamnesis* in Chapter 4.

He was convinced that autobiography is a retelling or reliving of events as they were personally experienced, or, as he suggests in the *Retractationes*, as they might have been experienced, with a mind to their intended instructional value. On this view, when an event occurs, a trace is stored in the memory, and later, when a stimulus of some kind, emotional or cognitive, re-excites the trace, as well as its temporal sign, the event is recalled.[43] This conception of episodic memory is not limited to personal stories but is also applicable to the foundational narratives of the Bible, which, in his view, operate on the same narrative principles and differ only insofar as they are related rather than lived, thereby demanding a different interpretive apparatus. This type of commentary is sometimes referred to as *enarratio*; this can either mean an account of events or their interpretation, and, in Augustine's *Confessions*, is conceived as a spelling out of the narrative that is made possible by the connection between episodic memory and narrative experience.[44] It is in this sense that he refers to his great commentary on Psalms as *enarrationes*, which constitute a meta-narrative, or internal conversation, within himself, that is carried on during his entire lifetime.

*   *   *

In sum, the chief difference between Augustine's thinking on the self and that of his Hellenistic predecessors arises from the origin of his views. He differs in what he says about memory, narrative, and history, but he differs most of all his utilization of the Bible as a repository of information on the sources of the self. His view is not based on naturalism, as in the Epicurean/Stoic tradition, on medical models of selfhood, such as those of Galen and his precursors, or even the Socratic method of self-examination, which regained popularity in late antiquity, but on personal inquiries into the permanence of the soul and the historicity of its origins, as recounted in Genesis. It follows that, in his understanding of the issues, the very idea of the self, considered as an independent object of thought, is a contingent notion. In his view, if a person pronounces the "*cogito*," and subsequently believes in his self's existence, there must also be, in the background of his subjective assertion, an underlying and objective reality, in which, in principle, all selves inhere. Lacking this, inquiry into the self might deteriorate into a type of skepticism which was well summed up by Hume, who said famously that when he looked into himself he found many perceptions but no self that linked them together.[45]

CHAPTER I

Reading with the Whole Self

One of the ways in which Christian thinkers attempted to create the sense of an integrated self was by means of ascetic practices in which mind and body could be brought into a harmonious relationship. My purpose in Chapters 1 and 2 of this book is to discuss one of these practices, namely sacred reading, and its relationship to questions of selfhood. In this chapter, I briefly review the principles of sacred reading (*lectio divina*) in the writings of John Cassian and Benedict of Nursia. In Chapter 2, I outline the way Augustine utilizes this style of reading as a framework for bringing together the contemplative dimension of literary experience and the notion of the creative imagination.

In Augustine's mature writings, ascetic practices are traced to biblical sources,[1] whereas in his early works they are chiefly associated with Platonism and Pythagoreanism. There is a reminder of the second of these philosophical connections at the end of *De Ordine*, written in the winter of 386–387, when his young friend Alypius expresses his admiration for the introduction to the classical sources of asceticism that their master has given to the group assembled at Cassiciacum. Among the steps in the direction of the contemplative life that Augustine has recommended is the traditional renunciation of wealth, honors, and the pleasures of the senses.

His inspiration for this advice, Alypius notes, is "the venerable and virtually divine teaching . . . attributed to Pythagoras," who, searching for "the shrines of truth," united a set of rules for living an ethical life with the knowledge of how such a life should be lived (*uitae regulas et scientiae*). As often in the Augustinian dialogues, the student echoes the master's own thinking. Augustine was convinced that Pythagoreans, Platonists, and Neoplatonists had all advocated ascetic programs in which worldly pleasures were to be abandoned, on the assumption that the soul, in thus purifying itself, would subsequently ascend to unity with higher principles or with God.[2]

Although he does not draw attention to the techniques of sacred reading in *De Ordine* or in other philosophical writings in this period, Augustine was by that time aware that Christian ascetics had found a pathway to detachment from the world through concentrated study and reflection on biblical texts.[3] After his ordination in 391, it is sacred reading that becomes the major meditative and contemplative discipline in his writings, complementing and in some sense replacing the comparable methods associated with Platonism and Pythagoreanism. Along with the adoption of monastic practices at Hippo, this type of reading assumes an ever increasing role in his implementation of the Christian ascetic life.[4]

Two acknowledged sources of this method of sacred reading in late antiquity are John Cassian and Benedict of Nursia. Taken together, they provide a helpful framework within which to examine Augustine's highly personal style of *lectio divina*. Cassian was his near contemporary, and Benedict, who used Cassian's *Conferences* as a source in writing the *Rule*, presented a more detailed and systematic account of the uses to which such reading could be put.

In the *Conferences*, reading is not isolated in the pursuit of the ascetic life; it is discussed alongside other devotional practices, including prayer, the chanting of psalms, and the divine office. By contrast, in the *Rule*, sacred reading has a coordinating function in the setup and practice of monasticism.[5]

Both authors speak of the necessity of the monk's renunciation of an autonomous or independent self. In the prologue to the *Rule*, Benedict specifically invites a person who is desirous of entering the monastic life to be prepared to give up the willfulness that is associated with the satisfaction of one's own desires (*abrenuntians propriis voluntatibus*). In his view, community life consists in a suppression of particular initiatives concerning the self in favor of shared values, which are based on the teachings of the gospels, the church fathers, and the lives of the saints, in particular St. Antony. The desert fathers and early coenobitic communities, such as those that Augustine observed on the outskirts of Milan in 384–385, were emphatic on linking the configuration of the self to the ascetic process of self-denial. The Milanese monks made a deep and lasting impression on him at the very moment when he was attempting to sort out the philosophical and biblical influences on his thinking about the self. As a preface to a discussion of Augustine's views in Chapter 2, therefore, it may be useful to review the interrelated descriptions of *lectio divina* that are found in the writings of John Cassian and Benedict.

John Cassian

John Cassian's dates are roughly 365–435. His *Collationes Patrum in Scetica Eremo*, in which his reflections on reading are chiefly found, was edited and published around 426. This work records a series of interviews touching on the topics of prayer, reading, and other aspects of the ascetic life that took place sometime after 399 between himself, his traveling companion Germanus, and some fifteen Christian ascetics, otherwise unknown, who were living in different localities in the desert near Alexandria. In his characterization of these remote communities, Cuthbert Butler notes,

> every man was left very much to himself and his own discretion: "they have different practices, each as he is able and as he wishes" (Palladius). There was no rule of life. The elders exercised an authority; but it was mainly personal . . . . The society appears to have been a sort of spiritual democracy, guided by the personal influence of the leading ascetics . . . . The monks used to visit one another frequently and discourse, two or three or more together, on Holy Scripture or the spiritual life.[6]

It is within this style of life that Cassian speaks of the uses of reading and prayer by individuals and groups of ascetics. The themes touched upon in the conversations include the specific topics found in the biblical texts under scrutiny as well as the spiritual principles they are thought to entail. The latter are occasionally expanded into more general statements on questions relating to the interior life. The view among infrequent visitors such as Cassian to the region's scattered monastic enclaves was that "the holy men were believed to have merited a peculiar indwelling of the Holy Spirit which guided their moral perception and lent authority to their words."[7]

In interpreting their statements on the power of reading and prayer, John attempted to create an image of an ideal Christian community in which monks were living in accord with the norms of the apostolic life. As portrayed in the *Conferences*, this style of life was based on a simple, uncluttered faith in Christ and was maintained, as far as possible, without possessions, even without books, which were frequently looked on with suspicion. In order to present a convincing picture of the pursuit of these ideals in the desert communities he visited, Cassian selected, modified, and interpreted much of the material he and Germanus recorded. The result was a distinctive literary genre among the writings of early Christian thinkers, namely the *collatio*, in a period that saw the appearance of diverse reflections on monastic experience. These included the *Historia Monachorum*, the *Lausiac History* of Palladius, the *Dialogues* of Sulpicius Severus, and the Cassiciacum dialogues of Augustine.

Like Augustine, Cassian's writings on this theme are the product of training in rhetoric and philosophy. To the student of ancient traditions in these fields, the work's title would seem to echo, if not the notion of a philosophical banquet, as in the *Symposium*, at least one of those many spontaneous occasions for dining and serious conversation that are made familiar to ancient and modern readers by narrators between Petronius and Augustine. An acquaintance with philosophy is likewise suggested by the background of Cassian's thinking, which consists in a generalized Platonic view of the soul's upward movement toward the One, in whose unity and perfection is thought to reside the world's permanent foundation.

His interpretation of this principle is chiefly grounded in the teachings of Origen of Alexandria, whose commentaries were instrumental in bringing Plato's theory of forms into the orbit of Christian theology, despite this writer's troubled status in traditional theological circles after 399. Cassian was deacon in Constantinople between 400 and 403 and is thought to have been favorable to the Origenist viewpoint. This may have been the reason for his apparently involuntary departure from the city in 405. He was also influenced by the idealistic spiritual writings of Evagrius Ponticus. Here, as in Cassian, emphasis is placed on an ascetic life based on faith and charity and characterized philosophically by the absence of passion (*apatheia*). Silent prayer is conceived meditatively as a way of emptying the mind and preparing for the individual's spiritual ascent. In both Evagrius and Cassian, this is looked upon as a process of mental purification set in motion by the combined activities of reading and prayer, even though its ultimate source is thought to be divine.[8]

The view of the self that is implied in the theology of Evagrius and Cassian is one in which a person's inner forces are constantly in battle. It is an epic and heroic struggle. Decisive victory can only be brought about by an effort of will. Thus, while the monk renounces one type of willfulness, which is a source of pride and potential individualism, he engages another, more exacting, in search of his soul's purification. The view of the ascetic life in Evagrius and Cassian is rigorous and uncompromising. Surrender to a single vice is considered to be the equivalent of surrender to them all. Negative behavior must be abandoned in all its forms; only afterward can the contemplative experience a type of *gnosis* and hope for eventual enlightenment. In Cassian's view, his most powerful enemy is his personal indifference to his fate. For, when he is not battling against vice, he is most vulnerable to giving in to temptation. In such moments he may be under the illusion that his mind is at rest, but in reality it is besieged by evil forces arising from the outside and from within the mind itself.

Yet this war between flesh and spirit, while potentially destructive of self, lays the foundation for a structured and integrated self. No miracles or divine interventions are needed; no natural forces acting from the outside. As Socrates and ancient Stoics taught, it is only necessary to believe that one can win victory over oneself. The desert monks are convinced that self-conquest cannot be imposed from above, even though, in the final analysis, it is conceived as a gift of God. The battle must be waged in open combat, day by day. The struggle is continuous. The only weapons at the monk's disposal are ascetic exercises, such as fasting, self-vigilance, and mortification. Chief among these techniques is prayer, which includes both liturgical devotions and sacred reading, for it is during prayer that the warring elements of flesh and spirit are most easily reconciled, proceeding toward equilibrium in stages, by means of meditation. This involves both mental and physical exertion, since prayer and reading take place through the voice as well as the eyes and ears. The road upward is steep: advance is slow, and proceeds step by step. The making of a self-perfected self may take years, even a lifetime.

As noted, in his reflections on these issues, it is not easy to separate what Cassian is reporting from his conversations with the desert monks from the moral and ethical ideas he himself wishes to implant into the *Conferences* (especially in conference 13, where he attacks Augustine's teaching on grace and helps to set in motion the debate on semi-Pelagianism, which erupted in 426–427). However, we can be reasonably sure that he is faithfully reporting the manner in which the desert fathers carried on meditative reading and prayer. In analyzing this type of ascetic activity we must remember that

> *lectio divina* . . . begins in the state of mind of the reader, who prepares himself for the Word of God, to read and to savour it, to pray, and to engage it in practice. It is not a question of exegesis,

even monastic, nor hermeneutics, nor of the theological or pastoral utilization of Scripture, but simply of a type of reading that is free and peaceful, but which nonetheless requires an effort of reflection, *meditatio*, issuing in prayer, *oratio*, in which the monks always liked to converse.[9]

It follows that there can be no single formula for describing all versions of this type of experience, since it differs in minor ways from one devoted person to another. On occasion Cassian records statements by the desert monks with whom he conversed in which reading appears to be a quasi-independent form of ascetic practice. This is the impression created, for example, at conference 14.10, where abbot Nestoros tells Cassian and Germanus:

> If you wish to arrive at true knowledge of scripture you must first make haste to establish an unmovable humility of heart . . . . However, take care that, in your eagerness for reading (*per studium lectionis*) . . . you do not find instruments of perdition (*instrumenta perditionis*) rather than the light of knowledge (*scientiae lumen*) . . . . When all earthly cares and thoughts have been put aside, devote yourself constantly to sacred reading (*sacrae lectioni*) in order that continuous meditation (*continua meditatio*) may fill your mind.

The principles involved in this type of prayer are summed up by abbot Isaac in conferences 9 and 10, the one outlining general principles of prayer and the other providing illustrations of these principles from the life of Christ and the lives of saints. Cassian's thinking is well illustrated by conference 9, in which the subject is the frequently reiterated theme of an enduring spiritual "edifice" in the mind of each monk.[10] The most important element in this construction is continual and uninterrupted prayer: in Isaac's view, this is the source and final objective of the perfecting of the heart.[11] It is a labor of both mind and body, whose combined efforts are ultimately directed toward maintaining an immobile tranquility of soul (*ad immobilem tranquillitatem mentis*).

The training may only proceed as it should if the monk's personal health and constitution permit, since it is necessary for him to keep his body as well as his mind in a permanent state of purity (*perpetuam . . . puritatem*, 9.2). The ascetic life, as thus conceived, consists in a combination of physical labor and untiring contrition of the spirit or heart (*tam laborem corporis quam contritionem spiritus indefesse quaeritur*, 9.2). These elements are united in a "reciprocal and indissoluble relationship,"[12] preparing the way for the mental and physical edifice that they subsequently represent.[13] This is a process of both thought and action, in which the monks attempt to rid themselves of habitual vices as well as the accumulated debris of their negative emotions. Only then, in Isaac's view, will they be able to lay a foundation for their spiritual lives on the solid ground of the heart, which, freed from outside influences, can become a source of ongoing simplicity and humility.

The plan that Isaac puts forward is an intentional design, inasmuch as the necessary elements have to be in place before mental and physical construction begins. How this comes about is the second topic of conference 9, and it is here that reading, or one should say, pre-reading, plays a central role. This phase begins with the liberation of the mind from a number of potential distractions, such as the needs of the body, the problems of everyday life, and unnecessary conversation. Also, as noted, involuntary emotions are to be kept under control, especially those expressing anger, anxiety, or depression. And, needless to say, there is no place for sexual or monetary concerns. Thus isolated from malevolent influences, the mind may show less inclination to wander from its chosen path.

However, there is one formidable impediment to the individual's spiritual progress, even if these preventive measures are in place. This consists in the memories of abandoned pleasures, which, Isaac is convinced, cannot be eradicated permanently or completely, no matter what precautions are taken in advance. The abbot reminds his visitors that

> we have to guard above all against our memories. Whatever we have conceived in our minds before the time of prayer is carried with us into the moment when we pray, since by necessity it has been incorporated into our mental records. Therefore, as we would wish ourselves to be during prayer, so we must endeavour to be before we pray, for the disposition of the mind during prayer depends on its state preceding prayer.

Negative thoughts, for example, those involving fear, sadness, or forms of personal indisposition, can be reintroduced involuntarily and effortlessly into our minds by means of a combination of memory and imagination. As mental events, these thoughts appear to us with clarity and vividness, as if they were taking place at that very moment rather than being recalled from a previous time.[14] In coming to life in this manner, they are difficult to resist and can easily prevent us from attaining the level of concentration that is required for genuine prayer. Such troubling images may redirect our thoughts to worldly matters that have been put aside and forgotten during the process in which the disciplines of the contemplative life are taking hold. It is because of such potentially destructive forces that Paul recommends to those pursuing a life of faith a series of uninterrupted devotions, admitting, as far as possible, no extraneous or unnecessary thoughts.[15] For the soul, Isaac observes, is like a downy and weightless feather, which can easily be blown about on the random and directionless winds of our cares and anxieties.[16] Like Dostoyevsky centuries later, he is convinced that this is one of the legitimate form in which we may speak of the devil's work in the world.[17]

But what is the nature of this prayer, which Isaac never tires of telling his visitors is the highest achievement of the monk's spiritual life? The question is asked by Germanus, to whom the abbot gives a practical if elusive reply. While there may be purity of the heart and soul in all those who pray with sincerity, it is impossible to distinguish one type of prayer from another, since all benefit from illumination on the part of the Holy Spirit. In his opinion, there may be as many kinds of prayer as there are states and conditions (*status . . . qualitatesque*) of the soul. Their variety is too great for accurate description, even by someone like himself, who is reasonably well acquainted with their different forms. Each person prays individually, and, in a sense, autonomously. As a consequence, the only way to judge the value and nature of a specific prayer is "in relation to the measure of its purity, in which an individual soul progresses on its own, with respect to its own state and condition, either influenced by forces from the outside or renewed from within by its own industry."[18] We pray differently if we are happy or sad, if satisfied with what we have or beset with temptation. Our attitude varies, depending on whether we are actively seeking virtue or grace or merely averting vice; whether we are thinking about the life of the blessed or hell and the last judgment, whether we sense that we are in peril and react defensively, or have security, and benefit from tranquility. In short, our point of view changes, chiefly in consideration of whether our minds are turned upward or remain below, entangled in worldly concerns.[19] In this context, Isaac suggests, an act of devotion is essentially a promise made to God[20] and a statement of intentions, which can take one of four forms: prayer itself, or a supplication, plea, or blessing.[21]

At conference 9.26, the visitors are given a brief but moving description of one of these styles of prayer, namely the reading of psalms. The lesson is delivered by Isaac, who prefaces his account by asking if there is anyone who might have the experience necessary to analyze the different forms of compunction that arise during prayer and therefore be able to give an account of their respective sources. Who, he asks, among the monks, can speak authoritatively of the means by which the soul is "inflamed" and "uplifted" in fervent devotion? Requesting the Lord's help, he recalls (*reminisci*) occasions when he himself has undergone this type of mental elevation. His words can be rendered in this way:

> I chant a psalm. A verse of the psalm inflames my heart. And when
> I listen to the music in the voice of one of my brethren, chanting a
> psalm, our souls are moved together. They arise, as if from sleep,
> and ascend, united in ardent prayer. I know, as well, that the
> singularity and seriousness of someone chanting the psalms can
> inspire great fervor in the minds of the bystanders, who are only
> listening.[22]

It is difficult not to be impressed by the sincerity of this description. However, it is necessary to note that this account differs from more intimate types of prayer that are outlined in conference 9. In contrast to the recitation of the psalms, the latter are intended to be frequent and brief.[23] Also, as prayers they are entirely internal, silent, and secret. For, following the Lord's instructions in the Sermon on the Mount, one should, so to speak, in preparing to pray, first go into one's room and shut the door.[24] In Isaac's interpretation of this statement, "to pray in our room" means to withdraw from the tumult of our thoughts and anxieties and to pray secretly (*secreto*) and intimately (*familiariter*) whenever, as individuals, we offer our prayers to the Lord (9.35). Not only are we to perform these duties in physical privacy: by "shutting the door" it is also suggested that we should pray entirely within ourselves, without opening our mouths or uttering a sound. Our inner silence will thereby offer a real and symbolic contrast to the potential disturbances coming from the outside world. In this state of perfect noiselessness we present our prayers and petitions to God, who has, of course, no need of our words, since he is able to look directly into our hearts.[25] Thus we are alone but not alone. Although we hear no voice but our own,[26] we are in silent dialogue with our Maker.

Similar principles hold for collective prayer, which is frequently mentioned in the conferences. These are discussed in a summary passage at *Institutes* 2.10–11, where the emphasis is again on the primary role of attention. When the monks celebrate their daily services, Cassian notes,

> everyone is silent, even though many brethren have come together. One would easily believe that no one was present except the person who rises to chant the psalm in their midst . . . . There is no spitting, clearing of throats, loud coughing, or tired yawning from wide-open, gaping mouths. There are no sighs, groans, or unnecessary noises, which might disturb those in attendance. No voice is heard other than that of the priest (who leads the prayer).

This is to restate in graphic and experiential terms the already mentioned directive of Isaac and other monks concerning their prayers, namely, in order for them to be efficacious, they must be undertaken in the right frame of mind. There is no place in periods of devotion for boredom, fatigue, or unwanted noise, which can only lead to inattentive prayer in others. No shift in mood is to be tolerated, which might interrupt the monks' focus on their entreaties to God:

> It is for this reason that the monks do not attempt to perform the Psalms (in the service) on their own, individually, but chant them together, continuously, as a part of the assembled congregation. In this manner each psalm is divided into two or three segments, and the recitation of these verses is interspersed with prayers. For what pleases the brethren is not the number of verses, however great they may be, but the intelligence or understanding with which they are grasped in the mind (*non enim multitudine uersuum sed mentis intelligentia delectantur*). It is this that they are after: "I shall sing with the spirit, and I shall sing with the mind." (1 Cor.14:15)[27]

At *Conference* 10.8, Germanus attempts to summarize Isaac's statements on the principles involved in the different sorts of daily meditations and to put them in order. In any art or discipline (*ars seu disciplina*), he observes, the beginnings are very simple. One is taught first what is easiest to learn, usually by means of a method that is gentle and encouraging. Later, nourished by reason, the mind addresses more lofty considerations, passing, so to speak, through "the portals" of a chosen profession and penetrating its inner regions. The transition from this primary form of education to the perfecting of one's skills is compared to learning to read and write. Germanus asks:

> How can a child pronounce those simple unions of syllables (that make up words) unless beforehand he has diligently acquired the knowledge of the marks or signs that represent the letters? And how will he learn to read with fluency if he has not first acquired the ability to unite these short and narrowly construed depictions of words? Further, how can a person who is ignorant of grammar hope to achieve facility in rhetoric or the knowledge of philosophy? The same holds for the supreme discipline, which unites us with God. (10.8)

Two thing are necessary if we wish to focus our thoughts on God through meditative reading.[28] First, we must keep our minds still and motionless (*inmobiliter custodire*). If our thoughts slip away for any reason, we must bring them back, preferably without having to go through the elaborate and wasteful process of relocating them in their proper places. In order to make this type of search unnecessary, we must retain them, so to speak, before our eyes (*prae oculis retentantes*), so that we have something to return to, quickly and without undue effort, whenever our attention has shifted, as it does from time to time, without our being aware of the cause, purpose, or direction.

To these classical instructions in meditative technique, common to both early Christianity and other meditative religions, such as Buddhism, Germanus adds a second concern, namely that of self-care. He asks how the self is to be managed and maintained within the different spiritual constitutions of individual persons. The answer is an extension of contemplative practice. If our minds wander from spiritual considerations (*de theoriis spiritualibus*) and we make use of a meditative discipline in finding our way back to their demands, we will have given ourselves the impression that we are returning to our former reflections as if we were coming back to our very selves after a time of absence. It is as if we had undergone a period of deathly sleep (*ad nosmet ipsos velut de letali sopore conuertimur*); and, like people waking from such unhealthy slumbers we naturally search at once for something that will reignite our minds (*expergefacti materiam quaerimus*) and, through memory, bring us back to the mental and spiritual state in which we were beforehand. In Germanus's view, it is the tendency of the mind to peregrinations, if uncontrolled, which is the chief obstacle to achieving and maintaining the meditative state of mind that is the precondition of prayer (10.8). This wandering has the effect of separating us from our inner selves, which are gradually revealed to us again in the process of prayer, as our mental energies are regathered together and concentrated.

This theory, Isaac notes, is well summed up in the directive of Psalm 69:2, by which we are told to keep God always in the forefront of our thoughts. An interpretation of this statement is attempted at conference 10.10 and 10.11, in which the abbot's source is the admonition of Moses at Deuteronomy 6:4 to love God with all one's heart. This, he says, is to be reflected upon "when either sitting at home or when passing on the way" so that love is written

> on the threshold and gateway of your mouth and on the walls of
> your house and in the inner regions of your heart in such a way
> that it will become a continuous prayer, an endless refrain, either
> when you bow down on your knees or rise up to perform the
> necessary tasks of everyday life.

This level of concentration requires a type of memory that differs from that of memorizing a text. This is a singular act, whereas what Isaac has in mind more closely resembles a repetitive or reiterative activity (as in the rosary). For in Isaac's view it is necessary for the soul to grasp the meaning of the biblical statement, not only in the mind, as writing that is read visually and so understood, but also, and primarily, in the heart, after it is said over and over again. The text has to be ceaselessly meditated upon, to the point that the subject acquires the strength of purpose to refuse any alternatives in interpretation, especially, Isaac notes, those that are richer and more ample in purview.[29] These are to be looked upon as temptations to be resisted.

Here we encounter again the theme of renunciation, this time in the form of a deliberate narrowing and impoverishing of the range of thought. (One might suggest, with some reservations, a comparison with the "emptying" of the mind, as in some forms of Buddhist meditation.) In Isaac's view, this is a move toward a desired state of simplicity and humility, whose features have been well summed up by Owen Chadwick:

> This study is not precisely intellectual. It has perhaps an intellectual
> issue or aspect, for the fathers of the *Conferences* frequently explain

texts hard to be understood. But the process is a continued meditation which forms the soul . . . . The word of God, stored within the mind, begins to present to the soul new meanings and to deepen its understanding. It is to be memorized, so that the texts spring to mind almost unbidden. Its thoughts drive out the wandering thoughts or prevent the entry of demonic thoughts.[30]

Moses's statement, Isaac argues, is a version of the first of the apostolic beatitudes, namely "Blessed are the poor in spirit, for theirs is the kingdom of heaven" (Mt. 5:3). It is the person who excels in this type of intellectual impoverishment who best fulfills the prophet's command to love God with all one's heart, no matter where he happens to be.[31] For what poverty, he asks, can be greater and more admirable than that of a person who recognizes the limitations of his strength and defenses; who is not immune to changes in circumstances but accommodates them; and who thus understands that at every moment his life and being (*uitam suam atque substantiam*) are maintained through divine assistance? It is a path that leads from sacred reading, as a discipline involving the body, to the monk's progressive embodiment of the virtue of humility in interaction with the mind.

A series of metaphors provides illustrations of these statements, for example, Psalm 103:18, in which it is said, "The mountain tops are for deer, while the rocks are for hedgehogs." A person who persists in a life of simplicity and innocence is a danger to no one: he merely wishes to be protected from his enemies, like a hedgehog hiding under a stone. The monk is similarly protected by the Lord's passion and, in meditating on this truth, encounters both the deer and the hedgehog in himself. Confirmation of this inner discovery is found by Isaac in Proverbs, where it is written: "Hedgehogs are a weak race and make their dwelling-places among the rocks" (Prov. 30:26). In interpreting such biblical statements, Isaac argues that no one is weaker (*inualidius*) in his spiritual health than a Christian seeking contemplative norms and values; no one is more infirm (*infirmius*) than a monk, who realizes that he lacks the means to avenge the wrongs against him and consequently does not dare to feel the lightest emotion at their injustice, even if it arises silently within himself.

Such a person, if his progress is to continue, must not only attain simplicity, humility, and a state of newly found innocence, as proposed in a number of the conferences. He must also exhibit the sort of discretion in his life choices that will insure that satanic influences are kept at bay. To extend the biblical metaphor, he must no longer think of himself as a lowly hedgehog but take on the image of a deer, as he feeds on the mountain tops of prophetic and apostolic thought. It is in this frame of mind that he will penetrate the deep emotions and dispositions of the Psalms, to take them to himself and, so to speak, for himself. He will chant them, not only envisaging them as composed by the prophets, but also, and more pertinently, as if he himself had written them—as if, in a sense, they were his own private and intimately composed prayers, uttered within the innermost regions of his heart. This message on the nature of compunction recalls the figure of the prophet, as a distant model for pious behavior, while being fulfilled in the daily activity of the monk's life.[32]

It is here that Isaac makes a second connection between prayer and sacred reading, supplementing his recollection of chanting a psalm at 9.6. At the point at which we perceive that the psalms were composed both for the prophets and for us, he proposes, scripture reveals its message more clearly than ever, so to speak, through its "veins and marrow." For the meaning of the texts comes to us, not by way of an exposition (*expositionem*) but through the example (*documentum*) that we have made of it ourselves. Filled with the sentiments that were felt when the psalm was sung or composed, we become, so to speak, its authors (*auctores*). We anticipate rather than follow its meaning: it is for us a set of intentions to be fulfilled in action. Its sacred words stir up the mental record (*notitiam*) of the attacks we have endured and are enduring daily, owing to negligence or misplaced fervor. We recall the good things that Providence has allowed us, as well as the memories of the things that we have, with our human subtlety and insidiousness, simply forgotten to do. We think of the blemishes on our character that have been left by our many personal weaknesses. We regret what has befallen us though improvidence and ignorance.

As we chant or sing, Isaac notes, we are reminded of all this (*decantantes reminscamur*). We discover the range of sentiments expressed in the psalm. We understand what is being said to us, and to us alone, as if we were looking at ourselves in a mirror of the utmost clarity (*in speculo purissimo*). As we are instructed through what we feel (*adfectibus eruditi*), these are things that we learn, not, so to speak, from having heard them (*audita*) but from having had them in view and felt them ourselves (*perspecta palpemus*). As a consequence, they are not like the sorts of messages that we send off to our memories for storage until they are needed by the mind; instead, we produce them spontaneously from the springs of emotion in our hearts (*interno cordis . . . adfectu*), as if they were sentiments that are found within us naturally and form a part of our being. We do not penetrate their meaning through the sense of the text that we have read (*eorum sensus non textu lectionis*) but through our preceding experience (*experientia praecedente*). This sort of prayer, in the spiritual purity to which it ascends by interior routes, requires no images or words (*quae non solum nullius imaginis occupatur intuitu sed etiam nulla vocis*). It consists in a fiery outburst in the mind's intentions and in an inexpressible moment of the heart's elevation (*ignito uero mentis intentione per ineffabilem cordis excessum . . . profertur*). It is a tiny bit of time in which the soul is able to pour itself out directly to God (10.11).

It would appear, then, for Isaac, as well as for his brethren in the desert, that prayer and sacred reading form a single continuous experience of mental and spiritual ascent. It is not reading that is the critical element in the process but the upward movement of the heart, in which is lodged the force of pure prayer. The mind must be kept focused during the devotional experience, and this is brought about by three ascetic activities, namely vigils, meditation, and prayer.[33] Acting in concert, these give strength and stability to the soul from the inside; and this continuity, Isaac notes, is best maintained within the normal routines of daily life rather than by conditions imposed from outside, such as might be dictated by desires or ambitions. The force that moves us upward, and prevents us from falling back, is continual prayer. Yet the condition of the soul during prayer is largely dependent on its condition before prayer begins. This implies that pre-reading has taken place, as a form of intentional devotion. The soul will only rise or fall in relation to where it was at its point of departure. And no one is hindered from working toward perfection because of an inability to read alone: this is just a means of attaining purity of heart and soul.[34]

Benedict of Nursia

Cassian's views form the basis of some of the important statements on sacred reading that are found in the *Rule* of Benedict of Nursia, written around 540. I now turn to these, after which I would like to say something about the type of self-transformation that is implied in this aspect of the program for the ascetic life.

Despite the important role that reading plays in cenobitic monasticism, Benedict devotes only one chapter of his *Rule* expressly to this subject (c. 38); this deals with reader of the week, that is, the person who reads scripture during meals and during prayers after mass and communion. Nonetheless, there are references to various sorts of reading in the *Rule* in which *lectio* normally refers to the reading aloud of a religious text by an individual before a group of monks,[35] even though, as I suggest below, other terms and expressions are sometimes used to indicate that reading is taking place, even if the term *lectio* is not expressly mentioned.

Reading also takes place privately, both aloud and in silence. When Benedict speaks of these types of reading, he qualifies *lectio* or *legere*, for instance in the phrase *legere sibi*, to read for oneself (48.5). It is assumed that the monks are aware of the type of reading that is being referred to. There is no general description of the reading process in chapter 38 or elsewhere in the *Rule*. We know that Benedict is normally referring to oral reading, since in this chapter as in others discussing reading he states that during such *lectiones* silence is to be maintained. It is important, therefore, to distinguish in the *Rule* between the rare and occasioned references to silent reading, by oneself, and the majority of references to reading, which refer to reading aloud. Also, the admonition concerning silence is not usually accompanied by suggestions of inner spiritual reflection; in chapter 38 it chiefly expresses Benedict's desire that there should be no unnecessary noise to distract the monks from the content of the texts being read or to prevent them from hearing the reader's words. Echoing Cassian's *Institutes*, he states that when the reading is taking place, there is to be no muttering or chattering; and if anything is needed, it should be requested, not by the voice, but by a sign.[36]

Other passages in the *Rule* confirm the sense of *lectio* as oral reading, either individually, for oneself, or publicly, before the congregated monks. At 4.35, Benedict admonishes his brethren to listen freely and willingly to the sacred readings (*lectiones sanctas libenter audire*). Reading aloud is thereby given equal status with oral prayer (4.55). In the *Rule* this type of reading and/or prayer occasionally has formal and even ceremonial associations, as at 14.1–2, where Benedict speaks of a procedure or method (*modus*) by which, on saints' days or other solemn festivals, there is a mixture of readings, psalms, refrains, and passages of scripture. As in Cassian, reading aloud is interdependent with psalmody (18.10; 18.18). The phrase *lectioni vacare* (to devote oneself to reading) usually refers to the reading or chanting of psalms, or to a combination of both (e.g., 48.10).

While Benedict does not always specify the presence of a text, it can usually be assumed that it is the oral reading of physical texts to which *lectio* refers rather than to the recitation of passages of scripture from memory. This is clearly the case in the more extensive periods of reading during the monastic year, such as the times reserved for *lectio* from the first of October to the beginning of Lent (48.10). Still another type of oral and formal reading consists in the reading of the *Rule* itself. Benedict states that the *Rule* is to be read to novices after two months (58.9), and that more generally the legislation is to be read and referred to whenever the monks are together (*saepius . . . in congregatione legi*), lest anyone claim ignorance of important details. Unlike Pachomius, who makes allowance for guests in his community to meditate on scripture in solitude, Benedict sets down that the "divine law" is to be read aloud before each newcomer for his instruction and edification (*Legatur coram hospite lex divina ut aedificetur*, 53.9).[37]

It should be noted that these readings are not intended by Benedict to be simply an oral recitation of the text. *Lectio* means reading with understanding. This is suggested by the way in which group readings take place; for instance, during the night office, after psalmody, a verse is read and the abbot offers a blessing; then, when everyone is seated, the brethren read three selections from the book on the lectern in turn (*Legantur vicissim a fratribus in codice super analogium tres lectiones*, 9.5). The reading of such texts is thereby distinguished from the psalms and prayers which precede and the responsories which follow (9.5–6), as contrasted with statements on the theme elsewhere in the *Rule*, where these types of reading sometimes overlap. Some thought goes into the choice of these texts, since Benedict adds that among readings appropriate for these occasions are selections from the Old and New Testaments along with passages of the church fathers. Another sign of the need for comprehension and reflection on the texts that are read is found in Benedict's recommendation that, after Compline, suitable readings may include the *Conferences* of Cassian or the *Lives* of the desert fathers, "but not the Heptateuch or the book of Kings, since it will not be useful for those of weak intellect to hear these writings at this hour." Reading is thus related to the monks' capacity for mental attention and understanding.

The sensorial and conceptual vocabulary employed by Benedict confirms these initial impressions concerning the nature of the reading that takes place in the monastic community. *Audire* in this context means to hear words spoken as they are read aloud. In the emphasis on hearing, it is tempting to see a frequently evoked Old Testament theme,[38] and this is surely echoed in Benedict's admonition to the assembled monks to "listen with care to the precepts of the master (Christ or abbot), and to pay attention to them with the ear of your heart."[39] Confirmation of this view is likewise found in the Prologue, where Benedict unites a number of scriptural passages by means of the sense of hearing; these refer either to the voice of heaven, of the Spirit, or of the word of God.[40] There are occasions when *audire* means hearing without implying that reading is taking place, as when the abbot assembles the community and explains certain matters, listening afterward to the advice of the brethren (3.1–2). But even here *lectiones sanctae* are in the background, since he is conceived as speaking for Christ (Lk. 10:16; cf. Reg. 5:6; 5:15). In this context, hearing scripture read aloud may provide the brethren with an interval in which difficulties in the texts can be thought about and perhaps overcome. In all cases this type of reading is a community event: Lauds and Vespers must never pass, Benedict states, without the superior's recitation at the end of the Lord's Prayer for all to hear (*omnibus audientibus*, 13.12). He likewise observes that reading in order or rank is less important than the quality of the reader and his ability to instruct his listeners (3.12; 47.2). These readings are likewise a way of limiting speech. Benedict states that monks should not relate by word of mouth anything they have seen outside the monastery (67.5). They are to resist hearsay, idle gossip, and needless grumbling.

As noted, there are connections between the various words for designating reading, whether these refer to reading from the page or to listening to someone else reading aloud. In these contexts the noun *lectio* is found 39 times in the *Rule* and *legere* 26, while there are 112 texts which contain the related terms *psallere* (11), *psalmodia* (3), and *psalmus* (98). Typical of the implied links between these various words for reading is the statement in chapter 13, where the subject is how Matins are to be performed on ordinary days. Here one finds reading mentioned in the contexts of singing, reciting, praying, or following along, as a text is read. It is assumed that the monks are either literate or illiterate but under instruction, and that the texts being read are comprehended without great difficulty; as a consequence, most of chapter 13 is devoted to technical considerations. For example, there is to be a recitation (*dicere*) of Psalms 66, 50, and, depending on the day, 5 and 35 (Monday), 42 and 56 (Tuesday), 63 and 64 (Wednesday), 87 and 89 (Thursday), and 75 and 91 (Friday). On all days this is to be followed by Psalms 148 to 150, by one reading from the Apostle Paul from memory, a responsory, an Ambrosian hymn, a versicle, the Gospel canticle, a litany, and a conclusion (13.2–11). To reiterate, in these instructions no mention is made of different styles of reading; it is simply taken for granted that they are variants on a single method. A similar set of interrelations exists for the terms *repetere* (18.10) and *recitare* (9.10, 17.4, 17.8, and 24.4).

There is recognition within the *Rule* of the subjective and objective elements in the reading process, although this is not emphasized or made a topic of comment. *Codex* normally refers to the book as an objective entity, quite apart from the reader's reconstruction, oral or mental, of the text that it contains (9.5; 9.8; 10.2). *Lectio*, the subjective element, refers to one's own reading or to that of the appointed reader. In both the objective and subjective dimensions of the reading process there is an implied connection between reading and interpretation as well as between reading and behavior. It is the second of these aspects of reading that is frequently on Benedict's mind in talking about reading as an aspect of the ascetic life, and here the subjective element plays a large role. For, while the book, in an objective sense, is the locus of authority (e.g., 9.8: *codices . . . divinae auctoritatis*), within the group it is the individual reader's reconstruction of the text that is the source of shared norms of conduct.

A comparable set of relations holds for Benedict's use of the substantive, *scriptum*, and the derivatives of the verb, *scribere*, which is frequently used as a past participle in the sense of a text, as the product of the act of writing (e.g., 2.28, 2.35, 3.13, 6.4, 7.59, 7.61, 31.4, 33.6, 34.1, 58.20, 60.3, 61.14, 63.17, 70.7). It is more difficult to define the range of meaning of another derivative, namely *scriptura*, which can refer to any transcribed text as well as to a passage of scripture; in the second sense *scriptura* is a synonym for *sacra pagina*, which, depending on its context, can mean both the text of scripture and its oral reading and commentary. It is in the setting of these multiple meanings that we must understand Benedict's words to the monks in the Prologue of the *Rule*, in which he urges them to awaken from their slumbers, since they have been roused to action by the words of scripture (Prol., 8; cf. 7.1), that is, by hearing the text read as well as by the message it contains. In this way scripture is said to turn the monks from their desires (7.19) to cause fear and dread (7.21), to admonish virtuous actions (7.25), and to bring about healing through its divinely inspired "medicine" (28.3). Within these different meanings for scripture, there are likewise allusions to a variety of relationships between the oral and the visual. Private reading, as noted, is presumably oral in large part, and is mentioned as an exercise for Lent, when the monks may each take a single codex from the library (48.14) and read for themselves (48.17). Here *legere* and *meditor* are viewed as a single continuous activity (48.23). Private reading (*legere sibi*) is permitted after Sext, provided that others are not disturbed by the sound of the reader's voice. In the time remaining after Vigils, those who need instruction from the psalter are advised to engage in *lectio et meditatio*. These types of reading are presumably visual and silent.

One of the important links between the objective and subjective elements in the reading process is provided by memory. In the *Rule* this relationship is more complicated than that described by Cassian for the desert fathers, in which the experience of scripture is largely one of performative memory. Perhaps as an expression of nostalgia for the monks of the desert, this type of reading is sometimes mentioned in the *Rule* within an oral and commemorative context. But the uses for memory in Benedict go beyond this and encompass a number of different functions, most related to textual experience and to what is nowadays called episodic memory, that is, to memory within personal narratives. One of the purposes of reading the *Rule* to the newcomer, literate, semi-literate, or illiterate, is to have it mentally recorded (58.9). As noted, there are frequent readings of the various chapters of the *Rule* for the whole community, in which ignorance consists in failure of recall (66.8). In these contexts one of the functions of *lectio* is the imprinting of precepts on the mind; recitation is largely a way of reinforcing their permanence and of testing the monks on how much they have learned. Hence reading and recitation are often alternated (10.2; 13.11: *memoriter recitanda*).

The abbot must be aware of his position in relation to the text of the *Rule* and act accordingly, without regard for the specific situation in which he finds himself (2.1; 2.30; 2.35). While he has to distrust his own memory, because of its potential weaknesses, he must bear in mind that his monks are likewise forgetful. He must not be too harsh in his judgments of the brethren's memories, and, when asking them to commit passages of scripture or the *Rule* to memory, he must take care, as it is said, not to "crush the bruised reed" (64.13, quoting Isa. 42:3). He has to be aware that the monks are continually engaged in memorization of one sort or another, and that this is a time-consuming and wearying activity for most. In addition to the *Rule*, the texts in question include passages from the psalter (8.3) and from other books of the Bible, as well as pertinent sayings of the church fathers. In directing them to their labors and maintaining their attention, meditation is mentioned frequently as an aid to memory. But the major role is played by oral and commemorative reading, which takes place formally in the divine office and less formally in the collective reading of texts in support of the practice of virtue (73.9); even, occasionally, in the recollection of ancient monastic practices (67.2). Of course, all the forms of the divine office are dependent on memory, including Lauds and Vespers (13.12).

Memory is thus conceived in parallel with the sacred page, *sacra pagina* (e.g., 12.1). The bridge between the two is the human heart. In the *Rule* the heart is conceived as both the repository of living precepts and the source of action that is based on them: it is therefore the principal link, through memory, between thought and action. The single mention of intentionality in the *Rule* is connected to prayer and the heart (52.4: *oret . . . in . . . intentione cordis*). The phrase *ex corde* throughout the *Rule* refers to knowing a precept or text by heart, i.e., through memory. However, in the context of scripture, *ex corde* is contrasted with *ex codice*, as during the summer months, when Benedict notes that books are not always used in readings and passages of scripture are recited instead from memory (*memoriter*). The heart is conceived as a treasure-chest in which this textual material is sorted, abstracted, and stored. This is not quite an archive but is well on the way to being a repository of factual memory with precise contents. Benedict makes frequent references to phrases like "the ear of the heart" (Prol., 1), "in the will of the heart" (3.8), "evil thoughts . . . in the heart" (4.50), "murmurs in the heart" (5.17), "speaking to oneself in the heart" (7.51), and so forth, and what is often meant is a variant of the idea of *lectio ex corde recitanda*.

Memory also works by means of signs (*signa*). The term is not employed in the sense of a verbal or textual sign, as in Augustine's *De Doctrina Christiana* books 2 and 3. In the *Rule* the sign refers to a level of meaning that falls below that of signification by means of language but nonetheless incorporates a role for memory. Thus, *signum* is any type of "signal" punctuating the phases of the monastic routine, for example, the sound of the bell in the middle of the night announcing the office (22.6), or, more simply, the gesture by the prior to rise for prayers (20.5). *Signum* likewise refers to the audible sign one is allowed to make during mealtime readings, even though, as noted, inaudible signs are preferred. As such, it is a sound that has a precise meaning, but one that does not interfere with the linguistic mode in which the message of scripture is conveyed (38.7). Finally, Benedict uses *signum* to indicate the mark which the unlettered novice makes in place of signing his name on the document committing him to obedience within the community (58.20).

Another indication of the connection between reading, speaking, and memory arises from Benedict's notion of error. In the context of the *Rule*, an error is definable as a mistake in the reading aloud of a written text and occurs when a reader mispronounces a word, say, from a psalm, responsory, or refrain (44.1). We must therefore understand literalism in the *Rule* as referring both to fidelity to the written text and to the manner in which it is pronounced. The punishment for errors in reading is severe, except in the case of children (*infantes*, 44.3) and adolescents (*adulescentes*; e.g., 30.2; cf., 22.7

and 63.8). In adults, competence in reading is related both to correct pronunciation and to levels of spiritual progress, in both the Prologue and the *Rule*'s final chapters. Benedict notes that there are other writings from which the willing student can receive spiritual direction, including, as noted, the Bible, the lives of the desert fathers, and the conferences of John Cassian. What page (*pagina*), he asks, from these writings, what speech (*sermo*) in scripture, resting on divine authority, is not a righteous guide for human life (*rectissima norma vitae humanae*, 73.4)?

The terms *pagina*, *sermo*, and *liber* here are rough synonyms, all referring to the link between words and lives, and within those lives, between reading and conduct. However, if we examine Benedict's vocabulary for these operations, it clear that they allow for considerable latitude. I take as an example of this his use of the terms *cogitare* and *cogitatio*, which are independent of the sacred reading process from which spiritual guidance is derived. In the *Rule*, *cogitare* means to have or keep something in the mind, in the sense of being aware of one's duties toward others (2.34) or bearing in mind the potential judgment of God (55.27), since the good monk must constantly reflect on how to give God an account of his decisions and actions (63.3; cf. 64.7; 65.22). *Cogitatio* refers to the self-reliant thinking that makes possible the individual's resistance to vice (1.5). Benedict also speaks of *cogitationes malae* (4.50) and of the sins and vices of both tongue and thought (7.12). However, these thoughts, good or evil, are always present to God, without intermediaries (7.4; cf., Ps. 94:11, 139:3). This is one of the many ideas that are taken over from the statements of the desert fathers in John Cassian and from passages of the Bible.

Another indication that it is life rather than a perceptual or cognitive experience that Benedict has in mind can be derived from the positive valuation that is placed on custom. The monk, he says, ascends by steps of humility, as these are developed in practice. In this process, the love of God, which he once expressed out of fear, is now expressed without effort, as though naturally and from habit (*velut naturaliter ex consuetudine*, 7.68). Virtue thereby becomes habit as well (7.69). Custom likewise indicates what is to be done in various stages of the divine office (13.3). Fasts too are customary (53.11). The visiting monk may remain with Benedict's community, provided that he is satisfied with the *consuetudo loci* (61.2). It is incorrect to think of these activities as dimensions of texts rather than lives. In reality, they are a combination of the two, in which the overall emphasis is on the *conversatio*, that is, on the monastic life as it is lived (1.3; 1.12; 21.1; 22.2; 58.1; 58.17; 63.1, etc.).

Again, *doctrina*, the source of discipline, means doctrine as it is embodied in the abbot, not in the text. It is lived out and publicly observable (Prol., 50). In the image of the ancient spiritual guide, Benedict is convinced that everything that the abbot teaches should somehow permeate his disciples' minds, since it is not chiefly his instruction but their obedience that will eventually be subjected to divine scrutiny (2.5–6). The best sort of abbot is one who teaches more by example than by words (2.11). Deans are to be chosen according to the merit of their lives and the wisdom of their doctrine (*secundum vitae meritum et sapientiae doctrina*, 21.4). Similarly, goodness in life and in teaching are the qualities that recommend the election of an abbot (64.2). Even the teachings of the church fathers are viewed as being directed chiefly toward observance and not uniquely toward the accumulation of doctrinal facts, as the monk proceeds on the road to perfection (73.2), ascending by steps to the summits of teaching and virtue (*doctrina virtutumque culmina*, 73.9). The reader of an informed text seeking spiritual progress is never isolated with the text alone, as he is envisaged in later periods, say the twelfth century or, more radically, the fifteenth and sixteenth. As soon as erroneous and sinful thoughts enter your heart, Benedict says, the individual monk must break them to pieces on the rock of Christ under the guidance of his spiritual father (4.50).

The combination of orality, custom, and lived experience pervades other notable concepts in the *Rule*. These are all kept at a relatively low level of abstraction. The adjective *rationalis* refers chiefly to verbal argument and the rationale derived from it (e.g., positively, 7.60; 31.7; negatively, 61.4; 65.14). *Exempla* are not written rules but, as noted, the examples provided by one's superiors (7.55), the Good Shepherd (27.8), and one's own acts of humility (60.5; 61.9). *Lex* means law in the sense of rules that are validated or invalidated by experience. Law is not simply what one wishes to do, as in some communities (1.8): it is the very symbol of the monastery, the text that is first read to visitors (53.9). It is the first thing that is told to potential brethren when they are admitted to the house. If they can keep the law, they can remain (58.10). The abbot, too, has to reflect constantly on the law, in order to be able to show the other monks "what is new and what is old" (64.9, quoting Mt. 13:52). *Factum* refers less to fact than to act, as in phrases such as *factum implere* (2.1), *in suis factis indicet* (2.12), and *praecepta Dei factis cotidie adimplere* (4.63).

Finally, let us observe that many of the features of Benedict's discussion of reading are found in his descriptions of the functions of writing. The abbot is to provide all things necessary for the monk's existence: cowl, tunic, sandals, shoes, belt, knife, stylus, needle, handkerchief, and writing tablets (55.19). It is recognized that the possession of writing instruments and reading materials is one of the clearest signs of the potential evil of private ownership, and through this, the sin of pride. As a consequence, it is recommended that there be no individual harboring of books, writing tablets, or pens (55.3). The role of writing as a potentially individualizing activity is deemphasized in other ways, for example, in the stress on its role as physical work within monastic routines. The only occasion when writing is given a precise function in Benedict's conception of the ascetic life is when the novice is first received into the community, and even then it is clear from the terms of the description that the act of writing is subordinate to the oral and ritual act of submission taken "before all." The newcomer must make this profession of faith by means of a verbal statement based on a document that has been drawn up in the name of saints whose relics are present as witnesses and in the name of the abbot, who is likewise present (58.19). The novice is normally required to write out the text of this document for himself; however, if he is illiterate, another can do it for him and he has only to add his mark (58.20). A comparable reluctance to grant autonomy to writing is found in chapter 73, where Benedict briefly sums up the purpose of the *Rule* and makes reference, as noted, to other Christian texts on the subject of spiritual perfection. In short, here as in the accounts of reading, the objective is the following of the monastic life. Reading and writing have only the status of *viventium . . . instrumenta* (73.6).

Self-Direction

Benedict's statements on the role of reading in the monastic life represent a development, transformation, and systematization of the views on the subject that are expressed more occasionally and episodically in John Cassian's *Confer-ences*. Taken together, these statements tell us a good deal about the relationship between sacred reading and self-direction in early Western monasticism. As a conclusion to this chapter, and before turning to applications of sacred reading in the *Confessions*, I would like to attempt to summarize the main features of this relationship under two headings: mind and body and the place of reading in the ascetic life.

As mentioned, the *Conferences*, as well, perhaps, as the *Rule*, were conceived within a background of Alexandrian Christian Platonism. Within that scheme, there is generally understood to be a division between the mind, as the governing instrument in human life and activity, and the body, which receives instructions from the mind and operates according to the dictates of the will. However, when an examination is made of relations between reading and self-direction within the *Conferences* and the *Rule*, the self appears to be conceived by both writers as a single entity involving both mind and body. The view of relations between the two can be described as holistic or integrative, since, at every stage of physical and psychological engagement in the ascetic life, the mental and physical appear to be operating in concert. Moreover, it is not a part of the mind or a part of the body which is implicated in this joint action: in every movement of mind and body, it is both mind and body that are equally involved. Also, there are not "higher" and "lower" operations, as in Plato's conception of reason and emotion; instead, every aspect of the person's self-organized activity is viewed as a willing collaboration between heart, mind or soul, and body.

Reading and meditation provide the overall framework as well as the rationale for these interdependent relations. This aspect of monastic culture has been given a classic statement by Jean Leclercq, who drew attention to the prevalence of literate modes of thought among the early Benedictine monks and to Benedict's own predilection for viewing monastic houses as individual communities organized around the written word:

> If then it is necessary (for the monks) to know how to read, it is
> primarily in order to be able to participate in the *lectio divina*.
> What does this consist of? How is this reading done? To under-
> stand this, one must recall the meaning that the words *legere et
> meditari* have for St. Benedict, and which they are to keep through-
> out the whole of the Middle Ages . . . . Most frequently, when *legere*
> and *lectio* are used . . . , they mean an activity which, like chanting
> or writing, requires the participation of the whole body and the
> whole mind.

A similar sort of integration is applied to the notion of meditation:

> In secular usage, *meditari* means, in a general way, to think, to
> reflect . . . , but more than these, it often implies an affinity with
> the practical or even moral order. It implies thinking of a thing
> with the intent to do it . . . . The word is also applied to physical

exercises and sports, to those of the military life, of the school
world, to rhetoric, poetry, music, and, finally, to moral practices.
To practice a thing by thinking of it is to fix it in the memory, to
learn it. All these shades of meaning are encountered in the
language of the Christians: but they generally use the word in
referring to a text.[41]

Reading and meditation, therefore, are viewed as coordinated aspects of
the ascetic life, whose purpose is to lead the individual toward a state of inner
perfection and tranquility. The framework for this transformation is the
concept of work, which appears in the *Conferences* both as a reality and as a
metaphor for the assimilation of the body into the spiritual life. Abbot Moses
echoes the words of Socrates in reminding Cassian that every art or discipline
has its purpose.[42] In this respect the ascetic is no different from the farmer or
the soldier, each of whom is trained in the skills necessary for his profession.
The farmer, Moses notes, braves summer's heat and winter's ice, subduing the
earth with his plow, just as the monk subdues his body with fasts, vigils, reading, and meditation. The monk accepts these bodily exertions "tirelessly and
gratefully." He has no need of worldly goods. He has no fear of "the vast solitude," of the desert. His spirit is prepared in advance.[43]

The ascetic life nonetheless presents a structured view of mind and body
in which certain activities play a special role. Their number includes reading,
meditation, psalmody, and the chanting of the divine office. These differ from
the other chief type of work, namely manual labor, in one respect, namely in
their relationship to time. In the case of physical work, it is present labor that
offers the possibility of future rewards, for example, to use Moses's metaphors,
a profitable crop or a battle won. In the case of reading and related activities,
the important temporal relations are between the present and the past on the
one hand, and the present and the future on the other. Like physical labor,
reading is a step in the direction of eventual salvation. However, readings, and
their derivatives, although they take place in the present, have an important
relationship to the past. They look back to an earlier age of the Christian religious life and to its practices, in which they are historically and theologically
grounded. Through them, the individual monk sees himself as the member
of a community that is composed not only of his fellow brethren but of communities in the past of his order, who are present and living with him through
the continuity in monastic institutions. In this way, reading is a link between
the communities of the living and the dead.

This experience can be described as a ritualization of memory. By this is meant that reading within the community is the actualization of emotionally charged moments from the past; these are memories of texts read within the religious house and more generally texts regarding scriptural history and principles. These moments of reading are brought to life and recharged with their original emotional qualities by means of the words of the sacred texts that are read aloud and by means of the other ascetic activities of which they form a part. As abbot Moses understands this phenomenon in Cassian's *Conferences*, reading and meditation thus create the occasion for a type of spiritual reminiscence (*spiritualis memoriae . . . occasio*). Their objective is to maintain a continuing state of compunction based on authoritative moments in the individual monk's previous experience and to integrate these moments from the past into the present, while at the same time directing them to a designated but temporally undefined goal in the future. Within this scheme for interrelating past, present, and future, the vigils, fasts, and prayers associated with commemorative readings contribute to the refinement and purification of the soul, interrelating mind and body, and look forward to potential salvation at the end of the penitential journey.[44]

We have then a hierarchical and Platonic scheme as a frame of reference, in which the body is in theory abandoned as the soul rises; however, in apparent contradiction, the self, which is a dimension of the soul, is viewed as an integrated entity containing both physical and psychological elements, which work together in this upward ascent and, in principle, in eventual salvation. Abbot Moses gets around the definitional problem by viewing this as an exercise of the heart, which means both learning by heart, so that lessons are remembered, and the activation of the heart, by which the words read are coordinated and given significance. In the passage from which I have already quoted, Jean Leclercq traces this connection to the Hebrew *haga*,

> which means, fundamentally, to learn the Torah and the words
> of the Sages, while pronouncing them usually in a low tone, in
> reciting them to oneself, in murmuring them with the mouth . . . .
> In certain texts (in the Western Latin tradition) that will mean
> only a "murmur" reduced to the minimum, an inner murmur,
> purely spiritual. But always the original meaning is at least
> intended: the audible reading and the exercise of memory and
> reflection . . . are involved. To speak, to think, to remember, are
> the three necessary phases of the same activity.[45]

Abbot Moses compares this type of meditation to the movement that takes place in a mill when water from the canal, falling into it, causes a circular motion in the wheel. As long as the water is in motion, there is "ceaseless labor," since it is the water's force that brings about all movement. Nonetheless, it is the owner of the mill who orders the milling of the wheat. The mill only grinds what is put into it, just as the monks live in obedience to the implicit command of God, who has enjoined upon them the ascetic life. The souls of the monks are surrounded by temptations that fall all around them, like the torrents of an uncontrolled stream entering the mill. In these conditions the individual soul is said to float continually in a mass of bubbling thoughts. Yet, even in this perilous and unstable state, in which it is capable of admitting good or tolerating evil, it has the free choice of taking to itself, and for itself, what it consciously desires. In Moses's view, sacred reading works in this manner. If we engage in meditation, our mind will operate like a mill that is incessantly nourished by flowing water, whose passage can be compared to the flow of thought from past to future. In the past is the recollection of the spiritual benefits that our souls once enjoyed, as memorialized in scripture. The flow of liquid through the mill and the milling process represent those that we will enjoy again,[46] when we re-ascend to God.

As abbot Serenus notes, nothing in the ascetic life is achieved without effort.[47] The human soul is in a state of perpetual flux.[48] In this condition it can remain inactive, if it wishes (*potest otiose consistere*, 7.4), or choose an active course. If there is no subject prepared in advance to which this ceaseless motion may be applied and with which it may afterward be occupied, the natural tendency of the soul is toward directionless wandering. It will fly hither and thither over everything it comes upon but not remain long in touch with anything. It is only after long practice on well-chosen themes that the soul trains the memory in the methods for attaining stability.[49] For the soul's inherent mobility is not due to God or nature but to our own inertia and imprudence (*desidiae uel imprudentiae*).[50] The figure Serenus employs to describe this struggle against random motion in the soul is that of embattled warrior, whose eventual victory is spiritual.[51] This is the source and rationale of the monk's efforts; it is a theology of spiritual engagement and perpetual labor,[52] which together curb the soul's unguided peregrinations (*euagationes*) while encouraging it and thereby preventing it from being overcome by fatigue, as it pursues the ascetic life. Both need and plenty spring from hard work: "He who cultivates his land will have bread in abundance but he who pursues inactivity (*otium*) will overflow with poverty."[53]

The self, as noted, is thus visualized as engaging in a continual struggle with itself and possibly against itself.[54] The only way to measure its progress is by means of planned and ordered work. This means that physical labor is not only a stage in the achievement of the spiritual way of life but also a means for the planning of that life. Just as the farmer is at work in the fields, the ascetic, as noted, attends to his chosen tasks by means of reading, meditation, and continual prayer. These exercises do not constitute perfection in themselves, even when they are performed assiduously and without deviation from accepted norms: they are merely the means to an end.[55] Just as the farmer chooses the tools appropriate to the kind of soil he wishes to cultivate, so the monk chooses among different exercises at his disposal in the perfecting of the ascetic life. The highest form of this spiritual labor is prayer, which aims at purifying the heart and achieving a total commitment.[56] In Serenus's words, the entire purpose of the monk's life can be described as perfection of the heart, or rather the perfecting of the heart, which consists in uninterrupted and continuing prayer. It is in this way that the monk strives for immobility and tranquility of soul, "on behalf of which he seeks and constantly enforces both the labor of the body and the contrition of the spirit."[57] In the *Conferences*, body and mind are united through this activity by an indissoluble and reciprocal bond (*et est inter alterutrum reciproca quaedam inseparabilisque coniunctio*, 9.2).

In sum, for John Cassian, as, by implication, for Benedict, it is the soul's potential mobility that is the source of ethical difficulties. In its ideal state, virtually never attained on earth, the soul is in theory in complete rest. In order to achieve this state or mind or soul, or at least to work toward it, a certain type of education is necessary. Like the farmer and the soldier, the individual seeking this inner tranquility must take up a form of training that leads to this goal. And, just as the farmer and soldier are taught certain skills, which make it possible for them to engage competently in their respective professions, namely to plow and to do battle, so the ascetic must acquire techniques of mind and body that enable him to achieve the objective of his own emotional and intellectual perfection, which, as Cassian sees it, is the highest form of the monastic life. It is a Socratic method of self-correction, but adapted to the Christian view.

The most important of these skills are related to the experience of reading; these consist in prayer, psalmody, recitation of passages of scripture, and the observance of the divine office. It is through such textual concerns that the other aspects of the monastic life are organized, informally in Cassian and formally in Benedict. In both this is a process of self-transformation; it is also a process of self-realization, since, once superficialities are stripped away, a person may recognize what is essential about the self—what belongs to one person, and to one person alone, as created in God's image and likeness.

Cassian and Benedict have much in common in the way in which this process is envisaged; nonetheless there is an important difference in their approaches. In Cassian's *Conferences*, reading leads, inevitably, if not directly, to the creation of an autonomous subject. This can be illustrated by recalling one of the features of meditative reading as described by Isaac, namely the bridging of the gap between readership and authorship. There is no comparable experience in the Benedictine *Rule*, in which, so to speak, the reader is so moved to mystical heights that he has the illusion that he has written the text he is reading and that, as a consequence, he and the text occupy an isolated capsule of time. By contrast, the emphasis in the *Rule* is on another aspect of the reading process, one which is equally powerful and possibly even in a limited sense revolutionary. This is the notion that reading, by creating a living "textual community," can influence the group rather than the individual in a collective pursuit of virtue and eventual happiness.

CHAPTER 2

The Contemplative Imagination

In the previous chapter I discussed aspects of sacred reading in the writings of John Cassian and Benedict of Nursia. This was merely a sketch of a large subject and, as such, was intended to act as a preface to the present chapter, in which I propose that Augustine, in his writing about the self, brings together the reading techniques of *lectio divina* and classical rhetorical thinking on the literary and creative imagination.

In support of that thesis, the chapter is organized in two parts. In the first, I review the approach to the imagination in the Roman rhetorical tradition, taking examples from Cicero, Quintilian, and Augustine himself. Then, using *lectio divina* as a foundational background, I turn to Augustine's transformation of Greek *phantasia* into Latin *imaginatio*, and examine the implications of his thinking on the imagination in selected theoretical statements on the subject as well as in illustrative texts from the *Confessions*.

The Rhetorical Tradition

Cicero

A convenient place to begin is the statement on imaginative representation in the opening paragraphs of Cicero's *Orator*. This short work was written in 46 B.C. in the form of a letter to Marcus Junius Brutus, one of Cicero's rivals, who had asked him on more than one occasion to describe the type of orator whose eloquence, in his view, was of the highest order (*eloquentiae genus . . . summum et perfectissimum*, 1.3). In Cicero's opinion, the question is interesting but rather difficult to answer in a definitive manner. There are many orators, and each has his own style of delivery. By what criterion can one decide which is "best"? This would be a daunting task in practical terms and even rather hard to formulate at a purely hypothetical level.[1]

In the end Cicero has an answer to propose, but it is not one that directly addresses the question Brutus has in mind. All those who work in the fields of literature or philosophy, he points out, are obliged, in the course of their activities, to recognize the limits of their natural endowments. It would be gratifying if one could write like Homer, philosophize like Plato, or deliver a speech like Demosthenes. However, in the period in which he and Brutus are living, there are no figures whose respective abilities are the equal those of such renowned figures in the past.

The acknowledgment of this fact should not be taken as a source of discouragement by those who, like Brutus, wish to compare the relative merits of orators in their own day. The achievements of such speakers, while falling short of the ideal standards of the past, can nonetheless be considered worthy of the praise of their contemporaries, if their contributions to the field of oratory come within reach of what can be judged to be the highest level that can be attained in their day (*magna sunt ea quae sunt optimis proxima*).

In attempting to delineate (*fingendo*) the best type of orator, therefore, it is not incorrect, in the first instance, to form an image (*formare*) based on eminent figures in the past. Yet he and Brutus must not lose sight of the task before them, which is the evaluation of public speakers living in the present. In that context, he continues, the pair may have overlooked an important dimension of their inquiry. The "unsurpassable ideal" of which they have been speaking, "which is seldom attained in a speech as a whole, is sometimes present in a part of a given speech and in some speakers"[2] in their own time.

Cicero then talks briefly about the second type of excellence and proposes a generalization concerning the principle on which he thinks it is based. In order to do this, he returns to the question of the imitation of the ancients, to which he has alluded through the figures of Homer, Plato, and Demosthenes, but now tackles the issues from another direction.

The image of a beautiful thing, he proposes, which may exist either in the mind or in physical reality, is never quite as good as the object itself. In his view, this is an inherent limitation of the mimetic tradition in art and literature. His example is the image of a person's face in the mind of an artist, which is never the equal of the face itself, no matter how skillfully it is drawn or sculpted.[3] Further—and this is his major point—the superiority of the original in comparison to the copy is not something that is perceived readily by the eye, the ear, or the other senses; it can only be embraced by the mind, that is, by thought or imagination.

Cicero's argument is illustrated by the examples of paintings with which he assumes Brutus is acquainted, as well as by the statues of the celebrated sculptor, Phidias (480–430 B.C.), which were widely regarded as achievements of unsurpassed beauty throughout the Hellenistic period. It is to the latter that he draws special attention. When Phidias was engaged in creating his renowned statues of Jupiter and Minerva, he suggests, the artist did not have his eyes focused only on living persons, who were acting as models of the deities and from whom he assumed the fine qualities of their features could be taken. On the contrary, there was, residing within his mind, a notion of beauty itself, unparalleled in its excellence (*in mente insideat species pulchritudinis eximia quaedam*, 1.3.8). It was on this that his inward gaze was focused, and it was this view in turn that guided his hand in producing the deities' shapes and appearances.

Cicero concludes that there are two sources of beauty in Phidias's sculptures. One arises from their outer forms, which are perceptible after they are finished and placed on view. The other has its origin in an interior and abstract source of beauty that exists in the mind of the sculptor before the statues of the gods are brought into being. Cicero is referring here to a principle of thought or imagination to which the sculptures give visual and spatial representation, while in itself this principle remains unrepresented.[4] In a comparable manner, he observes, we can imagine a perfect type of eloquence existing in the mind (*animo*), whereas by means of our ears we can only be the recipients of its copy or imitation (*effigiem*); and this, he notes, being outer, is inferior to what exists in thought (*cogitatio*). He adds, possibly as an afterthought, that these forms of things (*rerum formae*), which are inspired by the artist's inner resources, are comparable to what Plato had in mind when speaking about eternal and unchanging ideas.

This statement concludes the preface to the more detailed and practical outline of the qualities of a desirable orator, which occupies the remainder of the text of the *Orator*. As this is the only extensive discussion of the role of the imagination in the work, it may be useful to reflect on the conclusions Cicero has reached and their implications.

First of all, let us note that at *Orator* 1–14, as elsewhere in his writings, Cicero has no single term for referring to the activity of the imagination. The words he uses in the passages discussed, such as *cogitatio, mens,* and *animus,* are taken from conceptual domains in which the imagination is not usually the primary focus of interest.

Second, it is not entirely clear what is meant at 3.10 by the passing reference to Plato's "ideas." This would seem to be a combination of Platonic mental representations, in which the senses are not normally involved, and a composite notion, possibly influenced by both Aristotle and Stoic sources, in which the data of the senses are assumed to play a fundamental role in understanding things as they actually exist. In support of this view, let us note that, while beauty's inner source is described in the language of pure forms, the specific examples of excellence or perfection that Cicero has in mind are taken from the lives of real people, as noted, those of Homer, Plato, and Demosthenes.

There is still another unusual feature of Cicero's remarks. The description of an ideal type of oratory is made in the context not of speaking, as one might expect, but of painting and sculpture. Cicero has a lot to say about verbal eloquence later in the *Orator,* in the form of technical advice for those engaged in public speaking; however, in his introduction to the subject he prefers to tackle the issues in a theoretical manner and almost exclusively by analogy with the visual arts. As a consequence, it is not clear whether he is talking about imagination in the sense of the mind's power to form visual or auditory images, as a result of listening to someone speak, or the more general problem of images from the time of Phidias, as these are taken up, for example, by Plato, at *Sophist* 262a–d, or by Aristotle, at *De Anima* 3.3, either of which, individually or in combination, may lie in the background of his remarks. This question is complicated by the fact that the Stoic sources on which Cicero may be basing his view of tangible images may themselves have contained Aristotelian influences.

One further observation may be made about *Orator* 1–14, which provides an introduction to the second example of the use of the imagination among Latin writers that I wish to discuss. This concerns the relationship between the inner source of excellence about which Cicero is speaking and the concept of mimesis, to which I have already referred. If Cicero had been thinking along Platonic lines, as he suggests, there would be a connection between the ideal of the perfect orator and the living representation of that perfection. In order for that to exist, there would have to be a contemporary equivalent of Demosthenes (even though, he notes, Demosthenes has no equal among the ancients or moderns: *admirabile est quantum inter omnis unus excellat* (1.6)).

Inasmuch as this contemporary is comparable to Demosthenes, the operative principle at work would be the imitation of an ancient public speaker.

However, when he speaks of configuring (*fingendo, formabo*) this personage a few lines later, it is not the principle of mimesis that he has principally in mind. He is asking a more manageable question. This is whether, by making use of his own inner resources, the practicing orator can improve on the achievement of his contemporaries and come within reach of the elevated ideal he and Brutus are talking about. Recall that this is a quality of oratory that, according to Cicero, is evident only in some speeches, in fact in parts of a speech rather than the whole. His point is this: the superior orator works toward perfection from the inside, just as Phidias is thought to have envisaged from within the design of the statues of Jupiter and Minerva. If the sculptor had used living models, the result would have been mimetic rather than imaginative. It follows that in *Orator* 1–14 the mimetic and the imaginative are being contrasted, with the latter taking priority.

Quintilian

The second author whose statements on the topic of the creative imagination in Roman rhetorical writing I would like to examine briefly is Quintilian, who, influenced by Cicero, takes up the subject in the *Institutio Oratoria*, published around 95 A.D.

There are two relevant comments in this work. The first has as its topic the peroration (or conclusion) to a public speech, in which, Quintilian maintains, an expression of emotion is occasionally permissible (6.1.1; 6.2.1). He is aware that appeals of this type have been criticized by philosophers and court officials. The philosophers' disapproval is understandable, in his opinion, since in their eyes any argument based on emotion is inherently flawed. It is less clear to him why those involved in civil suits should entertain a similar point of view, since situations arise regularly in legal proceedings in which a resort to the emotions appears to be the only way of reinforcing the claims of truth, justice, or the public interest.[5]

Quintilian reminds us that for the ancients there were two kinds of emotions. One was called *pathos* in Greek and *adfectus* (emotion) in Latin. The other was *ethos* in Greek, and, since there is no corresponding term in Latin, is usually rendered as *mores* (moral habits or customs).[6] Quintilian concludes that what was known as ethics in Greek thought was usually referred to as moral philosophy in Latin. He concedes that the term *mores* can be an indication of almost any habit of mind (*omnis habitus mentis*); however, as he employs the word, it refers to a single property or peculiarity of morals (*morum quaedam proprietas*) within which there is a potential role for the emotions.

He makes a further set of distinctions between *pathos* and *ethos*. In his view, *pathos* is generally interpreted as pertaining to emotions that have been aroused (*concitos*), while *ethos* is reserved for those that are more restrained and composed (*mites atque compositos*). In the one, the emotions are vehemently agitated (*violenter commotos*), in the other, calm and placid (*lenes*). In the former, they appear to command (*imperare*), in the latter, to persuade (*persuadere*). Consequently, when we are under the influence of *pathos*, it is to be expected that we will find ourselves in a state of excitement or confusion (*perturbatio*), whereas when we are motivated by *ethos*, the result is usually an expression of benevolence and goodwill (*benevolentia*).[7]

Finally, in contrast to *pathos*, the expression of emotion associated with *ethos* requires less output of energy, although necessitating no less skill and experience. This is utilized more frequently by speakers than *pathos*, Quintilian observes, and is constantly in demand by their audiences. As a result, in one form or another *ethos* has acquired a role in almost all the cases that come before the courts. In his view, this popularity has come about because *ethos* is both an emotional and an ethical category, based, as noted, on the orator's innate sense of goodness (*quod ante omnia bonitate commendabitur*).

In sum: if the tone of a peroration is mild and courteous, as required for *ethos*, the sense of pleasure and affection that is produced in the minds of the hearers (*audientibus*) would appear to derive both from the facts in the case and from the speaker's moral character.

At 6.2.25, Quintilian adds a further point to this outline of the two types of emotion utilized by public speakers. This concerns what he considers to be a largely unrecognized insight on the topic of the audience's response to such emotional appeals. This, he notes, he is prepared to evaluate on the basis of his personal experience (*experimento meo*) as a speaker and a teacher, rather than through manuals of instruction. This practical experience has taught him that the best way to give rise to emotions that are truly and legitimately felt in others is to feel them first oneself.[8] It is pointless, he argues, for a speaker to give an imitation (*imitatio*) of grief, anger, or indignation, artificially making his looks agree with his words, if he does not accommodate what he says to his preexisting state of mind (*animum*). The purpose of this aid to eloquence (*eloquentia*), on those occasions when such expressions of emotion are appropriate, is to bring the latent potential of the mind (*vis mentis*) into accord with the truth of the morals (*veritas ipsa morum*) under consideration. From a different direction, therefore, but with a similar argument, he is, like Cicero, critical of mimesis.

To put his argument more generally, if we wish our words to have the power of authentically felt emotions in the minds of those to whom we are expressing them (whether as actors or speakers), we must make sure that an appropriate state of mind exists within us before they are actually expressed. This not only involves the work of the imagination: it also means that an implicitly rational decision has to be made about the connection of these emotions to the case, dispute, or ethical issues under scrutiny. It is only by means of such a preparatory engagement on our part that our outwardly spoken discourse, that is, our oration (*oratio*), can be said to have its origin in the same type of mental disposition (*in tali animo*) as it is supposed to produce subsequently in the minds of the persons who hear it, react to it emotionally, and ultimately pass judgment on it.[9]

Will the listener truly grieve, Quintilian asks, if he can find no trace of genuine grief in the words by which he is supposed to be moved? Will he display real anger, if the orator who wishes to arouse such an emotion fails to display it himself? Will he be moved to tears, if the pleader's eyes are dry? If none of these are possible, then, as noted, the first lesson for the orator to learn in expressing emotions in a public speech is that he must be capable of conveying to the audience the fact that he has thought out ahead and created within himself the same emotional range as he seeks in his audience.[10]

But how is it to be brought about that we feel such emotions, when emotions are not always, in fact only rather rarely, subject to our personal control,[11] as, for example, in the case of an outburst of anger? By way of answer to this question, Quintilian tentatively proposes the concept of inner visual representations: these, he notes, are what the Greeks call *phantasiae* and the Latins *visiones*, through which the images of absent things are represented in the mind in such a vivid manner that we seem to see them with our very eyes or to have them physically before us. In Quintilian's view, a person who is capable of creating such mental images will at the same time gain extensive control over the direction of his emotions.[12] He will be able to present words, things, and actions to himself as if they were true and real,[13] and this will set the stage for his rhetorical performances, in which he will be able to recreate genuinely felt emotions in his audience. Note that this involves a double representation, first in his mind and later in the minds of his listeners.

There is nothing surprising about this capacity, which, Quintilian maintains, we all have within ourselves in some degree, even though we may be unaware of its presence and uninterested in the uses to which it can be put. Every person has experienced image formation at one time or another, sometimes, he grants, in moments of leisure, when a variety of shapes and impressions move randomly in and out of our thoughts. Also, we engage in the projection of images in our fantasies and daydreams; on these occasions the images are frequently accompanied by unrealizable desires on our part, and it is easy for us to be taken in by them, even if we are aware that they are inventions. In this way we may become the victims of our own mentally created imagistic rhetoric. We can visualize ourselves traveling to exotic places which we do not know, crossing distant oceans of which we have only heard, engaging heroically in would-be battles with our enemies, giving public speeches for which we acquire fame, and even profiting from the riches we would like to have but do not possess.

But if it is possible for us to be misled by such images, Quintilian maintains, and willingly misled, it would seem, it is also possible for us to be taught some valuable lessons by them. The products of our imagination can be put to positive uses by lawyers, as, for example, when a speaker defending a client attempts to see within his own mind (*animo*) the circumstances that have given rise to the evidence presented in a case. He can, for instance, recreate the image of a murderer attacking his victim, the victim's vain plea for mercy, and the fatal blow, followed by agony and death. Through these false images—false, he emphasizes, because they cross the fine line between what took place, however improbable, and what might have taken place, however plausible—the lawyer, as defender of justice, is able make a convincing case for the defendant.

The term Quintilian employs to describe the vividness of such scenes when they are represented in the mind is *enargeia*, which, he notes, Cicero translates by *illustratio* (vivid representation) and *evidentia* (clarity, distinctness). As a result of this sharpness of view, the speaker not only gives a verbal account of what has taken place (*dicere*); he also appears to be showing or demonstrating the events (*ostendere*), and thereby more easily arouses the emotions of the listeners, since they can readily envisage themselves as being at the scene of the crime themselves.[14]

The topic of *enargeia* is taken up again at 8.3.62–71 within a lengthy discussion of literary style, choice of language, ornamentation, and *sententiae*.[15] In Quintilian's view, what we mean by ornamentation or elaboration (*ornatum*) in a formal speech goes beyond what is sharply defined and plausible (*perspecuo ac probabili*) and consists in three elements, namely clarity of conception, appropriateness of expression, and brilliance of embellishment.[16] *Enargeia*, therefore, which, he notes, is also called representation (*repraesentatio*) by some writers, is more than clarity (*perspecuitas*), since in the case of clarity the object perceived merely allows itself to be seen in the open (*patet*), whereas, in *enargeia*, it seems actively to show or display itself (*ostendit*), virtually calling itself to our attention. In Quintilian's view, it is a great gift for an orator to be able to express in words (*enuntiare*) the facts about which he is speaking with such accuracy, clarity, and precision (*clare*) that the audience has the impression that these facts are, so to speak, on view (*ut cerni videantur*). For oratory, if it is to be effective, cannot appeal only to the ears (*ad aures*). To reiterate: the judge of the case has to have the impression both that he is listening to an account of the facts and that, through the speaker's words, these facts are being placed before the eyes of his mind (*oculis mentis ostendit*). Quintilian terms this the image of something depicted entirely in words (*tota rerum imago . . . verbis depingitur*).[17]

Although Quintilian acknowledges a debt to Cicero in these discussions of *phantasia* and *enargeia*, his account differs in two important respects. Recall that, at *Orator* 7–10, Cicero utilizes the concept of an image in sculpture or painting to describe the perfection of an image that is only capable of being grasped by the mind. By contrast, in Quintilian, Gerard Watson points out that "we have a variation of the theme of *phantasia* producing what it has not seen: here it is a case of the listener seeing something that has not been said."[18] The difference arises between images *expressed* in words and images *arising* from words.

We may add to this observation the fact that in Cicero the chief interest in the discussion of images lies with the speaker, whereas in Quintilian there is a greater concern with the capacity of the audience (hearers or readers) to recreate the images in question in their minds. And this is a clue to another difference between their approaches. They are both aiming at Cato's image of the orator as an ethical person;[19] however, for Cicero this desirable quality arises chiefly from training in philosophy, whereas for Quintilian it is an aspect of rhetoric and therefore inseparable from the words that are actually spoken. For, in his view, as noted, *ethos* is superior to *pathos*, since it is through this type of expression of emotions that there is created in the minds of the hearers of a speech the same benevolent disposition that is at work in the mind of the speaker. It is out of this responsive situation that the evidence for the speaker's inherent goodness arises. It is a tricky argument, one, I believe, to which Plato would have been opposed on principle and on which Cicero would have expressed serious reservations.

Augustine: Two Illustrations

In the second part of this chapter I wish to suggest that these techniques of the imagination, namely *phantasia* and *enargeia*, are placed within the framework of sacred reading by Augustine in his consideration of the activity of the imagination in the creation of the self. I refer to this combination of disciplines as the work of "the contemplative imagination," giving equal weight in this notion to the roles played by sacred reading and images in the mind.

However, before turning to this topic, I think it would be helpful to provide illustrations of Augustine's independent use in the *Confessions* of the rhetorical figures discussed in the passages I have taken from Cicero and Quintilian, and to say a few words about the philosophical context in which he places these visual techniques, which differs considerably from that of the Roman rhetorical tradition. My first illustration is a discussion of the use of emotions in drama; the second is taken from the climactic moment in the *Confessions* when God permits Augustine to resolve the inner emotional conflict that is the source of the fragmented self of his preconversion years.

1. Text one: Confessions *3.1.1–3.3.5*

These chapters deal in order with Augustine's youthful love affairs (3.1.1) and with his attraction for the theater (3.2.2–3). On the former, he echoes themes widely found in Roman love poetry; however, no comparable background material has been found for his statement on the emotions that he experienced as spectator at dramatic performances. A number of ancient writings on the subject are ruled out. He did not know Aristotle's statements on the theme; in any case, Henry Chadwick notes, his view "is closer to Plato, *Republic* 10, 606–7 and *Philebus* 48a–b."[20] But, as he did not know these either, in my view it is possible that he was influenced by the account of emotions at *Institutio Oratoria* 6.2.29–31, to which he could easily have had access in his activities as a professor of rhetoric.

If that hypothesis can be accepted, his brief but incisive commentary on emotions in drama at the beginning of book 3 can be viewed, not as an isolated statement made on the basis of personal insights, but as part of a continuous and interdependent set of reflections on the subject in late Hellenism, which would of course include the already analyzed statements of Cicero and Quintilian. The emotionally charged episodes that are described in these chapters in the *Confessions* follow each other without pause in book 3, and can therefore be taken as sequential examples of moral waywardness which proceed from one type of psychological bondage to another. Augustine differs from Quintilian in treating both direct and indirect emotions and in passing in a rather different way from the personal to the collective expression of emotion. The second of these types will be taken up again in his account of the uncontrolled emotions experienced by Alypius during the cruel and bestial spectacle of the games, which his friend tries but fails to resist (*Conf.*, 6.9.14).

At 3.1.1 Augustine begins the discussion by describing his unreflective commitment to sexual encounters in Carthage as a form of emotional addiction, even enslavement. The path to this type of dependency was prepared by the moral atmosphere of the city—a frying pan, as he puts it, sizzling with illicit and disgraceful love affairs (*sartago flagitiosorum amorum*). He was then twenty-two. He had never been in love, and as a consequence longed for amorous experience: he was overcome with desire; in love with love itself (*Nondum amabam et amare amabam . . . . Quaerebam quid amarem, amans amare*).

In these charged phrases the theme of *ethos* makes its appearance within three philosophical and theological frameworks. These are (1) his hunger for spiritual nourishment, (2) his entrapment in the world of the senses, and (3) his willful polluting of the formerly unsullied waters of personal friendship by means of his uncontrolled desires. Worst of all, he appears to be aware of his dependency and to derive enjoyment from it:

> I rushed headlong into love, by which I was longing to be
> captured . . . . My love was returned and in secret I attained the
> joy than binds one in irons. I was glad to be in bondage, tied with
> troublesome chains. As a result I was beaten with the red-hot rods
> of jealousy, suspicion, fear, anger, and contention.[21]

In the second stage of this involvement at 3.2.2–3, the theme of *ethos* is extended, as it is in the *Insitutio Oratoria*, but the question Augustine asks is different from that of Quintilian. The latter wants to know why we should express emotions that we do not feel, such as feigned grief at a person's death, which run the risk of appearing inauthentic, even implausible, to others, especially those to whom one is trying to convey the opposite impression. By contrast, Augustine is asking how we can allow ourselves to express emotions in which we know we do not believe, and why, if we allow ourselves to express them, we consciously do so for pleasure, in open defiance of rational or objective moral considerations.

For Quintilian, emotions are admissible (in oratory) on the condition that there is some exercise of control. This is provided by the facts in the case, the legal system, and the studied timing of the appeal. Personal pleasure is not part of the equation. By contrast, Augustine assumes that emotion is capable of overriding the conventional frameworks for rational action within which we normally conduct our lives, including legal codes; the motivating force, thus deregulated, is nothing other than personal gratification. As this desire is not the work of reason, it follows that no mere assertion of reason is subsequently capable of controlling it. What is most disturbing about such expressions of emotion, from Augustine's point of view, is that they appear to arise from within ourselves by means of forces that are inaccessible to our conscious minds—from a region that we would nowadays associate with the "unconscious." It is because this inner realm is a mystery to us that we have the impression that the emotions in question are operating outside the traditional guidelines of our moral thinking, which Augustine, no less than Quintilian, believes to be principled by external and objective order, in Augustine's case by God.

Augustine asks why we go to the theater expecting to witness sufferings that we would not personally wish to endure. Why do we not try to avoid them, as we would in real life? On the contrary, we attend the play's performance in the anticipation that an invented scenario will be enacted. We desire a false expression of emotion in others in order to produce a falsely originating but genuinely felt emotion in ourselves.

A second set of issues arises for Augustine in relation to the fictional nature of the plays themselves; this of course does not occur in Quintilian, since legal cases are presumably concerned with established facts. How are we to judge the ethical value of our emotions, Augustine asks, even if these emotions are genuinely felt, if we know that the events on which they are based are false? Put in another way, why does our knowledge of the plausibility of the events not play a part in shaping our moral attitude toward them?

Augustine tells himself: When I suffer, I call it misery, and when I feel compassion for the sufferings of others, I call it mercy. But what am I to think of the misery or mercy that I feel when I know that the source of such sufferings is fictitious? I am not inspired to help the person who suffers in a play, and yet I am invited to grieve on his behalf. And the greater the pain experienced by the actors in the drama, and the more successful their performance in the audience's opinion, the greater is my pleasure in the grief that I experience. My dissatisfaction does not arise from the fact that that my feelings rest on false premises, as Quintilian might assume; however, it may arise from inadequacy of the performance. Nonetheless, my reaction at a play has one thing in common with Quintilian's notion of oratorical persuasion. My feelings are a response to the level of professionalism in the acting, just as Quintilian's putative judges and juries respond to the technical proficiency of the speaker in the case.

The relationship between performer and audience in these cases is not precisely the same. Quintilian's lawyer performs before a judge and jury, whereas the actors in the plays Augustine saw in Carthage perform before a group of spectators. The judge and jury are united in their response, whereas Augustine and his fellow theatergoers are not. Some may like the performance, whereas others may disagree. And a few, like Augustine, may ask themselves larger questions about the ethical dimension of playacting. The examples also differ if we consider the negative scenario, namely that in each case there is a failure to convince. Let us say that the lawyer loses his case, despite the adequate use of both *phantasia* and *enargeia*. He is in the same situation as the actors if they fail to entertain their audience. But whereas, in Quintilian's case, it is the performer's expectations that are frustrated, in Augustine's it is those of the audience. The bishop of Hippo has thereby gone a step farther than his predecessor in shifting the ethical responsibility for such emotions from performer to audience. That is an important move, one that is consistent with Augustine's thinking about the potential ambiguity of verbal signs.

Augustine also differs from Quintilian on the intentions that are involved in the expression of invented emotions. In the case of both the lawyer and the theatergoer, these are preceded by anticipation. The lawyer anticipates winning his case; the theatergoer anticipates a satisfactory performance. In a sense, gratification is felt before gratification can begin. In the case of the lawyer in the above example, this experience of emotion ends, unfortunately, with unsuccessful pleading. His emotions are shown to be false, not because they are inauthentic, but because they fail to convince.

Augustine has another type of scenario in mind. This arises from the fact that, in his view, image formation, as well as the subsequent work of the imagination, form together an inherent element in all human thinking. This is clear from his example. If I am a member of the audience at a play, he proposes, I may have experienced a foretaste of my satisfied emotions in my mind before the play begins, especially if I know in advance what it is about and the names of the actors, the nature of the roles they habitually play, and so forth. However, if the performance does not live up to my expectations, I am disappointed, not only because of the quality of the acting, but, also, and perhaps principally, because the experience of the play, as a fabrication, does not satisfy my personal illusions, which were clearly in place before it began. As a theatergoer, I know these emotions to be false in one sense, namely that they are based on a fiction, which is the play; but now, in the wake of my disappointment, I know them to be false in another, by not living up to or sustaining my own fantasies, which are the result of my innate tendency to form images. Far from rejecting the fictitious elements in a theatrical performance in these circumstances, therefore, I may anticipate and even embrace them.

Like the enslavement to love in 3.1.1, this is a framework in which my dubiously inspired but genuinely felt emotions can be expressed. It is only a step forward from Quintilian's view of emotions, but it is a major one. For in Augustine's view, the worst aspect of this type of inducement arises from the fact that the sufferings of the actors in the end become the principal objects of our desire. No less than in amorous pursuits, they are a form of enticement by the outer senses that exists for the sole function of satisfying those senses. They have no value except in relation to an experience of misery which we know to be inauthentic. The performance of a drama in the theater is therefore much like the performance of sexual desire in the individual, inasmuch as both are grounded on emotions arising from worldly situations. There is no flow from inner to outer, as in genuine or ethically informed feelings, but instead the opposite, a movement from outer to inner, and, in the end, toward an awareness that such inwardness as exists is entirely constructed. It is a form of mimesis, but one in which original and copy are confused. The indiscriminate lover and the impassioned theatergoer are alike in that they are unable to perceive the difference between appearance and reality. Living in illusions, they do not wish to be relieved of them, as Augustine notes:

At that time, poor thing that I was, I loved to suffer and sought out the occasions for such suffering. So when an actor on stage gave a fictional imitation of someone else's misfortunes, I was the more pleased; and the more vehement the attraction for me, the more the actor compelled my tears to flow.[22]

2. *Text two:* Confessions *8.7.17–8.12.30*

In the light of this evidence, we can propose that, in writing the *Confessions*, Augustine adopted an attitude toward the imagination that was a development, directly or indirectly, out of the discussion of the subject in texts such as *Orator* and *Institutio Oratoria*. Like Cicero, he was convinced that there is an inner model or ideal for all existing objects of beauty; and like Quintilian, he was dubious about expressions of emotion that are based on mere imitation. In a more general sense, the vividness of the narrative in books 1–9 suggests that he was sympathetic to the use of *phantasiae* or *visiones*, as well as to the clarity that Cicero called *illustratio* or *evidentia* and Quintilian *enargeia*. I turn to this conception of *visio* in the second part of this chapter and in Chapter 5.

Where he chiefly differed from Cicero and Quintilian on this topic was in his moral outlook. This is demonstrable in the *Confessions*; it is even clearer in *De Doctrina Christiana*, begun a year earlier, in which verbal ambiguity and truth are major themes. This work was Augustine's *Gorgias*, so to speak, in which he offered a critique of rhetoric within a compelling theory of signs; however, the essentials of his argument for right reason in this work are found in a different form at *Confessions* 3.2.3–4, where he sums up his thinking in terms of plays as fictions and actors as falsifiers of emotion. The chief question in his mind, from an ethical standpoint, is not why we are persuaded by such techniques, as it is for Cicero and Quintilian, but why, as members of the audience, and as Christians, we do not forcefully reject them as mere gratifications.

The description of emotional experiences in the opening chapters of book 3 is not an isolated incident in the autobiography, but forms a part of a series of scenes which have as their subject the education of Augustine's own emotions. These can be described as stages of a narrative history of the emotions in the *Confessions*, and as such they constitute a parallel for his intellectual evolution through Manichaeism, the *libri Platonicorum*, and the Pauline letters. In both departments, moreover, namely those of the emotions and the intellect, his difficult journey terminates in his conversion to the religious life in book 8.

The chapters concerned with his conversion (8.7.17–8.12.30) provide an excellent testing ground for the hypothesis concerning the staged use of the rhetorical techniques for image formation in the autobiography, and this is the second text I wish to discuss. However, before turning to these interlocked episodes, it is perhaps helpful to recall that the concluding scenes in book 8 have been the subject of a lengthy controversy in Augustinian scholarship. At the center of this debate was the question of their historical accuracy, and the parameters of the subsequent controversy dovetail nicely with what Augustine himself seems to have had in mind concerning fiction and truth in dramatic representations.

Since the publication in 1946 of Pierre Courcelle's seminal study of the sources and analogues of the narrative books of the *Confessions*,[23] few students of the issues are any longer convinced that the conversion episode and the events that led up to it took place precisely as Augustine describes them. Courcelle's method consisted in comparing the narrative account in book 8 with what we can learn of this critical period in Augustine's life from autobiographical statements elsewhere in his writings. The result of his inquiry was to question many of Augustine's assertions concerning his conversion and in the end to give us a much improved understanding of the factual background of the narrated scene. Yet it left unanswered a question with which this phase of Augustinian research had begun. This had to do with Augustine's reasons for departing from the provable record of his life (although that was not in itself unusual in ancient biography), and for substituting for the known and retrievable facts a story that was clearly the product of his creative or literary imagination. Put in a more general form, the question is why *phantasia* and/or *imaginatio* come to play so large a role in this critical episode in the *Confessions*.

The problem can also be posed at a philosophical level. We have to ask what Augustine had to gain through the use of literary and rhetorical methods that would have been condemned by the thinker whom he most admired for his views on the subject, namely Plato. Courcelle's response to this question was that his rhetorical skills were deployed in this instance for largely theological purposes.[24] This cannot be denied; yet it is doubtful that this can constitute the entire explanation for their use, since he could have accomplished the same ends through the use of purely discursive methods, without having recourse to rhetorical embellishments, as he does, for example, in books 8–15 of *De Trinitate*, whereas book 8 of the *Confessions* is unapologetically rhetorical in design and execution. In other words, it is not that Augustine made use of a rhetoric of the imagination, but that he used it deliberately and highly effectively. Despite the mystical dimension of the final scene in book 8, which takes us beyond language into the realm of faith, there is no point in the story of Augustine's conversion when rhetoric yields to discursive theological writing; not even, I would maintain, in the celebrated analysis of the "two wills," which immediately precedes the decision to enter the religious life, since this episode, in which there is a logical progression of ideas, achieves much of its philosophical force from Augustine's personal anxiety as the narrative approaches its climax. These chapters, therefore, are not only a work of the imagination: they are also, in some sense, Augustine's justification for the use of the imagination. That is the issue to which we must turn our attention.

A tentative answer to the question raised by Courcelle can be made if we recall that this approach to imagination has developed to this point in essentially three stages in the narrative books of the *Confessions*. The first stage is the criticism of ancient epic poetry in book 1; the second, the discussion of drama in book 3; and the last the conversion scene in book 8. The first is dominated by Plato's rejection of poetic imagery as being misleading, chiefly in book 10 of the *Republic*, and the second by Quintilian's rejection of false emotions for their inauthenticity and inability to persuade, in the texts discussed above. The second, as noted, outlines a complex theory of dramatic representation, in which a fictive external narrative in a play is replaced by a genuine internal narrative of the emotions in the interpreting subject.

The third stage in book 8 effectively combines the views of Cicero and Quintilian, while the shadow of Plato's rejection of poetry lingers in the background of Augustine's thinking, never forcefully restated but not entirely forgotten. His chapters in the conversion scene are comparable to Cicero's short discourse at the beginning of the *Orator* in one sense, namely that they are concerned with an inner ideal, which in this case consists in the highest form of religious commitment, pure faith. They are likewise comparable to Quintilian in the use of *phantasia* and *enargeia*, which render with unique vividness the particular pathway leading to Augustine's taking up of this commitment. What is perhaps unprecedented, at least in the light of books 1 and 3, is Augustine's view of himself as both subject and object of his emotional evolution up to and during the conversion scene. As the actor in the drama, this time his own, he is the person who performs emotions that are described, and, as author of the drama, he is the person who analyzes the effect of the performance, both on himself and on the reader.

This design is revealed in a single line of Psalm 115:16, which is quoted in the opening phrases of book 8: "You have broken my chains." These are the chains of sensual and emotional gratification, recalling the enslavements of sex and drama at 3.1.1–3.2.2: words that return in only a slightly different form in order to tempt him at the critical moment in his reflections on his future, when he is bemused by memories of sensual temptation (8.11.26). His desire at this point is not to be more certain of God, but to be more stable in him: *non certior de te, sed stabilior in te esse cupiebam.* For everything in his life up to that moment has been in the state of flux that is so memorably framed in the *Confessions'* opening lines in terms of the restless heart, which can find its peace only in God.

His wavering is now between his commitment to the church and his desire for wealth and worldly honors; these are traditional topics of criticism in ancient Platonic, Aristotelian, and Stoic ethics. He is also considering the stability of a good marriage, which will bring him wealth and an improved social position. He goes for advice to Simplicianus, the former bishop, who baptized Ambrose, and is sent in turn to the rhetorician, Marius Victorinus, the story of whose courageous decision to be baptized in public is a model he cannot yet imitate. In a state of ever increasing anxiety,[25] he receives an official called Ponticianus, who informs him of religious houses set up by Ambrose in the precincts of Milan. He is told the story of three nameless civil servants in Trier who were converted on reading the *Life of St. Antony.* He reflects on the numerous times he has been tempted by literary models of the Christian life and yet in the end postponed the critical decision to become part of it.

The problem arises from his will, a fact that he recognizes and mulls over in a lengthy interlude. But this is not an entirely original set of reflections. As he describes his situation, the seat of this inner struggle is once again the heart (8.8.19), that is, the source of his emotions; as a consequence, we find ourselves on the familiar ground of the discussion of real and false emotion in books 1 and 3. On this occasion it is not others' emotions that are under consideration, namely those of characters in the *Aeneid* and the new comedy, but his own. His emotional isolation within his own narrative is dramatized in each of the short episodes that follow the debate on the two wills.

Still imprisoned in his thoughts, he enters the garden adjacent to the house in Milan where he and Alypius have been living together. His erratic movements and facial expressions are signs of his inner turmoil. He has in the background of his thoughts the fateful sin of Adam: this tells him that the weakness of the will and the problems of the emotions have historical origins, which mortals cannot overcome on their own. He is tormented by the memory of his old loves, but his resolve is strengthened by the appearance of two personifications, Conscience and Continence. The climax of this series of scenes is a release of pent-up emotion and a pouring forth of tears, after which he hears, or thinks he hears, a voice telling him to pick up the text of scripture, open it, and read the passage that is before his eyes. Mindful of Antony's conversion along the same lines, he reads silently Romans 13:12–14, in which Paul admonishes his readers to forsake riots and drunkenness, eroticism and indecency, as well as useless ambitions. This is an expansion of the types of enslavements that he speaks about in book 3 (3.1.1–3.2.2).

To reiterate: this scene is a performance by Augustine for Augustine. The actor, pictured in the spring of 386, is witnessed by the author, writing in 397–400. In this way, the denouement of book 8 incorporates the scheme for persuasion through the emotions outlined by Quintilian, and does so in an original format, the autobiography. It is a format in which, through memory, the emotions act like signals that are sent and received by different states of the same person. In Quintilian there is no place for this type of retrospective imagination in the expression of emotion. In Augustine, by contrast, the emotional facts with which he is dealing turn out in the end to be fictions, since the series of events that generate these emotions is rearranged, if not invented, by himself. The imagination therefore plays a role in his theory of persuasion by means of the emotions that it does not play in Quintilian, or, for that matter, in any ancient author. In the end, Augustine's position is one that can admit the fictitious nature of literary representations, including of course his own, provided that the recipients, including himself, are aware of their ethical implications. As author in this context, and as his own spiritual director, he is clearly the implied reader of the *Confessions*, who, he believes, through a false story, may undergo a true conversion.

The Contemplative Framework

I now turn to the second topic of this chapter, in which my purpose is to provide an outline of the way Augustine uses sacred reading as a framework for the creative imagination in his configuration of the self. Once again my discussion is divided into two parts. In the first, I continue the analysis of *lectio divina* from Chapter 1 and provide one example of Augustine's adaptation of the technique from the *Confessions*.[26] In the second, I turn to the history of *phantasia/imaginatio*, drawing attention to the manner in which Augustine combines the program of sacred reading with the concept of the rhetorical or literary imagination.

I begin with a necessary word about the conception of the self within the religious writings of the period. In John Cassian, Benedict, Gregory the Great, and other pastoral authors, the prevailing attitude toward the self, as noted in Chapter 1, was essentially that of self-effacement. The readers of biblical texts thought of themselves as being insignificant before the omnipotent word of God. By reading in an ascetic or meditative fashion, in which the subjective and interpretive dimensions of the reading process were subordinated to the objectivity of the scriptural text, these readers indirectly acknowledged this relationship. In Cassian and Benedict it is through continual prayer that a person of a contemplative or spiritual turn of mind is able gradually to become acquainted with his true and inner self, which, as a dimension of the soul, is imprinted with the permanence of God's "image and likeness."

The energies of the monastic reader in search of self-knowledge were thus concentrated on cognitive and emotional interaction with biblical texts. The passages selected for these readings were read slowly and reflectively, with both body and mind. They were first voiced aloud, and at the same time thought about, then re-voiced in the mind, as this meditative thinking proceeded. As some monastic writers put it, the texts were masticated, as if they were a kind of physical nourishment, in the hope that spiritual "digestion" would ensue. This type of reading involved a great deal of repetition; it also meant that texts from different historical layers of the Bible were read and reread in essentially the same way. Although it was recognized by such writers as Jerome and Augustine that a diversity of statements and styles of expression were found in the Bible, they were convinced that the purpose of all of them was the same, namely the reinforcement of faith.

In its combination of the physical and mental, this activity can be contrasted with the reading that is associated with various forms of exegesis, interpretation, or hermeneutics. Despite a commitment to self-effacement comparable to what is found in *lectio divina*, there was in this approach to texts a process of self-exploration at work, which brought into play the reader's creative imagination. In the purest forms of *lectio divina*, such as those reported by John Cassian, one can speak of the attitude of the reader toward his personal self during the reading experience as passive or receptive. By contrast, in interpretive and reconstructive reading, the reader's disposition was active and outgoing, inasmuch as a part of the reading experience consisted in the internal examination of his subjective reaction to the text: a reaction which, needless to say, could be the result of a diversity of influences, including gender, educational levels, and material conditions. In distinguishing between these two types of reading, temporal factors also came into play, since, in *lectio divina* and interpretive reading respectively, the question of the nature of the self arose within different zones of time. In *lectio divina*, in which the text was read, recited, or committed to memory, the consideration of the self came about within the same period of time in which the oral reading was taking place. By contrast, in interpretive reading, whether it was carried on orally or silently, alone or in a group, questions of selfhood entered the process chiefly, if not exclusively, after the oral performative reading was finished.

The guidelines for *lectio divina*, that is, for noninterpretive sacred reading and self-direction, remained relatively stable throughout the Middle Ages; however, those concerned with interpretive reading underwent a considerable evolution, resulting in a complex three- or fourfold method for making sense of biblical texts. Two of these, the literal and anagogical, related directly to the reader's construction of self. By the fifteenth century the branch of sacred interpretive reading known as *lectio spiritualis*, which developed out of *lectio divina*, had been expanded to cover a wide range of reading, writing, and contemplative strategies in the field of religion. These interpretive procedures were eventually codified, as in the case of the *Spiritual Exercises* of Ignatius of Loyola, and in this form they represented an alternative to the conventional ways of approaching the self through more systematic thinking in philosophy or theology, in particular with those associated with the Aristotelian-Thomistic tradition. In the practices or exercises involved in *lectio spiritualis*, the question of the self was addressed locally and pragmatically in a textual context (as later in Montaigne, who practices a secular version of this type of meditative reading). In this approach, there was normally a dialogue between reader and text that effectively revived and extended the Socratic elenchus; however, in this case the interchange did not take place between individuals representing different positions, as in Plato, or in his late ancient admirers, such as Epictetus, but in a literary and commemorative genre of dialogue in which an individual carried on a conversation with himself alone.

As it grew into a major approach to the institution of readership in the late Middle Ages, this type of reading increasingly made use of both words and images. Here again, its practices differed from those of late ancient sacred reading, at least as recorded by John Cassian. In this style of reading the reader was chiefly concerned with images arising in biblical texts, whereas in later medieval interpretive reading consideration was given to images as they arose in the texts and in the reader's mind, as well as to the potential relationship between the two. It must be kept in mind that during the late ancient period, when there were precedents for *lectio spiritualis*, such images were almost exclusively depictions of religious subjects. Also, only a small number of the period's commentators on the question of images made a connection between the visual meditations inspired by sacred texts and the vehicle in which such images were coming into being, namely the reader's imagination. Among these were Augustine and Boethius, who set the stage for medieval explorations of the self in an autobiographical and imaginative form, frequently using images as their point of departure.

There is one other feature of this branch of sacred interpretive reading to which attention should be drawn in connection with the history of the self. This consists in the capacity of the contemplative methods to which I have been referring to overcome the diversity of medieval languages by means of an intellectual procedure that was in principle accessible to them all, namely reading. As noted, during the late Roman Empire and the early Middle Ages the unity of classical Latin was challenged by a wide variety of neo-Latin and proto-Romance languages. As a consequence of this linguistic evolution, it is not possible to look upon the medieval notion of the self—if indeed we may speak of there being only one such notion—as developing from a single conceptual model arising in grammatically inert classical Latin. The chief unifying force in thinking on the self was in fact derived from reading, or more precisely, from sacred reading, which was the most widespread form of the discipline in the late ancient and medieval periods. This heritage of connections between the reader and the self was passed on to the Romance languages, which constituted the medium in which problems of the self were increasingly presented after the twelfth century, however now within a greater diversity of interpretative procedures and more complex relations between authors and audiences, culminating in Dante's *De Vulgari Eloquentia*, published in 1305, which justifies the use of Tuscan alongside Latin. By means of this historical development, as it spread to other languages, reading gradually democratized thinking about the self in a manner that had not been possible in disciplines such as ancient philosophy and rhetoric, in which training was restricted to a tiny élite.

To summarize: the approaches to the self that arise, respectively, from noninterpretive and interpretive sacred reading are essentially those of self-effacement and self-construction. Augustine brought the two together into a single view of the self; however, the work of combination had already begun in sacred reading itself, since *lectio spiritualis*, in its early phase of development, shared the same meditative and contemplative methodology. It follows that, instead of configuring independent notions of self-identity for these practices, one might think of them, however cautiously, as representing different aspects of a single perspective. In this view, a late ancient and medieval notion of the self that is implicit in the discipline of sacred reading may not be one in which total self-effacement is considered desirable nor one in which there is envisaged a wholly autonomous type of self-construction. That is what we find in Augustine's ambivalent attitude toward the self, which consists, on the one hand, in elements of self-denigration arising from the view that sin is ineradicable in mortals, and on the other, in elements associated with the more individualistic notion of the self, based on such notions as subjective self-awareness and freedom of will.

The method most frequently utilized to achieve this equilibrium in Augustine is the same as in earlier noninterpretive and interpretive traditions, namely the use of reading, writing, and other contemplative disciplines. It is through this process that the individual practicing a form of sacred reading, whether this was reading itself or one of its derivatives (such as psalmody or liturgy), was able to humble himself before the biblical text and to eliminate from the encounter with God's word any unwanted features of his self. It is through the same method that the individual engaged in interpretive reading was able to concentrate his energies on an internal extension of the writings before him, which effectively became an extension of himself. Of course individual readers could and did interpret this ascetic program in different ways and, in one way or the other, all of them moved toward the poles of self-effacement or self-construction. But rarely do we find a reader who carries self-effacement to such an extreme that we know nothing about his personality from the record left by his writings. Equally rarely do we find a spiritual reader who is so taken up with internal self-construction that there is no echo of the foundations of his thinking in the sacred texts with which his speculations have begun.

An Illustration

As an illustration of this cooperative engagement in the creation of a notion of selfhood, I would like to look briefly at *Confessions* 5.1.1–5.2.2. This passage consists in two paragraphs of confessional prayer preceding Augustine's account of his meeting with the Manichaean bishop, Faustus of Milev, at age twenty-nine, possibly in 383.

The prayer is a brilliant combination of the reading techniques associated with both noninterpretive and interpretive reading. At one level, namely that of *lectio divina*, Augustine's devotional statement consists in a series of quotations from scripture, chiefly taken from the Psalms, but also from Paul, the Book of Wisdom, and Revelation; at another, it can be approached as a group of reflections on philosophical and theological topics drawn chiefly from Paul and Plotinus. In the sections of the prayer that arise from the method of noninterpretive sacred reading, Augustine's personality is dramatically subordinated to the passages of scripture to which he alludes through carefully selected phrases. In those arising from other sources, each statement makes a contribution to a presentation of self that is articulated within the themes of sin, redemption, and salvation. It is as a dimension of this theological design that Augustine's self-construction takes place at this critical moment in the *Confessions*, when he is about to abandon dualism for a more integrative view of the self within his return to traditional Christianity and eventual conversion to the religious life.

The use of the methods associated with *lectio divina* is made clear from the opening statement, in which he implores God:

> "Accipe sacrificium" confessionum mearum "de manu linguae meae." (5.1.1., 1–2).

> "Accept the sacrifice" of my confessions from "the hand of my tongue."

Here we have two phrases drawn from scripture, namely *accipe sacrificium* (cf. Ps. 50:21) and *de manu linguae meae* (Prov. 18:21), the latter being a virtual catchword for the type of oral reading and devotion associated with *lectio divina* (cf. Rom. 10:8). Further quotations in the opening phrases confirm the impression that the foundation of these two paragraphs consists in Augustine's previous readings, recitations, and memorizations of scriptural texts. He wishes to confess in God's name (*ut confitear nomini tuo*, Ps. 53:8); he begs God through his words to "heal" his "bones" (*et sana omnia ossa mea*, Ps. 6:3), so that they might declare, "Lord, who is like you?" (*et dicant: domine, quis similis tibi?*: Ps. 6:3; Ps. 34:10). He admits that he cannot hide from God's sacred fire (5.1.1, 4–7; Ps. 18:7). He praises God in love and confesses his mercies in praise (5.1.1,

7–8; Ps 118:17, Ps 118:75, Ps. 145:2, Ps. 106:8, 15, etc.). His weary soul rises slowly upward, supported by the works of God's creation and in the end transcending them (5.1.1, 11–13; Ps. 71:18; Ps. 135:4). He knows that only the restless and wicked attempt to flee the deity (5.2.2; 1, Ps. 67:2), but it is impossible to get beyond his reach (5.2.5; Ps. 138:7). In blindness the wicked stumble (5.2.6; Rom. 11:7–11). They have abandoned God but do not realize that he will not abandon them (5.2.7; Wisd. 11;25). In time he will wipe away their tears (5.2.16; Rev. 7:17; Rev. 21:4).

If we examine the contexts from which these references to scripture are drawn, it becomes clear that they form part of a larger design than is contained in the phrases themselves. This is suggested by means of the renunciation of sin and the consequent upward movement of the soul. The project is announced in the opening statement of 5.1.1, which combines the ideas of sacrifice and confession. In Psalm 50, which is the probable source of this connection, the psalmist says,

> Have mercy on me, O God.
> In your great tenderness wipe away my faults . . . .
> For I am well aware of my shortcomings,
> I have my sin constantly before me. (Ps. 50:2–5)

The other references to scripture at 5.1.1 reinforce these statements—the inability to conceal one's sins from God (Ps. 18:7), the necessity of thanks and praise (Ps. 118:175, etc.), and the notion of the mind's elevation (Ps. 71:18; 135:4).

Subsequently, two components of the design are revealed to the reader. One is the predictable theme of self-effacement. Within the biblical passages to which allusion is made, as well as within Augustine's comments, there is little overt talk of the self. The emphasis is on the words of scripture, as they are read and meditated. The author's self is not by any means obliterated: it is present as a thinking and feeling entity, whose vehicle is Augustine's voice, as conveyed in the cadences of his literary style. However, within the opening phrases of 5.1.1, it is also made clear by Augustine that this authorial and speaking self is not an autonomous force but is being configured, as noted, in a literary fashion beneath the omnipresent panoply of scripture, which acts as its framework and scaffolding. His words are offered to God by means of "the hand" of "the tongue" (Prov. 18:21), but it is the words of scripture that "heal" (Ps. 6:3). God has no need of his words in order to know what is in his heart (5.1.1, 4–7). As a consequence, there is no point in his talking about himself.

Yet, even during this process of effacement, a second theme makes its appearance; this consists in a subtle depiction of Augustine's inner self in *Confessions* 5.1.1–2, which is given literary shape by a combination of biblical and philosophical sources, essentially, as noted, those of Paul and Plotinus, which are organized by means of the principles of sacred interpretive reading. The way is prepared in 5.1.1 and developed in 5.2.2. In 5.1.1, Augustine observes that the heart of man may be closed but is incapable of permanently shutting out God. One of the paths by which God finds his way into the person's inner core is through the subject's awareness of divine creativity, which is present everywhere in life:

> Your creation never ceases to praise you. Every spirit continually
> praises you with mouth turned toward you; animals and physical
> matter find a voice through those who contemplate them.[27]

The praise that is mentioned here recalls the meditative space of the opening lines of book 1, in which there appears, tentatively at first but unmistakeable in its contours, the struggling self of Augustine himself:

> To praise God is the desire of man, who is a little piece of your
> creation. You inspire him to take pleasure in offering your praise,
> because he is your creation. (*Conf.*, 1.1.1, 6–7)

In a metaphor with possible Plotinian roots, Augustine thus envisages the fallen as having a shadowy, insubstantial existence, like areas of darkness in a bright and beautiful painting (5.2.2, 1–3).[28] Paraphrasing a passage from Romans 11:7–11, he pictures those who flee from God as inadvertently stumbling over him in their darkness. For they do not realize that God is to be found not in one place but everywhere:

> No space circumscribes you. You alone are always present, even to
> those who have taken themselves far from you . . . . Let them turn,
> and at once you are in their heart—in the heart of those who make
> confession. (5.2.2, 10–12)

Here, notably, one does not come upon the passages of scripture that are Augustine's point of departure at 5.1.1, but the inner life of the subject himself, as his self, informed by those passages, seeks to define itself and to define its relationship to God. In a final plea for self-enlightenment, Augustine asks:

> Where was I when I was seeking for you? You were there before
> me, but I had departed from myself. I could not even find myself,
> much less you.

The final message of *Confessions* 5.1.1–2 is that the authentic person whom Augustine is looking for has in fact been found, and this has come about by means of a movement in his thinking from *lectio divina* to interpretive and imaginative reading.

Phantasia/Imaginatio

I would now like to turn to the sources of this imaginative element. This involves approaching the issues from another direction, namely the transformation of the notion of the imagination itself, as represented by the Greek term *phantasia* and its Latin translation in Augustine's writings as *imaginatio*.

The roots of his thinking on the subject are not altogether clear. He did not have access to the central texts on *phantasia* in Plato, Aristotle, or the Stoics, in which the term is used chiefly in discussions of the theory of knowledge; he had to rely on the restatement of their views in the works of later thinkers, among them Cicero, Quintilian, and especially Plotinus, who, although a Platonist, placed a high value on knowledge acquired by means of the senses.

From this branch of Platonic thinking Augustine absorbed the view that it was necessary for the mind, in its interpreting function, to pass judgment on sensory impressions, in order not only to show what they have in common and how they differ, but to inquire into the source, nature, and validity of the impressions themselves.[29] From the Aristotelian tradition he appears to have adopted the distinction between *phantasia* and perception, proposing that the one, concerning sense impressions alone, is comparable to a physical capacity, such as sight, whereas the other, involving the interpretive capacity of the mind, can take place when nothing is actually seen, as in a dream or vision. This is his position in book 12 of *De Genesi ad Litteram*, as well as earlier, in the dialogue *Contra Academicos*, where he demonstrates an awareness of the Stoic doctrine by which the senses were considered to be a source of certainty concerning objects as well as the conceptions that they bring about in the mind, which were termed *kataleptikai phantasiai.*

A more direct source for his views on the imagination was a work by Plato with which it is certain he was familiar. This is the Latin translation of the *Timaeus,* which was widely read in late antiquity. Under its influence, and in harmony with his successive interpretations of the book of Genesis, Augustine grounded his thinking on interpretation in a manner that placed emphasis on the passage of objective time. On this view, there are essentially two kinds of knowledge, which correspond to different levels of being or existence. These are represented respectively by the eternal world of God and the temporal world of mortals. The one can be understood through the mind, and is the source of truth, while the other is grasped by means of the senses, and, as Plato argued, is sustained principally by *doxa* or opinion. Truth is perceived fully by God alone, although glimpses are occasionally permitted to mortals in exceptional circumstances. It is here that the Augustinian notion of the imagination came into play, both as an interpretive tool and, as noted, as an element in self-construction, in the *Confessions.*

As creator of heaven and earth, the god of the *Timaeus* is conceived as a supreme artist, and the created world is his acknowledged masterpiece. By contrast, human artists, working on more manageable projects, have to rely on a combination of perception and intuition. In this type of Platonism, when

> mingled with Stoicism, the status of *phantasia* was . . . elevated because *phantasia* was central to the Stoic theory of knowledge . . . .
> The once lowly *phantasia* (in Platonic and Aristotelian thinking) was to be praised as the faculty which could give us unexpected visions of reality. After that the development of the notion of the creative imagination was easy.[30]

However, there is one feature of *phantasia* that is found in Augustine but not in Plato, although it consists in a Christian adaptation of the scheme for creation that is similar in some respects to that of the *Timaeus.* This concerns the role of history, which, in Augustine's writings on the subject, acts as an intermediary between the eternal and temporal dimensions of existence. The Platonic elements in this design came to Augustine via philosophy, in particular from his reading of Plotinus and possibly Porphyry in the spring of 386; the historical perspective was a product of his studies in the Bible during the same period, in particular from his interpretation of the Pauline letters. In his synthesis of these traditions he argues that our primary source of information about the world consists in what we receive through the five senses (as well as a sixth, the internal sense, which transfers the data of the other senses to the mind); however, everything in the universe that is perceived through the senses and understood in the mind has been brought into being by means of a historical process. Augustine was also convinced that, however much we learn from the senses and however much we may be capable of subjecting that acquired knowledge to philosophical analysis, it is nonetheless the authoritative text of scripture, as a repository of historical facts, from which we learn the most concerning the reality of the existing world. This is because the Bible is the chief source accessible to mortals on God's original *and* continuing activity.

This notion of historically grounded but ongoing creativity differs from the view of creation that is found in Augustine's chief nonbiblical source on the subject, namely Plotinus, who, as noted, is an important commentator on the problem of *phantasia* and one of his chief sources of inspiration. A text that forcefully illustrates this difference is found at *Enneads* 3.8.3–4, where Plotinus discusses the creative dimension of nature. Here it is proposed that if nature causes other things to move and change while remaining unmoved and unchanged itself, then nature must be part of a creative and contemplative process which is itself changeless. But how can nature be said to be something that contemplates and at the same time something that is the result of contemplation? Plotinus argues that this cannot come about merely by a sort of reason or reasoning (*logos*). For, if by "nature" we mean what it is, we cannot separate what nature is from what nature does. Its making must, so to speak, be a type of contemplation and its contemplation a type of making (3.8.3):

> If anyone were to ask nature why it creates, if nature cared to listen and to reply to the inquirer, it would say: "You ought not ask but to understand in silence: you, I mean—just as I am silent and not in the habit of talking. Understand what, you ask? That what comes into being is what I see in my silence, as an object of contemplation . . . . My act of contemplation makes what it contemplates, as the geometers draw their figures while they contemplate."[31]

Plotinus may have in mind Plato's description of geometrical configurations at *Timaeus* 53C–55C, but, as Hilary Armstrong remarks, "the intuitive spontaneity of the process here, as contrasted with the careful and deliberate mathematical planning in Plato's symbolical description, brings out clearly an important difference in the mentality of the two philosophers."[32]

Plotinus likewise differs from Augustine, who would have read this passage with interest. In his writings on the topic, the notion of intuitive spontaneity is associated not with an abstract contemplative process, as in the quoted passage, but with the historical activity of God, as noted, in the original and continuing creative processes in the universe. In accounting for this development Augustine attributes Plotinus's idea of creativity in nature to the activity of the will in God, which, in a comparable manner, creates what and when it desires to do so and is not in any way dependent on the actions or thoughts of mortals. In Plotinus and Augustine the basic causal principle is similar: this is not a form of rationality, as in Plato, but a dialogic process within nature itself, about which Plotinus is led to ask:

> What does this mean? That what is called nature is a soul, the offspring of a prior soul with a stronger life; that it quietly holds contemplation in itself, not directed upward or even downward, but at rest in what it is, in its own repose and a kind of self-perception, and in this consciousness and self-perception it sees what comes after it . . . . If anyone wants to attribute to it understanding or perception, it will not be the understanding or perception we speak of in other beings: it will be like comparing the consciousness of someone fast asleep to the consciousness of someone awake. For Nature is at rest in the contemplation of itself. (3.8.4)

If we substitute God for the personified Nature in such a statement, and add Augustine's distinction between two types of sensory impression, *phantasia* and *phantasma*, we have the connection between Plotinus's notion of the creative process through nature and Augustine's notion of the creative process through history.

It would appear, therefore, that, using Platonic, Stoic, and Plotinian sources, although we are not sure in what order of priority, Augustine possessed all the necessary equipment for a new and interesting synthesis on the workings of *phantasia*. However, as I see it, while the elements of a consistent and consolidated view of the issues are present in his various statements on the theme of the imagination, the synthesis itself, which many scholars have hoped to find in these discussions, was never actually written. The closest

Augustine came to stating his views on the subject in a fully coherent form was in a literary rather than philosophical work, namely the *Confessions*. His systematic and philosophical statements on the theme are partial and incomplete. The lack of a fully worked out view of the problems in his discursive writings on *phantasia* can be demonstrated through a brief review of three of his major comments on the subject, which take place, respectively, in letters 6 and 7, in book 12 of *De Genesi ad Litteram*, and in book 8 of *De Trinitate*, to which I now turn.

1. Epistulae *6 and 7*

Augustine's earliest reflection on *phantasia*, and his only completely philosophical statement on the theme, takes place in an exchange of letters with Nebridius, in 389. In letter 3, written to his young friend two years earlier, Augustine had stated that "the sensible world is certainly—although how I don't know—an image of the intelligible."[33] He added to this Platonic dogma a series of questions and answers:

> Of what do we consist? Soul and body. Which is preferable? The soul, of course. What is praiseworthy in the body? Nothing but beauty. And what is the body's beauty? A harmony of its parts, along with agreeable coloration.

In his mind, the central issue was whether

> this form is better when it is true or false? Who would doubt that, when it is true, it is better. But where is it "true"? In the soul, surely. Consequently the soul is to be loved and esteemed more than the body. But in what part of the soul does this truth exist? In the mind and understanding. What is the opposite of these? The senses.

Nebridius had responded to these statements with a number of queries, but these, his student notes, had gone unanswered.[34] Yet the discussion had evidently advanced beyond the initial consideration of the sensible and intelligible components of reality,[35] since, in letter 6, where it is next taken up, Nebridius is able to refer to their previous exchange of views as having already passed through its preliminary stages. In a rhetorical flourish, he acknowledges the contribution to his thinking that has been made by his master's careful documentation of the teachings of Christ, Plato, and Plotinus; however, he prefers to turn his attention to two questions that have arisen out of their own long-standing discussion. These have to do with memory and images. In his view not every image requires memory, but no memory can exist without an image (*quamuis non omnia phantasia cum memoria sit, omnis tamen memoria sine phantasia esse non possit*). He asks Augustine whether he agrees.

The second of these questions is the more straightforward of the two. Nebridius is asking whether the operation of the imagination can take place without the participation of the senses.[36] If so, this would account for the fact that we sometimes have images in our minds that have not arisen from the outside but are produced when the mind is directed by the senses to the contemplation of its own internally generated forms.

The first question is more complicated, because it is more general in scope, and anticipates a problem that might have been raised by Augustine himself, if one takes into account the views that he subsequently expresses in letter 7. This concerns what happens in the mind when we remember what we have understood or thought about anything (*quid, cum recordamur nos intellexisse aut cogitasse aliquid?*).

Nebridius's answer to this hypothetical problem is not altogether clear and involves a pair of alternative routes from the senses to the imagination, between which he appears reluctant to choose. When we have understood anything that is corporeal or temporal, he states, we generate what pertains to mental impression or to imagination (*genuimus quod ad phantasiam pertinet*). Then we do one of two things: (1) we join words to understanding and thought; words, that is, which are not lacking a temporal dimension and which pertain to sense or imagination; or (2) we have experienced something through thought and understanding that is able to produce a memory in the imaginative part of the soul.[37] Nebridius is in a quandary on the matter and asks his teacher for help.

Augustine's answer is found in letter 7 and contains his earliest and possibly finest statement on the use of the creative imagination for literary and ethical purposes. He disagrees with Nebridius's notion that memory cannot exist without the images or imaginary appearances that his friend terms *phantasiae*.[38] However, in responding to this view, he points out that, while by means of memory we recall things from the past (*rerum praeteuntium*), nonetheless the memories by which we engage in this recollection appear in our minds as they exist in the present (*manentium*). As examples of this double view, Augustine notes that while he remembers his father, Patrick, who died sometime in the past, he also remembers that his father is no longer alive, and this occurs in the present. Again, he remembers Carthage, which he left as a young teacher of rhetoric, and yet he recalls that Carthage still exists, despite the passage of time since he left. In both cases something from the past is stored in memory, which is active in the present, and yet the two entities are remembered, namely his father and a city, from what he saw rather than from what he sees.[39]

His account of these relationships, which are attributed to *phantasia*, represents a change of direction, and in some sense an advance in thinking on the nature of the imagination in previous writing on the subject in the sources that we can ascertain that he had read. He agrees with Nebridius on one point: an object that is perceived cannot become a memory without at the same time becoming an imaginary appearance (*uiso illo imaginario*), which, he notes, is usually called *phantasia*. But he draws his friend's attention to the fact that there are types of memory for which no inner visual representation is needed. These consist in information of a conceptual nature, which, unlike sense data, may be lodged in our memories without our being aware of it. His example of this type of knowledge is taken from Socrates's account in the *Meno* of an uneducated slave boy who, without any instruction in geometry, was able to solve simple geometrical problems through a series of Socrates's questions and answers.

As I will argue in Chapter 5, Augustine does not adhere to the doctrine of reminiscence, by which, Plato proposed, such knowledge is transferred from one soul to another, but he is convinced that we possess certain mental endowments, such as the capacity for speech, numbers, or memory, which are lodged in us from birth and can be brought out by teaching, in which a kind of mimesis plays a part.[40] These capacities differ from the memories of specific things or events, whose existence in our minds depends on the past of our personal experience and the formation of mental impressions. As principles by which the mind works, the knowledge of speaking or numbers has a latent but permanent presence in our minds, and, as such, has no need of stimulation by means of the external senses or the resulting internal formation of images (*imaginatione*). In this sense, these fall outside the range of *phantasia*.

Augustine dismisses Nebridius's notion that the soul, if deprived of the outer senses, would be able to form accurate images (*imaginari*) of things in the external world. If that were the case, the mental images produced by those experiencing dreams or hallucinations, being internally generated, might be judged as reliable as those that are based on things that are actually seen. According to his understanding of Platonic principles, these images might be considered more trustworthy than those originating through the senses, owing to the possibility of errors in sense perception. Consequently, as Augustine sees the issues, the faculty of image formation (*imaginatio*), which originates entirely in the mind, cannot be viewed as a type of recollection in the mind (*commemoratio . . . in anima*), but must be seen as an inference based on potential or actual error (*falsitatis inlatio*), or, more accurately, on its mental imprint or impression (*inpressio*). In advancing this idea, Augustine is aware that, in the imagination of people who are awake, as well as in the mental processes of those who are asleep or insane, the mind is capable of producing forms that the subjects have never actually seen (*ut eas formas et facies cogitetur quas numquam uidimus*, 7.2.3).

It would appear, therefore, that *phantasia* operates equally well with realities, which we sense, and with fictions, which we invent. This is an important connection, to which Augustine devotes the remainder of letter 7, beginning with a recapitulation of his views in the form of a classificatory scheme. The types of images to which Nebridius is referring, which he, like so many others, calls *phantasiae*, can be divided into three classes (*in tria genera*), insofar as they are produced (1) by the senses or by sensing (*sensis*), (2) by reflection or thought (*putatis*), or (3) by calculation or determination (*ratis*, 7.2.4).[41] As examples of (1) he offers things that he has actually seen, such as the appearance of Nebridius, the grammarian Verecundus (whose villa at Cassiciacum he was lent in the winter of 386–387), or the city of Carthage (where he once studied and taught). For (3) he gives the examples of numbers and dimensions; the latter are of two sorts, namely those found in nature and those produced by the mind. As an instance of the former, he suggests the shape of the universe or numbers, and of the latter, geometrical figures or musical rhythms.

In case (1) potential error is avoided by physical appearance and in (3) by logic and reason. A lengthier explanation is provided for case (2), which Augustine evidently finds difficult to discuss as precisely as (1) and (3). In attempting to give an account of this type of *phantasia* (which he laconically characterizes through the past participle of *putare*, meaning here to think, suppose, or illustrate), he provides the reader with his first extensive description of the literary and philosophical imagination in his writings.

To this faculty, he notes, belong the images of things that we suppose to have been so, or even in reality to have been so (*quae putamus ita se habuisse uel se habere*), the former suggesting, as elsewhere, the possibility of being taken in by one's own perceptions and fantasies. We either think up these *phantasiae* ourselves (*ipsi fingimus*) or configure them (*figuramus*) indirectly, for example, when a story is read to us, or when we hear, compose, or have an inkling of a fabulous tale (*cum legitur historia et cum fabulosa uel audimus uel componimus uel suspicamur*).

Augustine divides these products of the imagination into two kinds, namely figures taken from literature and figures invented to support an author's position. The first includes images that appear in the mind (*ut occurrit animo*) based on the reading of literary texts or in attendance at the theater, for example, the face of Aeneas, the figure of Medea in her chariot of winged serpents, or characters in the comedies of Terence, such as Chremes or Parmeno. The second includes a variety of images to which the erudite (*sapientes*) resort in communicating what is true by what is false, for the sake of the ignorant or uneducated (*stulti*). The latter are frequently based on superstition but alleged to be fact by the speaker; examples include the inferno of Phlegeton and the wooden stake that allegedly supports the northern sky, (and notions of this sort, he observes, arise with unusual frequency in the minds of such unreliable observers of the outside world as poets and heretics). It is legitimate, he proposes, to use these and equally improbable notions when we are engaged in configuring or thinking of something (*fingimus et putamus*), or when support is sought for one or another position in open debate (*inter disputandum*, 7.2.4). But these thoughts are not of course to be trusted, since, as pure creations of the imagination, they are falser than images based on the senses (*at istas imagines quis dubitauerit istis sensibilibus multo esse falsiores*, 7.2.5).

In a final statement Augustine attempts to give a psychological dimension to these invented images. How does it come about, he asks, that we think of things that we do not see? This could not take place unless there were a certain power inherent in the mind of diminishing and increasing (*nisi esse uim quandam minuendi et augendi animae insitam*, 7.3.6). This perceptual capacity can be observed, for example, when a bird such as a crow comes into view, since it seems to increase in size as it comes closer. By subtracting or adding to its features, which we recognize, it is even possible, by means of a mental configuration alone, to produce the features of a bird that no one has ever seen.

Such invented or fictional images are able to break into our thoughts spontaneously (*in talibus animis figurae huiusce modi uelut sua sponte cogitationibus inruant*), proving to Augustine's satisfaction that it is possible for the mind of the person imagining (*animae imaginanti*) to produce things by addition or subtraction which in their totality have not been experienced by the senses, even though from time to time parts of them may have been perceived. As an example, Augustine offers himself, who, as a child reared near the Mediterranean, was able to imagine the sea from seeing only the movement of water in a small cup, whereas, until he came to Italy, the taste of strawberries and cherries, which he did not know in his youth, was impossible for him to imagine.

2. De Genesi ad Litteram, *book 12*

In letters 6 and 7 Augustine and Nebridius discuss the imagination through epistolary dialogue. One has the impression of a well-articulated but reasonably spontaneous exchange of views on a long-standing philosophical problem. There are references to supporting texts in letter 7 (e.g., the plays of Terence), but by and large the two parties in the conversation base their statements on their own reasoning.

By contrast, Augustine's lengthy discussion on the imagination in book 12 of *De Genesi ad Litteram* takes the form of a commentary on a biblical text, namely 2 Corinthians 12:2–4, where Paul relates the following story:

> I know that fourteen years ago a Christian man was laid hold of
> and as such taken all the way to the third heaven, whether in the
> body I do not know or whether out of the body I do not know—
> God knows; and I know that this man was caught up into
> paradise, whether in the body or out of the body I do not know—
> God knows—and that he heard unutterable words that a man is
> not permitted to speak.[42]

This statement is the point of departure for a lengthy discussion of visual representations in which the Pauline text is analyzed at three levels: (1) the original experience of mental elevation, (2) the interpretation of this experience by Paul, and (3) the philosophical implications, as implied by Paul according to Augustine.

The discussion is divided into two sections. Chapters 1–5 are concerned with Paul's assertions about what he did and did not know about the transport of the unnamed Christian to the third heaven, and in some sense to paradise, and with whether these experiences differed or were the same. Chapter 6 introduces the more general problem of *visiones*, which takes up the remainder of the book (cc. 6–37). Since *visio*, in the sense of an appearance or something seen, is an acceptable translation of *phantasia*, the second section of *De Genesi* 12 has to be considered one of Augustine's lengthy statements on this aspect of the creative imagination.

By way of introduction to this theme, he proposes that there is one type of *visio* that excels all others. This takes place when something is seen, not as an image of an object, imaginatively (*imaginaliter*), but in itself (*proprie*). This is a reiteration of one of the ideas put forward by Cicero, Quintilian, and Augustine himself on the question of artistic or poetic inspiration, now, however, illustrated by a biblical text and as a result placed in an exegetical context. From a philosophical point of view, Augustine is saying that the sort of *visio* which is seen in itself is not seen through the body (*non per corpus videtur*), that is, by means of the external sense of sight (12.6.15), but internally, in the mind.

After making this clear, he abandons the purely philosophical discussion of the issues and introduces a classification of *visiones* based on levels of meaning in the scriptural maxim, "You shall love your neighbor as yourself" (Matt. 22:39). When this precept is read (*in hoc praecepto cum legitur*), he notes, it becomes apparent that there are three classes of visions (*tria genera visionum*).

1. The first is that which takes place by means of the eyes and consists in the visual perception of the letters of the written text (*unum per oculos, quibus ipsae litterae videntur*). In this case a physical object is physically perceived.

2. The second is that which arises in the spirit of man, when a neighbor is thought about, even though he may be absent (*alterum per spiritum hominis quo proximus et absens cogitatur*). Here a physical being is recalled as a physical presence but not as a physical reality, perceptible to the senses.

3. The third arises through the focusing of the mind's attention, by which the love in question is itself brought into view (*tertium per contuitum mentis, quo ipsa dilectio intellecta conspicitur*). Here the meaning of an abstract notion is arrived at by inner vision or perception alone.

It is these divisions that Augustine subsequently employs as a model for understanding the type of *visio* that is involved in Paul's story at 2 Cor. 12:2–4. The next stage of the argument takes place at *De Genesi* 12.6.15. Here he reiterates the threefold division of images that is discussed in letter 7, namely those arising from sensory impressions, suppositions or recollections, and the by-products of thought. However, a modification is introduced: the images in the third category, that is, those originating in the mind, are understood to arise from *either* seeing or reading. This raises the possibility of moving back and forth between philosophy and exegetical theology on the assumption that, with respect to *visiones*, comparable operations of the mind are involved.

This interdependence, I suggest, accounts for a change in the threefold scheme as initially proposed: it shifts the subsequent discussion of *visiones* into a form in which greater weight is given to theology than to either philosophy or rhetoric. The change is not evident in Augustine's reflections on the first type of *visio*, which, he notes, can take in everything in earth or heaven that can be seen with the naked eye, or with the second, which consists in corporeal things, even if absent, that require the operation of memory and image formation.

The first case is self-evident and requires no commentary on Augustine's part. He takes as the second the occasion when we visualize earth or heaven while in the dark; at that point, he correctly observes, we are seeing not with our eyes, that is, with our bodies, but with our minds or souls (*ubi nihil videntes oculis corporis, animo tamen corporales imagines intuemur*). What we have in view may consist in the true (*veras*) images of things we have previously seen, which have been retained in memory, or, alternately, those that are made up (*fictas*), as it were, by thought or imagination (*cogitatio*).[43]

When we turn to the third category, we encounter an implied orientation toward exegesis which characterizes much of the subsequent discussion of *visiones*. For this type of *visio*, by which we have in inner view of our love for our neighbor, is the product not of seeing but of reading, instruction, and subsequent reflection. In Augustine's view, this type of *visio* is superior to *visiones* 1 and 2, since its content cannot be seen as an image similar to itself but is seen in itself (*eas res conspicitur*). For love, he notes, is not visualized in one way when it is present and in another way when it is absent: it can only be seen clearly in one way, since its image is entirely produced in the mind. It has presence and permanence in itself.

The types of *visiones* to which Augustine has been referring by means of illustrations from scriptural texts are now denominated as *corporale*, *spirituale*, and *intellectuale* (12.6.16). Of these terms, the first presents no problems, since it is entirely dependent on the senses, while the third, called *intellectuale* or *intelligibile*, is proper to the mind, which only sees through itself (*mens quippe non videtur nisi mente*, 12.10.21). However, the term *spirituale* requires a word of explanation (12.6.18).

Two connotative fields are singled out for discussion, one historical, the other psychological. The first arises from the contrast between the "natural" and "spiritual" in conceptions of the body, to which Paul refers in stating: "What is sown as a natural body shall rise as a spiritual body" (1 Cor. 15:44). In Augustine's view, this refers to the state of the body after the resurrection, when it will be revived in the spirit alone and have no need of corporeal underpinnings. In this respect the meaning of "spirit" is roughly equivalent to that of "soul," as suggested by a number of scriptural texts (e.g., Ps. 148:8; Eccles. 3:21).

The other sense of "spirit," which is more relevant to the discussion at 12.6.16, is one in which the term "spiritual" is used for describing the activity of the mind itself, in the exercise of reason and judgment which characterizes the understanding of every sort of image. For there exists in every mortal, Augustine notes, what may be termed an eye of the soul, to which pertain the image and knowledge of God,[44] and this has its origin in the soul's very creation. In support of this notion he makes reference to two Pauline texts in which attention is drawn to the notions of *imago* and *agnitio* (image and knowledge). These are Ephesians 4:23–24 and Colossians 3:10, where, respectively, the apostle speaks of putting on the new man (*induit novum hominem*), created in accordance with God's design, and renewing the interior man in the knowledge of God according to the divine image by which he was originally created (*qui renovatur in agnitione Dei, secundum imaginem ejus qui creavit eum*).

Spirituale here is opposed to *corporale*, as Augustine notes, citing texts such as Galatians 5:17, where Paul speak of the desires of the flesh working against the spirit, and John 4:24, where the apostle refers to worshipping God in spirit and in truth (*in spiritu et veritate*). While truth, as an idea in the mind, is in principle separated from the body, there are occasions when an element of corporality is present; an example arises, as previously noted, if I think of the neighbor whom I love as myself, even though he may be absent (cf. Matt. 22:39). In this case I am seeing an object in my mind which has a body and I am seeing it in itself, rather than as an image; yet I am not seeing it as I would other bodies by means of my body (cf. 12.6.15).

In Augustine's view, the paradigm for this way of thinking about *visio* is the resurrection, whose language is echoed in Paul's twice reiterated comment at 2 Corinthians 12:2–4, namely "whether in the body I do not know or out of the body I do not know, God knows." We can conclude that the emphatic statement "God knows," in which the ideas of "knowing" and "not knowing" are effectively swept away, is a reference to a specific type of metaphysical experience. This arises from the fact that, in Paul's view, the explanation of the vision of the third heaven, being "unutterable," is unable on that account to be revealed to him or to anyone else by means of human language.

This is a commonplace of Augustine's thinking about language, which is explored in detail in book 1 of *De Doctrina Christiana*. Once the distinction between these types of communication enters the discussion, it is inevitable, in Augustine's way of looking at things, that philosophy will be complemented, if not at times replaced, by hermeneutics, since the observation on communication depends on the interpretation of biblical texts in which God is said to "speak," either through language, action, or symbols. This is the type of discussion that takes place in the following chapters, in which an account is given of the second type of *visio* within the threefold scheme by means of Augustine's theory of signs. As this option appears in book 2 of *De Doctrina Christiana*, where it is discussed at length, it is conceived as an aid to the interpretation of passages of the Bible.

Augustine introduces this perspective on the problem of *phantasia* by announcing to his readers that the different meanings of the word *spirituale*, which he has derived from selected biblical texts, do not in his view fully exhaust the senses of the term in the second kind of *visio*. As a consequence, he adopts a different type of explanation of these images, which takes its point of departure from Paul's statement at 1 Corinthians 14:14: "If I pray in a tongue, my spirit prays but my understanding is unfruitful" (*Si enim oravero lingua, spiritus meus orat, mens autem mea infructuosa est*). Augustine interprets the word "tongue" as referring to some form of obscure and mystical signification (*intelligitur . . . obscuras et mysticas significationes*). In using the word, he proposes, Paul is speaking to the type of signification that can instruct no one if the potential for understanding in his mind has effectively been removed (*si intellectum mentis removeas*), since, at that point in the process of communication, the subject would be hearing what he does not in fact comprehend (*audiendo quod non intelligit*).

Here, at a human level, we have a parallel for Paul's statement at 2 Corinthians 12:2–4 to the effect that the unnamed individual who experiences the vision he describes did not know whether the perception of the third heaven took place in the body or out of the body, since God had not revealed its meaning to his understanding; that is, there was no interpretable connection between the event, which he accepted as fact, and its meaning, which, at that point, remained a secret or hidden, since the words that were spoken were not those by which it could be adequately described.

The point is underlined by another quotation from Paul, namely 1 Corinthians. 14:2: "For he who speaks in a tongue does not speak to men but to God; for no one understands, although the spirit is speaking mysteries." Augustine notes: "[Paul] makes it sufficiently clear that in this passage he is referring to a sort of tongue in which there are significations, such as the images of things and their likenesses. When these are not in the understanding, they are said to be in the spirit (*cum autem non intelliguntur, in spiritu eas dicit esse*)."[45] While it is the signs of things and not things themselves that are produced by the tongue, which is the bodily member that is put into motion when we speak, it is clear that in this passage Paul was referring to the production of signs before they are understood (*signorum prolationem priusquam [res] intelligantur*). In this case, in Augustine's view, a revelation (*revelatio*) could take place involving knowledge, prophecy, or doctrine (*vel agnitio, vel prophetia, vel doctrina*; 1 Cor. 14:6).

At 12.11.22, Augustine again illustrates the difference between corporeal, spiritual, and intellectual *visiones* by means of the already quoted maxim,[46] "You shall love your neighbor as yourself" (Matt. 22:39), however this time adding a further word of explanation. When the statement is read, he recalls, the letters are seen corporeally, the neighbor is thought of spiritually, and love is brought into view intellectually.[47] Once the letters have been read, they are absent from view and their corporeal presence has vanished; however, they can still be thought of spiritually, just as the neighbor in question, although conceived spiritually, can be present.[48]

By contrast, in the case of the notion of love these options are not available. Love cannot be seen as a substance in itself (*per substantiam suam*); that is, it cannot be viewed by means of the bodily eye, and is therefore not a *phantasia*. Nor can it be thought of by means of an image of the body that is similar to it, but which exists solely in the mind, to which Augustine gives the name *phantasma*, since it is in the intellect that this type of *visio* is known and perceived.[49] The eyes of the body are incapable of seeing by means of either spiritual or intellectual vision; instead, they act as messengers, so to speak, announcing what has been perceived externally, as objects, to the internal and judgmental sense of the spiritual sense of sight.[50] Augustine will elsewhere speak of this as the work of the internal sense, which coordinates the inputs of the exterior senses and relays them to the mind, where they are sorted, judged, and recorded.

By overseeing and directing the data furnished by the eyes, and by transferring these from the corporeal to the spiritual level, spiritual vision acts as a parallel for this work of interpretation. This situation arises from the transfer of bodily images to the mind, which is capable of placing them in an ethical context. Augustine hints at this connection between the perceptual and interpretive functions, which is brought about by the will, in the remainder of chapter II. If the soul were irrational, like that of animals, the message from the eyes would go only to the spirit, and not at all to the intellect, which presides over the spirit. Consequently, after the object in question has been taken in by the eyes (*phantasia*) and an announcement has been made to the spirit, the spirit produces a secondary image (*phantasma*), which is passed on to the intellect. It is in the intellect that the decision is made as to whether the object that has been seen is the sign of a thing (*rei signum est*). If so, its meaning is either understood immediately in the intellect or is sought out by means of a method that is utilized only by the mind.[51]

This type of transition is illustrated by the story of Belshazzar's feast from Daniel 5:5–28. This episode is understood by Augustine as an example of a corporeal vision interpreted by an intellectual vision. The hand that the king sees writing on the wall of his palace is taken to represent the imprinting on his spirit of the image of a corporeal object, namely letters, by means of the bodily sense, that is, the eyes. When this corporeal vision was finished, Augustine argues, the image of the letters remained as a spiritual vision in thought (*in cogitatione*). In this way two types of *visio*, namely *corporale* and *spirituale*, were completed, representing the transition from one type of text orientation, namely the physical text, which is perceived by the sense of sight, to another, the imaged text, which is understood in the mind. The visual sign is produced before the eyes of the body in the same way as, within Augustine's general theory of signification, the oral sign is presented to the ears. In his view, this *visio* was seen in the spirit by Belshazzar but not yet understood, since it had appeared only before the king's corporeal eyes, even though his mind was active in inquiring into its meaning. In other words, interpretation in the mind begins proactively, even before the *signum* actually enters the mind, where it can be interpreted and understood. The *visio intellectualis* of which Belshazzar is incapable is then experienced by Daniel, who interprets the handwriting on the wall as a prophecy (12.11.23).

This example completes the transition from philosophy to exegesis in content as well as in method, since what we have in fact is an illustration of reading by means of a reading. Augustine next turns to a number of ways in which the mind can contribute to modifications in the scheme of corporeal, spiritual, and intellectual *visiones*, thus returning the discussion to philosophy. One of these connections arises through the degree to which we are conscious of the passage from one form of vision to another. Let us take the situation in which we are awake, and the mind is not alienated (*alienata*) from the bodily senses but remains in touch with them. In this condition we are able to distinguish a corporeal from a spiritual vision, that is, from the type of vision in which we think of absent bodies by means of the imagination (*qua corpora absentia imaginaliter cogitamus*). The ability to make such a decision lies within our mind's capacities, whether (1) we are recalling things that we know from memory, whether (2) we are thinking of things that we do not know but which are given shape by the thinking that takes place within the spirit itself, or whether (3) through decision or conjecture, we fashion in our minds things that do not exist anywhere in any form (*sive quae omnino nusquam sunt, pro arbitrio vel opinatione fingentes*).

This last can take place when a thought is given too great an extension, or when too much attention is paid to it (*nimia cogitatione intentione*); alternatively when, owing to illness, a person's mind is affected by delirium and fever. It is also possible for the opposite to take place, that is, for one to be in a state of mind in which attention is paid only to one's internal thoughts and the mind is completely cut off from the activity of the senses. In this situation, one can experience a corporeal vision, but the objects that are in view will not be perceived by the subject, even though the eyes may be wide open. Here the mind is concerned with the images that are presented to the spirit, or recalled there, or with images created in the mind itself. Such images may have a special meaning for those who are ill, asleep, or in a state of ecstasy, and, if they are understood, it is owing to the spirit's activity in unfolding their meaning to the mind (12.12.25). Augustine thus reserves a considerable latitude of interpretation for spiritual visions in a pathological context.

Chapters 13 to 22 of *De Genesi* 12 deal with particular problems within the field of imagination. These include divination (12.13), evil as a source of deception (12.14; cf. 12.25), carnal desires experienced in dreams (12.15), the delusions of people suffering from delirium or physical pain (12.17), and impediments to sense perceptions (12.20). At 12.16 an important note is added to what has been said about the retention of images in the memory and their role in the stabilization of the life of the imagination. What is remarkable about a spiritual vision, Augustine observes, is this: spirit takes precedence over body and the image of a body comes after the real body; yet that which is second in temporal succession is produced within that which is prior in nature, that is, the real body. However, because spirit is superior to body, the image of the body that is formed in the spirit excels the body itself in its substance.[52]

This conclusion relates to the notion of spiritual reading insofar as there is auditory retention of the syllables of words that are read, which is essential for their meaning. For unless the spirit continually formed within itself and retained in memory an image of the word perceived through the ears, one would not know whether the second syllable was actually second, since the first would no longer exist once it had impinged upon the ear and passed away. All conventions of speech, all harmony of song, and every orderly movement of the body, Augustine argues, could be dissolved and come to nothing, if in the spirit there were not a memory of past motions to act as guide for those to come. The essential point is this: the spirit would not harbor the memory of such past motions unless it had formed them in the imagination within itself.[53] And it is not only these actions with which it is concerned but also those of the future, well before those actions take place.[54] The ultimate source of these images in the soul remains a mystery, Augustine maintains, just as in everyday speech there are many words that we regularly use and whose origin we do not know (12.18.39).

3. De Trinitate, book 8

Neither letters 6 and 7 nor *De Genesi ad Litteram* 12 take up the role of the imagination in the sort of ideal person Cicero has in mind in his opening statement in *Orator*, when he is speaking of the perfect orator. However, this question is addressed briefly in book 8 of *De Trinitate*, a work written between 399 and 420, in which books 8–15 take up among other things the problems of cognition associated with the threefold image of the Trinity.

Throughout *De Trinitate*, Augustine adheres to a variant of the scheme for the perception and comprehension of images outlined in letter 7. This is summarized at the beginning of book 11, where he notes that, when we see an object, three things are involved: (1) *res*, the object itself, (2) *visio*, the sighting by which it is perceived, and (3) *animi intentio*, the attention or intention of the mind, which directs sight to its object.[55]

The discussion of these elements initially takes shape in book 8, where the reader is reminded that the names of the three persons of the Trinity are used in two ways. They are the particular names given to the Father, Son, and Holy Spirit, and are the names that are "spoken of relationally between each other" (*quae relatiue dicuntur ad inuicem*, 8.1.1). Therefore, when we say, for example, that the figures of the Trinity are both good and omnipotent, we are not speaking of qualities in three different persons but of relations in one God. Such statements are made according to their essence (*secundum essentiam*), since to say that they exist (*esse*) is to say that they are great, good, wise, and so forth. In other words, names imply qualities, and vice versa.

How then can it be that in the Trinity, with respect to these qualities, two or three persons are not greater than one alone? In Augustine's view, this paradox cannot be grasped by the sensory perceptions of mortals, which are limited by the habits or conventions of the flesh (*consuetudo carnalis*, 8.1.2). The senses can only perceive created things (*ipsa . . . creata*) from the outside; they are incapable of seeing from within the truth by which they are created (*ueritatem autem ipsam qua creata sunt non potest intueri*). For it is only truth that truly exists, and in this truth no one thing has more being or existence than another. As a consequence, we cannot say of the Trinity, as we might say of two pieces of gold, that one is greater than the other.

In understanding the Trinity in this relational manner, we get no further ahead in our thinking by the use of the literary imagination. We cannot conceive the three persons of the Trinity, for example, as we would a threefold division in fables (*fabulae*), as in the story of Heracles's overcoming the three-headed monster, Geryon.[56] Nor can we envisage the triune God along the lines of anything that we see (or do not see) in the heavens. For even if, in the sort of thinking that is associated with image making or with the imagination (*imaginationis cogitatio*), one were able to magnify the light of the sun as it is conceived in the mind as much as possible, in order to make it seem, in degrees, to be brighter or stronger than it ever was before, and even if this increase in brightness, which is entirely dependent on the mind, were to take place by as much as a thousand degrees, the radiance in the end would not be the equal of the light of God. Augustine adds that other analogies based on literary or metaphorical schemes are likewise to be rejected in this type of comparison, for example, the notion of spirits without bodies. All such views are inexact and misleading, since mortals are encumbered by corruptible bodies and dependent on the uncertain data of the senses. They are unable to understand fully and completely how God can be truth, since they are impeded by the mists of bodily images (*caligines imaginum corporalium*) and the clouds of phantasms (*nubila phantasmatum*). We perceive the truth of God in an instantaneous flash of insight, but this is a fleeting moment in our experience and does not last. We rise temporarily, but inevitably fall back to our habitual and earthly way of thinking (*relaberis in ista solita atque terrena*, 8.2.3).

This statement is a mixture of ideas from Plato and Plotinus. Augustine's point of departure is Platonic doubt about the value of sense data. But his scheme includes the Plotinian notion of mental elevation, through which the individual moves upward from the senses to the mind and beyond. It is the metaphor and metaphysics of seeing that gives a framework to his statements on these themes and leads him in due course to a problem similar to that posed by Brutus to Cicero concerning a perfect orator. However, in the end his solution is the result of a nonphilosophical line of reasoning, and it is here that I would like to bring a more general question to his discussion of *phantasia*.

The section in question begins in book 8, chapter 3, with an enumeration of things that can be called good. Among these are creation, living things, a healthy life, friends, and their affection—even the eloquence of a polished lecture, as Cicero and Quintilian propose, which succeeds in moving the audience toward the conclusion desired by the speaker. On the other hand, when we say that we love God because he is good, we are not distinguishing between one sort of good and another, as in these examples of good things, nor are we trying to persuade anyone of anything using emotional appeals. On the contrary, we recognize that God is nothing more or less than good itself (*ipsum bonum*).

In the next stage of his argument Augustine departs from the classical lines of thought utilized by his predecessors in the rhetorical tradition and strikes out in a direction of his own, basing his conclusions on considerations of will and language. He asks us to think about what takes place when we hear the words, "good soul." In his view, two things are understood, namely "soul" and "good." It is one thing to be a soul, another to be good. The soul does not bring itself into being by its own act of will; however, in order to be a good soul, it has to perform an act of will, which consists in turning itself toward the good. The human soul has this unique characteristic, namely, that it can freely choose to be good or bad, and thus to incur praise or blame. However, in order to become good, after deciding to do so, the soul has to look for guidance from something that it is not, namely, the good, since, as agreed, it is not innately good. The only thing toward which it can turn (*conuertat*) is the good itself, which it loves, desires, and therefore approaches (*cum hoc amat et appetit et adispicitur*).

As a consequence, Augustine proposes, we can assert that there can be no goods that change over time (*mutabilia bona*) unless there exists a single good that does not change over time (*incommutabile bonum*). It is to this that the soul must convert itself in order to become good (*se igitur animus conuertit ut bonus sit*). Augustine conceives the decision to be good on the part of the soul as its entry into a state of self-awareness, which requires a continual effort of will to be maintained and perpetuated. The soul must remain steadfast in good, and inhere in it, so that it can profit from its presence. It is in fact from this willful participation in the good that the soul derives its being, as contrasted with the contrary, namely absence of the good, which would render it incapable of being.[57] This decision in favor of the good is an act of faith, not a source of knowledge, on the part of the soul. For we do not know the good toward which we are directing our thoughts, any more than, as Paul says, we can see God "face to face" (1 Cor. 13:12).

If that is the case, how can it be said that we love (*diligamus*) something that we are unable to see (*uidebimus*)? For who can say in truth that he loves what he does not know (*Sed quis diligat quod ignorat?*). Something can be known and not loved, but can something be loved and not known? It follows that no one can love God before, in some sense, knowing him (*nemo diligit deum antequem sciat*). And what does it mean to know God (*deum scire*), if not to see him in the mind or soul (*cum mente conspicere*) and, in this fashion, to perceive him with certainty (*fermeque percipere*)? It is possible for those who have pure hearts and practice faith, hope, and charity to see God, and it is to this end that works of religion (*divini libri*) are studied for the soul's benefit (*in animo aedificanda*). The result is that it is possible for someone of faith to believe in God without knowing him, and in this sense God is loved before he is known.[58]

With this conclusion Augustine arrives at a problem shared by a number of ancient schools of philosophy, namely the care of the soul. Care must be taken, he notes, lest the soul, in trusting in what it does not see, perceives something that it has configured for itself which it itself is not (*ne credens animus id quod non uidet fingat sibi aliquid quod non est*), and thereby love what is false. This would be tantamount to placing faith in *phantasia* or *imaginatio*. In rejecting this alternative, Augustine falls back once again on a variant of the Platonic mistrust of the senses. When we believe in corporeal things of which we have heard or read but have not seen, he notes, our minds represent them as things with a bodily delineation and features (*fingat sibi animus aliquid in lineamentis formisque corporum*). It will occur to anyone engaged in this type of thinking or configuring (*cogitanti*) that the image in the mind may be either false or true, but even if it is true, no profit can be derived from it, since there is no way that an objective verification can be made. For who, for example, on reading the writings of Paul, or hearing accounts of his life and works, is not capable of creating a picture of the apostle's face in their minds (*non fingat animo et ipsius apostoli faciem*)? There would doubtless be many possible portraits of this type, all based on purely subjective considerations. However, in Augustine's view, the correct way to approach this sort of problem is not to begin with invented images of what Paul looked like (*facie corporis*) but, guided by faith, to take as our point of departure the sort of life that he led, through God's grace, and the kinds of deeds that he performed (*ita uixerunt et ea gesserunt*), all of which is attested in scripture.

On this view, what is the source of our affection for the apostle? Is it because he was once a living human being? That cannot be possible, for since he died in the past, the memory of death is with us in the present, as argued in letter 7. Also, the source of our affection for him is his just soul, which is unaffected by the passage of time. We know what a soul is because there is a soul in each of us. This is not something that we can see with our eyes; nor do we acquire our knowledge about the soul either from its features or from its similarity to other souls. Yet, paradoxically, there is nothing that is so intimately known by each of us as our souls, since it is by means of our souls that we know everything else that we know.[59] We recognize the movements of bodies from their resemblance to our own movements, as it appears before our eyes; however, no one can perceive the movement of the soul, even though, within our souls, we are aware that movement is taking place. Consequently, if we know the soul of another person, we do so based on our knowledge of our own souls, believing of that person what we do not in fact know of him.[60] For we not only know that we possess a soul but can learn something about what a soul is from our reflections on it.

However, when we turn to the question of a "just man," as we do in forming an image of Paul, a different criterion applies. As noted, we know what a soul is simply from the fact that each of us has a soul. By analogy, we cannot understand what a just man is unless we are just ourselves.

Augustine's subsequent argument is complicated and can be summarized in point form as follows. First, on the question of a "just man" belief is not

sufficient: we need certain knowledge. But how is this to be acquired? Augustine is convinced that we cannot love what we cannot observe by means of
sight. This is a reinterpretation of Paul's view of faith. Yet how are we to see
the just soul of the just man, since nothing pertaining to his state of mind
appears before our eyes? In Augustine's view, and this is his second point, the
answer lies within the will. If a man is not just and desires to become just, he
must express the intention of becoming just, which implies that he desires or
loves a just man who actually exists, since, again, we must judge by what we
see since we cannot see into his soul. It is only in this way that someone who
is not yet just can say that he knows what a just man is. However, Augustine
notes that the Platonic problem remains, since we have to ask in what sense
such a person can say with confidence that by this process he actually "sees"
the attractive ideal of justice. The only possible answer is that we know what
a just man is from within ourselves (*In nobis igitur nouimus quid sit iustus*).
For when he seeks to utter the words "a just man," Augustine only finds the
meaning of the words he is speaking in his own mind or soul. The same is
true if he asks another person the question. He too must find the answer within
himself. To seek what is justice, therefore, involves a method, but it is one in
which the relevant questions and answers arise entirely within the mind of
the individual.[61]

This is an exploration of the Pauline scheme as well as an original application of the Socratic elenchus. However, at this point in the discussion
Augustine also moves in a different direction from either Cicero or Quintilian
on the questions of images by taking up the notions of both *phantasia* and
phantasma, considered in relation to each other. These terms, which frequently enter his reflections on internal representations, are applied to the image of a person that is formed of purely abstract qualities. Again Augustine
notes that he can find the image of Carthage in his mind, because he has lived
there, but Alexandria, where he has not lived, can only be configured as a
product of his imagination. The important point is that in both cases it suf-
fices for him to pronounce the syllables of the place names in order to bring
before his internal view an image of the locality. Once this image is in his
mind, he is able to describe these cities in detail for others, who can in turn
judge the accuracy of his descriptions, if they are familiar with them. Further, he notes, while he is engaged in speaking these syllables, he is at the
same time able to gaze within upon the mental pictures of these cities, as they
are conjured up, both from the realities he knows, in the case of Carthage,
and from studied inventions, in the case of Alexandria; and, believing these

for what they are worth, respectively, he concludes that he will likewise have trust or faith in the descriptions of cities in the words of others. The essential link is between language and putative reality, not, as in Plato, between appearance and reality, since, within this scheme, the statuses of the images of Carthage and Alexandria are equally valid with respect to the syllables pronounced.

But when it is a question of a just man, Augustine proposes, the concepts of *phantasia* and *phantasma* do not apply in precisely the same way. In his view, the remarkable thing about the soul, in its attempts to frame a mental picture of Paul, is that it can visualize his "just soul," and it also perceives that this is not the same just soul that, with some effort, his own soul may be able to perceive within itself. In other words, the same rules for other minds that apply to images generated within the soul, for which there is no external model, apply to those which are generated from either sense perceptions or the accounts of others, as in the cases, respectively, of Carthage and Alexandria. Although Augustine does not have a specific term for this type of image generation, it might tentatively be called a work of the creative imagination, inasmuch as it is an image, which he has conceded, but one that is based on no antecedent model which he can recognize, since, as he notes, he cannot recognize the quality of justice in another person, even one who is dead, without first being able to recognize it in himself. In the end, therefore, the mental picture that he forms of Paul is composed of a combination of faith and intentions, and, as such, is superior in his view to images made up from sense data that are perceived first- or second-hand by the perceiving subject.

*   *   *

What conclusions can we draw from these three discussions of *phantasia*? First, it is clear that Augustine has taken important steps in progressing beyond Platonic, Neoplatonic, and Stoic notions of visual appearances and has entered into the realm of the contemplative imagination in his discussion of texts. In this respect he is following Cicero and Quintilian; however, in pursuing this course, he takes an intellectual route that differs from that of his Roman predecessors in as much as it involves reading.

In his exchange of letters with Nebridius, his analysis of the problem of memory images is based chiefly on psychology and philosophy; in the examples taken from *De Genesi* 12 and *De Trinitate* 8, it is based exclusively on statements in biblical texts. The earlier stage of his thinking is a reflection of his confidence in reason before his baptism and ordination; the later discussions are illustrations of his thinking on reason within the principle of authority. Reason is not entirely replaced by authority as the discussion moves forward from his pre- to post-conversion period; however, instead of being utilized to advance arguments that are true or false according to their logic alone, reason is used as a tool to defend statements which are assumed to be true. To Augustine's way of approaching the question of the soul's powers, they constitute the most authoritative statements on the subject, and while they may demand a rational explication, they do not demand a rational defense of their truths, which are historical rather than philosophical in nature.

Augustine's solution to the philosophical dimension of the problem, therefore, is not, strictly speaking, philosophical. Where he truly succeeds in transcending ancient thinking on *phantasia* is in shifting the burden of his argument from philosophy to literature, as he does in the *Confessions*. In this work it is not his arguments about the truth or falsity of images that are the center of attention, but the manner in which he applies his theory of *phantasia* and *phantasma* to his own experience. His presentation is compelling, as Quintilian might say, because it is convincing: the emotions that he generates in his readers are those that he truly appears to have felt himself. In the end it does not matter that he has dealt with the philosophical dimension of the subject in a fragmentary and incomplete fashion, rather than approaching it in the more disciplined manner of figures whom he admires on the subject, especially Plato and Plotinus. For his long-range purpose in taking up the topic is not to provide a purely philosophical account of *phantasia*, but to use what he knows about it from philosophy and psychology in the production of an entirely new type of theological literature, in which the various episodes in a story are woven together by memory and history. In this he is the Christian successor, not only to Plato, but also to Seneca and Plutarch.

CHAPTER 3

The Philosophical Soliloquy

One of the ways in which late ancient authors approached questions of the self was by means of a form of the Socratic elenchus that I have elsewhere called the inner dialogue.[1] Augustine makes extensive use of this type of dialogue, for example in *De Ordine* and the *Soliloquia*, where his interlocutor is the personification of his rational faculties,[2] and in the *Confessions*, where he is in conversation with his own past.

In this chapter I offer a sketch of the evolution of this literary form in the late Hellenistic period and in late antiquity, drawing on illustrations from the writings of Seneca, Epictetus, Marcus Aurelius, Plotinus, Augustine, and Boethius. My concern is with the relationship between the literary and philosophical elements in the inner dialogues utilized by these authors and can be viewed as a contribution to the inquiry in recent years into literary forms of expression in philosophy, in particular in Plato and the Platonic tradition.[3]

Although it was Augustine who invented the term *soliloquium*[4] to describe the literary and philosophical soliloquy, the form was already well established as a genre of discourse by the fourth century A.D. There are speeches that qualify as soliloquies in Homer, as well as in Aeschylus, Sophocles, Euripides, and Aristophanes.[5] Soliloquies are attributed to Pythagoras[6] and the Presocratics.[7] Socrates comments positively, if briefly, on their function in the *Sophist*, *Theaetetus*, and *Philebus*. Plato makes use of the technique in the *Crito* and *Hippias Major*.[8]

The number and variety of internal dialogues employed in philosophy increased during the Hellenistic period and late antiquity. By the time Augustine composed the *Soliloquia*, in the winter of 386–387, the soliloquy had become an independent literary genre in both Greek and Latin thought and was recognized as an alternative, or complement, to the open dialogue.[9]

Augustine is highly original in the uses to which he puts inner dialogues and does not appear to be imitating earlier writers who employ the technique. However, among authors whom he is known to have read, it should be noted that Cicero speaks highly of inner dialogue, although he does not utilize the form often, and Horace, who occasionally speaks to himself in his verse, on one occasion comments on soliloquizing as a method of composition, as he strolls along the Via Sacra in Rome.[10]

In my view, the rise in interest in the soliloquy within the field of philosophy was the consequence of two parallel and interdependent developments arising in the Hellenistic period. One was the revival of the Socratic method of teaching, common to different schools, in which inner dialogue easily became an extension of outer or formal interchanges of this type.[11] The other was the widespread use of internal or reflective interpretive methods for accompanying the classroom discussion of a variety of ancient texts, including those of philosophers. The history of the soliloquy in the late ancient period can be viewed as an intermingling of these traditions, in which training in grammar, rhetoric, and interpretive methods provided a common background for the use of the technique of self-talk in philosophical schools with diverse intellectual allegiances.

In attempting to provide a history of the use of this form in philosophy, it is important to bear in mind that, after the death of the founders of the major schools, the teaching of philosophy was gradually transformed into an academic type of pursuit, in which there were professors, a curriculum of set texts, and institutional arrangements for instruction. Students were initiated into the doctrines of the different schools through the study of the writings of their founders—figures such as Plato, Aristotle, Epicurus, Zeno, and Chrysippus.[12] Instruction normally took place in two stages: a master first read and commented orally on a school's foundational or canonical texts, possibly drawing on his personal notes; then he engaged in a discussion with his students on the doctrines found in these texts, sometimes illustrating his views by means of examples.[13]

In both segments of the lesson the master was obliged to make use of interpretive techniques; these could be based on the written materials on which he was lecturing or, in combination with these, on other readings. What Augustine calls a *soliloquium* was one type of interpretive procedure within the second stage of instruction, in which a verbal exchange of ideas between a master and his students was replaced or supplemented by a silent dialogue within individual students' minds. The passage from an outer to an inner mode of communication often went unremarked, since ancient reading and commentary were frequently carried on orally while the lesson was in progress, as contrasted with later periods, when commentary was often a separate activity that took place after the initial reading of set texts.[14]

During late antiquity, and continuing into the Middle Ages, it was a short step from these *voces paginarum*, as they were sometimes called, to voices in the minds of readers and interpreters of texts.[15] There are references to the use of inner dialogues for interpretive purposes in both Greek and Latin authors; for example, as noted, in Plutarch's pedagogical treatise, *How a Young Person Should Listen to Poems*, where students are advised to talk to themselves (*pros heauton eipein*) after the master's exposition of literary texts,[16] or in Augustine's early dialogue, *De Ordine*, where his friends and followers are likewise invited to mobilize their internal resources after classroom readings of Virgil, Cicero, and the Bible.[17] In training in philosophy this sort of activity often encouraged rote learning rather than original inquiries; however, a few thinkers working within the system attempted to revive the aims of the Socratic method of instruction and complemented their lessons by means of inner dialogues. It is with their achievements that I am concerned.

Seneca

It is helpful to begin a discussion of the literary and philosophical elements in the period's soliloquies with Seneca, since he provides the most detailed description of the soliloquy as a technique of self-examination among the writings of Hellenistic thinkers.[18] This is of course a Stoic version of the inner dialogue, and it is valuable as a point of departure for a broader inquiry into the genre because "eclectic" Stoics like Seneca considered themselves to be among the authentic heirs to the Socratic tradition.[19]

The relevant passage appears in *De Ira*,[20] where Seneca recalls the practice of self-scrutiny in a little-known Stoic teacher, Quintus Sextius the Elder (fl. ca. 50 B.C.). This is recommended as a way of calming unruly emotions and establishing a tranquil frame of mind. Seneca notes that "the senses have to be governed in a way that brings about firmness or stability (*firmitatem*)," as contrasted with an approach that can contribute to their "enfeeblement, owing to . . . the subject's mental disposition (*animus*)."

In pursuit of this goal, Sextius went over his daily activities and routines every night before going to bed, asking himself such questions as "'What bad habit did you cure today?', 'What vice did you resist?', 'In what way are you a better person?'" By following his example, Seneca argues,

> our anger will be somewhat reduced and made more manageable, if we know that the emotion will come before this kind of judgment every day. In the light of this fact, what could be more attractive than this practice of thoroughly sorting out each day (*hac consuetudine excutiendi . . . diem*)? How beautiful is the sleep that follows this recollection (*recognitionem*), how tranquil, how profound and undisturbed (*quam altus et liber*), when the mind has either approved or criticized itself, and when this secret investigator and judge of oneself (*speculator sui censorque secretus*) has become acquainted with one's behavior (*cognovit de moribus suis*).

Seneca adds that he personally makes

> good use of this potential (*potestate*). Every day I plead my case before myself (*cotidie apud me causam dico*). When I no longer see the light, and my wife, conscious of my habit, has fallen silent, I examine the whole of my day (*totum diem meum scrutor*) and judge the value of my deeds and words (*factaque ac dicta mea remetior*). I conceal nothing from myself, I omit nothing. For why should I fear any of my errors, when I am able to say the following words to myself: "See that you no longer do this." "I will overlook it this time." "In that debate you spoke too belligerently. In future do not argue with the uneducated: those who have not learned anything evidently do not wish to learn anything." "You criticized that person more frankly than was necessary; consequently you have not improved him but only caused offence." "Moreover, see that you not only speak the truth but that the person whom you are addressing is in a frame of mind that is receptive to the truth. A good man is always happy to be corrected; however, the worse the man is, the less he takes to any sort of advice."

As practiced by Stoics and by members of other philosophical schools interested in the Socratic heritage,[21] this type of self-scrutiny is a personal affair: it takes place in solitude, its medium is the human voice, and it works by means of questions and answers within the mind. In Pierre Hadot's words,

its purpose is nothing less than "the mastery of the subject's inner discourse,"[22] and as such it forms a critical part of a program for personal advancement by attaining an equilibrium between mind and body. It is a
technique midway between the traditional form of spiritual guidance[23] and a
more personal type, later developed by Augustine, in which direction is
largely carried on internally by the subject himself. If philosophy is divisible
into *scientia* and *habitus animi*,[24] as Seneca proposes, routines of this type are
among the practices that ensure the soul's advancement by means of its own
activity: *animi bonum animus inveniat.*[25]

Seneca's outline of Sextius's practice is evidently the result of reading, personal contacts, and instruction. This is revealed by his form of presentation, in
which he describes soliloquizing as a received doctrine and provides a discussion of its usefulness, thereby reiterating the two stages of the master's normal
form of teaching. Also, in his handling of the frequently encountered theme
of spiritual direction,[26] he pictures himself acting as a guide for his friend
Novatus, to whom *De Ira* is dedicated, just as Sextius is mentor for him. This
is the setup for discipleship that is found throughout the *dialogi* and *epistulae.* Finally, he cannot resist the temptation of playing before an audience. As
he reports, he and Sextius reexamine their daily activities before going to bed;
however, in his case this takes place in the presence of his wife, who is accus-
tomed to his routine and remains quiet in order to permit him to concentrate
(*et conticuit uxor moris iam mei conscia*). She clearly represents ambient talk,
dramatizing his need for outer silence while engaging in self-scrutiny.

It is also clear that a deliberate design is at work in the literary setup of
the *dialogi.* These writings may not have been conceived as "dialogues" in the
traditional sense of the term, but as a hybrid of external and internal types of
discourse.[27] In view of this intermingling of genres Miriam Griffin legitimately
asks:

> Into what category does the description *dialogi* put these works,
> which have no named characters, no organized conversation,
> no definite setting? What relation can this use of the word bear to
> Cicero's, for whom it meant live debate or a type of literary
> composition exemplified by his own philosophical and rhetorical
> works? In the early Empire, the word still seems to be used, as it
> always had been, of philosophical works with named characters
> and organized debate.[28]

Seneca does not take up the question of genre; however, he hints at the manner in which soliloquies may have made their way into his process of composition in an aside at *De Tranquillitate Animi* 1.14, where he states:

> In my literary studies I think it is surely better to fix my eyes on the theme itself (*res ipsas*) and, keeping this uppermost when I speak, to trust meanwhile to the theme to supply the words so that unstudied discourse (*inelaborata . . . oratio*) may follow wherever it leads.[29]

Here inner dialogue is viewed as both a compositional and an instructional device, and that is how it is envisaged in the *dialogi*. Within these works the represented conversations normally takes one of two forms. In the simpler version, the soliloquy consists in a pair of speaking voices within Seneca's mind, as in *De Vita Beata*.[30] Here the soul, interrogating itself,[31] develops its inner resources,[32] frees itself from emotion,[33] and acquires virtue,[34] as Seneca (or the reader) takes control of the shaping of his (or her) life.[35] In the more complicated version, the internal speeches take place within an external dialogue, as in *De Tranquillitate Animi*, where the (imagined) interlocutors are Seneca and the prefect Serenus (d. A.D. 63). Here soliloquies arise in the mind of each speaker during (or after) conversations and follow a similar strategy for the soul's improvement.[36] Serenus is said to learn of the source of his illness (enslavement to emotion)[37] by means of self-inquiry (*inquirenti mihi*),[38] and Seneca confirms that the situation arises from the emotional disposition of his mind (*adfectum animi*) by means of silent questioning within himself (*quaero . . . tacitus*).[39] The starting point for the discovery of the malady and the healing process that follows is self-assessment *Ante omnia necesse est se ipsum aestimare*.[40] Once emotional health is restored, these internal conversations maintain the soul's tranquility and contentment.[41]

A still more complicated scheme is worked out in the *Epistulae Morales*,[42] where Seneca acts as both teacher and thinker, imparting doctrines while at the same time taking part in the discussions as a participant. He can thereby benefit from the very instruction he desires for his disciple.[43] He alternates between being a real and a fictional person, while his correspondent plays the role of alter ego. Talking to Lucilius, therefore, Seneca is frequently talking either to himself, to himself through his pupil, or to himself and his pupil at the same time. In the early letters the image of a living correspondent is kept before the reader, whereas in the later and lengthier epistles the personal connection is less emphasized. In these letters the presentation of Stoic doctrines takes precedence over the open discussion of Stoic, Epicurean, and Aristotelian themes.[44] In this respect, the rhetorical techniques utilized in the *dialogi* and the *Epistulae Morales* can be considered variants of the same model, in which personal characterization of the speakers in the dialogue has both a philosophical and a dramatic function.[45] What differs in the letters is the part played by the implied reader, which is considerably amplified while nonetheless remaining within the compass of the Stoic notion of spiritual direction.[46]

Epictetus

A different approach to the philosophical soliloquy is taken by Epictetus, who lived between roughly A.D. 50 and 120. In his *Discourses*, self-scrutiny and teaching are taken up in a series of open dialogues, while inner dialogues are often employed in handling topics in pedagogy or theology.

Through the recording of these outer dialogues, the *Discourses* allow us, as readers, to become witnesses to the classroom discussions that took place between Epictetus and his students during normal periods of instruction in philosophy.[47] The participants in these classes were chiefly young men from the city of Nicopolis, where Epictetus taught after the expulsion of philosophers from Rome in 94. Owing to his fame as a teacher, there were frequently visitors in his school from privileged families elsewhere in the Empire.[48]

The lessons were based on the teaching methods of Socrates, for which Epictetus never tires of expressing his admiration.[49] However, the *Discourses* differ considerably from their acknowledged source of inspiration, and chiefly in four ways. The dialogues that have come down to us are on the whole shorter than those of Epictetus's model; they are recorded in a less literary style than that of Plato (i.e., in colloquial Greek or *koine*);[50] they contain more repetitions in themes and methods than do the originals;[51] and their subject matter is in general more limited in scope.[52] It has been observed more than once that these qualities give the *Discourses* a false appearance of spontaneity, and thereby make them "deceptively simple to read."[53] We are apt to overlook an important fact: in Epictetus, the inner dialogue, as a by-product of the exterior dialogue, is presented as an alternative, perhaps deliberate, to the Socratic form of dialogue, principally by deformalizing its language and style of presentation.[54] Not only is the language of discourse simplified. There are no privileged partners in these conversations, which take place with persons named[55] and unnamed,[56] as well as with a variety of invented figures.[57]

Epictetus thereby suggests that the study of philosophy can be more open and accessible than in the form in which it is presented in the more elitist writings of Plato. He nonetheless adheres to Socrates's view that persons pursuing the philosophical life must engage in some form of regular self-examination, for which, in the *Discourses*, soliloquies are sometimes employed.[58] His point of departure in these exercises is Socrates's teaching on the dual function of reason. In this view, reason is self-reflective, that is, it is able to understand itself,[59] while, as a tool for rational or logical thinking, it works alongside other disciplines that employ comparable principles of organization, such as those of the liberal arts.[60] Within this framework the inner dialogue in Epictetus serves a traditional instructional purpose,[61] supplementing the master's formal lessons[62] while at the same time addressing a variety of everyday ethical and philosophical problems among his students.[63]

In Epictetus's view, inner discourses of this type are solo performances, like short dramatic speeches, whereas the open dialogue is comparable to the chorus in an ancient drama, in which there is a joint expression of views by a group of people at once.[64] He makes ample use of both forms, and does not always distinguish clearly between them. Inner dialogue is mostly reserved for moments when his students mull over their lessons in solitude,[65] notes in hand, so that they can at once read, write, and commune with themselves.[66] In the master's view, they should engage in inner dialogues while he is teaching[67] as well as during the classroom discussions that follow.[68] It is in this manner, he points out, that he himself often reflects on personal ethical questions, such as the theft of his bedside lamp from his study,[69] as well as more general philosophical matters, such as the role of hypothetical syllogisms in framing arguments.[70]

His use of soliloquies in these contexts is not formalized, and arises in most cases out of the type of discussion that take place in normal conversation. A typical example of his approach is found in the opening chapter of book 3, where Arrian records the visit to his school by a student of rhetoric from Corinth.[71] The young man arrived in the classroom too ornately dressed for the master's austere taste; however, instead of offering direct criticism, Epictetus asked the newcomer with mock innocence whether there was not a more worthwhile inner criterion for judging something of beauty than the clothes he was wearing.[72] He had in mind the student's capacity for understanding the nature of justice, which, if allowed to mature, would presumably enhance his attractiveness to others as well as to himself.[73] However, in order to comprehend a beauty of this type, the young man would have first to conduct a Socratic inquiry into the kind of person he was, scrutinizing himself rigorously from within.[74] After delivering his comments on the theme, Epictetus concluded with these words:

> Beyond that (i.e., inner transformation) I do not know what more I
> can say to you; for if I say what I have in mind, I will hurt your
> feelings, and you will leave, perhaps never to return; on the other
> hand, if I remain silent . . . I will not be saying anything to you as a
> philosopher . . . . If some time in the future you come to your
> senses, you will have good reason to blame me. "What did Epicte-
> tus observe in me," you will say to yourself . . . : "Although he saw
> me . . . in so disgraceful a state he . . . let me remain this way and
> never said a word."[75]

Both these putative conversations—that of Epictetus allegedly talking to himself and that of the student, imagining himself talking to his master—provide illustrations of a principle that is central to Epictetus's thinking about the philosophical life. This is the concept of *prohairesis*, a term that is difficult to translate by a single word but which means in his writings a combination of will, moral purpose, and ethical commitment. It is a notion that has distant, and perhaps untraceable, Aristotelian roots but clearly develops in an original manner in the *diatribai*,[76] where it refers globally to "the possibility of free moral self-determination"[77] and oversees faculties involved in ethical decisions, including both speech and sight.[78] In Anthony Long's words, *prohairesis* thereby becomes Epictetus's foundation for self-care:[79]

> Rather than treating the moral point of view as a disposition that
> is distinct from self-concern, he presents it as all of a piece within
> the natural or proper understanding of one's human identity. That
> identity is one's volition or *prohairesis*, the only inalienable thing
> that we have and that we are. It is in virtue of *prohairesis* that we
> are capable of conscience and self-consciousness—knowing
> ourselves, reflecting on who we are, and reasoning about how we
> should organize our lives.[80]

This is a version of what I am calling an "integrated self," which Augustine will develop along somewhat comparable principles of self-maintenance, however, using the notions of will and linguistic philosophy as his foundations for ethical conduct. Epictetus may have anticipated this view, although he is not a direct influence, by linking the notion of *prohairesis* to that of *prolepsis* (preconception), that is, to the manner in which the subject is presented with the possibility of a way of imagining or talking to himself about how events that may potentially affect his emotional state may in fact take place. The combination consists in

> applying . . . preconceptions to particular cases . . . in conformity with nature, [and distinguishing between] things that are and are not under our control. Under our control are moral purpose (*prohairesis*) and all actions with moral purpose (*panta ta prohairetica erga*).[81]

These forces permit the individual to choose freely between good and evil,[82] and to prepare for unexpected turns of events,[83] reducing anxieties.[84] A role for interior conversation is thereby created, since these are the sorts of events about which people hear, read, and talk with themselves.[85] In Epictetus's view, such thinking comprises an appropriate "topic of investigation for the person who embarks on philosophy (*zetesis tou philosophantos*),"[86] and frames hypotheses (*anastrephometha*) about the kind of life he wants to lead.[87]

A second function for soliloquies is found in Epictetus's statements that contain a combination of philosophical and theological reflections. The early thesis of Christian influence on these parts of the *Discourses* has been abandoned;[88] however, it is recognized that Epictetus uncannily parallels New Testament and patristic phrasing in such matters as his conception of the Stoic god as a "father," who knows us, observes us, and listens to our supplications,[89] including inner speeches uttered for his consideration. While this god is identified through pantheism with the workings of nature,[90] he is envisaged as operating through divine will[91] and arranging everything in the universe in a manner that permits mortals to understand his diverse purposes by means of their own investigations.[92] Epictetus frequently displays his piety and humility before this awesome force in terms reminiscent of the Psalms:

> I came into the world when it so pleased him,
> I will leave it at his pleasure;

while I lived this was my purpose—
to sing hymns of praise . . . .[93]

Also, in parallel with Judaism, Christianity, and Greek polytheism,[94] he envisages god as speaking through his chosen disciples, the philosophers, who interpret the *logos*, which is his word.[95] In expressing these views, Epictetus frequently addresses the deity through prayers, and in these are found, as later in Augustine, some of his most profound and poetic soliloquies.[96]

He is convinced that "it is impossible for man to conceal from god, not merely his actions, but even his purposes and thoughts."[97] The deity has endowed us with an innate capacity for tranquility and happiness;[98] however, the constraints of the mortal condition have to be recognized:

> Over the things that we seriously care for no one has authority; and
> the things over which other men have authority do not concern
> us . . . . Has god not given you that which is your own, unhindered
> and unrestrained . . . .? Your faithfulness is your own, your
> self-respect is your own. Who can take these things from you?
> Who but yourself will prevent you from using them? . . . Since
> you have such promptings and orientations from the divine . . . ,
> you can produce your own preconceptions (*prolēpseis*)."[99]

Those engaged in inner dialogues on these themes are likened to "spectators" in the crowded "theaters" of their own thoughts.[100] They effectively become audiences for their own speeches,[101] in both his theology and philosophy.[102] In this respect, Richard Sorabji notes, Epictetus is comparable to Cicero inasmuch as he

> recognizes the same mixture of choice and nature, and uses the
> same metaphor of an actor's roles,[103] but with the complication that
> he sees our roles, character, ability, occupation and status, as to
> some extent assigned by God.[104] Nonetheless we all have choice.
> We must tell ourselves who we want to be (*tis einai theleis*) and then
> act accordingly . . . . There are, as in Cicero, a general reference
> point (*koinē anaphora*), viz. acting like a human being . . . and an
> individual reference point, concerning our occupation (*epitēdeuma*)
> and will (*prohairesis*).[105]

In Epictetus's words:

> When you mix in society or take physical exercise, or converse
> with others, are you with you . . . and yet are unaware of it? This is
> not a god outside, of course . . . . but one inside, whom you can
> listen to within yourselves . . . , whom, while hearing, you may
> dishonour . . . . Even before his image you would not dare to do
> some of the things you do: is it not worse to do them in his presence,
> since he is always present within you?[106] When we are alone,
> therefore, talking silently to ourselves, we are not truly alone. Just
> as we listen to ourselves, god listens to us.[107]

Such self-address begins in a Socratic fashion with the acknowledgment
of ignorance.[108] In order to advance we have to narrow our focus to essentials[109]
and acquire the skills needed for dealing with our specific problems. Epictetus is fond of comparing these to the ability to read and write, or to playing a
musical instrument, noting on one occasion: "If you want to be a good reader,
you have to read; if you want to be a good writer, you have to write,"[110] and on
another: "What . . . is it that makes a man free from hindrance and restraint
in writing? The knowledge of how to write. And what in playing on the harp?
The knowledge of how to play the harp. So too in living it is the knowledge
of how to live."[111]

If we are to benefit from dialogue with ourselves, therefore, we have to
practice inner conversation day after day:[112] to observe ourselves, as god observes us;[113] to think about ourselves,[114] having purged our minds of illusions[115]
and sensory impressions (*phantasias*).[116] "In the way in which we respond to
questions involving sophistry," he notes, "we should exercise ourselves daily to
counteract the false images produced by our senses."[117] We cannot free ourselves from such sources of error merely by discussing the views of philosophers, past or present, nor can we acquire the necessary knowledge from
different sorts of books.[118] We have to withdraw from external things entirely,
and turn our attention to inner moral purpose (*prohairesin*), cultivating and
perfecting ourselves through personal analysis.[119] Without the processes of
reasoning and judgment that such an exercise entails, the works of eminent
thinkers have no more value in the shaping of the ethical side of our lives than
the telling of mere stories (*historias*).[120]

In Epictetus's view, "that is why philosophers advise us not to be satisfied
with mere learning (*mono to mathein*) but to bring to it meditation (*meleten*)

and training (*askesin*)."[121] Echoing, but transforming, the second part of the normal instructional process in philosophy, he notes:

> A little while ago it was god's will for you to be at leisure, to converse with yourself, to write about these things, to read, to listen, to prepare yourself. You had sufficient time for that. Now he says to you: "Come at length to the contest, show us what you have learned, how you have trained yourself."[122]

The exercises have to be performed slowly and patiently over a long period, since we can only observe ourselves taking control in stages.[123] In this process inner sight precedes inner words, and inner dialogue, which follows, is an enabling device, comparable, as suggested, to the overcoming of illiteracy.[124] Above all, we have to learn to live in society and yet remain apart from it, dialoguing within ourselves:

> A person can often find himself in the company of people who are misled in a variety of ways. Such people are ignorant of their sources of error, how they have come by them, and how they can be rid of them. While we are in such company it is always a good idea to engage in self-examination and self-questioning. I can ask myself: "Am I like them? Am I the person I imagine myself to be? Is my conduct appropriate? Am I prudent and temperate? Do I have self-control? Am I sufficiently educated to meet whatever comes, or is that just a claim that I am making?"[125]

Marcus Aurelius

The third author whom I have singled out for attention in the late ancient history of the inner dialogue is Marcus Aurelius, whose *Meditations* marks a new phase in the integration of literary and philosophical techniques.[126]

The *Meditations* is thought to have been written a few years before the emperor's death in 180,[127] possibly under the title, "Thoughts to Himself" (*ta eis heauton*). The book has been described as a set of exercises on "self-discipline and self-address" and as a "private work of self-analysis and devotion;" however, it might equally well have been called "*Soliloquies*," since, as R. B. Rutherford notes, its contents "are not predominantly reflections, pensées, or miniature essays . . . but statements in which the author tends to be talking to and at himself ."[128] The *Meditations* is in fact the earliest (extant) philosophical treatise that is entirely composed in this type of discourse.

In giving this form to his thoughts, Marcus moves well beyond the influence of Epictetus, to whose *Discourses* he was introduced by his tutor, Rusticus.[129] Epictetus normally makes use of soliloquies in his external speeches, or in some relation to them, whereas in the *Meditations* Marcus does not record conversations with anyone else. His readers are given the impression that they are eavesdropping, unnoticed, on a series of interchanges taking place within his own mind.[130] They are instructed as much by the manner in which he draws them into the problems he is dealing with as by the solutions he proposes.

It is by means of these studied, inner reflections that he effectively becomes his readers' spiritual guide. Unlike his predecessors in this activity, such as Socrates, he is a self-effacing type of guide, who never states his purpose openly or spells out his method but encourages his readers to follow him along the silent meditative path he has chosen for himself. One of the sources of the *Meditations'* popularity over the centuries has arisen from its capacity to teach philosophy in this informal manner, in which the reader is gradually initiated into a type of contemplative practice that begins with reading itself.

The *Meditations* is the first work in the history of the subject in which such reflective experience transcends the oral didactic methods of the Hellenistic classroom in this intimate manner. Again the comparison with Epictetus is instructive. On reading the *Discourses*, one is aware that the discussions in which the master is involved with his students followed the reading of set texts, perhaps after a short break, and that the themes touched upon in these discussions were mostly suggested by the readings themselves. In this context, as noted, we find Epictetus engaging in soliloquies, and encouraging them in his students, chiefly as a supplementary demonstration of what he is talking about in open conversation. By contrast, in the *Meditations* there is no reference to institutionalized teaching after book 1; nor is there a second type of framework in the form of an editor, who, like Arrian, takes down his master's thoughts, as a secretary, and later organizes them for publication. As a result, in the *Meditations*, the process of reading, commenting, and editing is incorporated into the work itself. The most important influence in the creation of this "method," if that is not too strong a term,[131] is Marcus's habit of scrutinizing texts as he was taught and making notes or memoranda (*hypomnemata*).[132] It is by means of this term that he frequently refers to his book, or to the notes that went into it, as well as to Epictetus's *Discourses*.[133] However, in contrast to his mentor, who makes use of recognized philosophical strategies in his teachings, the *Meditations* is an original combination of the literary and philosophical in which it is difficult to separate the one from the other.

There is a two-stage process in Marcus's lessons, therefore, but it differs from what normally takes place in classroom instruction in philosophy. The practice of close reading and note-taking, in which Marcus apparently engaged over a long period,[134] creates the first stage of the disciplinary framework of the *Meditations*. The second consists in his habit of meditating while writing (and vice versa).[135] In this respect he again differs from Epictetus, whose formal and informal discussions have an oral flavor.[136] Arrian is emphatic on this point, claiming that the *diatribai* were taken down more or less as they were delivered and not altered for the purpose of publication, remarking: "Whatever I heard him say I used to write down, word for word, as best I could, endeavouring to preserve it as a memorial (*hypomnēmata*), for my own future use, of his way of thinking and the frankness of his speech."[137]

By contrast, Marcus begins and ends the process of philosophizing with writings in mind, and, in this respect at least, he is a textual thinker.[138] His inner dialogues, although presumably spoken within his mind, are derived from a combination of his readings, conversations, and experiences, in which the three are inseparably linked, as much later in Montaigne. Also, unlike Epictetus, who, it is assumed, commented exclusively on philosophical texts, Marcus's reading included history, philosophy, literature, correspondence, and perhaps theology.[139] This mental library, in which genres and disciplines were not clearly distinguished, formed the backdrop of his inner dialogues, which flowed through his mind in what has aptly been called a set of themes and variations.[140] From these took shape new memoranda, also mentally recorded, which were expressed in epigrammatic statements, in reflections on selected themes, and in longer passages on topics to which he repeatedly returned, such as the brevity of time.[141] Constructed in this way, the *Meditations* is not simply the record of a spontaneous outpouring of words or ideas, as it sometimes seems to be, but a sophisticated interplay of style and thought.[142] It is, in this sense, a philosophical archive for Marcus, as well, perhaps, for his readers, to which they may return at leisure, when ethical guidance is needed.

Little of this complex process of composition reaches the surface of the text.[143] As noted, the first impression that one has on taking up the *Meditations* is that the author is writing for himself alone,[144] and this, in a limited sense, is the case. The tone of the work is personal, intimate, and even somewhat esoteric, inasmuch as its philosophical sources are not always declared, and, as a result, Marcus's thinking is sometimes difficult to follow. The impression of a personal work of reflection is strengthened by the repetition of major themes, the loose organization of chapters, and the unadorned Greek style, which, Matthew Arnold observed, is "without . . . great charm."[145] However, after crossing the threshold of the author's private world, when one has entered into his innermost thoughts, the reader gradually becomes aware of an instructional dimension, which attempts to connect Marcus's inner dialogues to the larger question of rational self-government (*to hegemonikon*).[146] As he puts it, "the governing self becomes invincible when it withdraws into itself,"[147] adapting to circumstances,[148] excluding the irrelevant, and tailoring its thinking to essentials.[149] The cultivation of the inner life is the precondition for this type of thinking:

> Men look for retreats for themselves, either in the country, at the seashore, or in the hills . . . . Yet all this is unlike the philosopher, who can at any moment retreat into himself. For nowhere does a person withdraw into more quiet or more privacy than in his own mind . . . . Continually, therefore, grant yourself this refuge in order to restore yourself.[150]

It is within the mind, therefore, provided it is governed by discursive reason,[151] that the light of truth is slowly revealed.[152] The outside world is left behind, chiefly in order to permit the individual to perceive that he has within himself a force that is "stronger and more divine than the things which create passions and make a mere puppet" out of him.[153] To recognize this, it is necessary for him to retreat into his inner self,[154] and, once there, to reside within himself and reason with himself. For (as Epictetus remarked): "Things, as objects, stand outside our doors, themselves by themselves, neither knowing nor reporting anything about themselves. What then does report about them? The governing self."[155]

Only by this means can one create the tranquility of mind necessary for reliable ethical judgments.[156] As the sun rises for each new day, the emperor is in the habit of saying to himself: "I shall today meet many inquisitive, ungrateful, violent, treacherous, envious, and uncharitable men."[157] The question in his mind is what he should do in such situations. At the beginning of

book 5 he frames his response with a combination of assertiveness and detachment:

> When I dislike getting up, I have this thought ready: "I am rising
> for a man's task. Why then am I out of sorts if I am only going to
> do what I was born to do . . . . Or was I made just to stay in bed,
> under the covers, and keep myself warm?" "But this is more
> pleasant," I say to myself. And I answer: "Were you made for
> pleasure, that is, to react rather than to act?" . . . . "Do you refuse
> to assume a man's responsibilities?"[158]

He asks himself:

> "To what purpose, then, am I now using my soul?" In every
> instance ask yourself this question and cross-examine yourself:
> "Am I deploying what is called the ruling or governing part of the
> soul? And what sort of soul do I have? A child's, a boy's, a woman's,
> a tyrant's, a domestic animal's, or a wild beast's?"[159]

We should query ourselves regularly, asking "How does this act affect me?"
or "Will I regret it?"[160] Self-interrogation is a method for sifting realities from
images, impressions, dreams, and fantasies.[161] In accord with Stoic teachings,
these exercises of the mind or spirit should not be concerned with the entirety
of a life, or even a few episodes, but uniquely with specific situations in the
here and now, since, like Seneca, Marcus is convinced it is only in the present
that we truly live.

   This concern is expressed in numerous ways, for example, when he
asks:

> Will you, my soul, one day be good, simple, single, naked, and
> more visible than the body by which you are contained? Will you
> ever feel only love and devotion? Will you ever have no needs or
> desires, neither longing nor lusting after anything . . . ? Will you
> ever be happy with the present ?[162]

Again, he speaks about mental memoranda, which are self-conscious acts of
will in which

we . . . create opinions . . . and, so to speak, inscribe them in our minds. Yet we can choose not to inscribe them, or, if we do so without thinking, to erase them whenever we wish.[163]

Or he reflects on life's transitory nature, as in a passage written at Carnutum, near the border of Pannonia, during the battle with the Quadi in the 170s:

We ought not to think about the fact that each day a little of our life has passed away and that what is left is less and less. Instead we should think of this. Even if we live for a longer time, it is not at all certain that our minds will be equal to the task of unravelling events, or for speculative thinking . . . . If our minds decline, our bodies may continue as before: we may still be capable of respiration, digestion, perceptions, and desires. But we will gradually lose the right and appropriate employment of ourselves—our sense of duty, our ability to analyse sense-impressions, and our awareness that it may be time to end our lives. All of these topics require the capacity to reason and to make judgements, and these begin to fail before all the rest. And so we must press onwards, because at every moment we are coming closer to the end.[164]

Plotinus. Augustine

I now turn to Augustine, who takes the philosophical soliloquy in a new direction in the *Confessions*, thereby inaugurating a lengthy period in Western literature in which it is recognized as an independent literary and philosophical genre. The chief influence on this dimension of his thinking is a series of reflections on self-consciousness is the *Enneads* of Plotinus.

Early in his career Augustine reveals that he is an accomplished practitioner of the inner dialogue, which, as noted, was used extensively in *De Ordine* and *Soliloquia*, written in 385–386.[165] The use of soliloquies is one of the ways in which these and other Cassiciacum dialogues are distinguishable in their technique of argumentation from Cicero's *Tusculan Disputations*, which was their literary model. Within these early writings one finds a wide range of inner conversations on philosophical, theological, and rhetorical topics,[166] which include Augustine's formative thinking on will, time, and the existence of the self.[167] This type of dialogue is employed later in his writings in determining the limits of human language to deal with metaphysical questions,[168] which appear to Augustine to be more manageable when speaking to himself than when speaking to others.

One of the best-known examples of this sort of thinking arises in his discussion of the nature of time in book 11 of the *Confessions*, in which he talks at once about the nature of dialogue and time, asking famously:

> What is time? Who can explain it easily and briefly? Who can comprehend it even in thought in a manner in which the answer can be articulated in words? Yet what do we speak of, in our familiar everyday conversation, more than of time? We surely know what we mean when we speak of it. We also know what is meant when we hear someone else talking about it. What then is time? Provided that no one asks me, I know. If I want to explain it to an inquirer, I do not know. But I confidently affirm myself to know that if nothing passes away, there is no past time, and if nothing arrives, there is no future time, and if nothing existed, there would be no present time.[169]

Augustine's lengthiest exercise in the genre of inner dialogue was of course the writing of his life history as an extended Christian version of a Socratic exercise in self-examination. An equally important influence on his thinking was Plotinus, who employed this philosophical form for the dual purpose of instructing others and himself.[170] Porphyry, his biographer, provides us with a brief but helpful outline of his approach to self-talk in the following passage:[171]

> He was concerned only with thought (*monon tou nou*) . . . . He worked out his train of thought from beginning to end in his own mind, and then, when he wrote it down, since he had set it all in order in his mind, he wrote as continuously as if he was copying from a book. Even if he was talking to someone, engaged in continuous conversation, he kept to his train of thought (*pros to skemmata*). He could take part in the conversation to the full, and at the same time keep his mind fixed without a break in what he was considering. When the person he had been talking to was gone he did not go over what he had written, because his sight . . . did not suffice for

revision.[172] He went straight on with what came next, keeping the connection, just as if there had been no interval of conversation in between. In this way he was present at once to himself and to others.

We are not dealing here with the rhetorical presentation of the dialogue, as in Seneca, the classroom version of the genre, as in Epictetus, or the internal ruminations characteristic of Marcus's *Meditations*, but with a form of composition that evolves in the mind before it is expressed in words, and for which, in consequence, the creative phase can be said to take place entirely in silence, as subsequently in Augustine. The only words that are mentioned in Porphyry's account of Plotinus's methods are those of the external conversations in which the philosopher took part at the same time as he was engaged in his reflections, which, if Porphyry is to be trusted, had no influence on the argument that he was developing within himself. It would be admissible to speak of this mode of composition as an "inner dialogue," but only in a special sense, inasmuch as it takes shape in the individual's thinking without the necessity of a present, remembered, or imagined debate, in contrast to inner dialogues in the Socratic and Stoic traditions, which require the active participation of alternating voices.

We cannot be absolutely certain on this question, since Plotinus himself does not refer to his methods of composition, at least in the edition of his teachings that was organized by Porphyry. However, the possibility cannot be ruled out, since there is a brief utilization of the Socratic elenchus at *Enneads* 3.8.4, quoted in Chapter 2, where the topic is the role of nature in creation and its relationship to the activity of contemplation. Here there are internal questions and answers in which Nature is pictured as talking to herself, as in the inquiry into the nature of time at *Confessions* 11. Augustine frequently engages in internal conversations of this type, either talking to himself or picturing a conversation taking place in the mind of God. A later passage in the *Enneads* involving the notion of silence may have been critical in alerting him to the possibility of using inner dialogue to explore the problem of self-knowledge within the Christian paradigm of sin and redemption. This occurs in a unique autobiographical statement at *Enneads* 4.8.1, where Plotinus portrays his temporary mental elevation in these words:

> Often I have woken up out of the body to myself and have entered
> into myself, going out from all other things; I have seen a beauty
> wonderfully great and felt assurances that then most of all

I belonged to the better part; I have actually lived the best life and
come to identify with the divine; and set firm in it I have come to
that supreme actuality, setting myself above all else in the realm of
Intellect. Then after that rest in the divine, when I have come down
from Intellect to discursive reasoning, I am puzzled how I ever came
down, and how my soul has come to be in the body when it is what
it has shown itself to be by itself, even when it is in the body.[173]

This account does not involve two *voices* speaking within the mind but
two *perspectives* on events taking place in the mind. It does not proceed by
means of a rational argument; on the contrary, discursive reasoning is the point
of departure for a higher experience, which, Plotinus suggests, is not so much
lacking in words as existing at a level that is beyond words, again anticipating
an Augustinian view, in this case on the limitations of human language. Also,
one has an impression in this passage of heightened emotion combined with
mystical engagement, with the result that, unlike many traditional internal
dialogues, in which oppositions of ideas are stressed, the quoted passage emphasizes affective and intellectual integration in a manner that is not dissimi-
lar to what takes place in Christian tradition as a by-product of ascetic
exercises, such as early sacred reading, as practiced by the desert fathers.

Central to this conception of the soliloquy are two configurations of
time; these consist in the transitory and the timeless, both of which reappear
in Augustine's reworking of the Plotinian model of the soliloquy. In Seneca, Epictetus, and Marcus Aurelius—to take the three examples already
mentioned—there are abundant references to the passage of time as a factor
in life over which mortals have no control; however, these commentators on
the theme do not construct their inner dialogues around the phenomenon of
internal time-consciousness itself, as do, in different ways, Plotinus and Augustine, in a distant anticipation of the view of Edmund Husserl, which was
later reused in an existential context by Martin Heidegger, Jean-Paul Sartre,
and Emmanuel Levinas. In his distinctive rendering of the issues, Plotinus
appears to be engaged in an introspective experiment in both self-consciousness
and metacognitive self-awareness.[174] Also, while he seems to be talking about
his normal state of being in the world, he is actually experiencing an enhanced state of mind, which involves the upward movement of the soul. The
journey toward heightened awareness and the return to normality are presented as a brief account, or narrative, of the soul's elevation and subsequent
descent, and this is related by the experiencing subject in the first person.

In adapting inner dialogue to these ends, Plotinus takes the first tentative step in the direction of Augustine's conception of autobiographical and spiritual narrative.[175] The second step is taken by Augustine himself, who, based on the theology of the incarnation, introduces into the temporal scheme the history of the body, which is excluded from Plotinus's more intellectualist speculations.[176] Like Plotinus, we might say, Augustine is interested in exploring self-consciousness, but unlike him, he gives this form of interiority a human voice, in fact, his own voice, as reproduced in the subjective tone of his Latin style, which, in itself, is a kind of embodiment. This resonant and commemorative style, which, as noted, is unique among late ancient writers, is a constant reminder in the *Confessions* that Augustine's tormented soul cannot ever free itself entirely from his body, as envisaged in Plato's myth of the cave in the *Republic* and in a more ethereal context in Neoplatonism.

Ambrose, who was a close reader of the *Enneads*,[177] considered Plotinus's account of the soul's elevation to be an allegorical restatement of Paul's description of the man who was taken up to paradise at 2 Corinthians 12:1–4, which has been discussed in Chapter 2.[178] According to Pierre Courcelle, the Ambrosian sermon in which the comparison is found may have been heard by Augustine in the spring of 386, thus suggesting that this was one of the channels by which the Plotinian notion of mental ascent made its way into the "vision at Ostia" at *Confessions* 9.10.23–25.[179] In that passage Augustine reworks the scheme as the story of a pair of self-conscious mental ascents, namely those of himself and his mother, and he does this in each case in two stages, proceeding from words to wordlessness, thus paralleling the contrast between discursive reasoning and intellect at *Enneads* 4.8.1.[180] He thereby incorporates the instructional mode of the soliloquy into the philosophical, as he and Monica each speak to themselves simultaneously within their minds or souls.[181]

This was the culminating point in a period of development in Augustine's thinking about inner dialogue in which the technique acquired a place in a hierarchy of types of words. Within his reflections, this intellectual ladder leads upward from spoken words to silent and interior words, next to abstract words in the mind, and finally to the Word of God, which lies beyond the language of mortals.[182] Augustine develops this model of language in a number of early writings and presents it in a formal, synthetic manner in books 2 and 3 of *De Doctrina Christiana* and in book 15 of *De Trinitate*.

Along with this configuration, and, in my view, as a by-product of it, he established the West's first consistent and fully articulated theory of the relationship between narrative time and hermeneutics. An early phase of his thinking on these subjects appears in his Cassiciacum dialogues, where he is still speaking principally as a teacher of rhetoric to his Milanese students; however, this is superseded by his development of a method for interpreting biblical texts, which, according to the *Confessions*, took shape slowly and hesitantly around the same period. His mature thinking on biblical narrative is found in his sermons, his several Genesis commentaries, and in particular in his *Enarrationes in Psalmos*,[183] and must therefore be considered a fundamental orientation of his reflections rather than a phase that was limited to the writing of his autobiography.

As applied to his life history, Augustine differs from his predecessors in the use of this interpretive technique in two respects. First, he takes up his life as a whole (at least down to the moment of his conversion) rather than speaking of isolated episodes, which are used as moral example by Seneca, Plutarch, Marcus, and other Hellenistic thinkers. Also, unlike Stoic writers of autobiographical self-examination, such as Sextius in Seneca's *De Ira*, he does not limit his attention to the present but is focused equally on the ethical implications of narratives in the past, present, and future.[184] Again differing from his predecessors in this genre, he is concerned with a "hermeneutic" understanding of such events, in which, as Paul Ricoeur has observed, there is no lived experience without some accompanying form of self-reflective interpretation.[185] One of the recognized features of his thinking on this theme concerns the use of memory, which is not limited to notes on reading or experience but functions as a form of reconstruction of the continuity of his thoughts and feelings. In this respect, he is the Latin successor to Plutarch, although the latter's writings were unknown to him, in extending and deepening the hermeneutic dimension of memory until it becomes a framework for self-consciousness itself.

In achieving this goal, and, in doing so, making the philosophical soliloquy into an independent literary genre, Augustine takes a position on the ethical value of literature that differs from that of Plato, the Middle and late Platonists, and the Stoics. He agrees with earlier thinkers on the inappropriateness of epic for teaching ethics because (as Epictetus summed up Socrates's words in books 3 and 10 of the *Republic*) "the *Iliad* is nothing but a sense-impression and a poet's use of sense-impressions."[186] However, he responds, not by rejecting literary studies and their images on the whole, as an initial reading of books 1 and 3 of the *Confessions* might suggest,[187] but by creating a role for rhetoric and the creative imagination in Christian thinking, which is discernible after 396 both in the *Confessions* and in book 4 of *De Doctrina Christiana*.

This view of poetry arises from his conviction that the Bible's beauty owes a great deal to divinely inspired rhetoric,[188] and, as noted in Chapter 2, reflects a broad re-evaluation of the literary imagination which had already begun in Stoic and Neoplatonist thought. This rethinking had for the most part been concluded by the time of Philostratus (d. ca. A.D. 244), who distinguished between two sorts of mental images, one that he called *mimesis* (imitation), which reproduces what is seen, and another called *phantasia* (here translatable as "imagination"), which reproduces what is seen physically as well as what is not seen, except in the mind.[189] In reworking these distinctions, as noted, Augustine effectively retains Plato's suspicion of literary images, while agreeing with Aristotle's view, possibly reproduced in the interpretation of Plotinus, that *phantasia* can interface with sense and intellect in producing a reliable type of mental impression. From these different streams of thought Augustine fashions his working definition of *phantasia* as something seen and *phantasma* as something imagined as if it has been seen.[190] The other essential element in the Augustinian conception of the imagination is very possibly drawn from Plotinus, and consists in his subjective interpretation of his personal experience as his mind ascends beyond the senses and proceeds upward toward God.

These developments reach their culminating point in the role assigned to the literary dimension of the imagination the *Confessions*, in which the combination of lived experience and memory images is effectively transformed into practical form of instruction. On this view, just as the Bible illustrates moral truths by means of timeless and unforgettable narratives, the literary imagination of the individual reshapes his or her personal history into a memorable educational genre, by which, Augustine is convinced, we can give an ethical orientation to our lives.[191] Self-analysis and self-address are united, and are jointly concerned with what is experienced in an expansive present as well as with the later interpretation of that experience. This dual feature of Augustine's thinking marks a transition from earlier spiritual autobiographies to the notion of *bios* as reading, writing, and rereading, or, as some would prefer, a kind of interweaving,[192] in which interior dialogue, reason, imagination, and interpretation work together.

Boethius

I conclude this sketch of the use of philosophical soliloquies in late ancient authors with a few words about the chef d'oeuvre that brings this tradition to an end, namely Boethius's *Consolation of Philosophy*, written in 524.[193]

This work is an isolated masterpiece in its century's literature, and, as Henry Chadwick noted, "something of that isolation belongs to [the author] even during his lifetime."[194] Accused of treason and placed under house arrest in 523, he wrote *The Consolation of Philosophy* in the knowledge that on its completion he would very likely be put to death. In this dark moment of his life, the writing of his book was an attempt to reinstate philosophy as the arbiter of justice, liberty, and civic responsibility in the face of tyranny[195] and arbitrary judgment, as well as to make a contribution to the traditional philosophical problem of how to achieve the good or happy life.[196]

As a work of literature, the *Consolation* is a hybrid of two philosophical genres originating in antiquity, namely the "consolation" (*consolatio*) and the "protreptic" (*protrepticon*).[197] The consolation was an essay or letter mourning the loss of a relative or friend, drawing attention to the transience of human life, and suggesting reasons for accepting one's loss.[198] The protreptic was an encouragement to convert to the philosophical life, which could be written in a number of literary forms, including the dialogue.[199] Book 1 of Boethius's work is a "consolation," in which Lady Philosophy offers the author spiritual "medicine" to strengthen his soul in the face of adversity.[200] Books 2 to 5 comprise a loosely organized "protreptic," in which a number of the traditional themes in this genre are touched upon, including the concepts of freedom, necessity, and providence.

A good illustration of Boethius's approach to the dual functions of inner dialogue is found in the carefully staged entrance of Lady Philosophy in book 1 prose 1. She appears before him as an allegorical figure, whose gown aptly summarizes her traditional functions; and she informs him that his morbid state of mind is understandable to a personage of her background, since he has temporarily lost his source of identity and is effectively alienated from himself.[201] Boethius pays close attention to what she has to say, and as the dialogue proceeds, his disposition improves with the aid of her therapeutic words.[202] At length he is inspired to ask why such a grand "mistress of virtues" has taken the trouble to visit him in the solitude of his spiritual exile.[203]

She makes it clear that she has come to offer him consolation in his predicament, over which he has apparently lost control. She reminds him that injustices have been committed against philosophers in the past; she also explains why his sense of isolation is largely self-induced.[204] She notes that he has disregarded one of her fundamental lessons; for, "if a person resides within the protection of her ramparts, he need never fear a sentence of banishment; but once he ceases to desire a home there, he likewise ceases to deserve it." Mere erudition, she adds, is no help in these circumstances: "What I look for is not library walls adorned with ivory and glass, but your mind's abode; for I have installed there not books, but what gives books their value, the doctrine found in my writings of old."[205] As the letters *pi* and *theta* on her gown suggest, Boethius's problem arises from an inability to relate ethical theory to practice. Philosophy is not something to be read about, as he may have thought during his years as a scholar: it has be studied for self-instruction, and above all to be lived.

The inspiration for the figure of Philosophy in this scene is probably derived from Plato's *Crito*, where Socrates relates that in a dream he thought he saw "a beautiful and comely woman dressed in white,"[206] forewarning him of his impending execution, which he refuses to forestall despite the compelling if sometimes confused arguments advanced by Crito himself. In this sense, we may view book 1 of Boethius's *Consolatio* as a distant and highly contextualized response to Plato's *Apology*. However, the source for the philosophical lesson in this prose, which leads Boethius toward a philosophical and theological *protrepticon* in books 2 to 5, is above all Augustine's *Soliloquia*, where Reason interrogates its author from within his mind just as Philosophy questions Boethius, until she discovers the source of his illness and an appropriate form of therapy for his soul.[207] In focusing his attention on his personal misfortunes, Boethius has apparently forgotten that it is God who presides over the universe and has endowed the world with its purpose, in which he plays a very small part.[208]

The Augustinian inspiration is made clear in Boethius's proof for the *cogito*, which is adapted from the opening statement at *Soliloquia*, book 2. By means of this discussion Philosophy leads him out of his melancholy state by proving to him that he knows one thing for certain, namely that he exists as a rational mortal creature, and therefore, in this respect at least has ethical control over mind or soul, even in the face of his impending fate. She thus reuses the argument of Augustine in the *Soliloquia* to the effect that there are two things of which every person is certain, namely that he is alive and that he is not immortal.[209] Here is the interchange, beginning with her words:[210]

> "So will you first allow me to ask you a few simple questions, so as to probe and investigate your mental state? By this means I can decide upon your cure."

> "Ask away at your discretion," I replied, "and I shall answer you."

Philosophy asks Boethius whether in his view events take place in a random and haphazard fashion in the world or whether they are divinely guided by means of reason, and if so, how this is brought about. Boethius admits that there are many things he does not understand about universal order, but that he is sure of one thing, "God is the source." If that is the case, Philosophy adds, disturbances of the type he is experiencing can alter his disposition, but they cannot destroy his inner sense of being. She asks:

"Do you remember that you are a man?"
"Of course I remember," I replied.
"Can you define what a man is?"
"Are you asking if I am aware that I am a mortal creature endowed
    with reason? Yes, I know that, and I proclaim it."
"But are you aware of being anything more?" she asked.
"No, nothing more."
"Now I know," she said, "the further cause of your sickness, and it
    is a very serious one. You have forgotten your own identity."[211]
("*Iam scio," inquit, "morbi tui aliam uel maximam causam: quid ipse
    sis, nosse desisti."*)[212]

This restatement of Augustine's argument can be viewed as a final echo of the Socratic tradition of self-address in late antiquity.[213] However, if we recall Socrates's words on the subject, especially those that are attributed to him as he awaits his unjust but apparently wished for verdict in the *Apology*,[214] it is clear that we are dealing with a different conception of the role of reason in philosophical discourse, and it is on that point that I should like to end my survey.

In employing inner dialogues, Augustine and Boethius are not trying to solve problems through rational arguments, as Socrates claims in his defense that he was doing for his youthful followers in Athens; on the contrary, the allegorical figures representing, respectively, Reason and Philosophy, frame provisional solutions to problems that their authors are convinced reason ultimately cannot solve. In the *Soliloquia* and perhaps more persuasively in *De Magistro*, Augustine provides an explanation for this position, suggesting that inner dialogues are clearer, more precise, and less prone to distractions than open dialogues; nonetheless, in their grasp of realities, these forms of discourse are constrained by the fact that they originate in the language of mortals and are therefore unable to rise above human concerns. Similarly, influenced perhaps by Augustine, Boethius complains to Philosophy that her verbal arguments are circular and therefore unanswerable.[215]

The purpose of these criticisms of the Socratic approach to discovering truth is to advance an argument based on metaphysics Socrates himself would not have accepted. Through internal dialogue, which turns on itself, as Augustine reminds his son in *De Magistro*, they propose a model for the circularity of all human reasoning and advance the view that an understanding of reality can only come about by means of a type of communication that is superior to words, transcending them and deriving ultimately from God. Recall that in the *Theaetetus* Socrates proposes that inner dialogue is an essential features of human thinking: a type

> of talk which the soul has with itself about the objects under consideration . . . when it thinks it is simply carrying on a discussion in which it asks itself questions and answers them itself . . . . And when it arrives at something definite . . . we call this its judgment. So, in my view, to judge is to make a statement, and a judgment is a statement which is not addressed to another person or spoken aloud, but silently addressed to oneself.[216]

To this expression of confidence in human reason, Augustine replies, seconded by Boethius, that in the last analysis rational accounts of realities by means of words are just words—signs, symbols, or mental representations, and, *pace* Socrates, these words do not acquire a greater power of signifying if they are spoken within the mind to oneself. A measured and defensible response to Augustine's Sceptical claim will not made until 1641, when Descartes restates the Socratic argument in favor of making certain judgments about realities by means of inner dialogue in *Meditationes de prima philosophia*.

The initial prose of the *Consolation of Philosophy* thus provides an illustration of the fact that the soliloquy develops as a literary and philosophical genre in late antiquity in a form that is derived from but differs in structure from the Socratic dialogue, and this difference has a great deal to do with methods of instruction in philosophy. I have proposed that the earliest Latin thinker who utilizes the philosophical soliloquy in this educational fashion is Seneca, in his dialogues and *Moral Epistles*. He is followed by a number of figures who make use of this literary model for philosophical thinking; among them I have singled out Epictetus, Marcus Aurelius, Plotinus, and Augustine. Epictetus employs inner dialogue as a supplement to his external dialogues, and among their other functions these internal speeches provide a means of expressing his notions of *prohairesis* and *prolepsis* as well as establishing a literary foundation for his personal and affective theology. Marcus Aurelius conceives inner dialogue as an autonomous literary genre; his originality arises chiefly from his methodology, in which he intermingles literary and philosophical techniques, and from his view of the reading process as a communicable form of spiritual guidance.

Augustine gives the literary genre a name, *soliloquium*, and makes it the foundation for a conception of autobiography that is indebted to the silent, inner conversational technique and the accompanying notion of self-awareness in Plotinus. While not losing touch with ancient uses for the form, he renews all its traditional applications in a Christian context, including the ancient routine of self-scrutiny and the Socratic approach to problem-solving by means of logical questions and answers. He is followed by Boethius, who effectively terminates the late ancient tradition of the inner dialogue. Using Plato and Augustine as his points of departure in the opening scene of *The Consolation of Philosophy*, he unites the soliloquy with the genres of the *protrepticon* and *consolatio*, effectively bringing the three forms together in a single literary vehicle. The contributions of Augustine and Boethius in turn prepare the way for the development of the philosophical soliloquy in later thinkers such as Anselm of Canterbury, Peter Abelard, Dante, and Petrarch, in whom its logical implications and literary form move in new directions.

CHAPTER 4

Self and Soul

The rise in interest in the self in late antiquity took place in conjunction with adjustments between the notions of self and soul. Augustine's reflections on the theme represent one of the decisive phases in this development. In this chapter I turn to two aspects of the bishop of Hippo's thinking on the subject. In the first part I discuss his statements on self and soul in two early writings, *De Immortalitate Animae* and *De Quantitate Animae*, composed respectively in 387 and 388; in the second, I turn to the revision of his views in the light of his conversion to the religious life.

By way of introduction, I would remind the reader of one of the recurrent problems that arises in dealing with this as well as other philosophical topics in Augustine's writings. It is usually difficult and in some cases impossible to pin down the sources of his thinking.

To take the present topic as an example: he is unacquainted with the accounts of the soul at *Republic* 577a and 590c–592b, as well as with the dramatic statement on the self made by Socrates at *Phaedo* 115b–c, where the aging sage, facing execution, calmly bids farewell to his young associates, reminding them of the necessity of self-care.[1] It is of course tempting to think that the bishop of Hippo may have been influenced by these or other well-known reflections on the themes of the soul and self in antiquity. However, while there has been a great deal of research on the question, there are few irrefutable conclusions.[2] Augustine was likewise unfamiliar with the literary tradition of self-representation in Greek that began with the deliberative monologues in Homer, in which, as Christopher Gill has shown, there is considerable skill in the practical reasoning and decision-making associated with the concept of the self.[3] As noted, in book 1 of the *Confessions*, Augustine tells us that he was discouraged from the serious study of Greek epic, even though he acknowledges the skill with which the stories in the *Iliad* and *Odyssey* are told.[4] In the early books of his autobiography he prefers to see himself as a Christian successor to Aeneas rather than to Achilles, Hector, or Ulysses.[5] In any case it was not a truly epic representation of himself that he was after. During the period in which the *Confessions* was written, that is, between 397 and 400, he had not yet abandoned the picture of himself that is presented in his early dialogues, written in 386–387, in which he is configured as a latter-day Hellenistic sage, leading his students (and readers) through the intricacies of ancient ethical thought in a Socratic fashion by means of a combination of rational arguments and confrontations. In fact, with the exception of the *Aeneid*, the type of literature that most accurately anticipates his statements on the self in the early dialogues as well as the *Confessions* is one that is comprised of works in which his philosophical views are expressed in a rhetorical setting. His formal (although not substantive) predecessors in this tradition include Lucretius and Plutarch, neither of whom he knew, as well as Seneca, whose *Moral Epistles* he could have known but does not quote directly. The writer who influenced him most in the blending of these persuasive and philosophical techniques was undoubtedly Cicero, whose style in the *Tusculan Disputations* he imitated in his early writings and whose ethical outlook he continued to admire well after his conversion.[6]

There are nonetheless some features of his approach that set him apart from Cicero and other Hellenistic writers on the self. He is famously concerned with proving that the self exists, against the Sceptical argument that the self's very existence is subject to doubt. His response is summed up in the statement, *Si fallor, sum*, which is recognized to be the distant antecedent of Descartes's similar expression of the same principle in the phrase, *Cogito, ergo sum*. Also, in his understanding of the self a large role is reserved for intentions, which are conceived in a combination of mental and linguistic terms. On this view, we think of the words that we want to say before they are uttered; similarly, he proposes, we reason in terms of plans, agendas, and potential courses of action in looking ahead to what we want to do. Thirdly, in Augustine's conception of the self, special attention is paid to the interrelated themes of memory and narrative. These are the subjects to which he devotes a part of book 6 of *De Musica*, which is taken up in Chapter 5 of this study, and book 10 of the *Confessions*, in which the topic is framed within a general theory of recollection. On this theme, I have suggested, he echoes views similar to those expressed by Seneca, Plutarch, and Marcus Aurelius, all of whom were convinced in different degrees that our knowledge of the self is largely the result of the interweaving of our personal memories. Yet Augustine goes one step farther than these thinkers in proposing that the inner "me," which he recognizes as a version of the self, and the memory on which this knowledge depends, are virtually the same thing: *Ego sum qui memini, ego animus.*[7]

The Philosophical Element

Although there is considerable overlap in Augustine's thinking about the soul and the self, a number of important distinctions are made between the two entities. The soul is eternal; it is nonmaterial and not subject to extension or division. By contrast, the self is impermanent. It has a clearly material component, consisting in embodiment, and a less clear, presumably nonmaterial component, in which it acts as a framework or container for the mind and its products. As such, it is subject to extension and division between birth, when its corporeal encasement is initiated, and death, when the body dies.[8] Moreover, unlike the soul, which is essentially good, as created by God, the moral condition of the self depends on the exercise of the will in combating evil and embracing high ideals.

There is nonetheless considerable continuity, and even possibly some overlap, in his thinking about soul and self. This is suggested by the vocabulary with which the two are described. Like ancient authors in general, Augustine has no specific term for designating the self; he gets around the problem of terminology through the use of pronouns, for example, at *De Ordine* 1.3.6 or *Soliloquia* 1.1.1. By contrast, there are three principal words that are employed for designating the soul, namely *spiritus, anima,* and *animus,* the latter pair being used at times interchangeably.[9] Other terms for the soul include *mens* and *ratio,* which normally refer to the soul's preeminent parts,[10] although on occasion they are used for the soul itself. The qualities attached to the soul are indicated by means of adjectives, for example, *anima rationalis, irrationalis, intellectualis,* or *spiritualis.* There is no precedent for such a varied group of terms for the soul in earlier writers, especially in Augustine's chief sources for his vocabulary, Varro, Cicero, and Porphyry.

To add to this picture, there are a number of occasions in Augustine's writings when he appears to have in mind the concepts of both soul and self. A concise statement on this potential interconnectedness is found at *De Genesi ad Litteram* 7.21.28 (which can be compared to *De Trinitate* 10.3.5–11.16), where it is noted that

(the soul) is unable to be ignorant of itself, even when it is seeking to
know itself. When it is seeking itself, after all, it knows that it is
seeking itself. This is something that it could not know, if it first did
not know itself. It does not seek itself or look for itself anywhere else
than within itself. As a consequence, if it knows it is looking for
itself, it clearly knows itself. Moreover, the whole of the soul knows
all that it knows; that is to say, it is in seeking or looking that it
knows itself; therefore, the whole of it knows itself and it knows the
whole of itself. It does not know anything else, only itself, which, as
noted, it knows thoroughly and completely. The question arises:
If it knows itself, why does it continue to seek itself if it knows itself
while it is seeking itself? For, if it were ignorant of itself, it could not
possibly know itself, while it was seeking itself.[11]

The background to this statement is found in Augustine's several rehears-
als of the principle of the *cogito*. The connection between this laconic expression of the principle of self-existence and the more discursive presentations of
the issues in a passage such as the above arises from one of the fundamental
characteristics of the soul in Augustine's view, namely that it is the source of
life in all living things. As mortals we are all aware of one thing: we are alive.
This is a self-evident truth, about which we can have no doubt. However, if
life, in this sense, is a timeless principle, the awareness of its permanence is
nonetheless a product of self-consciousness, which operates over time. The
point is made at the beginning of book 2 of the *Soliloquia*, when Reason asks
Augustine:

> Do you, who wish to know yourself, know that your self exists?
> I know.
> How do you know?
> I do not know.
>
> Tu, qui vis te nosse, scis esse te?
> Scio.
> Unde scis?
> Nescio.

I have translated the second pronoun *te* in the first question as "self" because
the personified figures of Reason, which is speaking from within Augustine's

soul, is, in this period of his thinking on the issues, designated both as reason and as self. Reason here represents the living, reasoning person, who is the rational, self-aware Augustine living in space and time. What we have in the Socratic exchange at the beginning of *Soliloquia*, book 2, therefore, is a dialogue between Augustine and Reason which is at the same time a dialogue between soul and self. Augustine's response to Reason's question, namely *scio*, is not an affirmation of what the soul is, since he does not know what it is (*nescio*), but an affirmation that he knows he exists through the permanent existence of his soul. This is essentially a proof of his self-awareness, and in this there is a second perception or conclusion. This concerns the fact that his self is finite and subject to ineluctable demise.

De Immortalitate Animae

One of the early writings in which the relationship between soul and self is discussed in detail is *De Immortalitate Animae*, which begins with a reiteration of the principle of the Augustinian *cogito*. However, instead of speaking of life, in its continuity and permanence, as in the *Soliloquia*, Augustine takes as his example of the human potential for reason the nature of a discipline (*disciplina*) such as mathematics, which, if it exists anywhere, exists "in that which has life and always exists."[12]

The rational soul, he proposes, is like such a discipline in one respect, namely that it remains unchanged, even though it may be responsible for changes in things that undergo change.[13] If there is such motion, it has to be understood as having been brought about in association with, or because of, movement in the mind; and even though the change in question may have been intended in the mind, the mind itself is not necessarily moved in bringing it about. If that were not the case, the mind or soul would not be timeless but subject to death, like other products of the brain, such as self-awareness itself.[14]

In Augustine's thinking, there is no such thing as a mutation of the mind (*animi mutatio*, 5.7). But is there any way in which the mind recognizes its own immutability? His initial response to this question is in two parts. He first reiterates his defense of reason's changelessness.[15] He speaks of this as the view within the mind by which it beholds the true or changeless, not through the body, but through itself. This is understood in the mind either through the contemplation of the true or through the true itself, as the subject of this inward inspection.[16]

As a second topic, he asks whether it would be possible for the soul to contemplate the true through itself in one of these ways if there were not some antecedent connection with the true already in place. His answer is affirmative, but with a proviso: everything that we think about or contemplate in this manner may be said to be grasped either through thought or through sense and intellect. The things that are understood by means of the senses are perceived as existing outside us and as being contained in some locality, and it is this that makes their perception possible. By contrast, the things that are grasped in the intellect are understood as having been placed nowhere else but in the very mind that understands them, and are therefore not so contained.[17]

How then is the inner connection (*conjunctio*) to be brought about? Aspects of this question are discussed in chapters 7 to 16, in which the relationship between soul and self is taken up in greater detail. The argument can be summed up as follows. On the one hand, as proposed, soul, mind, and reason are changeless, in contrast to the body, which grows and diminishes over time (7.12). However, it is necessary to distinguish between the body's form, which does not disappear, and its material frame, which does (8.13). The body therefore can be looked at in two perspectives, namely temporal and nontemporal, and, in the latter, as a reflection of God's intentions for a type of permanence within an impermanent mortal frame (8.14). It is this that provides the rationale for Augustine's later argument in favor of the integrated and embodied self, in which two dimensions of time are involved. Here is his statement on the issues:

> If the body has been made, it has been made by the act of someone
> who is not inferior to the body . . . . It follows that the body,
> considered in a universal manner (*universum . . . corpus*), has been
> made by a better and more powerful force and nature than itself, or
> at least by one that is not corporeal . . . . For nothing can come into
> being by itself. Moreover, this force and incorporeal nature, that is
> the power that effectively brings the body into being (*effectrix
> corporis*), is universally present and preserves the body universally.
> For, after the making, it did not disappear.

The mind, therefore, does not differ fundamentally from the body in this respect but merely possesses the quality of changelessness in a higher degree, from which it derives its immortality. In the relation between body and soul, ordered mutability imitates the immutable (*ordinate mutabilitate id quod immutabile est imitari reperitur*, 8.15). Moreover, just as the soul sees itself, not through the body, but through itself, that is, the mind, so, within the body, the soul is capable of a comparable type of self-observation, which results from its powers of introspection. In other words, with respect to the soul, there are two types of introspective self-inquiry to be taken into consideration. There is a higher type, which is carried on within the soul itself, and a lower type within the self. Discussing the difference between them, Augustine notes (10.17):

> Perhaps we ought to believe, as some have suggested, that life consists in a type of mingling in the body (*temperationem corporis*). This would not have occurred to them if they had been able to see those things which are true and endure forever, once the mind had withdrawn and purged itself of the habit of bodies (*corporum consuetudine*). For who, looking thoroughly into himself (*Quis enim bene se inspiciens*) has not experienced that his understanding of a given thing was more adequate to the degree that he was able to remove and withdraw the intention of the mind (*intentionem mentis*) from the body's senses?

De Quantitate Animae

In the discussion of the soul's nature in his early writings, Augustine claims the patronage of Plato; however, he has replaced Plato's division of the soul into the reasoning (*logistikon*), spirited (*thumoeides*), and appetitive (*epithumetikon*), as found, for example, at *Republic* 4.435a–441c and 9.580d–583a, with a simpler dichotomy between the rational and irrational, which can in theory be applied to either the soul or the self. This is also the case in his account of the soul and self at *De Quantitate Animae* 33.70–34.77.

In an earlier discussion of the theme in this work, Augustine fails to offer a convincing account of the union of body and soul through sensation alone (25.48). In the later chapters he reframes the question, making use of a hypothetical dialogue between himself and his interlocutor, Evodius, in order to broaden the analysis into the nonsensory.[18] It is in this connection that he touches upon relations between soul and self.

As in *De Immortalitate Animae*, a distinction is made between our knowledge of the soul itself, which is very limited, and our knowledge of its functions, which is extensive. In the section of the dialogue under discussion he divides these into a number of states or levels of understanding. In the first there is virtually no knowledge regarding either soul or self. For, although we are alive and are aware of this fact, we are unaware of what the soul is doing precisely, in order to keep us alive. It is by means of the soul's presence that the principle of life is bestowed on the terrestrial and mortal bodies of both animals and humans (*corpus hoc terrenum atque mortale praesentia sua vivificat*). This is the level at which the soul sustains life, distributes nourishment, prevents disintegration, aids growth and reproduction, and preserves harmony and beauty (33.70).

The second level of the soul's activity consists in what it is able to do by means of the senses, and this too is shared by animals and humans. However, it differs from the first level in providing a clearer and more evident means by which the life of a person is understood.[19] In these functions the soul operates both externally and internally. Acting externally, it directs its attention (*intendit*) to sensory reactions such as touch, heat and cold, rough and smooth, hard and soft, and light and heavy; it distinguishes flavors, odors, sounds, and shapes through the senses, respectively, of taste, smell, hearing, and sight. Acting internally, it is able to detach itself from the senses and their continual movements for a certain length of time, thereby providing the senses with an opportunity to restore themselves while directing its attention to the images of things taken in by means of the senses. It sorts them out, allowing for both realities and fictions, as in dreams.[20] In the process of sifting, the soul, in withdrawing into itself, enters into dialogue with itself (*secum*) at two levels, one internal, in which it speaks to itself, and another, directed outward toward the self, as it exists in space and time.

In framing the second level of the soul's activities in this manner, Augustine takes a step in the direction of incorporating the movements of the soul into those of the self. This move is parallel to his remark in *De Immortalitate Animae* on the way in which the nontemporal and the temporal are combined in the process of embodiment. Here, however, he points out different levels of involvement. On the one hand, the soul delights in the facility of motion that is naturally accorded to the movements of the body, in which harmony is created with no effort on its part. By contrast, in a motion of another sort, namely, sexual relations, the soul is apparently unable to bring about harmony (*concordia*) entirely on its own and needs the compliance of the self. Augustine notes that in such unions, the soul "endeavors to make two natures into a unity by means of community and love."[21] The soul likewise takes part in the birth of offspring and cooperates (*conspirat*) in fostering, protecting, and nourishing them

(*fovendis, tuendis alendisque*). In both of these activities the form of cooperation that is envisaged is between the soul, operating from the inside through
the mind, and the self, operating from the outside through the body. As if
emphasizing the point, Augustine adds that these types of activities involve
habit and memory: habit, that is, from the bodily standpoint, and memory
within the mind or soul:

> To the things among which the body acts, and by which the soul
> sustains the body, the soul connects itself by habit (*consuetudine*),
> and from these, as if they were its members, it is reluctant to be
> separated; and this force of habit, which is not broken either by
> separation from the things themselves or by intervals of time, is
> called memory.[22]

The third level of the soul is uniquely human and chiefly concerns
memory, which, in this context is not to be thought of as referring to the habits
created by reiterated acts, such as are characteristic of level 2, but to the in-
numerable things that are impressed on the soul and retained by it by having
our attention directed to them or by means of signs (*sed animadversione atque
signis commendatarum ac retentarum rerum innumerabilium*, 33.72).

Of the seven levels of the soul, it is this that is most clearly integrated
with the self and includes a great many features of civilization in which the
body takes part. These encompass the techniques of craftsmen, farmers, and
builders of cities, the arts of communication, including words, gestures, (non-
verbal) sounds, paintings, and statues, as well as the languages of different
peoples and their teachings, both new and revived. Also taken into account
are books and records, which are useful for the preservation of memory and
the regard of posterity, the duties, privileges, honors, and dignities of mortals
in both public and private life, civilian and military, secular and religious.
Last, Augustine turns to the force of reason and thought, to eloquence, poetry,
varieties of song, and forms of acting and mime that are designed for entertainment, as well as the knowledge of surveying and arithmetic, not forgetting the
human tendency to conjecture, based on the present, what has happened in
the past or will happen in the future (33.72).

Augustine then progresses to the fourth level, in which the relationship
between soul and self is taken up on the higher plane of true goodness and
testimony (*bonitas . . . atque omnis vera laudatio*, 33.73). Here the soul acts, not
only on its own behalf, as part of the universe, but on behalf of the universe

itself, while at the same time it stays aloof from the world's goods, which are not comparable in excellence to its own. For, the more it turns inward to itself for the things from which it derives enjoyment, the more it withdraws from things tainted with worldliness, thereby cleansing and purifying itself.[23] By this means the soul distances itself from the negative features of self, and, in consideration of human society (*societas humana*), it does not will for mortals what it would not will for itself. At this level of its activity, the soul thus submits to authority (*auctori*) and to the precepts of the wise (*praecepta sapientium*), convinced that through these statements God is speaking for himself (*et per haec loqui sibi deum credere*).

Yet, in the course of purging itself (*purgationis negotio*), the soul also expresses more distinctly than at its lower levels a fear of death (*metus mortis*), which, although not overwhelming, is never far from its thoughts and actions. The more ardently the soul seeks God's justice, the more anxious it is about not reaching this goal (*sollitius quaeritur*). In this state, the soul lacks the tranquility that is absolutely necessary as a precondition for investigating the most obscure and hidden aspects of its being (*propter metum minus est investigandis obscurissimis rebus pernecessaria*). The higher the soul progresses on its cleansing and healing journey, leaving behind the negative associations of self, the more anxious it becomes, as it realizes the distance that exists between the states of purity and defilement. So unsettled is its state of mind, Augustine proposes, that when self and body are finally left behind, there remains the danger that God may find the uncluttered human soul more of a burden to bear than the combination of soul and self (33.73).

At the fifth, sixth, and seventh levels in Augustine's scheme, the soul has left the body behind, and as its ascent is undertaken, we hear less of the self. The end of the fourth level would therefore be an appropriate place to pause and consider what Augustine has said about relations between the soul and the self. First, it is clear that he has a twofold conception of the soul, which is based partly on his philosophical sources and partly on a more literary approach to the subject that is largely his own invention. On the one hand, the soul is an immaterial, invisible, and non-extendable entity; on the other, it appears in a type of personification, that is, an allegorized self that transcends the self, and in this form, like the literary representation of Augustine himself, exists in perpetual inner dialogue with itself, from which, as much as in the example of the *cogito*, it derives the proof of its existence. This dialogue is of course the mirror image of the inner conversations that Augustine has with himself in other dialogues and in the *Confessions*. One can therefore ask whether, in this aspect of his conception of the soul, it is not the self that is the image of the soul, as he more than occasionally suggests, but vice versa.

The Theological Element

So far in this chapter I have been discussing Augustine's views on the self and soul as reflections of antecedent notions in Plato and later Platonism, in which the self is looked upon as an image in the mind. As transformed by Plotinus, this became a foundational concept for Augustine's early speculations on the nature of the self. As a complement to this discussion, I would now like to devote a few pages to the biblical component in his thinking on the subject, both during his initial speculations on the theme and afterwards. For, if one dimension of his argument in favor of an integrated self arose from his modification of Platonic thinking on the nature of the soul, another was derived from the Bible, in which he found the doctrine of the soul's origin as well as important lessons on asceticism and contemplation.

In the end, the product of his reflections on the self in the mature period of his thinking in theology is a hybrid, in which the doctrines concerning the soul that are absent from the Bible are framed in the language of Platonism, while those concerned with the self, which are infrequent in his philosophical sources, are largely taken from the Bible. The result of this intermingling of sources is a view of the self in which there is no longer a notion of a cognitive core in the person in which the essentials of the self are located and in which they function independently of the body, as in Platonism. The self is looked upon as a composite entity resulting from a synthesis of the psychological and physical elements in the person's makeup. Within this conception of the self, a special role is given to three mind-body elements in the self's construction: these are will, memory, and narrative.

The larger context of Augustine's views is the emergence of a distinctively Christian position in thinking about the self during the patristic period. Christian writers, in contrast to philosophers, universally recognized a historical element in their reflections on the self that was derived not from ancient views on the mind or body but from the interpretation of Christ's crucifixion and resurrection. For, according to the synoptic Gospels, it was not the Lord's soul that was put on the cross but his living historical person—his embodied self, one might say, which had been sent to earth to dwell for a time in a mortal frame. It was this incorporated self that reappeared before Mary Magdalene three days after his execution.[24] The telltale detail in this episode is the empty tomb. Had it been Christ's soul alone that went upward, his embodied self, which was subsequently seen by a number of people, might have remained permanently behind.

Particularly important in the formation of Augustine's view of the self was his reading of the letters of Paul during the 380s, in which he found the basis for his trenchant opposition between the will of the body and the will of the soul, which forms the central element in his preconversion reflections on the self in book 8 of the *Confessions*. It is in Paul that Augustine first came upon the method of resolving this tension by means of the spirit, for example, at Romans 12–15, where the apostle asks his followers to offer their very selves to Christ, "with mind and heart" (Rom. 12:1). There is a lengthy, synthetic picture of Augustine's thinking on this theme in book 13 of the *Confessions*, where his commentary on Genesis is interspersed with reflections as these arise from Paul and from other biblical texts.

However, well before this concluding statement in his autobiography was written holistic conceptions of the self had taken shape in his thinking, as suggested by the analysis earlier in this chapter of passages taken from *De Immortalitate Animae* and *De Quantitate Animae*. This type of reflection is echoed in other early writing. How else can we interpret the conclusion to *De Beata Vita*, his earliest dialogue, where it is affirmed that lasting happiness—the often reiterated goal of ancient philosophical reflection—demands above all the acceptance of Christ's humanity and divinity?[25] Even before this dialogue was written, Augustine recalls, in book 3 of the *Confessions*, his state of mind at age nineteen, noting retrospectively that it was the absence of mention of the crucifixion of Christ that dampened his initial enthusiasm for the recommendation to take up a life of philosophy in Cicero's *Hortensius*, a work which, by his own admission, oriented him more than any other toward a lifelong search for wisdom.[26]

We do not have to look far in the Gospels for the sort of statement which Augustine would have found valuable in his reflections on the theme. One such *locus classicus* is the collection of sayings involving the self found at Matthew 16: 24–28, Mark 8: 34–39, and Luke 9: 23–27. In the version in Mark, which is the earliest of these interconnected statements, Jesus addresses his disciples (and others present) in these words:[27]

> Anyone who wishes to be a follower of mine must leave self behind (*autou eipen autois*); he must take up his cross, and come with me.

Whoever cares for his own safety is lost; but if a man will let
himself be lost for my sake and for the Gospel, that man is safe.
What does a man gain by winning the whole world at the cost of
his true self (*ten psychen autou*)? What can he give to buy that
self back?

If we compare this statement to the references to the self in Plato that
were directly or indirectly accessible to Augustine, we can see how far Gospel
thinking on the theme would have oriented him in a different direction. Both
pagan and Christian spokesmen on the subject of the self are equally concerned with self-care and with the possibility of limited self-improvement.
However, in the philosophical tradition it is argued that the individual should
be able to attain this objective on his own, without outside help, whereas all
three versions of the Gospel sayings maintain that betterment, possibly leading to salvation, can only be achieved through unwavering loyalty to Christ.
Also, while it is presumed that the philosophic style of self-cultivation takes
place over time, since it involves training or practice (and this is echoed in
Augustine's thinking about the ascetic life), there is nothing in the statement
in *First Alcibiades* or in Plato's authenticated writings on the theme that
resonates like the decisive "before" and "after" of the three Gospel statements,
all of which suggest a sudden, decisive, and irrevocable change of direction
for one's life. In this respect, Matthew repeats Mark almost verbatim: in both
versions there is an identical emphasis on the role of the will in the process of
conversion, with the result that the demands made in the sayings are only relevant for a person who voluntarily and self-consciously decides to become a
follower of Christ.[28]

In this passage of the Gospel, it can be argued, we are not in fact presented with a philosophical conception of the self at all. This is clear no matter
how we translate the texts in question. I have quoted from the version of Mark
in the 1961 edition of *The New English Bible*, which translates the Greek pronoun for self and the noun for soul (or life) by the single word "self." In the
Latin Vulgate, completed early in the fifth century, Jerome is more careful in
his choice of words, expressing the pronominal form for self in the first quoted
phrase in Greek as *semetipse* and the second as *anima sua*. But whether we prefer a less or more literal rendering of the statement, it is clear that Jesus is
speaking to his followers about the type of self which each of us knows
inwardly, day by day, in a preconceptual manner. If there is a philosophical
element in the quoted statements, it is chiefly concerned with the factor of

time: this enters sentence 1 of the quoted passage as an aspect of the narrative, since the potential follower of Christ leaves the self behind, and reenters in sentences 2 and 3, where the envisaged follower realizes that what is implied in this transition is the overcoming of time.

Mark makes a distinction between two types or groups of persons, namely the "crowd" and the "disciples."[29] The followers of whom he speaks are not all intended to become disciples,[30] but they are supposed to pattern their lives on the life of Christ. It is this pattern that the Gospel passage repeatedly emphasizes, and it has essentially three components. The first is self-denial (*aparnesastho heauton*). Jesus does not ask his followers to give up material things or to adopt an ascetic lifestyle, although these are mentioned elsewhere, but literally to surrender "the self," to disown it. This is a more radical reshaping of self than is implied in the "spiritual exercises" of which Socrates and later philosophers speak and which remained popular in Stoic thinking down to Seneca. It also differs from the gentler process of meditative withdrawal through *lectio divina*, at least in the form in which it is later outlined in the writings of Benedict.

The person who desires to become Jesus's follower must, so to speak, "take up his cross." Since this can imply a readiness to accept crucifixion, one can consider this a figurative way of saying that a follower of Christ must be prepared lose his or her life, as indicated in the next verse (*apolesei ten psychen autou*). The image of a humiliating death, usually reserved for criminals, therefore reinforces the image of a willful or voluntary sacrifice of one's self, which is implied in the Christian concept of self-denial. While this was often the case in the subsequent history of martyrdom, it is not principally a physical death that Jesus has in mind here, but, as suggested, a death of the self by means of an extreme form of discipleship. This is conceived as an unwavering allegiance, which Jesus demands of his followers, even if it leads to torments or sufferings. It is in that sense that we should understand the third component of the statement, namely the directive for the convert to "follow" Jesus (*akoloutheito*), as mentioned in the opening phrase.

Augustine singled out the directives for self-reform in the Gospels and the letters of Paul for comment, especially in his sermons, in which he attempted, often fruitlessly, to bring about behavioral improvements in his recalcitrant parishioners in Hippo Regius. Recalling his own experience, he perhaps also had in mind that it was a directive comparable to the ones I have quoted, namely Matthew 19:21, which inspired the conversion of Antony, as related in the second chapter of Athanasius's *Life*. It was the translation of the *Vita Antonii* attributed to this author, which played the major part in the conversion of the bureaucrat Ponticianus at *Confessions* 8.6.15 and, if we can believe the story, in his own conversion at *Confessions* 8.12.29. These literary connections—and they are, I think, provably literary and rhetorical, as Courcelle maintained—are summed up in the celebrated "*tolle, lege*" scene, where Augustine says:

> Audieram enim de Antonio, quod ex euangelica lectione, cui forte superuenerat, admonitus fuerit, tamquam sibi diceretur quod legebatur: *Vade, uende omnia, quae habes, da pauperibus et habebis thesaurum in caelis; et ueni, sequere me.*[31]

> For I had heard how Antony happened to be present at the Gospel reading, and took it as an admonition addressed to himself when the words were read: "Go, sell all you have, give to the poor, and you shall have treasure in heaven; and come, follow me."[32]

This recollection of the *Vita Antonii* is followed by Augustine's quotation of Romans 13:13–14, in which he is literally asked to "put on" (*induere*) the Lord Jesus Christ. It is an appropriate metaphor if what is meant is "reclothing" the self, as Paul himself suggests.[33] There is no more enduring expression for the integrated or embodied self in early Christian writings, as Augustine recognized in frequently reusing Paul's words in his writings on the theme.

Antony is asked to situate his life within the pattern of a single model life, as were many ancient philosophers, for example the far-flung readers of the letters of Epicurus. The ensuing struggle (as related by Athanasius) is between the saint and the demons, who attempt unsuccessfully to prevent him from following his chosen path. The comparable episode in Augustine works differently. There are no demons, and in place of a single life we have several lives: the life of Christ, of course, but also the lives of Antony, Marius Victorinus, and the anonymous bureaucrats in Trier, who find the *Vita Antonii* by chance in an abandoned cottage. In Augustine these lives inform his own life, as if they represented—to reuse Paul's metaphor—its outer garments. What has changed between Paul and Augustine is, so to speak, the composition of this clothing: its fabric is no longer made of lives that have been known at first hand, but exclusively of lives that have been heard or read about. One of the original features of Augustine's conversion episode in comparison with ear-lier stories on this theme is the buildup of overlapping narratives, each of which reinforces the other in the reader's mind.

These stories are in Augustine's thoughts at the moment of his conversion. As a consequence, the episode, as narrated, has to be considered in both a his-torical and a rhetorical context, and, as such, as his definitive commentary on the notion of the embodied or integrated self. The event itself, as remembered by Augustine, is structured by his memory, and two sorts of memory images are involved. One of these, *phantasiae*, consists in images of things he has seen, while the other, *phantasmata*, is made up of images of things he has learned about from the reports of others.[34] In the conversion scene, the mental impres-sions denominated as *phantasiae* are represented by his old self, which he knows well and can remember from what he actually witnessed himself, while *phan-tasmata* are represented by his new self, inspired by his readings, which he does not yet know. Following Paul, the one is the self he wants to leave behind; the other is the self he wants to become. This is the first time in the conceptual his-tory of the self as an autonomous theme in philosophy in which the beginnings of self-reform are brought about by an image in the mind that the thinking subject recognizes as a figment of his (or her) imagination, even though the possibility has been suggested, as mentioned, by Cicero, Quintilian, and other writers on the topic. And that is the way it has to be, for, had Augustine known beforehand what he was able to become through conversion, based on the firm impression of what he had been in the past, his conversion would not have been necessary. What he has added to the Gospels and Pauline accounts of self-reform is a combination of intentionality and imagination within an embodied self whose reality is realized physically and historically in time.

As noted, he acquires knowledge about the possibility of shedding his old self and acquiring a replacement with the help of the reports of others. These combine verbal reports, such as that of Ponticianus, and written reports, such as the biblical and hagiographic texts he has been reading in an intensive but disorderly fashion since the spring of 386. It is of course the action of grace rather than the reading of these writings that eventually permits him to con-vert, at last overcoming the stubborn will of his body. However, within this process, the writings with which he has previously been acquainted play a critical role in his interpretation of the event, both before and afterward, and this too concerns imagistic representation.

In this respect his account of conversion differs in an important respect from that of Athanasius. For Antony hears the Gospel text as it is read aloud and abruptly changes his life, without the use of intermediaries, whereas Augustine's conversion is preceded by an interlacing of already interpreted lives, whose force on his thinking is well advanced by the time he picks up Paul's letter to the Romans and opens the codex to the page on which the decisive passage is found. These texts influence him before his conversion as well as afterward, when he writes up and reinterprets his original experience, possibly altering its narrative details to suit the imaginary design.[35] It is possible to label this subsequent elaboration as "rhetoric," and to envisage the scholar's task as peeling off these added literary layers to the story in order to get to the bare facts of the conversion experience. But if we do that, in search of historical veracity, we lose something of the conversion's meaning, at least as Augustine appears to have conceived it. For, in this climactic scene in his autobiography, he is talking not only to himself but to a wider audience of potential converts in the present and future, encouraging them, in the form of a narrative protreptic, and telling them that, if they wish to shed their former selves, they will need both the will to take up new lives and an imaginative setting for the life that each of them wants to live.

The Pauline metaphor of the worn garment, as noted, is an appropriate way of describing Augustine's transition from a philosophical to a theological outlook, within which his configuration of the self takes shape. In literary terms, this involves a move from a "thin" to a "thick" description of the self. By the term "thin," I mean the type of delineation of the self that one frequently finds in ancient philosophical writings, such as *First Alcibiades*, in which the notion of the self is presented in abstract terms. Augustine utilizes this approach to the self in his proof for the self's existence by means of the *cogito*. By contrast, the "thick" description is one in which his self-perception is bound up with a multitude of concrete details—the observations and interpretations that arise in his experience of everyday life. In the narrative books of the *Confessions*, therefore, we may speak of dual notion of the self which incorporates the thin description, as it found in his ancient sources and his own writings, into a larger imagistic canvas that includes his fears, desires, hopes, doubts, and uncertainties, as he draws near the turning point in his life. In the end, the uniqueness of his identity is conveyed, not through philosophy alone, but through a combination of philosophy and creative imagination.

CHAPTER 5

Rhythms of Time

Introduction

In 415 Augustine wrote a letter to Jerome on the topic of the soul's origin. In the course of his discussion he proposed that the principles involved in the harmony of the soul are comparable to those operating in the sphere of music (*musica*). These are governed by the science or sense of good measure (*scientia sensusve bene modulandi*):

> If a man who is skilled in composing a song knows what lengths to assign to what tones, so that the melody flows and progresses with beauty by a succession of slow and rapid tones, how much more true is it that God permits no periods of time in the process of birth and death of his creatures—periods which are like the words and syllables in the measure of this temporal life—to proceed either more quickly or more slowly than the recognized and well-defined law of rhythm requires, in this wonderful song of succeeding events.[1]

In this statement Augustine is restating in a modified form an ancient Stoic doctrine. Living a happy and virtuous life, in which the soul is at peace with itself, implies that one is "living harmoniously with nature."[2] The link between the Stoic and Augustinian statements of this view arises from the notion of harmony as an element that crosses the boundary between the physical and the psychological dimensions of existence.

In this chapter I explore the meaning of the Augustinian notion of "harmony" in a pair of texts that illustrate different stages of his thinking on the subject. The first is the summary of his views that appears in the prose poem, *Sero te amavi, pulchritudo* at *Confessions* 10.27.38–10.29.40, which was presumably written before 400; the other is the lengthier exploration of the theme in book 6 of *De Musica*, which was begun in 389 and completed, after revisions, in 408 or 409.

Augustine's formulation of the principle of harmony differs from its distant Stoic predecessor in two respects. He rejects naturalism as the principal creative force in the universe, in favor of God's will, and he gives a central role in the construction of universal harmony to the factor of time. His best-known discussion of time is at *Confessions* 11.14.17–11.20.26; however, it is in an alternate version of his views, in book 6 of *De Musica,* that is found his major statement on musical and mathematical harmony.

Although there may be echoes of Stoic thinking in Augustine's notion of harmony, his views on time also have a great deal in common with Platonic doctrines. There is a similarity between the theory of time that informs several of his early works and the statement on the subject that is attributed to Parmenides and reported by Plato in the dialogue of the same name at 151e–155c.[3] In this section of his lengthy speech, the aging and distinguished Parmenides is elaborating his conception of the One for Socrates and his assembled friends. During the course of his argument he asks whether the One can be said to exist in time and, if so, what relationship the One might have to the three major dimensions of experienced time, namely past, present, and future. I quote a part of his statement, in which it is only necessary to replace the notion of the One with that of God to arrive at an approximation of Augustine's views in book 10 of the *Confessions* and in book 6 of *De Musica*, to be discussed below:

> Since the one *is* one, of course it has being, and to "be" means
> precisely having existence in conjunction with time present, as
> "was" or "will be" means having existence in conjunction with past
> or future time. So if the one is, it is in time. Time, moreover, is
> advancing. Hence since the one moves forward temporally, it is
> always becoming older than itself . . . . Also, it is older, when,
> in this process of becoming, it is *at* the present time which lies
> between "was" and "will be," for of course, as it travels from past to
> future, it will never overstep the present. So, when it coincides with
> the present, it stops becoming older: at that time it is not becom-
> ing, but already *is*, older. For if it were getting ahead, it could never

be caught up by the present, since to get ahead would mean to be
in touch with both the present and the future, leaving the present
behind and reaching out to the future, and so passing between
the two.

Augustine's view of time differs from that of Parmenides in one major
respect: this concerns the relationship that he envisages between time and
memory. Here, in addition to the Stoic background on *phantasia* mentioned
in Chapter 2, the ultimate origin of his thinking may be found in two other
Platonic dialogues, in which mention is made of the ancient doctrine of anamnesis. This is the theory that humans possess knowledge from previous
incarnations of their souls, and that learning consists of rediscovering that
knowledge in the mind.

Anamnesis is briefly discussed by Socrates at *Phaedo* 72c–73c and *Meno*
81b–c. In the second of these texts, the sage maintains that anamnesis is not
just a theory devised for and by intellectuals but is also looked upon with favor
by other types of thinkers, among them priests, priestesses, and poets, all of
whom are convinced that

> the human soul is immortal; at times it comes to an end, which
> they call dying, at times it is reborn, but it is never destroyed . . . .
> As the soul is immortal, has been born often, and has seen all
> things here and in the underworld, there is nothing which it has
> not learned; so it is in no way surprising that it can recollect the
> things it knew before, both about virtue and other things. As the
> whole of nature is akin, and the soul has learned everything,
> nothing prevents a man, after recalling one thing only—a process
> men call learning—discovering everything else for himself . . . ,
> for searching and learning are, as a whole, recollection.[4]

While Augustine's views on time are reasonably close to those related in
the *Parmenides*, which he did not know at first hand, those that he expresses
on memory differ in important respects from the statements on anamnesis in
the *Phaedo* or *Meno*, parts of which he may have known, either directly or
indirectly, through the philosophical writings of Cicero. One of these differences arises from the connections that he sees between memory and language, which are not foreshadowed in any Platonic texts dealing with the

subject. Here, the central influence on Augustine's thinking appears to be his own personal style of skepticism.

A good example of his approach to the topic of memory in this context is found at the end of *De Magistro*, where, after a lengthy debate with his gifted son, Adeodatus, the young Augustine comes to the conclusion that we are never taught anything by verbal signs alone, unless we have an antecedent knowledge of the realities for which they stand. On this view, words are just indications of meaning, which ultimately depends on the mind and on memory, and beyond that, on the higher knowledge of God, in whom alone true and complete understanding of things is found.[5] Accordingly, the doctrine of anamnesis is expressed in his statement on the theme in a paradoxical form, which can be summed up as follows. Either the person seeking the knowledge of a word's meaning knows what he is looking for, since the required information is already lodged in his memory, or, alternatively, he does not know what he is looking for, since the information is not located there. In both cases it is memory and not language that is the ultimate source of the knowledge.

In his early writings, Augustine may have entertained the notion that we learn nothing from our teachers that we do not have already in our memories, as he suggests at the end of *De Magistro*, but he had abandoned any trace of the idea by 397, when he began the *Confessions*.[6] For in books 1–9 he tells the story of a progressive education involving eminent teachers, such as Ambrose of Milan, as he works his way successively through the writings of Cicero, Manichaeism, Neoplatonism, and Paul. He came closer to the negative view expressed in his debate with his son in his last writings on the subject, in particular in the *Retractationes*, written in 426–27, where, under the influence of his doctrine of grace, he modified the early and rather literary account of his achievements in the dialogues and *Confessions*. He now offered his readers an edited and altered version of the story of his youthful intellectual enterprises in which there is less emphasis on cumulative learning through established philosophical methods, such as the Socratic elenchus, and more on the insights that were arrived at by means of hermeneutics and the interpretation of passages of scripture. He also downplayed the element of the *Bildungsroman* that is so evident in the narrative books of the *Confessions*.

The link with anamnesis was nonetheless maintained through the notion of cultural memory, which informs the early books of *The City of God*. Another historical context for anamnesis arose from the liturgy, in which those celebrating the divine office or engaged in other forms of devotion were invited to recall an event at which they were not present, the Last Supper. Augustine rethinks this tradition of latent memory along two lines. First, he incorporates into the notion of liturgical anamnesis a literary program of depth and intertextual complexity, as I attempt to show in the first part of this chapter. Also, on a more general level, his poetic evocation of passages of the Bible in the prayers and devotional statements in the *Confessions* anticipates the early modern notion of reminiscence as a reflective or contemplative form of recall that is largely dependent on personal memory. The classic statement on this type of poetic memory was made centuries later by Wordsworth in the Preface to *Lyrical Ballads*, where it is described as

> the spontaneous overflow of powerful feelings: it takes its origin
> from emotion recollected in tranquillity: the motion is contemplated
> till by a species of reaction the tranquillity gradually disappears,
> and an emotion, kindred to that which was before the subject of
> contemplation, is gradually produced, and does itself actually exist
> in the mind.[7]

Needless to say, in the linguistic and liturgical modifications of the ancient doctrine of anamnesis, Augustine moves in a different direction from that taken at *Meno* 81b ff. and *Phaedo* 72c–73c. Recall that in the *Meno*, Socrates provides an illustration of transmigrated memories by means of a slave boy, who, having no training in geometry, is led to the solution of geometrical problems by means of questions and answers alone. The experiment proves to Socrates's satisfaction that the necessary knowledge could not have arisen from his abilities but represents a kind of inheritance of the required information from a previous soul in which it was lodged. This contrasts with Augustine's view of retained memories, as expressed, for example, at *De Immortalitate Animae* 4.6. Here it is argued that an art or discipline (*ars*) may simply be present in the mind on one occasion and absent on another. In Augustine's view, this sort of memory lapse is a frequent phenomenon and takes place through forgetfulness or lack of adequate training (*quod per oblivionem atque imperitiam*). The causes are twofold. Either something is in the mind but is not in present thought (*aut est aliquid in animo, quod in praesenti cogitatione non est*), or something is in the mind of which the mind itself may not be aware (*Potest igitur aliquid est in animo, quod esse in se animus ipse non sentiat*). This recalls the paradox concerning memory in *De*

Magistro, in contrast to Socrates, who focuses on a slave boy's latent or hidden memories.

Augustine's chief concern lies with the relation of memory to attention. If we know two disciplines, he proposes, let us say music and geometry, and focus on one of them, our understanding is chiefly the result of our mental concentration. Also, because we presumably have some knowledge of these disciplines lodged in our memories, we have a second level of awareness to contend with. For, while we are focusing on one discipline, we are conscious that we are not focusing on the other. In contrast to Plato, therefore, Augustine is interested in the source of our knowledge of a discipline at a given moment in time as well as in a more general problem: this is whether two states of attention are not involved in *every* situation involving remembered information. This might be termed a problem of the mind's presence or absence. Augustine allows that music or geometry may have been incompletely or imperfectly learned; however, this does not change the central issue, since, in the cases of such partial mastery, the learner will not have forgotten that he was once aware that he had the knowledge of both disciplines. This means that, in relation to attention, the cases of *oblivio* and *imperitia,* which he takes up in his discussion, are essentially the same.

To put this point slightly differently, in Socrates's view one can acquire the knowledge of geometry from scratch, without any previous instruction, by means of questions and answers, since the required information may already be in one's head, merely awaiting rediscovery. But this argument works only if a figure like the slave boy is totally ignorant of the discipline when the questions begin, and learns everything that he knows through the process of deductive reasoning, in response to logically organized questions. For his part, Augustine is not concerned with this type of instruction, which begins, so to speak, with the assumption of a *tabula rasa.* He prefers to take up the more normal situation in education in which a hypothetical student has acquired the knowledge of geometry or music, as he notes, partially or completely. What he wants to know is the status in the memory of one of these disciplines, when it is not being thought about, while the other is in the mind and being put to practical use. In principle, he proposes, a person could have access to either form of knowledge, if he simply redirected his attention to it, whereas for Socrates's slave boy this is not apparently an option. In the end, it is the will that plays a central role in Augustine's theory. He concludes that

> when, either reasoning within ourselves (*nos ipsi nobiscum ratio-cinantes*), or having been asked pertinent questions by someone else

concerning any one of the liberal arts (*ab alio bene interrogati de quibusdam liberalibus artibus*), we find the things that we find nowhere else but in our minds (*ea quae invenimus non alibi quam in animo nostro invenimus*), a distinction has to be made between discovering (*invenire*) something and making it (*facere*) or begetting it (*gignere*).[8]

Literary Reminiscence

As Augustine views anamnesis, therefore, the issues differ from those that are found in the writings of Plato, and chiefly in two respects. As the quoted passage from *De Immortalitate Animae* suggests, anamnesis does not involve memories shared by two souls, which are presumably occupying separate zones of time, but those that are retained within the lifetime of a single individual.[9] Also, a notion that is employed in classical thought to describe the transfer of information from one *soul* to another has become the model for a type of literary reminiscence, in which words, phrases, and longer passages are transferred from one self to another through the artificial memory of writing. To put it simply, in the Augustinian interpretation of the idea of anamnesis, the soul is replaced by the text and the notion of transmigration by that of commemorative reflections in the mind of the reader.

As a preface to the main subject of this chapter, which consists in a discussion of this topic in book 6 of *De Musica*, I would like to provide an illustration of the way the principle of literary anamnesis operates in one Augustinian text. The passage that I have in mind is *Confessions* 10.27.38–10.29.40, which is usually identified through its incipit, *Sero te amaui, pulchritudo*. This is a prose poem in which Augustine recapitulates in mystical language a part of the discussion of memory in book 10.

In reading this passage, it should be kept in mind that book 10 comprises an independent treatise within the *Confessions*, supplementing a good deal of earlier writing on memory in philosophy, including Aristotle's *De Memoria et Reminiscentia*, the anonymous *Rhetorica ad Herennium* (book 3), Cicero's *De Oratore* (book 2), and Quintilian's *Institutio Oratoria* (book 11). Augustine's contribution deals at length with the psychological dimension of the subject (10.12.10–10.19.40), as well as with the problem of overcoming negative habits through a combination of ancient spiritual exercises and intellectual discipline (10.30.41–10.43.70).

The literary role for reminiscence appears near the end of the first of these two segments, and is summed up at 10.27.38, which I prefer to present as free verse:

Sero te amaui
pulchritudo tam antiqua et tam noua
sero te amaui.
Et ecce intus erat et ego foris
et ibi te quaerebam
et in ista formosa quae fecisti, deformis inruebam,
Mecum eras, et tecum non eram.
Ea me tenebant longe a te.
Quae si in te non essent, non essent.
Vocasti et clamasti et rupisti surditatem meam,
corucasti, spenduisti et fugasti caecitatem meam,
fragrasti, et duxi spiritum et anhelo tibi
gustaui et esurio et sitio,
tetigisti me, et exarsi in pacem tuam.[10]

Translation:
Late have I loved you,
beauty so ancient and so new,
late have I loved you.
And see, you were within and I outside
and I was seeking you there.
and upon the beautifully formed things you have made I threw
    myself, formless.
You were with me but I was not with you.
These things kept me far from you,
things that would have no being, if not existing in you.
You called, cried out, and broke through my deafness,
You glittered, gleamed, and drove out my blindness,
You were fragrant, I drew in my breath, and I pant after you,
I tasted you, and I hunger and thirst for you,
You touched me, and I burned for your peace.[11]

In a subtle interweaving of scriptural images inspired by the *Song of Songs*, the Psalms, and a variety of other biblical texts on memory, these lines faithfully

echo the penitent words addressed to God in the prayers that open a number of books of the *Confessions*. Here is an example from 1.1.1:

> Magnus es, domine (cf. Ps. 47:2) et laudabilis ualde: (Ps. 95:4;
> Ps. 144:3) magna virtus tua et sapientiae tuae (Ps. 146:3) non est
> numerus. Et laudare te uult homo, et homo circumferens
> mortalitatem suam.[12]

> Translation: "You are great, Lord, and highly to be praised." "Great
> is your power and your wisdom is immeasurable." Man, a little
> piece of your creation, desires to praise you, a human being
> "bearing his mortality with him."[13]

A comparable effect of layered readings, in which biblical texts are sandwiched
between Augustine's own meditative phrases, is produced in the devotional
segment that opens book 10. Here we sense that he is already moving in the
direction of the theology of loss and retrieval that is so simply and movingly
expressed in *Sero te amaui*. The use of this technique of internal quotation was
widespread among Christian authors in late antiquity. Words, expressions, and
on occasion lengthier texts from the pagan classics and/or the Bible were inserted into an author's compositions on the assumption that they would be
recognized immediately by their learned readers.

   Both the quoted texts of scripture and the surrounding statements are interpreted as a single integrated piece of writing. Augustine employs this
method of intertextual referencing in a manner that is highly developed in
the *Confessions*. He sometimes utilizes as background pagan texts alone, as in
Soliloquia 1.1.3–6 or those taken from the Latin classics and the Bible, as in *Sero
te amaui*. Both of these prayers echo in different registers the statement on
spiritual ascent at *Enneads* 1.6.8, where Plotinus asks how one can speaks of

> the inconceivable beauty which stays within the holy sanctuary and
> does not come out where the profane may see it. Let him who can
> follow and come within, and leave outside the sight of his eyes and
> not turn back to the bodily splendours which he saw before. When
> he sees the beauty in bodies he must not run after them; we must
> know that they are images, traces, shadows, and hurry away to that
> which they image. For if a man runs to the image and wants to

seize it as if it were the reality . . . then this man . . . will sink down
into the dark depths where the intellect has no delight.[14]

Augustine blends this type of thinking with literary and rhetorical texts, as at
Confessions 9.3.5, where he describes the pleasures of Cassiciacum by means of
an erudite allusion to *Aeneid* 6.638, thereby intermingling different notions of
the "ideal landscape."[15]

*   *   *

In the prayer that begins book 1 of the *Confessions* this method of layered references produces the effect of a pair of texts being read at the same time. One of
these is read silently in the reader's mind, based on memory, while the other is
listened to, as an auditory experience in the present, as if the reader's voice
were that of another person. Also, while Augustine is envisaged as reciting his
prayer, the reader, who is presumably well acquainted with scripture, is mentally going over the psalms to which allusions are being made. The two texts,
the one that is read silently, and the other that is pronounced, come together
in their messages as well as in their prose rhythms. In both cases the dominant
rhythm is that of the Latin text of the Bible, in particular that of the Psalms.

In bringing about this effect in his readers, Augustine makes simultaneous use of three successive phases of composition. The first consists, as noted,
in the oral reading and memorization of the Psalms, the letters of Paul, and
other relevant biblical texts. In the second, the expressions taken from these
texts are inserted into the prayer, based upon associations of words and images formed in Augustine's mind. In the third, the stylistic rapports with biblical prayers, in particular those of the Psalms, are reaffirmed, along with the
introduction of philosophical and theological themes originating in Augustine's thinking. During the transition from the first to the second phase, the
expressions borrowed from the Bible retain a part of their original content but
are transferred to Augustine's prayer, in which they reappear in a context that
is still related to their biblical sources in fundamental ways but nonetheless is
distinguishable from them in the mind of the reader of the composite text. In
passing from the second to the third phase, the setting is once again changed
from the biblical quotations that provide its landscape to the thought and expressions of Augustine himself; and yet, all the while that this is taking place
in the reader's mind, the echo of the Psalms can still be heard by means of the

vocal reproduction of their poetic rhythms. It is possible to see this literary method in action at *Confessions* 9.4.7–11, in which Augustine describes an emotionally charged reading of Psalm 4 in the presence of his mother, Monica, during their stay together at Cassiciacum.[16]

A variant of the scheme is employed in *Sero te amaui*; however, here Augustine goes beyond its applications in the prayers that begin books 1, 5, and 10 as well as other texts of this type earlier in the *Confessions*. The poetic rhythms that one encounters on reading the text are in this case at a high level of detachment from the content of the biblical quotations from which they are taken. As a consequence, the reader's mental record of these texts is constituted almost exclusively from the flow of *auditory rhythms* that takes place in the preceding prayers, which thereby act as the model and spiritual guide. For the attentive reader, the text of these prayers is not completely forgotten and continues to echo in his or her mind. But the content of these texts is not recorded in the text of *Sero te amaui*.

In this way, Augustine adapts the notion of anamnesis to literary ends that are possibly related in his mind to liturgical devotions. He rejects the ancient doctrine of the reincarnation of souls; however, by means of his theory of signs he retains one of the principal characteristics of this theory: this is the Platonic doctrine according to which the knowledge that one has acquired is reactivated through a type of remembering. As noted, he introduces into this doctrine a type of transmigration that does not imply the presence of souls, which in Plato retain the knowledge that they have acquired from a previous life, but of texts, which retain the memory of the pagan or Christian works that have been previously read. Augustine assumes that, although souls do not migrate, rhythmical patterns in sacred texts, being divine in origin, have the capacity to do so, and, insofar as they are patterns, they acquire, as a by-product of this capacity, a type of preexistence, to the degree that they were in place before the invention of the diverse literary situations in which they subsequently appear. In book 6 of *De Musica*, to be taken up in the second part of this chapter, Augustine argues that the memory of a pleasant and fitting prose rhythm is derived ultimately from the imitation of eternal harmonies, which are transmitted to mortals through the medium of sound.[17] *Sero te amaui* is an illustration of this phenomenon: what we remember, when we hear the passage recited, is the reiteration of the poetic prose in the preceding prayers, which preface other books of the *Confessions* and in doing so act as staged introductions to Augustine's spiritual progress. The message that is conveyed in these prayers is hidden in memory, in the sense that it does not function as working or conscious knowledge; it therefore may be said to consist of a latent memory, which may be brought back to mind by comparable prose rhythms.

At the moment in which he has an auditory perception of *Sero te amaui, pulchritudo*, the reader therefore has a simultaneous experience of presence and absence, of sound and silence, which recalls the use of comparable ideas in Augustine's philosophy of language and attention, as well as in his interpretation of Plotinian texts on the notion of spiritual ascent. He thinks of the preceding prayers, which are based on biblical passages and resound silently in his mind. With these echoes in his thoughts, he may likewise recall parts of the narrative of books 1 to 9 (parts, I would suggest, rather than the whole, although, within Augustine's developing hermeneutics, the whole may be recognized through its parts). For, just as the biblical references in *Sero te amaui* are rendered subtle to the point of barely being perceived, so there is little or no precise recollection of the events which are recounted in these books—aside from a single reference to Augustine's conversion at 10.29.40. The earlier events are present in the reader's mind as a silent narrative, and it is in this unexpressed manner that they act as a powerful statement of regret in *Sero te amaui*. In reiterating the sound patterns of the preceding prayers, Augustine thus recalls his own narrative and announces to his readers the central lesson in the latter part of book 10. This concerns the reform of habitual patterns of thought and action by which memory has become enslaved.

The recitation of this prose poem thereby becomes the point of departure for a new mental habit which incites the individual toward self-direction and reform. At the same time the pronouncing of these lines is an attempt to recall something that has been forgotten, that is, the biblical texts which are not evoked directly in the spoken passages. Forgetting and remembering thus form a pair of consolidated activities which rest on the rules of composition. As such, they draw attention to a fundamental feature of Augustine's theory of signs: as noted, when we hear a word that represents a thing, we understand the signification through an act of memory. To return to the lesson of the *Meno*, we seem to recognize an object of knowledge of which we are unaware: the words teach us how to recall the things that are hidden in our memories up to the point at which we bring them into our conscious thoughts. For Plato, we relearn things that we know, since we have learned them in another life; for Augustine, we recognize what we know as a result of our innate faculty for transforming thoughts into language. We thereby utilize memory in order to cross the frontier between the unconscious, in which thoughts are inaccessible, and the conscious, in which they are configured as words.

In order to remember one text, therefore, it is necessary to forget another. But the former text is not entirely forgotten. *Sero te amaui* is an expression of regret for an occasion in which love has failed, as well as a wish to revisit that occasion again by means of memory, to relive and transform it through reinterpretation, into a more positive experience. As a consequence, we can say that it is in the act of forgetting that we find the genesis of Augustine's poetic and theological desire, to which he refers on numerous occasions in the *Confessions*, as his chief source of motivation. The text that is rediscovered and rehearsed in memory is an act of regret towards both an actual occasion and an implied text of that occasion that has somehow been lost. All poetry in this genre becomes a lamentation on poetry that is not present within the interior of poetry that is present. In a symbolic sense, writing poetry or poetic prose resembles the narrative of the fall: there is something forgotten that is potentially recoverable, which is life before the fall, and there is anxiety in the act of remembering what once was but no longer exists.

*   *   *

The decisive moment in book 10 of the *Confessions* is the mention of Luke 15:8–10 at 10.18.27, the parable of the woman who lost one of her ten pieces of silver. This reference precedes the story of the prodigal son (Lk. 15:11–18), one of Augustine's preferred biblical accounts of alienation from God and eventual return.[18] It is not the theological utilization Augustine makes of the prodigal son that is unusual in comparison to other references to this text in patristic thought, but the idea according to which the relation between Old and New Testament, Jews and Christians, can be modeled on the basis of auditory poetic patterns, and placed in an order in which a later motif resembles a preceding one by means of its musical rhythms, while containing a different message. The author thereby becomes the agency of a type of creation in which poetic rhythms are adjusted to the music of more noble biblical passages, which are, in Augustine's view, their eternal source, in the same way as he asks God to adjust his soul to its divine exemplar at the beginning of book 10.

One memory takes the place of another, and a new life takes form from a former life. The text of *Sero te amaui* combines the thought of Paul and Plotinus, insofar as it speaks of the paradox of a beauty which is at once old and new: *tam antiqua et tam noua*. Poetry represents an experience in which the individual life is absorbed in a much larger configuration, just as the rhythms of *Sero te amaui* reflect the rhythms of biblical prose, thereby becoming a canonical text which serves as an intermediary between the unpronounceable Word of God and the words spoken or written by man. With *Sero te amaui*, Augustine deliberately creates a pause in book 10, which is the first of the nonnarrative books in the *Confessions*, and he does so by introducing a highly subjective narrative interlude, which is based on the principle of regret. The narrative element suggests more than it says. Although, as noted, we do not hear Augustine speaking of specific events, we are presented with a synthetic declaration on their significance. This is expressed through the Pauline notion of renewal, which is combined with the Augustinian notion of grace, consisting in a decision by God that we cannot anticipate, as was the moment of his conversion to the religious life in book 8.

This narrative declaration is interpreted in the interior of the nonnarrative context of book 10, which concerns the concept of memory. It must be understood as a reaffirmation of the possibility of personal and autobiographical memory functioning as an ethical element in our lives. Augustine seems to be telling us that what inspires us to reform is not only an abstract theory of memory or a program of improvement but a perpetual rhythm of sorrow and regret: this is a type of remembering, personalized through the sense of hearing, concerning something forgotten that has been reactivated in the mind by means of the poetry of the Psalms. It is a utopian theme expressed in terms of an ideal musical harmony. Although we cannot force our natures to utilize memory to reach God (10.8.12), this type of memory is nonetheless critical in our ascent, since it makes us conscious of our need for harmony, and from the awareness of this need we can make some degree of progress. We cannot prepare ourselves intellectually for grace. Yet we have the possibility of expressing our regret for our failings and thereby laying the foundation for our renewal.

In this respect, *Sero te amaui* is both a turning point in the discussion of memory in book 10 of the *Confessions* and a preface to the discussion of time in book 11. The proof for the existence of present time enters Augustine's thoughts by means of the recitation from memory of the first line of the Ambrosian hymn, *Deus creator omnium*. Here again, it is the poetic rhythm of the text that provides Augustine with the solution, for which *Sero te amaui* can be considered a model text, composed along the same principles by himself. It is at the end of this prose poem (10.27.38) that Augustine begins his ascent toward God by means of the five senses, hearing, sight, smell, taste, and touch. These are the sources of his former enslavement through habitual memory,[19] and it is by means of the echo of eternal harmonies in this text, acting sensorially, that he is set free. In this sense, as noted, we may think of *Sero te amaui* as an example of a technique employed by Augustine in order to replace classical anamnesis with a personal style of literary reminiscence. It works by means of an alternation of forgetting and remembering, in which the prose rhythms of the Latin Bible, which are present in the reader's memory, are reutilized in the context of the personal life of the text's author, namely Augustine. This method has evident implications for his notion of the self; these are spelled out in *De Musica*, book 6, to which I now turn.

De Musica

I begin this part of the chapter with a brief reflection on *De Ordine*, book 2, where Augustine puts the types of question asked in *De Musica* in context by observing that an adequate foundation for a Christian philosophy and for harmony in life can only be laid by means of training in the liberal arts. In the spring of 387, awaiting baptism, he had planned a group of studies in these disciplines in order to give substance to this program, which was intended to lead students towards God *per corporalia . . . ad incorporalia*.[20] Like the conversations with his junior associates that took place at Cassiciacum, these treatises were conceived as a set of Socratic dialogues between a master and students, which were to be taken down, revised, and subsequently published.

The tentative and incomplete nature of some of these writings has to be taken into account in evaluating Augustine's early statements on memory, which are considerably revised and extended in book 10 of the *Confessions*. He had worked on drafts of two of the *disciplinarum libri* before returning to Africa in 388, namely *De Grammatica* and *De Musica*,[21] the latter of which he regretted not finishing at the time he relocated, owing to his ecclesiastical duties.[22] He also took back with him the introductions that he had composed to the books on dialectic, rhetoric, geometry, arithmetic, and philosophy. These manuscripts appear to have been lost in the move, as was the unfinished study of grammar; however, in his later reflections on this period of transition, he did not rule out the possibility that these works, or parts of them, had been preserved by others.[23] This may have been the fate of *De Dialectica*, which has survived in a fragmentary and incomplete form but nonetheless with a good deal of its argument intact.

In this cycle of studies, which is unique among educational writings in late antiquity,[24] Augustine restored to the study of philosophy the range of subjects associated much earlier with Stoicism, which included grammar, rhetoric, ethics, semantics, and epistemology, as well as selected topics in natural science. An introduction to these projected works is found in the speech that he conceived for the allegorical figure of Reason in book 2 of *De Ordine*. In this lengthy discourse, Reason witnesses the birth of the liberal arts, which are viewed within a hierarchy of disciplines, all of which are based on the type of rationality she herself represents (2.11–2.20). Reason first describes the functions of grammar, dividing the subject into copying, calculating, and literary composition; she then turns to the sounds of animate and inanimate beings, as well as percussion instruments, passing to rhythm and harmony and concluding with geometry, astronomy, and mathematics. In the last phase of her presentation she takes up the concept of number, which is envisaged as the integrating principle behind these diverse illustrations of God's eternal wisdom. When the exposition is concluded, Augustine's friend, Alypius, expresses his admiration for the role given to the mathematical component in the organization of the liberal arts.[25] He traces this approach to the venerable figure of Pythagoras, but Augustine acknowledges that its true source is Varro.[26]

There is a comparable but much briefer account of Reason's upward movement in book 6 of *De Musica*, which likewise focuses on her ascent from the sensory to the nonsensory realm (6.10.25–6.10.26). In addition to recapitulating this and other doctrines found in earlier writings, this dialogue contains a lengthy account of a subject that is touched upon but not discussed in detail in *De Ordine* or elsewhere: this is the rationale for rhythm and harmony in quantitative verse, and its relationship to the temporal and eternal. The important phases of Augustine's exposition on these themes in *De Musica* take place in books 1 and 6.[27] Book 1 attempts to distinguish arts that utilize a knowledge of harmony, both theoretically and practically, from those whose rhythms depend on motions that are instinctive, habitual, or mimetic. Book 6 divides this musical knowledge into the sensory, mental, and spiritual, and discusses the manner in which one ascends through each level toward God. The orientations of books 1 to 5 and of book 6 are reflected in their respective sources: in the earlier books these are drawn principally from pagan verse and ancient treatises on metrics, whereas in the final book Augustine analyzes a single line of Christian verse, *Deus creator omnium*, from Ambrose's evening hymn,[28] in the context of his own reflections on theological themes.

Within the variety of discussions that make up book 6, Augustine devotes particular attention to the topics of time, memory images, and the soul's equilibrium, including within the last subject an original excursus on the emotions. His position is a union of neo-Pythagorean and Platonic views in which mathematical conceptions provide the foundation for a philosophical doctrine that continually reasserts the contrast between the sensible and the intelligible.[29] While advocating the view that the greatest hindrance to the ascent of the soul derives from the body, from which the soul can be freed through the use of reason, Augustine nonetheless proposes the view that, because harmonies are sensed before they are understood, it is from the body that the process of ascent must begin. The connection between the sensible and the intelligible is provided by the analysis of the temporal aspects of meter, in particular, by the treatment of duration in book 1. This segment of the discussion is based on the distinction between simultaneous and successive sounds as they impinge on the sense of hearing: the one produces harmony, the other, melody.

Augustine suggests, in effect, that the methods used to write quantitative poetry in order to create an aesthetically pleasing auditory effect can tell us something about the emotional and cognitive makeup of the soul, whose purpose is the establishment of well-being in the individual. This relationship rests on the assumption that the harmonic rhythms that make up the norms of acceptable verse and the forces at work in creating the soul's equilibrium share a common mathematical principle. In Augustine's view, this principle can be grasped at a certain level through sense perceptions, but a fuller understanding depends on the mind, especially on the faculty of aesthetic judgment in concert with will and reason. It is through the cooperation of these cognitive activities that *musica* comes to be a branch of knowledge, a *scientia*.[30]

In relating poetry and music by means of these principles, Augustine was preceded by Plato, who saw this as training for the young and as a preparation for a reasoned understanding of virtue in adulthood, whereas Augustine analyzes the problem of the soul's harmony uniquely in relation to the adult listener to performances of harmonious music or quantitative verse, asking whether the appreciation of their inherent beauty is the result of nature or reason. In focusing on an adult audience, *De Musica* thus differs not only from Plato but from Augustine's other dialogues, in which there is frequently envisaged an educational progress from a real or symbolic youth to adulthood, in what may be described as a shadowy anticipation of books 1–9 of the *Confessions*. And although Augustine echoes Plato's three criteria for musical art, namely the moral, the pleasurable, and the artistic, he does not argue on behalf of the individual's ability to "gauge the correctness of the composition" and thereby "judge its moral goodness or badness,"[31] but proposes instead that there is a relationship between poetic or musical composition and the principles of mathematical harmony. These in turn, in combination, reflect the ideal equilibrium of the human mind.

De Musica is unique among treatises on music and poetry in late antiquity in incorporating into a Platonic scheme some central principles of Stoic views on poetry, in particular, the notion that problems in poetics are inseparable from those of the study of language.[32] Among the elements that are possibly Stoic in origin that are found in books 1 and 6 are the general distinction between signs and their signification, as well as the notion that a poem is a composition that may exist simultaneously in speech and thought. The three central elements associated with the Stoic approach to language, namely *phone*, *lexis*, and *logos*, reappear, although somewhat transformed, in Augustine's discussion of quantitative verse from the viewpoint of its acoustical impression, its disposition or arrangement, and the significance of the verses. Augustine was convinced that philosophy can be taught in either well-composed verse or prose: the first operation is explored in *De Musica*, book 6, while the second is found in *De Doctrina Christiana*, books 2–4.

In both approaches, the auditor or reader is attracted by the beauty of the literary creations, which rest on eternal principles, and at the same time convinced by their truths, which are logically defensible. Literature and philosophy can thus work together in the teaching of wisdom, as Reason suggests toward the end of *De Ordine*, book 2. As noted, Augustine absorbed some of the criticisms of literary studies that he found in his sources, in particular in Plato and Cicero, but he likewise brought about an advance in thinking on the subject. This consists in uniting ancient views on quantitative verse with the notion of the soul's moral education by means of narrative. Literature is thus viewed as a bridge between the harmonies of nature and the potential harmony of lived experience, the latter depending on the individual's discipline and judgment. Just as we enjoy the sensory effects of a well-balanced line of verse, then reflect on the principles of harmony involved, we can appreciate the manner in which sense data impinge successively on our lives, detaching us from the temporal process and permitting us to profit from harmonies that have a beneficial effect on the soul. Humans, therefore, who are doomed to perish in time, can thereby be taught to appreciate the nature of God's intelligible beauty by means of the existential perfection and harmony of his eternal forms.[33]

Augustine conceives this complex exercise in meditation as a method for promoting and for sometimes achieving self-understanding. It is perhaps for this reason that he takes relatively little interest in the dramatic qualities of the exterior dialogue in *De Musica*. With the exception of some light moments in book 1, we do not find the thrusts and parries that enliven the philosophical discussions in *De Beata Vita*, *Contra Academicos*, and *De Ordine*. Also, in

contrast to the mise en scène in these dialogues, we are given no indication
of where they take place or their intellectual background. The "master" and
"disciple" lead the reader forward directly to the center of the dialogue's subject,
as do, on a different topic, Augustine and his partner, Evodius, in *De Libero
Arbitrio*. Even in comparison to other dialogues that are conceived along the
lines of a spontaneous associations of ideas, such as *Contra Academicos* or *De
Ordine*, *De Musica* appears to be rather loosely organized (or not to have
benefited from a final phase of revision and reorganization). There is no ded-
icatory epistle, as in other Cassiciacum dialogues, which, in the case of *De
Ordine* 1.1, introduces the major lines of the argument. The work's preface is
found at the beginning of book 6; its purpose is to summarize the material
covered in books 1 to 5 and to categorize the types of readers whom Augustine
has in mind as the dialogue's potential recipients. These are readers, he assumes,
who, like his students, are capable of following the stages of the discussion as it
proceeds from corporeal to spiritual matters.

These generalized readers take the place of the patrons and friends mentioned in the prefaces to other dialogues. They also replace the living audiences of his classes in Milan and at Cassiciacum, and, in a larger context,
the potential or implied readership of his cycle of works on the liberal arts,
as originally conceived. In contrast to earlier dialogues, he takes pains not to
identify the parties in the debate, even though it is clear that he is the master,
leading the discussion, and that the student is a member of his inner circle in
Milan and at Cassiciacum, one, in fact, who has much in common with the
young poet Licentius.[34] This undramatic way of framing the argument can
be looked upon in one perspective as a stylistic defect; however, indirectly, it
serves one of Augustine's purposes in book 6, namely, the deemphasizing of
sensory phenomena, as represented by the unnecessary verbiage that often
characterizes the open dialogue. This type of discussion is replaced, deliberately, it would seem, by the type of discourse in which one finds an analysis
of the interior movements of the soul, as, in dialogue with itself, it struggles
to understand the principles by which it can achieve a harmonious balance.[35]
Through the manner in which the dialogue takes place, therefore, as well as
by means of its argument, Augustine suggests in book 6 of *De Musica* that
there is an art of living, revealed in narratives, just as there is an art of musical
harmony, revealed in well-composed verse. He is also convinced of the opposite, namely that disharmony, like falsehood in one's outward life, can produce instability in the soul by means of negative emotions and actions.[36]
Harmony can result from opposites, of course, in life as in rhetoric, and in the

former producing a kind of eloquence and beauty that depends on events rather than on words.[37]

A Science of Rhythm

The skills Augustine has in mind in this type of ascent depend on relationships that arise both in language and in mathematics. He is convinced that it is from a combination of the two that the abstract or organizing principles of harmony are established. How this comes about is the subject of the initial conversation between the master and the student in book 1, where Augustine invites the reader to consider two ways in which the meaning of a word can be made clear by means of its sound, that is, by its quantity and accent.

His examples are the words *modus, bonus,* and *pone. Modus* and *bonus* differ in sound and spelling but represent the same metrical foot (the pyrrhic, composed of two short syllables). By contrast, *pone* can be a verb or an adverb, depending on whether the accent is placed on the first or the second syllable, *póne* or *poné.* This is an illustration of the fact that words with different meanings can be spelled in the same way. In both examples it is by means of the sound (*sonus*) that the hearer of the word establishes its meaning (*significatio*).[38]

Do these topics fall within the discipline of grammar?[39] It does not appear so,[40] since it is possible to represent a pyrrhic foot by physical means, for example by striking a drum or plucking a string.[41] Moreover, by employing other ways of counting, one can create a greater number of types of feet than are found in the writings of the established authorities on the subject, the grammarians (cf., 5.1.1). In order to do this it is necessary to distinguish between the name traditionally given to a foot (*uocabulum*), which arises in grammar, and a foot's temporal dimension (*temporum dimensio*),[42] which concerns relations of number. The latter belongs to another discipline,[43] which Augustine calls *musica*.

But how is music in this sense to be defined? What is the force and rationale of this discipline (*disciplinae vis et ratio,* 1.2.2)? Augustine's answer is that *musica,* which, throughout *De Musica,* refers to both music and to metrical poetry, depends on *scientia bene modulandi,* a knowledge of measurement or mensuration, through which its harmony is produced.[44] Of course, it is possible to have harmony where such knowledge is not involved; examples include song, dance, and the sounds made by percussion instruments.[45] These are arts that can be described as *modulans,* that is, possessing regular or rhythmical measures, and, as Augustine will later demonstrate, they require knowledge; however, they do not necessarily depend on formal knowledge,[46] and as a consequence differ from *musica*.

The student agrees: *modulor* is derived from *modus*; this connection suggests that even popular art, to the degree that it reflects measurement, displays a certain orderliness. The master responds to this assertion with the analogy of "speaking" and "oratory."[47] An uneducated person may be asked a question, and, if he answers, even with a single word, he is doubtless speaking; however, he cannot be called an orator, since there is no evidence of training in eloquence in what he says. In a comparable manner, we can refer to measure (*modus*) in relation to many things, but regularity of measure (*modulatio*) relates only to *musica*.

At the root of this distinction lie different senses of the verb *modulor* in relation to the harmonies of any musical discipline: these pertain respectively to the *measuring* of the temporal intervals of rhythms by means of voiced accents (or their substitutes, e.g., drum beats), which constitute mere sounds, and the *rules* for regulating such sounds in accordance with melody, pitch, and rhythm, which are a type of organized knowledge.[48] Augustine effectively combines these senses into a single concept of rhythmical movement, which appears to be applicable to spoken words as well as to poetry, chanting, and dance.[49] As he notes in *De Ordine*, these disciplines, like music, are not merely arts, which can be learned through memory and practice, but branches of knowledge in themselves, since they are based on inherent regularities that can be modeled by means of mathematics.[50] Accordingly, *De Musica* extends the meaning of *numerus* from number itself to a variety of numerical relationships, as well as to the theory of harmony and proportion on which they are based. Augustine likewise adds a dimension of meaning to the noun *numerositas*;[51] this refers to the harmoniousness resulting from the interaction of diverse parts, units, or divisions in a "mensurable" work of art.

In the light of these considerations, the master offers the view that a comprehensive definition of music would have to address these questions: (1) What is meant by the measurement of rhythm (*quid sit modulari*)? (2) What is implied in measuring rhythms well (*quid sit bene modulari*)? and (3) Why do considerations of this type make music a branch of knowledge (*scientia*, 1.2.3)?

He is convinced that he has answered questions one and two by arguing that *modulari* implies *bene modulari*, since, in regulated measurement (*modulatio*), the measure (*modus*) consists in a movement (*motus*) that is adapted to regular temporal requirements. *Modulatio* can be defined as skill or experience in moving: *modulatio . . . dicitur movendi quaedam peritia* (1.2.3). This skill has two characteristics. First, we recognize through our sense of aesthetic judgment that such movement takes place as it should; otherwise it does not fall within the category *bene moveri*.[52] Also, this aesthetically pleasing movement takes place in and for itself, as if the work of art in question expressed a desire for completion, rather like the ordered unfolding of a genetic code.[53] The pair agree that some sort of knowledge is involved in such motions, whether these consist in playing an instrument or fashioning an object from wood or silver, since, in all cases, the artisan or artist gives evidence of his knowledge through the plan of the work in question, which clearly exists in his mind before it results in the exterior movement that creates the work.

But at what point does *musica* cease to be *scientia*? This is the point of question three. Augustine has a longer reply to this query, in which he utilizes a hierarchy of artistic harmonies consisting in those of bird songs, instrumentalists, and rational harmonic principles.[54]

A bird is able to sing a song that is well modulated, but it evidently has not acquired this skill by means of a *liberalis disciplina*.[55] A similar skill is possessed by some animals, for example, by bears and elephants, both of whom can be taught to dance. These are performances that involve an appreciation of music but not an understanding of music as a branch of knowledge. In a comparable way humans sometimes listen to popular songs, just to relax. In this case, the pleasure (*libido*) arises through a certain sense (*sensu quodam*) of music rather than through an understanding of musical harmony (*de ipsis numeris*).[56] Neither in animals, therefore, which lack reason, nor in humans, who possess it, can this type of music be called a branch of knowledge (1.4.5).

The case of instrumentalists is more complicated, since their skill is the product of art (*ars*) rather than nature (*natura*).[57] The master asks whether such skill can truly be called an art, since playing an instrument also involves imitation (*imitatio*). The student points out that most art, including, of course, the performances of birds and animals, is understood in this perspective.[58] The question is whether any of these arts, insofar as they are merely imitative, can be said to make use of knowledge. After a discussion of the alternatives, the pair conclude that birds, being nonrational animals, lack reason: they are capable of imitation, and this is doubtless a type of art, but it is not art that involves knowledge, since no rational thinking takes place. By contrast, humans possess reason. Yet some forms of art practiced by humans require only imitation, that is, the training of limbs of the body. Master and student agree that, if all imitation were art and all art used reason, then every artistic effort, including the songs of birds, could be said to be based on knowledge. But that is not the case; therefore, some way has to be found to distinguish art that utilizes knowledge from mere imitation.[59]

The student sees a flaw in this reasoning, which involves the roles of memory and habit in one art form, the playing of an instrument. Clearly performers rely on these capacities. Where then, within their skill, can we locate *scientia*?[60] The relevant question is whether hearing and memory, on which their ability to perform depends, are associated with the body or the mind. The pair agree that hearing involves both, while memory is chiefly mental, since memories, although originating in sense impressions, are subsequently transferred to the mind, where they are stored as images.[61] But this argument loses its force when it is recognized that, in playing a musical instrument, it is habitual memory that is chiefly involved, and this requires training a part of the body. Moreover, the capacity for memory training is shared by nonhuman animals, even though they lack reason, for example, by the swallow, which finds its way back to its abandoned nest each year. As a consequence, the pair may have been too hasty in relegating bird songs to the domain of mere imitation. For if memory is used in finding a nest, it is surely involved in repeating a song.

It would be more accurate to say that when a piece of music is played the performers are guided by what gives them pleasure through their senses, that is, by what they hear; afterward, they commit to memory the movements of their fingers through which these sensory effects are produced. They practice those movements, thereby engaging in a type of imitation. In performance they give the appearance of possessing both technical skill and knowledge. However, if true *modulatio* exists in and for itself, as argued earlier (1.2.3), instrumentalists, even if they have knowhow, cannot be said to possess the type of knowledge that pertains to music, unless it can be shown that they have in their minds beforehand the information that enables them to play in an acceptable fashion. If not, we can say that their skillfulness is the product of practice (*usus*) rather than *scientia bene modulandi* (1.4.8).

The student protests that even this skill is mental, not corporeal. But the master reminds him that there is no necessary connection between the capacity to think and to play. If a good mind were all that performers needed, every intellectual would be a good instrumentalist. In music, as in other arts, the problem is not knowing what to do but knowing how it is done.[62] A person who plays an instrument skillfully, therefore, displays manual dexterity that results from practice informed by theory rather than from theory alone, and this skillfulness is the result of the combined activity of his sense of hearing and his memory,[63] that is, both body and mind. An individual may know music but not know how to play an instrument, but anyone who plays an instrument has to possess an implicit knowledge of music. Something similar can be said of audiences: the listeners may have no formal training in music, but they are able to distinguish between a good and a bad performance. Their response is evidently based not on an understanding of musical theory[64] but on their natural capacity for musical judgment, which operates in the first instance by means of their sense of hearing.[65]

*   *   *

This discussion provides an introduction to Augustine's solution to the problem of the soul's equilibrium. This arises from the connection between the principles of rhythm and the subjective experience of time. This topic occupies the remainder of book 1, is taken up again in book 6,[66] and in the latter texts moves Augustine from his earlier Platonic assumption of a division of the work of the mind and the body in music toward a view of the manner in which they are interrelated. This, in turn, becomes his basis for the integrated view of the self, which is among the subjects to which he turns in book 6.

This phase of the dialogue returns to the subject of time measurement at 1.1.1 and attempts to distinguish two features of temporal experience, duration and nonduration (*diu et non diu; diuturno et non diuturno*, 1.7.13). The master argues that the length or shortness of a period of time can be calculated by humans provided that there is an agreed unit of measurement.[67] Movement B can be said to be twice as long as A, if we know beforehand the length of time of A. If we do not, then the space of time between A and B is *indefinita et indeterminata* (1.8.14).

He then distinguishes different types of numerical sequences, using as his point of departure the concepts of equality and inequality.[68] First come rational and irrational (*rationales, irrationales*, 1.9.15): the one is represented by the sequence 2, 4, 6, 8, the other by 3, 10 or 4, 11. The numbers in these sequences are termed connumerate and dinumerate respectively, depending on whether they are inclusive or exclusive in relation to their base quantity (*connumerati, dinumerati*, 1.9.16). Connumerate numbers are subsequently divided into two types, that is, sequences like 2, 4, 6, 8, and 6, 8, 10, and so on. In the one, the sequence is composed of 2 + 2, 4 + 2, 6 + 2, etc., in the other, of 2 X 3, 2 X 4, 2 X 5, etc. The master calls the first set of numbers complicate (*complicati*), the second, sesquate (*sesquati*, from *sesque* 1.10.17).[69] He points out that in the case of rational motions (*rationales motus*), the sequence would be infinite unless a fixed ratio (*certa ratio*) imposed measure on form (1.11.18).

The master is not only proposing a set of relations that will be transformed in book 6 into the principles of harmony by which the soul maintains internal equilibrium: these relationships equally underlie Augustine's theory of narrative, in which they appear as three distinct components, the beginnings, the stages of development, and the understanding of narrative time. His thinking on these questions can be summarized as follows.

1. A narrative, like a numerical sequence, begins at an arbitrarily chosen point in time. The question of beginnings (*principia*) in the numerical sequence is taken up at *De Musica* 1.11.19. The parallel in narrative theory is found at *Confessions* 11.3.5–11.6.8, where the topic is the creation of the universe in Genesis 1:1: *In principio*.

2. The stages of a sequence consist in a beginning, middle, and end: *Ergo ut totum aliquid sit, principio et medio et fine constat* (1.12.21). In Augustine's interpretation of this principle within numerical theory, the whole cannot be understood without the parts and the parts cannot be understood except in the relation to the whole. Thus, the sequence 1, 2, 3 consists in three discrete numbers; however, for the series to be understood as a mathematical sequence, each number has to be conceived in relation to the one that comes before and after. Also, it is evident that memory plays a role in reconstructing meaning.

Augustine justifies these components of his theory by arguing that the number one represents a beginning, but has no middle or end; the number two is a second beginning, whose relationship to the number one is created only in sequence; the number three is the sum of one and two and thus holds third place in the series. The situation of the number three, which is both temporal and spatial, does not occur in the case of any subsequent number, for example, four; and, as three is the combination of the two *principia*, that is, one and two, four may be said to be a whole and perfect number, inasmuch as it embodies both:[70] *magna haec ergo concordia est in prioribus tribus numeris* (1.12.22). All subsequent numbers, such as four, are related to the series 1, 2, 3 by means of proportion (*analogia*). The theory thus proceeds from small units to the consideration of a higher unity,[71] and this unity is understood through memory, once the physical sequence has ended.

3. The third component concerns the intervals themselves. This topic is not fully explored in book 1: it is the subject of a technical discussion in books 2 to 5, and a theoretical synthesis in book 6. Introducing the theme at 1.13.26–27, the master recalls that the discussion has been concerned principally with a problem in counting. He asks why it is acceptable to introduce intervals of ten between one and infinity (i.e., 1–10, 10–20, etc.). The pair agree that after

1, 2, 3 the nature of numerical progression changes with 4; but the master points out that the sum of 1, 2, 3, and 4 is 10, thereby providing a clever if unconvincing solution to the problem of numerical units.

Both parties agree to revisit the description of movements that can properly be attributed to the discipline of music. Mathematics has clarified the issues, but the pair have not solved the problem of quantities when these are not specifically concerned with numbers. As a consequence, Augustine returns to grammar in search of an alternative approach. His example on this occasion is the iambic foot (composed of a short and a long syllable in sequence). He first considers the problem from a mathematical standpoint, proposing a thought experiment in which two periods of time that have the ratio 1:2 are measured by means of our observation of two individuals who are asked to run respectively for one and two hours.[72] The problem with this method is that we would require the presence of a timekeeping device, since our personal estimates of the two periods of time would doubtless vary. We could not be sure that the ratio 1:2 was established, and as a consequence we would be unable to derive an agreed aesthetic pleasure from a certain knowledge of mathematical harmony.

As an alternative, let us say that a person creates the impression of an iambic foot by clapping his hands, dancing in rhythm, or moving his limbs in some other way, as suggested earlier.[73] In this case, it might be possible to determine the measure of time, since it is short, or, if not, to observe that there are alternating intervals in which the second period doubles the length of the first. This determination would be made by the senses, that is, by the ears or the eyes, when the clapping is heard or the movements are seen. Needless to say, this level of aesthetic pleasure does not require a previous knowledge of the type of rhythm in question. It is comparable to the appreciation of a performance displayed by listeners who have no knowledge of music, inasmuch as it indicates that they have an implicit understanding of musical harmonies.

The purpose of the master's comparison between these two types of measurement is to locate the source of this pleasure (*delectari, voluptas*) and to suggest that it is somehow connected with the *scientia bene modulandi*, that is, with the knowledge that pertains to the well measured movements that comprise the inner logic of music's discipline (*ad ipsam rationem disciplinae*): movements, let us recall, which are not made in the service of a principle that lies outside the work of art but are experienced and enjoyed entirely within it (e.g., dance, 1.2.3). True, these movements, as they pass from the senses to the mind, leave traces of their presence in our senses; yet, despite this transitory phenomenon, the principles involved remain unchanged in their internal mathematical relations. In order to find the source of these regularities, it is necessary to follow those traces from the senses to the mind, and from the mind to the "abode" of the *ratio disciplinae*.

Augustine lays the foundation for this discussion at the beginning of book 2, where he again takes up the contrast between the mathematical and grammatical approaches to meter and accent introduced at 1.1.1. He has already proposed that grammatical knowledge of musical harmony is limited, because it consists chiefly in imposing names, whereas mathematical descriptions are much greater in number, since they arise from many permutations and combinations. These perspectives have to be combined if the pair are to achieve a full understanding of musical harmony in poetry.

This question is associated in the master's mind with another issue: this is the relevance of the open dialogue to the method by which they are attacking the issues. Toward the end of book 1, the student criticizes the dialogue, which, owing to digressions, has not advanced beyond the mathematical understanding of harmonics (1.12.26). In book 2 the master returns to this question. If they agree that there are different approaches to the issues based on authority and reason, is the student prepared to accept what has been established on the topic of metrics through long-standing custom? Or would he prefer to carry out the inquiry by means of reason alone, as if they were previously uninstructed on the issues?[74]

The student, opting for the open dialogue, draws attention to the fact that the field of knowledge that is called grammar in Greek and *litteratura* in Latin claims to be the custodian of traditional learning on this question. But a subtle (if cynical) wit could demonstrate that this knowledge only reflects what has been previously thought: for dull minds this is its charm.[75] Revisiting an earlier example, the pair examine the verb *cano* (I sing), from *Aeneid* 1.1: *Arma virumque cano, Troiae qui primus ab oris.* There are two possible pronunciations, depending on whether one follows *grammatica* or *musicae ratio*. According to grammar, the first syllable has to be short. As *custos historiae*, the grammarian bases his argument on the writings of those who have come before, which is the source of his *auctoritas*.[76] But according to the discipline of music, which takes account of a word's *rationalis dimensio et numerositas*, the sole criterion for deciding whether the first syllable is short or long in various contexts is the *ratio mensurarum*, the rationale of its measurements. If the context calls for two long syllables in *calno*, the pronunciation will offend grammar but not musical logic, in which the time values of the words that enter the ears are determined numerically by means of the rhythm.[77] However, it is clear to a lover of poetry like Augustine's student, especially if it is Licentius, that the enjoyment of Virgil's opening hexameter results from a plan of composition, the *ratio versus*, that unites the two disciplines harmoniously. The pleasure of the line would be greatly reduced, for example, if *primus* were replaced by *primis*, thus changing a short syllable to long, altering the musical rhythm. But Augustine leaves for book 6 an explanation of the difference, which involves the psychological experience of time: *id est . . . quod ad diu et non diu pertinet* (2.2.2).

A Lesson in Reading

Book 6, to which I now turn, represents the culmination of Augustine's thinking on these questions involving harmony.[78] Up to this point, the master observes, the pair have been traveling in the company of grammarians and poets by necessity rather than by choice,[79] since this was the only route that lay open to them in their attempts to exhaust the discussion of the physical properties of verse. In book 6, pagan poetry is abandoned in favor of a single line of a Christian hymn, just as the variety of literary topics in books 1 to 5 is superseded by reflection on a single theological doctrine, namely the conception of God as the principle of creation. Both aims, the grammatical and the theological, are neatly incorporated in the phrase *Deus creator omnium*, as well as Augustine's perhaps less well articulated desire to write another commentary on the opening chapters of the book of Genesis.

With the discussion of duration in book 1 as his point of departure, he subsequently analyzes this single line of liturgical verse in a variety of contexts. He pays special attention to the phenomenon of silence: this is expressed metrically through pauses between syllables and cognitively by means of a progression from the senses to the mind, where the understanding of the line takes place.[80] Recall that his argument, which is reiterated with minor changes throughout book 6, provides the foundation for the theory of subjective time that is reproduced in book 11 of the *Confessions*.[81] As *Deus creator omnium* is read aloud, the sound of the syllables marks the passage of time in accordance with the rules for *scientia bene modulandi*. However, when the physical sound has ceased, the meaning of the line as a whole is constituted in the mind with the aid of memory. It is by using memory as a connective between the senses and the mind, therefore, that the hearer realizes the meaning of the words as they were intended to be understood by the speaker. In book 6 of *De Musica*, Augustine is concerned with the manner in which this transition takes place and what it signifies for our comprehension of time. In order to achieve this end, he tackles issues that are not raised in the *Confessions*, where his analysis of the same line is more centrally concerned with the experience of time itself.

The relevant discussion in *De Musica* begins in book 1, where it is suggested that verse, dance, and artistic activities leave traces of an ideal scheme of harmony in the senses.[82] There Augustine is interested in the origin of these traces, whereas in book 6 he turns to the ways they are reflected in the audience. In the earlier books he likewise argues that verse rhythms are not understood in increments of sound but as a harmonic whole. In book 6, he develops this argument considerably, proposing that the upward movement of the mind from sensory to nonsensory levels can be considered a disciplined activity, even a type of spiritual practice, which attempts to integrate the ascending harmonies arising in the human soul with those descending from God. He thus provides a set of footnotes to his notion of Pauline and Plotinian ascent, as outlined in book 12 of *De Genesi ad Litteram*.

What is new in his account of this exercise, in comparison with what is found in the other dialogues written in Milan or at Cassiciacum, is the emphasis placed on the theological component, in particular, on the doctrines of original sin and the incarnation. Augustine traces the source of human disharmony to the disobedience of the first couple in the garden of Eden (cf. 1.6.13) and the implications of this event. He is convinced that there is a relationship between the experience of time in the reading of a line of verse and the cosmic process by which God became man. Just as the eternal rules for harmony exist temporarily in the senses, when a line of verse is read, so the incarnate God passed from the divine to the human level, existing impermanently in time. And just as Christ moved downward toward humans, thereby transforming his eternity into life in a temporal mode, so humans, by directing their thoughts upward and engaging in contemplative practices, are able to move from sensory toward nonsensory experience. Thus mortals, who are, so to speak, trapped in history, are temporarily released from time during the period of their meditative withdrawal. As Augustine illustrates in the vision at Ostia, this is an anticipation of everlasting timelessness after death, when the elect will rejoin their maker, and the sensory rhythms that mark the aesthetic shape of their lives will be reabsorbed into a single, eternal principle of harmony.

Augustine's consideration of this relationship holds an important implication for his subsequent understanding of spiritual practices, especially in the *Confessions*. In his early writings, these exercises are usually conceived as atemporal forms of thought, such as the dialogue, the soliloquy, and the thought experiment. In this type of presentation the passage of time is suspended in the hypothetical present in which the mental exercises themselves take place, as a kind of *epochē*. However, in book 6, the theoretical groundwork is laid for a type of contemplative practice in which the factor of time is critical for the realization of the desired state of mind. The models for this exercise are a line of verse and a theological doctrine, both of which involve a relationship between the temporal and the eternal. In each case, this relationship depends on memory; as a consequence, memory becomes a central element in Augustine's conception of spiritual practice itself. In *De Musica*, this memory concerns verse; in books 1–9 of the *Confessions*, it records an entire life; and in book 10, it attempts to reform habitual conduct around a new narrative pattern. In each of these phases of Augustine's thinking the passage of time is utilized as a means of superseding its own temporal limitations, since, in the absence of the awareness of time's passage, the subject has an impermanent experience of the timeless.

In addition to deepening the theological context of *De Musica* in this manner, and suggesting, between the lines, that the question of harmony, inasmuch as it is historically grounded, involves both the self, over time, and the soul, out of time, book 6 makes an attempt to alter the relationship between Augustine and his readers, in comparison to the way it is framed in his other dialogues. Unlike books 1 to 5, book 6 is not addressed to students, as a manual on rhythm, harmony, and proportion, but, as noted, to a more general audience of *docti*, *periti*, and even *semidocti*, who presumably have been instructed in the doctrines of the earlier books. In Augustine's view, these readers can proceed to a more advanced level of understanding in which authority is not identified with handbooks of grammar but with theological truth. This introduces the notion of progressive learning, which is a major theme of books 1 to 9 of the *Confessions*.

In order to clarify the nature of the ascent from the earlier books of *De Musica*, the master employs a metaphor utilized in other dialogues. This concerns the passage of the potential reader/participant from adolescence (*adolescentes*) to mature benevolence (*benevoli homines*). As in the *Confessions*, he uses the life cycle to describe the reader's self-education, which begins with

the liberal arts and is completed by interior instruction, occasionally complemented by direct illumination. At the beginning of book 6 he likewise offers
his readers one of the numerous criticisms of the open dialogue that are found
in his early writings: master and student, he notes, have spent too much time
in a patently puerile type of discussion (*plane pueriliter*); readers are once
again to pardon his apparent lightheartedness (*nugacitas*) in view of the deep
obligations (*officiosus labor*) of the present endeavor. One new idea is introduced: open discussion is viewed as a constraint on spiritual ascent, which is envisaged, as in the last segment of *De Magistro*, in a hermeneutic manner: it
begins with carnal matters and literal understanding: *quibusdam gradibus a
sensibus carnis atque carnalibus litteris*;[83] and it finishes with divine instruction in which no natural intermediary is needed (*nulla natura interposita*). In
this process the notion of number acquires a connotative field that moves from
what is countable to the rhythm, harmony, and plenitude of God.[84]

Augustine's design for this ascent is presented in book 6 in a pair of lessons in reading: in chapter 1, this appears as an outline of the potential readers of *De Musica*;[85] later, a second lesson takes place in the reading of the line
Deus creator omnium.

In his discussion of readership, as noted, the chief distinction in types of
audience is between persons with a genuinely spiritual outlook, to whom the
book is dedicated, and the majority of students, who are incapable of proceeding beyond the physical aspects of rhythm, as outlined in books 1 to 5.[86]
Augustine encourages readers strong in faith but weak in erudition, whose
love of God, he is convinced, will eventually triumph over ignorance.[87] However, book 6 is not written for (1) lower levels of readers, those, for instance,
who are weak in spirit, or (2) for those who entertain the hope of inward
tranquility without labor or hardship,[88] or (3) for devotees of secular literature (like the poet, Licentius) who are unaware of its potential snares.[89]

In justification of these divisions, he asks his readers a question, which is
based on a consideration of *Deus creator omnium*. When the line is read, the
reader is aware that there are four iambic feet and twelve intervals of time.
How do these produce the resulting harmony? In response, he proposes to discuss four aspects of sound (*genera*). These consist in sound considered in itself
(*in sono*), in the sense of hearing (*in sensu audientis*), in the act of being pronounced (*in actu pronuntiantis*), and in memory (*in memoria*).[90] The notable
feature of this enumeration is the emphasis on reception. This represents a shift
from an objective to a subjective set of issues. In books 1 to 5, the awareness of
a perceiver of a line of verse is occasionally discussed, but what is chiefly under

scrutiny is the numerical relationships arising in harmonies themselves. By contrast, in book 6, Augustine makes subjective understanding his major concern and considers its problems from different angles.

First of all, whereas the divisions of meter in books 1 to 5 are taken up independently of each other, the four *genera* of book 6 can be considered individually or cumulatively. This means that the harmony of *Deus creator omnium* could be recreated in the listener's mind in the form 1, 1 + 2, 1 + 2 + 3 or 1 + 2 + 3 + 4.[91] Second, the problem of communication is considered from a number of vantage points: *genera* 1 and 2 concern the hearer, 3 pertains to the speaker, and 4 applies to both parties. Finally, the later scheme, in contrast to earlier discussions, proposes a hierarchical arrangement, inasmuch as relationships 1, 2, and 3 deal chiefly with the physical properties of sound, while 4 is concerned with a mental activity in the reader. In proceeding from books 1 to 5 to book 6, therefore, Augustine advances, as he has said, from the corporeal to the incorporeal (*a corporeis ad incorporea*, 6.2.2; cf. *Retr.* 1.6).

In the light of these schemes, the four possibilities are distinguished in the following ways:

1. *In sono.* This is the type of sound that is created by bodies of some sort when they strike the air, such as drops of water (as in the opening chapters of *De Ordine*, from which a lengthy discussion of order ensues). This beating results in brief intervals of time within a measured rhythm, and, inasmuch as this rhythm is produced by physical means, it can be assumed to continue even if no one is present to hear it.[92] As noted, this beating can reproduce the equivalent of poetic meters (1.1.1;1.13.27).

2. *In sensu audientis.* This is the type of sound that creates the impression of rhythmic patterns in the listener's ears. Augustine asks whether those patterns arise in the source of the sound, in the ears, or in a combination of both. It is granted that the ears have a power of perception (*vis percipiendi*). This is proven by the fact that those who can hear have a different sensory experience from those who are deaf, even during periods of silence.[93] But do the ears have this inherent capacity to perceive harmonies, as contrasted with their capacity to perceive what is harmonious based on their reception of sense impressions?[94] If so, do other senses work this way (e.g., touch)?

If the capacity for aesthetic judgment did not exist in the ears, the student notes, we would be unable to say whether a given sound was harmonious or not. As a consequence, whatever it is that permits us to express our approval or disapproval when a sound is heard can be called the rhythm or harmony that exists in the sense itself, and this capacity arises by nature rather than by reason.[95] For his part, the master shifts the responsibility for such judgments from a shared relationship between performers and audiences to the recipients of sounds alone.[96] The student's reply (6.2.3) likewise deals principally with the receiver's *vis approbandi et improbandi*. Augustine has in mind something that takes place after the initial aural experience of a text, as if, in the absence of the sounds, the listener or reader based his aesthetic judgments on what he has already perceived. The first distinction in 6.2.2 between *genera* 1 and 2–4, which in principle applies to sounds, is thus turned into a means of establishing ethical and aesthetic judgments within the more restricted medium of the received text.

The master responds to the student's observation by introducing another theme from book 1. This concerns the difference between the physical and the psychological measurement of time,[97] which is later discussed in greater detail. At the physical level, a line of verse can be read at different speeds: each reading occupies a separate interval of time (*spatium temporis*), although both lines have been composed in the same metrical feet (*ratio pedum*, 6.2.3; cf. 2.2.2). The effect in the ears is produced only in reaction to the physical presence of sound, and, needless to say, if there is no sensory stimulus, there is no reaction.[98] Furthermore, hearing one voice (*vox*) differs from hearing another, just as hearing differs from not hearing: the effect (*affectio*) cannot be extended or shortened, since it is measured by the sound that produces it, not the type of foot. If the source of this sound is a harmonious voice (*numerosa vox*), then the effect has to be harmonious (*numerosa*). In this respect, waves of sound are like tracings on water, which do not exist until the impressions from corporeal sources are formed and then cease to exist when they disappear.[99] The psychological effect is brought about differently by the natural power which is, as it were, adjudicating (*naturalis . . . vis quasi judiciaria*). This is present in the ears and remains there, whether there is sound or silence. When there is no sound, we cannot speak of a harmony in the ears brought about by physical means.[100] Yet, even in the absence of an external cause, the mind is capable of appreciating harmonic order.

3. *In actu pronuntiantis.* The third genus consists in the effort, practice, and action of the person who pronounces the line of verse.[101] The master points out that when we are silent, we are nonetheless capable of producing certain rhythmic harmonies in our minds, and these appear to possess the same duration in time as they would if they were produced by means of the voice.[102] It is evident that these rhythms owe their existence to an operation of the mind, since they produce no sound and have no effect on the ears.[103] They therefore

constitute a third type of rhythmical pattern, in addition to those *in sono* and *in audiente*.

4. *In memoria.* The consideration of the fourth genus, that is, harmonies preserved in the memory, arises out of a question concerning the third type of sound. The master again asks whether harmonies that are produced in the mind alone can exist without the help of memory. He considers the possibility that their source is physiological, like pulsations in the veins; alternatively, they can be said to be regulated by the soul, like our breathing. But in neither case would memory be required. Yet rhythmical harmonies are clearly able to be lodged in the memory; the proof is that, once we have heard them or thought of them, we can recall them whenever we wish.[104] These harmonies can be said to exist without the support of other types of rhythm, since they are retained in the memory after the latter have disappeared.

5. *Quintum genus.* Augustine also introduces a fifth genus at 6.2.2, which is identified with the natural judgment found in the sense of hearing when pleasure arises from the balanced effect of numerical harmonies (or, alternatively, from displeasure at their absence).[105] The presence of this faculty, noted at 1.13.27, is thereby reaffirmed.

We have, then, a fivefold rather than fourfold scheme of harmony, which, as modified in presentation, consists in (1) making a sound, which is attributed to a body; (2) hearing, which affects the soul by means of the body; (3) the production of rhythm, which has greater or lesser duration; (4) the remembering of harmonic patterns; and (5) judgments about such harmonies.

A Sabbath for the Soul

The master now turns to the second theme of book 6, namely the aesthetic hierarchy of types of rhythm. It is here that he will transfer his attention from the soul, about which his remarks have hitherto been concerned, to a combination of soul and self.

He begins this phase of the discussion by asking which of the harmonies that they have analyzed excels the others. The student selects the fifth, arguing that it is this that judges those that have come before. The master then asks a further question, namely, which of the other four in his view is the best; that is, which is most helpful in the individual's attempt to ascend from the corporeal to the incorporeal. The student chooses rhythms in the memory, since they last longer than those sounded, heard, or produced.[106]

This is an important move, which has to do with more than duration. The student has effectively opted for things made over those being made[107]—a view he will later modify. The master draws attention to an unexamined assumption in his thinking: this concerns the impermanence of all the harmonies under consideration. When he or the student speaks of a rhythm of "greater" or "lesser" duration, they are referring to relative lengths of time. This is like saying that a day in good health is preferable to many in illness, or that one can read more than one can write in one's waking hours.[108] True, a sound that is retained in the memory lasts longer than one that is heard, but this is because the images of the sounds in question outlast their physical sources. These sounds are nonetheless corporeal in origin, and cannot be given preference over rhythms that arise in the soul. For both the sounds that created them and their images in the memory disappear over time, the one by cessation, the other by being forgotten.[109]

The master has in fact returned to the problem of narrative introduced in book 1 through the notions of *cessatio* and *oblivio*, which deal with the same topic but approach it from different directions. In the case of *cessatio*, the rhythms proceed in a sequence in which one image is replaced by another, even before the sequence is terminated. The preceding images yield to the succeeding ones until they all disappear and the rhythm ceases to exist. In *oblivio* the whole is likewise effaced, but little by little, and this takes place while several other rhythms may be maintained in the memory. Some memories vanish after a day, others after a year or more.

In all cases, the disappearance takes place in imperceptible steps.[110] But there is a difference in the way in which it occurs. In *cessatio* the end is perceived all at once, whereas in *oblivio* the individual is able to configure the rhythm in question without error, since the entire unit does not vanish in an instant. Also, in *oblivio* the strength of an image begins to weaken from the moment that it is lodged in the memory; by contrast, in *cessatio* the passage more closely resembles the way in which one year ends and another begins at a precise moment in time. Accordingly, when we speak of *oblivio*, we use expressions like, "I scarcely remember," which means that we have a vague recollection along with the awareness that our memory has partly been effaced. For this reason the master finds it necessary to conclude that every type of harmonic rhythm, including the genus in memory, is transient, but in different ways.[111]

In 6.4.6, Augustine thus suggests that time and our awareness of time are alike in a fundamental respect—their impermanence. Moreover, he has now affirmed the thesis, announced earlier, by which the key to the psychological understanding of time is memory. Two examples of this idea are presented, namely reading and writing (*lectio, scriptio*) and good health and its opposite, physical infirmity (*sanitas, imbecillitas*). The first example is in his opinion easy to deal with, since it is clear that more information can be covered in one day of reading than in several days of writing. He grants that the question of well-being is more complicated. As noted, in an objective sense, one day of health is preferable to many days of illness; however, from the subjective viewpoint of the person who is contrasting the two, the possibility of illness may be present in his mind while he is experiencing a period of good health. What the individual is thinking about at this moment, therefore, is not health alone, but health and nonhealth, which exist in two parallel and potentially livable narratives, one of which prevails over the other because of external circumstances. In this manner of thinking on the part of the subject, the present is colored by a past event that may or may not have taken place, that is, a period of illness, and this event acquires the mental status of a memory image, whether or not this image refers to a reality. As this pair of scenarios is enacted in thought, the passage of psychological time is presented to the subject as an alternative to physical time: the many days of illness actually take up more time than the one day of health, but, because health is preferable to illness, the single day of health is given a higher psychological value. This is essentially what Augustine says about the interpretation of time in two different readings of the same line of verse. And this is the method of interconnected recollections which, somewhat transformed, he will recreate brilliantly in books 1 to 9 of the *Confessions*.

Having discussed the fourth and fifth *genera*, the master turns to the first three in his earlier classification (*in sono, in sensu audientis,* and *in actu pronuntiantis*), asking the student for the second time which of these in his view is to be preferred over the others (6.4.7). The student shifts his position and opts for a combination of *sensus* and *memoria*, thereby uniting elements of types 1–3 with those of 4 and possibly 5. He recalls that the first genre consists in sounding numbers (*sonantes numeri*); on hearing them, he now argues, we sense them, and when this takes place, we feel their effects. As a consequence, they can be said to be the original source of the harmonies experienced in the ears; however, these in turn are the source of harmonies in the memory, to which, he now proposes, they should be preferred, since they are their cause.[112] The student has effectively argued for the primacy of the sensory impressions in creating mental images, a view that harmonizes with what Augustine argues elsewhere regarding the notion of *phantasia*.

The student nonetheless recognizes a problem in this way of approaching the issues. How is it that *sonantes numeri*, which are corporeal or incorporated, can be considered more praiseworthy than those *numeri* which, while they are being sensed, are discovered to exist in the soul?[113] Furthermore, why is the corporeal placed above the spiritual, as if the former gave rise to the latter?[114] The master replies to these questions by means of an excursus, which presents a summary of Augustine's views on the manner in which the body can be rehabilitated within a theology that favors the superiority of the soul. This discussion, which begins at 6.4.7–6.5.10 and continues after an interruption at 6.5.13–6.5.15, once again places the relationship between body and soul in the context of the fall and the incarnation.[115] It also introduces to book 6 important considerations involving the relationship of soul to self.

Before the events in the garden of Eden, Augustine proposes, the soul governed the body in harmony. Even after original sin, the body retains something of its prelapsarian state of beauty and harmony, and this preserved integrity acts as a potential influence on the workings of the soul,[116] now governed, however, by freedom of choice. Later, in the incarnation, divine wisdom humbled itself by taking a human form, and, by suffering and dying, offered mortals an alternative to the pride that was the original cause of their downfall. By framing his statements about the body within these two interlocking narratives, Augustine devalues the body but does not rule it out of consideration in the problem of ascent from sin to salvation, as in the case of Platonism and Neoplatonism. One can sum up his thinking on this topic, as expressed in *De Musica* 6, as stating that, while the soul remains superior to the body, all that takes place in the soul is not considered superior to all that takes place in the body.[117]

His case is strengthened in his view by the fact that the initial fault in universal history, that is, original sin, did not arise from an event that occurred before the union of body and soul but afterward, and took place as the result of a willful decision, in which, according to Christian commentary, there was an awareness of the potentially harmful consequences of disobedience to a divine command. It is the will, therefore, that ultimately determines our state of spiritual health or illness, depending on whether, so to speak, the soul turns its attention towards its master, the soul, which lies above, or its slave, the body, which is below.[118] Only through a conversion upward does the soul attain at length what Augustine calls *otium liberum intrinsecum*, a kind of sabbath for itself, free from all constraint, which arises from within (6.5.14).

A number of traditional philosophical issues have to be reconsidered in the light of these views, the first of which, the master argues, is the question of how we judge truth or falsity in a world that has permanently abandoned the possibility of attaining absolute truth. He asks us to consider a typical problem of representation, namely seeing a tree in a dream,[119] thus once again taking his discussion in the direction of the notion of *phantasia*. In this example, the form of the tree has been made in the soul; however, that same image, which is seen in the mind while the person is asleep, was originally created in the body, that is, by the physical sighting of an actual tree.[120] This tree was seen with corporeal eyes; therefore, the higher truth in this case arises from the body, although in principle the body is inferior to the soul.[121]

Moreover, the image of the tree that was seen is better, therefore, not because it was made in the body, but because it is truer, whereas the image of the tree in the soul is false because all images are false, not because it was created in the soul. "Better," in this context, does not imply that the body has primacy over the soul: instead, it is the indication of an image that is nearer, more suitable, or more fitting, both in relation to the body's and the soul's notion of truth,[122] since what produces *numeri*, that is, the numbers or harmonies in question, takes precedence over the *numeri* that are produced.[123] Where the soul differs from the body is in its awareness that through the body it has received something that it lacks, and, on receiving it, turns from the carnal senses and reforms itself in accordance with the divine harmonies of wisdom.[124] In Augustine's view, this is what is meant by Ecclesiastes 7:26: "I have gone round and round so that I might know, consider, and seek both wisdom and number."[125]

It does not follow that the "vital principle" in the tree is superior to the vitality of the person who hears the verbal rhythm represented by the word "tree." If that were the case, hearing would consist of nothing but what is produced in the soul via the body.[126] The master points out that when we hear something the body does not act like an artisan, shaping the raw data of the senses for the soul.[127] The body is animated by the soul through the doer's intention (*intentione facientis*, 6.5.9).[128] Augustine recalls the principle advanced by the student, by which the producer of a *numerus* takes precedence over the rhythm produced (6.4.6). The soul is not always affected by the body, but occasionally acts on it and in it, as if the body were subjected to its domination through divine providence. The soul sometimes operates with ease and at other time with difficulty, since influences on the body act first on the body and only afterward on the soul.[129] When the soul is opposed, it becomes, so to speak, more observant and attentive to what it desires, and this attentiveness results in what we call distress or fatigue, whereas, when body and soul are in harmony, the dominant emotion is pleasure.[130]

These ideas imply an active theory of sensation, based on Augustine's conception of the will. The deferral of the body to the commands of the soul is not automatic, but results from communication between *anima* and *natura corporea*, both portrayed as having their directives, as Augustine will later acknowledge in his discussion of inner conflicts at *Confessions* independently of 8.9–10. It is at *De Musica* 6.5.9–10, written, it is assumed, independently of the account of his conversion, that he provides his readers with his most detailed analysis of the potential of the soul for dealing with the body's movements. As in the autobiography, he emphasizes the role played by the accompanying emotions, *dolor*, *labor*, and *voluptas*, as an aspect of this interchange and as a signal on the soul's part, indicating whether or not the will has been obeyed. Finally, he gives a large role to attention, which is an aspect of the will's activity and the force of concentration of the mind that precedes deliberated action. *Anima*, in fact, which is presented in the suggestion of an allegorization, occasionally acts like a person entering into a meditative state in its relations with *natura corporea*, since, like Augustine himself in his many experiments with detachment, the soul is essentially attempting to distance itself from sense perceptions. When confronted with a bodily action that is contrary to its will, *Anima* reacts by refocusing its attention elsewhere. But, if the action harmonizes with its will, it is more attentive to it: *attentius agitur* (6.5.9).

This process is looked upon as a type of internal narrative which affects the future course of our actions through the interaction of body and soul, and it is this mutual influence to which the name "sensing" or "perceiving" is given (*sentire*, 6.5.10).[131] This sense, therefore, is something that exists within each of us individually, even when, as is often the case, it is not activated by an external or internal impulse—a view that is expanded in book 2 of *De Libero Arbitrio*. When the soul activates our sense of perception, it does so in a manner that is attentive to the sensory reactions that take place in the body. In this manner, the soul fits external impulses to the appropriate sense, for example, light to the eyes, or sounds to the ears. On the other hand, when there is introduced into the body anything that is perceived as "otherness," the soul reacts more attentively, and, adjusting itself to the agency in question—whether this operates through the senses of hearing, smelling, tasting, or touching—it responds positively or negatively, depending on whether it perceives the influence to be in harmony with the body or not. And the soul, in doing this, "displays" or "exhibits" these operations to the body as it is reacting rather than submitting to the body's reactions themselves.[132]

Inasmuch as sound produces an effect in the ears, the ears can be defined as an animated member of the body (*animatum membrum*). In inquiring into the relationship between the activity of the soul, in which the capacity for hearing arises, and the ears, in which it is realized, the master notes the parallel between the motion in the air, which produces sound, and the motion in the ears, which produces hearing. However, in the activity of body and soul, sound exists as long as there are vibrations in the air and in the ears, whereas the vital activity of the soul, which assures the sense of hearing, exists before these vibrations begin and continues after they have finished. As long as the senses are being activated in sound, the soul's continuity is maintained in silence;[133] and, whenever it senses something, the soul is aware of what can be called their *motus*, *actiones*, or *operationes*. When the senses of sight, hearing, smell, taste, or touch are brought into play, these operations take place in response to antecedent conditions in which the senses are acted upon by outside forces (e.g., light, sound, odor, and so on). However, when the soul is affected by its own operations, it is acted upon by itself, not by the body; nonetheless it acts by accommodating itself to the body. In doing so, the soul is reduced in its own eyes, although it is never lowered to the body's level.[134]

At the end of his discussion of the soul's harmony and disharmony, Augustine returns to the question with which the pair were previously concerned. The master again asks the student which of the three remaining types of rhythm in their earlier analysis is the most excellent, those that occur in memory, in sense perception, or in sound (*in memoria . . . , in sentiendo, . . . in sono*, 6.6.16; cf., 6.4.7). The student does not place physical sound after memory and sensation, as he did initially, but he still appears to be uncertain as to which of the two is superior. In the end, he adopts the line of reasoning that he had previously advanced, preferring the causes (*facientes*) to their effects (*facti*; cf. 6.4.7). On this view, primacy is given to rhythms present in the soul at the time of hearing rather than to those retained in the memory, which are their by-product. Two questions naturally follow from this conclusion. Does it imply that rhythms in the soul are superior to those in the memory only while we are listening to them, since it is then that the former clearly cause the latter? And, if numerical relationships that we sense through such listening are in part operations of the soul, how can we distinguish harmonies that arise from sense perceptions from those in the soul that do not operate through the senses or the memory of sense impressions, but instead by means of harmonic intervals within the soul itself?[135]

It is clear that the discussion is at an impasse, since, beyond sense impressions, the pair agree that they have no experiential knowledge of what creates harmonies in the soul. The master attempts to solve the problem by means of a classification of types of rhythm according to their degrees of merit (*meritorum gradibus*). In order of preference, these are (1) *judiciales*: judicial, i.e., those by which judgments are made; (2) *progressores*: progressing, i.e., those that are advancing; (3) *occursores*: occurring or encountered, i.e., those that have been heard;[136] (4) *recordabiles*: recordable, i.e., those in the memory; and (5) *sonantes*: sounding, i.e., those that exist in physical sound.[137] He thereby introduces a parallel for the earlier fivefold scheme for *numeri*, i.e., *sonare, audire, operari, meminisse*, and *annuendo vel abhorrendo quasi quodam naturali jure*.[138]

In trying to determine which is best, he asks the student whether any of these *numeri* in the second scheme are free of temporal constraints, or whether, like sequences of sounds described earlier, they all decline over time and disappear.[139] The student initially advances the view that only the *judiciales* are permanently sustained. In order to challenge this statement, the master returns to an earlier problem, namely whether it makes any difference to the meter of a line of verse if a word is pronounced at different speeds (cf. 1.7.13–1.8.14; 2.2.2). His example is once again a word written in iambic meter (e.g., *parlens*).[140] If he says this word twice, taking twice as long for the second pronunciation, he does not appear to offend the student's sense of judgment by ignoring the law of meter.[141] It is clear, therefore, that these rhythms are superior to the other four types insofar as they are not constrained by a given span of time.[142] Nonetheless, as also pointed out earlier (1.13.27), there is a limit to the length of time over which a judgment concerning regularity of measurement can be expected to carry conviction, owing to the upper boundaries of sense perception. If one diminishes the speaking time by successively reducing the time taken to pronounce the syllables by a ratio of 2:1, the reader soon passes beyond the capacity of the hearer to make accurate judgments about the meter.[143]

Most people, he observes, are offended by lame meters after hearing them and judging them in relation to what they know to be harmonious or not. But what is the source of this capacity—nature, training, or both (*natura, aut exercitatione, aut utroque*, 6.7.19)? Recall that when the master earlier asked whether the knowledge implied in his definition of music arose from imitation or reason, the student answered that in his opinion both were involved (1.4.6). It was also decided after a lengthy debate that the instrumentalist's knowledge arose from both practice and artistic understanding. The question now before them is whether a similar combination of practice and theory can account for the appreciation of numerical harmonies themselves. The master points out that it would be possible for one person to judge and approve prolonged rhythms, while another might be incapable of doing so; moreover, the person lacking the capacity might be able to acquire it through practice. However, in both cases, the skills would have to be applied within certain definable limits of time.

The master subsequently outlines the larger reasons for entertaining this view in a lengthy discourse that begins at 6.7.19. This consists in an extension of the concept of *proportio* or *analogia*, which was introduced into the debate at 1.12.23. On this view, every living thing, according to its particular class, is endowed with a sense of place and time in a relationship of proportion within the universe.[144] The body's mass is proportionate to the overall mass, of which it is a part; its age, to the age of the universe, of which its life span is a part; and its action, to universal motion, of which its movement is a part. It is through the totality of these relationships that the universe, that is, what is called "heaven and earth" in Scripture, achieves its greatness,[145] since the parts can be reduced or increased proportionately, and yet the universe remains as great as ever. The reason for this state of affairs is that no place or time is absolutely large or small within the universe: each is relatively larger or smaller in proportion to something else.

Moreover, it is owing to these proportionate relationships that humans are incapable of judging periods of time superior to those that fall within the range of their senses. It follows that *numeri judiciales*, although superior to other types of harmony, are not eternal, even though, the master admits, it is difficult for mortals to discern the reasons for their limited life span.[146] The master adds that custom or habit (*consuetudo*) has a secondary, craftsmanly, and habitual constitution (*quasi secunda, et quasi affabricata natura*),[147] since the habits formed by means of our tastes and judgments evidently undergo change over time, one fashion frequently replacing another.[148] It is clear from this statement that the *natura* about which he has been speaking is *humana natura* in the sense of *hominis natura mortalis*, as a consequence of sin. Human nature thereby reflects the proportionate structure of the universe as well as the biblical account of the entry into the world of humans' *carnalis vitae actiones*.

The bringing together of the notion of mathematical harmony by means of ratios and the historical legacy of the fall of the soul from virtue is a reminder of the large role played by relations in Augustine's theology of the self. Humans are condemned to live in a carnal, sensory world, because of their pride and disobedience in the garden of Eden. It is for this reason that all the harmonies that they are capable of understanding, including *numeri judiciales*, are governed by temporality. However, this weakness has to be conceived and understood within the overall mathematical structure of the universe, in which all rhythms, from the lowest physical level upward, are interrelated through the principle of proportion. Within this scheme, *numeri judiciales* can be understood by analogy with the account of Reason in *De Ordine*, which rises above the senses and the mind only to realize its own limitations before the eternal.

While the master has difficulty proving that *numeri judiciales* are not eternal, he has no doubt concerning the mortality of the other four types of rhythms, which, he proposes, are all subject to some form of superior judgment. As for the *numeri progressores*, when they strive to produce a harmonious operation in the body, their parameters are determined secretly by the agreement of the *numeri judiciales*.[149] It is this form of cooperation that prevents us from walking with unequal steps, moving our jaws out of synchronization when we eat, and so forth. By contrast, *occursores numeri* are not produced by their own initiative but passively. They too are subject to the *numeri judiciales*, but only insofar as they are retained in the memory.[150]

This point can be illustrated by the pronunciation of a syllable, which, no matter how short, resounds between two moments of time. The sound is extended over a very short period; as a result, what we would call the waves are borne imperceptibly through beginning, middle, and end. Moreover, in recognizing this fact, we reflect rationally on what is taking place, independently of the physical events themselves. Thus it can be shown that it is by means of reason, not the senses, that spaces of time and place are subject to division. The master emphasizes the point by reminding the student that human hearing is unable to distinguish the beginning and end of the pronunciation of a single syllable. In order to do so, the sense of hearing has to be aided by memory. At the moment at which the end of a syllable makes a sound, it is by means of memory that the motion produced by the beginning still endures in the mind. If that were not the case, we could not accurately use the past tense in stating that we "had heard" anything.

The role of memory in *numeri occursores* is likewise illustrated by means of attention deficit. It often happens that, when we are in the presence of people who are speaking to us, our minds are absorbed with other thoughts.[151] The problem does not arise from the fact that, at the moment of hearing, the soul does not put in motion rhythms that react to what the other person is saying, but that this motion's impetus is arrested by the directing of our attention toward another subject. On the other hand, if the motion produced by the speaker's words had remained with us, it would have remained in the memory; as a result, we would have recognized and sensed that we had heard something.[152]

The role of attention, which provides the connection between the different *numeri*, is subsequently explained by comparing two experimental situations. It is possible that a person's mental reactions may be too slow to appreciate the fact that a syllable, no matter how briefly it sounds, can be shown by logic to have a beginning and end. For our hearing cannot register, and therefore our souls cannot experience, the sound made by two syllables at the same time. The second syllable is not heard until the sound of the first has ceased.[153] And, just as, in vision, light aids us in understanding intervals of space, so, in hearing, memory aids us in understanding duration. Alternately, if a person hears a rhythmic beat over a long period which is succeeded by a second rhythm whose intervals are equal to or double those of the first, then the subject's attention shifts to the second and represses the memory of what has come before. In a comparable fashion, we can look at one part of an object and then at another, trying to decide whether it is round or square. However, if we forget what we first saw in focusing our attention on the second perspective, we cannot come to any conclusion about its shape without the aid of memory, which effectively establishes a sequence of time between the two experiences.

Numeri judiciales that are situated in intervals of time, therefore, cannot bring about judgments without the aid of memory, except in the case of the advancing rhythms by which their own progress is measured.[154] This is likewise the case for *numeri recordabiles*. When we recall something, we call it up from memory, as if it were stored away. At such a moment we have recourse to something similar to the original motion of the mind, and we call this "remembering."[155] We reproduce in thought, or by some physical means (for example, by a movement of the limbs, as in dance) the rhythms that we performed on an earlier occasion. And we are aware that these movements are not coming into our minds for the first time but that we are returning to them again.

At the time we transferred them to our memories, we may have had difficulty in repeating them and even needed some guidance, in order to get them right, whereas now, with this problem overcome, these rhythms present themselves in an agreeable fashion, following both their proper time and order; so easily, in fact, that the rhythms that inhere most tenaciously in our memories come forth spontaneously, even if we are thinking about something else at the time.[156]

                              *   *   *

It is now clear that *numeri judiciales* interact with the four other types of rhythm. But is there anything superior to these, that is, a principle of judgment within them by which they can be evaluated? This is the question that is taken up in the final segment of the dialogue.

The student is greatly impressed by the force and potential of judicial rhythms, since it is to these harmonies, he believes, that the senses dedicate their services. Consequently, he is doubtful that a superior sense of harmony can be found. In response, the master invites him to consider again the first verse of Ambrose's hymn *Deus creator omnium*. When it is sung or chanted, all five types of *numeri* appear to be involved: *sonores*, of course, in the sound; *occursores*, in the hearing; *recordabiles*, in the recognition; *progressores*, in the pronunciation; and *judiciales*, in the pleasure.[157]

The student asks why the term *judiciales* is not applied to reason rather than to pleasure within this scheme. Also, he fears that such an assessment of reason would amount to nothing more than a more careful judgment of numerical harmonies by means of themselves, when it is clear to him that our judgments based on reason and pleasure arise from the same source.[158] The master first dodges the question, pointing out that, in enumerating the five types of *numeri*, he was making distinctions that pertained to the movements and affections of a single nature, namely the soul.[159] He quotes the student's own words at the beginning and end of book 1 to the effect that that they should not waste their time quibbling over words.[160] Instead, they should recognize that the principle of reason is superimposed on the sense of pleasure, since reason would be incapable of judging inferior harmonies if it did not possess more enduring harmonies in itself.[161]

What characterizes reason is not only the ability to make rational distinctions but the type of self-consciousness that separates the knower from the known. If, by this criterion, one includes reason among the *numeri*, there are not five types but six, which can be arranged in a hierarchy that proceeds from the sensory (*sensuales*) to those that fall under the rubric of the judicial (*judicialium nomen*), the latter including reason itself. Reason is at the top of this ladder; at the bottom are *numeri sonores*,[162] which, the master now suggests, should rather be called *corporales*, because they normally involve visible motion (*motus visibilis*), as in the example of the dance (6.8.22; cf., 1.2.2). The earlier position of the student, by which *numeri sonantes* were given priority, because they give rise to the other rhythms, is definitively rejected.[163] The master concludes with an allegorical account of the way in which Reason assesses numerical harmonies as an aspect of her appreciation of her own beauty, proceeding upward from the senses to the mind (6.10.25–26).

The master then returns to the division of numerical relationships outlined in book 1, now placing them in a larger context. He points out that something similar can be said concerning the intervals of silence between words: our sense of harmony is not offended by the awareness of the absence because what is demanded by the law of equality is supplied, not by sound, but by the duration of a space of time.[164] In listening to sounds followed by periods of silence in the reading of poetry, therefore, the hearer applies the same rules, simply filling out mentally the length of time that sounds would have created physically. By this type of mental examination, a short syllable, when followed by a rest, can be interpreted as a long syllable, whereas, if the same syllable had less than two time intervals, the law of equals would not apply because there would be nothing with which it could be compared (cf. 2.2.2; 6.2.3). In the master's view, this law, which was proposed in numerical fashion in book 1, also applies to varieties of sentences, although the principles involved are less evident to the senses.

Augustine provides two examples of the limitations of the human perspective in this context (6.11.30). First, if a person were placed in a corner of a large, attractive building, and kept in position like a statue, he would be unable to appreciate the harmonious beauty of the whole, since, from his perspective, he could see only one part of the architectural design.[165] Second, if the syllables of a poem were to come to life when they were pronounced and acquired the ability to think about the harmonious effects of the sounds that they were making, they would be unable to appreciate the beauty of the poem of which they are the parts. This appreciation would demand an understanding of the entire work, when the reading was completed, while their perspective is limited to the passing effects of the individual sounds.[166]

Proceeding downward through *progressores*, *occursores*, and *sonantes numeri*, one comes closer to the information provided by the senses. Yet, since one and the same soul receives and records these impulses, albeit from different sources, they are all subsequently made accessible through memory. (For this reason, the master observes, the human memory is considerable help in dealing with the complexities of everyday life).[167] Our mental records retain what is known from experience or what is grasped by the senses, even if they only have the status of opinion (*opinio*), and are liable to error.[168] With respect to memory, as noted, such errors consist in two types, which are called *phantasia* and *phantasma,* the one arises from the images of physical objects that find their way into the memory, while the other arises from the motions of the mind based on the images already in the memory.[169] Through rhythmic recurrence, the mind is even capable of creating *phantasmata* that are images of images (*imagines imaginum*).[170]

Augustine admits that it is difficult to find an explanation for the origin of these types of images. He nonetheless engages in some speculation concerning their functions, and thereby adds a footnote to what is said about mental impressions in letter 7 and elsewhere. He is certain that if he had never seen, a human body, he would not be able to configure its visible form in his thoughts. He is aware that whatever he creates in his mind is based on what he has seen, as a product of his memory. He is likewise conscious of the fact that, within the operations that take place in the memory, it is one thing to discover a *phantasia* and quite another to create a *phantasma*.[171] He has no doubt that the soul is capable of such operations: he is equally sure that it is an extreme form of error to mistake *phantasmata* for things that are actually known.[172] We sometimes speak of knowing (*scire*) when we are referring either to things that have been sensed (*sensisse*) or imagined (*imaginari*). Thus he can say that he knows his father in one way, because he has seen him, and his grandfather, who is deceased, in another, through memory and imagination. But neither truly exists: the images are respectively *phantasiae* or *phantasmata* (6.11.32). As a consequence, he is convinced that mental images should on the whole be distrusted, or, when they are the object of thought, scrutinized carefully through the understanding (*intelligentia*). He thus returns to a Platonic position, but one in which the senses and the body play important roles.

This train of thought brings the discussion back to the moral predicament of humans, and, in particular, to the role of transitory pleasures based on images. In addressing this problem anew, Augustine describes a contemplative practice for separating the mind from the body, which is a complement to the philosophical soliloquy but oriented in the direction of pure meditation. This exercise has to do with our attempts to isolate ourselves from the images of physical things in our memories, even though these impermanent images can represent objects of lasting beauty. In Augustine's view, the presence of such images, as they move in and out of our conscious thoughts, is a reminder that the deity has not entirely abandoned us: their fleeting nature is likewise a warning that we cannot return to stable truths without withdrawing from their sensory associations. This process can be completed in three stages, as described elsewhere in his early writings on the theme: suspension of thought, concentration on spiritual matters, and persistence, so that the habit is broken and misleading images disappear.[173]

The master recalls that the memory is the recipient of both corporeal and spiritual types of motion. Because sensory movements take place in space and over time, these motions cannot be considered the source of the eternal harmony that the soul finds within itself (6.12.34). Where, then, does this permanent harmony arise? Doubtless, someplace superior to bodies. But is this in the soul itself (*in ipsa anima*) or above it (*supra animam*)? The student asks once again how it is that the numerical harmonies found in quantitative verse remain in the mind after the sound of the words has passed away. The answer is that certain rhythms, which do not endure, result from harmonies that do.[174] As proposed in book 1, the artistic skill (*ars*) in question arises in the disposition of the artist's mind (*affectionem . . . animi artificis*). This disposition could not exist in the mind of someone unskilled (*imperitus*) in the art of writing verse, nor could it be completely forgotten (*oblitus*), if it had once been possessed (cf. 1.4.5–7).

But if it had been forgotten, even temporarily, how could it be recalled? The master proposes a solution based on classical anamnesis, asking whether the artist in question could have recalled his skill on being asked about it. Would the rhythms return to him via the questions he was asked? Alternatively, is the artist likely to be reminded of them by means of a movement within his own mind, as if he were rediscovering something he had lost?[175] The student thinks that the artist would find these rhythms within himself, and, as his phrasing suggests, in relation to the self (*apud semetipsum*). But if that is the case, what is the role of questions and answers in this type of recall? The master asks the student whether, on interrogation, it is possible to teach an artist which syllables are long or short, if he has completely forgotten them, since their quantities have long been agreed upon through custom. If this arrangement had not been fixed and stabilized through nature or teaching (*natura vel disciplina*), is it not possible that even learned persons in contemporary times would have elongated the syllables that the ancients shortened, and vice versa?[176]

The student agrees that many things that are forgotten can be recalled through questioning, as Socrates suggests. But the master retorts that there are some things that one evidently cannot recall, for example, what one ate for dinner a year ago. Memory, therefore, is not an infallible source of knowledge, especially when a lengthy period of time elapses between image formation and recall. The student notes that it would not have been possible for him to remember the rules for short and long syllables either, if he had entirely forgotten them. By this route the master returns to the question with which *De Musica* begins, namely, whether a knowledge of poetic rhythms depends on inherited teachings or on an innate understanding of mathematical harmonies, which can be arrived at by means of reason alone. He asks the student to consider the word *Italia*, the first syllable of which is pronounced long by some of their contemporaries and short by others. This difference in pronunciation is evidently a question of linguistic conventions that change over time. By contrast, the law of numbers, which determines harmonies, remains unchanged: one plus one equals two, both now and in the past.

These rules are applicable to all the domains of thought in which numbers are pertinent, it would appear, with the exception of the quantities of syllables. A person untrained (*imperitus*) in mathematics would be able to master them, not because the methods had been forgotten but because they had never been learned, since they depend on logic rather than conventions of speech. But is this not true of meters too, since they reflect both the changeless and the changing elements in quantitative verse? In this context, the master asks how the rhythms of metrical poetry could be imprinted on his mind in order to give rise to a mental disposition capable of producing what is called their art.[177] Could this knowledge arise from someone who was asking him questions (as in the case of geometry in the *Meno*)? By a different route, we return to Augustine's perpetual query on the advantages of dialogue and soliloquy.

The master has an answer that is directed toward the option of the inner dialogue. In his view, the person to whom this question was proposed would act within himself, in order that he might understand if what was being asked was true before giving his answer.[178] This reasoning takes him close to the proof for the existence of God based on the truth of number (a problem that was possibly being worked out by Augustine about the same time but along different lines in *De Libero Arbitrio*).[179] On this view, the *numeri* about which they are speaking are *aeterni* and possess no hint of *inaequalitas*. As a consequence, they have to have been imparted to the human soul from a source that is eternal, which can only have been divine.[180] It is clear, therefore, that a person who, on being questioned by someone else, is moved from within himself toward God, would not be able to understand an uncommunicable truth unless it had been previously retained in his memory, even if he were prompted from the outside.[181] This is an example of reminiscence, but, again, not of the type described by Socrates in the *Meno* or *Phaedo*.

The master thus suggests that the person who carries on a dialogue within himself concerning what is unquestionably true is in fact searching within himself for the traces of God's eternal laws. As in the *Soliloquia*, this type of conversation is a way of indicating the importance of external reasoning as well as its limitations in the light of interior instruction. It is not clear to him why anyone would separate himself from the obvious benefits of this type of contemplative practice, and as a result make it necessary for the method of teaching from within to be recalled by means of memory. He asks whether the mind or soul needs to be brought back to itself in this way because it has permitted its attention to be drawn to other matters. And what sort of thinking would account for its turning away from the contemplation of the highest type of equality to something evidently inferior?[182] The answer is that the soul, when it is in communication with itself, acknowledges the existence of changeless equality, but it also recognizes the problem of its own changefulness: it knows within itself that in its interior reflections its attention is directed toward both the timeless and the temporal. Passing from one to the other, it evidently performs operations in time, which are neither eternal nor changeless (6.13.37). There is a capacity in the soul by which it understands both the eternal and the fact that the temporal is inferior to the eternal, even when it knows that the latter resides in itself. The soul's prudence consists in desiring what is superior rather than what it knows is inferior. The soul therefore retains the potential for virtuous behavior within itself.

Why, then, does the soul not adhere immediately to these eternal rhythms, since it already knows that it should do so? Because we direct our care and attention mostly to the things that we love: these are objects of beauty, which give us pleasure by means of the senses. As a consequence, we search for what is harmonious (*convenientia*) according to the measure of our nature, and we avoid what is unharmonious (*inconvenientia*). Where there is equality or similitude, there is also harmoniousness: *Ubi autem aequalitas aut similitudo, ibi numerositas* (6.13.38). It is the love of acting in response to what is successively felt in its body, therefore, that turns the soul away from the contemplation of eternal things, soliciting its attention through its concern for the pleasures of the senses.[183] The soul experiences these *passiones* through a series of *numeri*.

Its initial reaction takes place by means of *occursores numeri*, that is, harmonies of reception. The second response is brought about by *progressores numeri*, that is, by harmonies that are put forth by the soul itself. Its attention can be rerouted by the two sorts of memory images, *phantasiae* and *phantasmata*, both of which are attributable to *recordabiles numeri*. Finally, the soul is diverted by the vain love for the knowledge of things, and this is governed by *sensuales numeri*, in which are found the rules by which it takes pleasure in the imitation of art: whence is born curiosity, the enemy of tranquility, and vanity, which is powerless over truth.[184] This love of acting or responding, which inevitably turns away from truth, is inspired principally by pride. It is because of this vice that the soul prefers to engage in the imitation of God rather than to be of service to God.[185] The soul is thus represented as having in itself the self-awareness of a person who hesitates over the options of spiritual or corporeal attractions in life. This awareness amounts to the introduction of the notion of the self into the concept of the soul. Despite twists and turns in its argument, as well as creating the impression of being a still unfinished piece of thinking, book 6 of *De Musica* is the most important statement of this principle in Augustine's early writings, whose assumptions underlie his achievement in the *Confessions*.

CHAPTER 6

Loss and Recovery

One of the functions of meditative reading in late antiquity was for the purpose of healing. Meditation was proposed for the treatment of specific conditions, such as melancholy, as well as for creating a general equilibrium in individuals between mind and body. The type of meditation used for healing was usually the by-product of sacred reading.

This chapter is devoted to exploring the connection between reading and healing in the centuries between late antiquity and the early modern period. In taking up this subject, I am returning to the questions concerning reading and the self that were discussed in Chapter 1, however from a different direction. This consists in placing the uses of meditation within the context of the history of medicine as well as that of religion. In introducing the theme of healing to this collection, I am aware that I am diverging from the philosophical perspective on the self that is found in Chapters 2 to 5. The detour is justified in my view, since it is through the practice of meditation in clinics and hospitals that a significant contribution has been made to contemporary thinking on the topic of an integrated self.

Meditation and Healing

I begin by reminding the reader that in Western medicine disease is normally accounted for by means of changes in chemical and biological processes. In recent years, another focus for the understanding and treatment of illnesses has arisen through forms of alternative, complementary, or unconventional medicine.[1] This type of healing, which has always existed on the margins of biological medicine, has been the subject of scientific inquiry for two to three generations and forms part of a movement in both Western and non-Western societies in which a reassessment is being made of the potential contribution to health of such factors as diet, exercise, climate, and the life of the mind.

Within the health sciences, studies in this field are classified under the heading of "mind-body medicine." This is a scientific program, whose achievements can be illustrated by the experimental research of figures like Jon Kabat-Zinn and Richard Davidson.[2] It is also an eclectic endeavor, which draws on the healing traditions of religions, ancient cultures, and indigenous peoples. These approaches to healing have in common a concern for the interconnectedness of mind and body, in contrast to thinking in some branches of biological medicine, which is alleged to maintain a dualistic outlook.[3]

Owing to the longevity of interest in this sort of healing, it is not surprising that studies in mind-body medicine frequently go beyond physical health and illness and address broader philosophical questions, including the search for a happy, fulfilled, or meaningful life, which is a reiterated concern in Plato, Aristotle, and other ancient thinkers.[4] Mind-body medicine claims to have discovered, or rediscovered, important connections between mind, body, and philosophical themes such as these, which were known in former times, or in non-Western cultures, but have been overlooked in the development of rational or scientific medicine, especially during the experimental epoch that began with the publication of William Harvey's *De motu cordis* in 1628.

However, even those who are enthusiastic about this field acknowledge that it suffers from two limitations. One is a lack of controlled and randomized trials,[5] which has prevented mind-body medicine from being accepted by many trained physicians. The other consists in the failure of historians to chart the history of mind-body techniques within Western medicine, which would have provided reasons why these approaches to healing took so long to enter the scientific field. In this chapter I limit myself to the second question, and, within that, to one type of mind-body technique, namely meditation. I ask why scientists and historians alike have so little understanding of the cultural roots of the meditative methods of healing that are presently under investigation and have been deployed, sometimes with considerable success, in contemporary clinics and hospitals.

*   *   *

Meditation has a fully continuous history in Eastern religions and a less continuous history in Western philosophy and religion. In the East there is a

lengthy tradition of thinking on the ethical and religious value of contemplative practices as well as on their role in creating an equilibrium between mind
and body. In the West, a comparable history exists and reaches its high point
of development during the Middle Ages in the three "Abrahamic" religions,
Judaism, Christianity, and Islam. However, after the Reformation, the practice
of meditation in the West is reduced in both Catholic and Protestant communities,
owing to changes in religious attitudes and the introduction of the printed book.
A new phase of meditative or contemplative thinking based on the appreciation of nature rather than on religious principles takes place in German and
English Romanticism in the nineteenth century. These two developments
form the background to the introduction of Eastern types of meditation in
clinics and hospitals in our time.

In all traditions of meditation, instruction begins with two points, namely
the focusing of attention and the awareness of the inner life of the mind.
Mental concentration results from a variety of simple exercises, such as deep,
regular breathing, listening to a sound, looking at an object, or, in Christian
meditation, reading a sacred text. The awareness of mind and body is taught
by a number of methods; for example, in Buddhist mindfulness meditation,
which is a popular form of practice in the West, an attempt is made to empty
the mind of its contents and to permit thoughts entering the field of consciousness to come and go, without any effort being made to arrest them, reflect on
them, or orient them to some form of activity. After a few lessons, those
practicing meditation can experience an awakening to the life of the mind as
well as to a sense of interconnectedness with the animate and inanimate
things around them. Accomplished meditators claim to reach higher states of
self-awareness or self-consciousness; some have even spoken in mystical terms
of attaining a sense of transcendence or timelessness.

Beyond the initial stages in the learning process, which, I would empha-
size, are largely practical in orientation, there are some notable differences in
these training exercises in individual traditions. One of these concerns movements. In hatha yoga, meditation is linked to disciplined physical movement,
whereas in Buddhist mindfulness, one is asked to sit perfectly still and
cross-legged on a mat, frequently in a darkened room. Sufis induce a meditative state of mind through a five-step, mentally concentrated dance. In Zen,
the goal of inwardness is achieved, not by movement, but by reflecting on a
koan, a story containing a paradox that cannot be resolved through the use of
reason. By contrast, during the Middle Ages, Jewish, Christian, and Muslim
meditation was associated with sacred reading and liturgical devotions, and

in both Byzantine and Latin Christianity with contemplation on external or internal narrative images, which complemented the texts that were read during the office and became in themselves an important focus of attention.

The medical research community has been studying visual, textual, and abstract methods of meditation for some time. The emphasis in contemporary investigations is on the physiological or psychological effects of such techniques. Less interest has been shown in their origins, evolution, and applications within different religious or cultural milieux, even though pioneers in their use in the field of medicine, such as Herbert Benson, were invariably taught how to meditate by means of apprenticeships with experts within such communities (in his case with Hindu holy men).[6] As a consequence of this orientation in the field, successive generations of clinicians and experimenters in mind-body medicine have become increasingly removed from the cultural roots of the techniques they are using, even though at times attempts have been made to recreate them. Within the ever-growing literature on the subject there is seldom mention of the historical background of the type of meditative technique that is being recommended; an example is the widespread use of the term "mindfulness," frequently without reference to its context in classical Buddhism. In the medical literature on the subject the different styles of meditation tend to be merged in a single model, and the products of meditative experience are usually described in terms of their behavioral results rather than their historical associations. This has resulted in a consolidated view of meditation in which an ancient and diversified discipline has effectively entered an ahistorical phase in its development.

The separation of the cultural and medical approaches to meditation has had a considerable advantage from a scientific point of view. It has permitted medical research to proceed with investigations into the influence of meditation on a variety of pathological conditions without having on each occasion to take into account issues that do not fall within the orbit of medicine. As a result of these types of inquiries, the list of mind-body treatments involving meditation has grown over the years in which experimentation in the field has taken place, and positive results are nowadays routine. To give just a few examples: meditation based on visual imagery has proven valuable for pain relief, the control of anxiety and depression, as well as in preventing nausea in chemotherapy;[7] it is also employed regularly in the treatment of asthma, eating disorders, and post-traumatic stress.[8] Lifestyle changes combining diet, exercise, and various styles of meditation have been shown to lead to the regression of coronary atherosclerosis, thus complementing earlier experiments in which it was proven that disciplined meditation can decrease heart rate, blood pressure, and oxygen consumption.[9] Recent experiments have even suggested that practiced meditators are able to alter a small number of involuntary mechanisms in the autonomic nervous system.[10] There is a growing if controversial literature on the use of meditation in the treatment of schizophrenia,[11] as well as in other mental disorders. Meditation is regularly employed in programs of rehabilitation from substance abuse and alcoholism. Inmates in prisons have for some time been engaged in the writing of autobiographies as exercises in meditation, often with beneficial results.

Attempts have been made to isolate "meditation" and to study it as a distinctive physiological state. It has been established that meditation differs from sleep, as well as from forms of relaxation when one is awake. This is the case, for example, when subjects are watching films or television, in which it has been calculated that there is only roughly half the decrease in the rate of respiration that occurs in meditation. Changes in skin resistance and conductance have been recorded during yoga and Zen meditation, as well as distinctive electroencephalographic effects, including an increase in the amplitude of the slow brain waves that are associated with feelings of well-being. In the field of psychology, researchers have noted that people who meditate often have a more focused attention in the present, rather than the past or future, and a better attitude toward work. There is increased emotional stability, especially among deviants and criminals, and a greater interest in the ethical, familial, and social dimensions of life. In general, those who meditate are said to be concerned with long-term rather than immediate needs. In contrast to the general population, they are less prone to forms of aggressive behavior. They own fewer firearms. They appear to have fewer anxieties about death than those who do not engage in some form of contemplative practice.[12] These features of meditation have been summed up by Daniel Goleman as the acquisition of "emotional intelligence."[13]

The existence of a growing literature on the topic in contemporary scientific research has in turn altered the context in which historical, religious, or anthropological inquiries into the traditional mind-influencing techniques of meditation and visualization are carried on.[14] The entire enterprise, consisting of both the humanistic and scientific studies, has acquired a type of social relevance that differs from the functions of meditation or contemplation in more traditional situations, where the practice tends to be restricted to participation in religious ceremonies. In the ancient West as well as in contemporary non-Western communities, knowledge of the techniques of meditation is normally restricted to a small number of people in society who are usually members of an élite, such as priests. By contrast, contemporary meditation has become a mainstream activity: it is taught in formal and informal groups everywhere by professionals and amateurs, and, with the exception of specific traditions, such as Catholic *lectio divina*, it is no longer associated exclusively with religious or cultural settings.

The recent rise of interest in meditation cannot be described as a mass movement, but it has had a democratizing effect within the field of personal health, since a great many people in different walks of life are for the first time interested in its potential. The reason for this is clear. If meditation has a provable therapeutic value in medicine, then it is lives that are ultimately at stake, to say nothing of the sums spent annually on health insurance, a part of which can presumably be diverted to other social needs if inexpensive alternatives to costly drug or surgical interventions are found. As a consequence, for the first time in history, interest in the medical potential of mind-body practices threatens to overshadow the public understanding of their traditional cultural or religious contexts. In premodern societies little was known about mind-body therapy by scientific standards as presently understood; however, there was a large literature on mind-body relations in the fields of religion, pseudo-science, magic, and prognostication. Nowadays, the scientific appreciation of mind-body practices is expanding at all levels of society, while the understanding of the historical background on which these practices rest is increasingly confined to the academy. Those who are engaged in the application of meditative disciplines to the treatment of disease do not have time to investigate their cultural background, while those engaged in research on the history of meditation generally lack the scientific education necessary for understanding what is involved in their clinical use.

From another viewpoint, however, the research community in alternative medicine is increasingly convinced that the traditional associations of meditative methods of healing play a role in determining their effectiveness. The precise nature of this relationship remains unclear, and, as noted, is not the major focus of scientific interest. However, repeated experiments have established that mind-body therapies are not "magic bullets," like antibiotics, but are one of a group of healing procedures that depend for their effectiveness on the patient's beliefs and mental disposition. The best known treatment of this type is the placebo,[15] in which patients are treated with a pill that has no known medical benefits but are told the contrary. In experiments with placebos it is usually found that a percentage of patients taking the false remedy show improvements that are comparable to those who have taken the real thing. While there is no irrefutable evidence that it is the placebo that has brought about the positive changes, there is no doubt among researchers in the field concerning the effects of the pseudo-remedies on the brain. It is for this reason that they have proven effective for such conditions as recurrent pain, immunosuppression, chronic fatigue syndrome, and depression.[16]

A great deal remains unknown about this broad category of healing, in which doctors and patients are aware of the effects of the treatments in question but have no scientific appreciation of how they have come about. In the case of the placebo, effectiveness depends on the presence of a figure of authority, usually the doctor, as well as on the dialogue between doctor and patient that deals with the expectations of each party concerning a possible cure.[17] Like the true treatment it replaces, the false remedy is rather like a promissory note—a solemn engagement on the part of the physician to perform services in the future. As such, it brings into play the patient's wishes and long-term goals in a form that is well known in religious traditions of thought. These preconditions of trust, on which the healing is presumably based, can be re-created artificially in a clinical setting, where their credibility rests largely on the prestige of scientific medicine. However, a clinic or hospital has the disadvantage of not being the normal environment in which persons exercise cultural or religious convictions, and sooner or later these structures of belief are weakened, reducing the effectiveness of mind-body treatments.

There is another dimension of this type of healing that must also be taken into consideration, and this, as noted, recalls a number of ancient schools of thought. Quite apart from their medical applications, meditative techniques, as they arise in clinical settings, may be playing a role in society's search for a supplement, or even a replacement, of the metaphysical framework of institutionalized religion. In other words, the use of meditative techniques in medicine may be associated with a broader movement in contemporary belief systems in which emphasis is placed on a secularized and largely personalized type of spirituality. Within medicine itself, men and women appear to be rediscovering a dimension of the healing process that people once knew about and believed in, along with the forgotten matrix of ideas in which they had their social underpinnings.[18]

Some doctors adhere to a purely biological model of healing that rules out a role for such concerns; however, increasingly beliefs, including those of health care professionals themselves, are receiving attention as factors potentially affecting the health and well-being of patients. It is not unusual nowadays for medical personnel to form groups in hospitals and to engage in quasi-literary studies of the dramas, narratives, and rituals that take place during the healing process. A vocabulary once reserved for religion has been transferred uneasily to medicine, and, although the pace of change has been slower, medical perspectives based on mind-body relations have seriously invaded the field of religion for the first time in centuries. This change in attitudes suggests that there is something about contemporary society's beliefs, or their absence, that has compelled the health sciences to take on a part of the task traditionally assigned to the spiritual side of life.

*   *   *

If there is a degree of bewilderment on these relationships in the public mind, some of the responsibility must rest with historians for failing to provide thinkers in the field of medicine with a map of the earlier territory they are traversing. There are popular books on the history of mind-body medicine in the West, but no scholarly account of contemplative practices that takes as its point of departure contemporary changes in attitudes toward disease and healing. One of the reasons for this absence is that such an account would not find a place in standard reviews of the advancement of medicine. Healing practices that share a frontier with the spiritual or contemplative life do not play a large part in official histories of medicine in the premodern period. The familiar topics are the rudiments of anatomy and physiology, the Hellenistic pharmacopoeia and classification of diseases, the deployment of surgical interventions, and the development of social welfare programs to aid the poor, malnourished, and chronically ill.

To move farther back in time, mind-body procedures do not figure significantly in the writings of the founders of Western medicine, Hippocrates and Galen, both of whom championed what eventually became the medical model of illness. This is based on the view that every pathological condition has a traceable cause and that this can be determined through the use of diagnostic tools, narrowing the range of treatment to the source of the illness.

Hippocrates is the model for this approach. Within the sixty books of writings on medicine, there is an occasional mention of mind-body issues, for example, in the advice to physicians on the benefits of taking case histories and paying attention to a patient's psychology. Also, the Hippocratic Oath, in defining the norms of professional conduct for future generations of physicians, draws attention to their moral responsibility and to the adoption of an ethical mode of life (*bios*). Nonetheless, healing is considered to be essentially a technical art (*techne*), which is "result-oriented . . . , learned, practiced, and transmitted by individuals," while in its scientific dimension it is said to "transcend . . . their private lives, representing a transpersonal community."[19] The orientation of the text of the *Oath*, as well as the influential inscription in a sanctuary dedicated to Asclepius's cult at Epidaurus, is toward directed self-conscious activity rather than any type of meditation, contemplation, or philosophical inwardness. These writings

> make human cognitive activity central to their expectations. . . .
> The oath-taker's promissory self-vision prominently includes
> numerous cognitive acts, such as making distinctions and passing
> judgments, engaging in analogical reasoning, teaching those who
> wish to learn, lecturing and sharing learning with students,
> avoiding giving certain kinds of advice, being alert and continuously
> watchful, distinguishing between intentional or voluntary and
> unintentional or involuntary injustice, hearing and seeing things
> and deciding about which of these on which he should remain
> silent, reflecting on the consequences of fulfilling his oath and of
> committing perjury, and so on. In short, the oath-taker not only
> envisions himself as an agent (or potential agent) performing deeds
> or refraining from acting, but also as a cognitive being, reasoning,
> discerning, hearing, seeing, differentiating, deciding, judging,
> comparing, anticipating, and so on.[20]

In the light of such considerations, it is appropriate to speak of Hippocratic medicine, in both its design and practice, as being based on observational rather than philosophical or psychological criteria. This was the chief objective of the schools established at Cos and Cnidus, where physicians were instructed in the physical examination of patients, the observation of abnormalities, and the search for the causes of disease.[21]

Once this tradition of medical thinking was established, its basic principles were followed in succeeding centuries. Galen was more philosophical than Hippocrates, but he too considered the empirical approach the most secure foundation for medical science. This view is documented in two works that develop Hippocratic themes, *On the Elements According to Hippocrates* and *On Mixtures*; in his great study, *Anatomical Procedures*, Galen likewise adopts a purely scientific outlook, despite the limitations in his anatomical experience that arose from his lack of opportunity to dissect cadavers.[22] The Arab physicians who played an important role in the discipline of medicine after the seventh century, for example al-Razi, 'Ali ibn al-'Abbas, Abu-l-Qasim, and Avicenna, considerably expanded diagnostic procedures and treatment in hospitals, but they did so within a Hippocratic and Galenic framework. This approach remained the norm among medical practitioners in the West until the seventeenth century, when it was reaffirmed by William Harvey, who considered his study of anatomical procedures to be a revision and improvement on Aristotle. The progress of medicine has subsequently relied entirely on biology, chemistry, anatomy, and physiology, despite the occasional expression of interest in mind-body factors in figures such as Thomas Sydenham and Claude Bernard, and in a different context by Freud.

If we examine the use of healing within religion, a comparable picture emerges. Meditation was practiced in Hellenistic Judaism and in first-century Christianity; however, there is no record in the period's religious history for the use of disciplined meditation as a technique for curing specific illnesses. In the New Testament, the methods most frequently mentioned for healing are miracles and the casting out of evil spirits. There are some 65 reports of miraculous cures in the Gospels and 49 in Acts.[23] Other methods of healing that are frequently mentioned are prayer, exorcism, and occasionally the revival of the dead. In Matthew and Mark the use of prayer in healing usually concerns individuals, whereas miracles typically take place before an audience, as in the accounts of Peter, Philip, and Paul. One of the questions that remains unanswered in these episodes is about the role of the surrounding community in establishing the preconditions of belief in which these arbitrary and dramatic scenes are enacted.

These miracle stories are largely popular in focus. Among educated people in both Jewish and early Christian communities during the period in which the Gospels were written, the prevailing view of disease was that of Greek and Roman society in general. This relied almost exclusively on the methods of physical medicine. Illness was associated with internal causes and visible symptoms, and cures involved the removal of these through a variety of scientific and pseudo-scientific means, rather than by the establishment of the long-term conditions for health and well-being associated with mind-body techniques.[24] The picture changes somewhat during the patristic period, when there are occasional references to healing involving the use of contemplative practices. However, for the most part, stories of healing in the lives of the saints likewise involve miracles, while among radical ascetics there is, in addition, a distrust of medicine, since it represents a causal force that rivals healing by means of divine intervention.

Within the period's spiritual writings, there are nonetheless passages in which serious consideration is given to mind-body relations, as in John Cassian, although these do not often raise medical questions.[25] A comparable orientation is found in Byzantine hagiographic sources, in which there are discussions of the emotional and cognitive implications of disease as well as reflections on meditative technique involving visualization, especially during the period of the iconoclastic controversy. It is difficult to generalize about the medieval centuries that follow; however, as noted, advances in medicine usually concerned the etiology of disease and the setting up of centers of care rather than mind-body issues.[26] Again, there are occasional accounts of interest in this area, for example, in the book written for Frederick II by Adam of Cremona on the regime to be followed by pilgrims and travelers to insure their stamina and mental stability.[27]

At the beginning of the modern period, mind-body practices were mainly found in the ill-defined territory between magic, medicine, and religion.[28] They did not form a part of learned or scientific medicine. If they played a role in the treatment of disease, it was largely because the majority of ordinary people could not afford the services of doctors. Even those who could were sometimes reluctant to call upon them, since it had become clear that they had no true understanding of the causes or cures of disease. Keith Thomas notes that

> the population at large disliked Galenic physic for its nauseous remedies and were frightened by the prospect of surgery. Some of the most intelligent laymen of the day expressed total contempt for conventional medicine. . . . King James I regarded academic medicine as mere conjecture and therefore useless. Francis Bacon thought that "empirics and old women" were "more happy many times in their cures than learned physicians." Some scientists and intellectuals followed the example of Paracelsus and were prepared to learn from herbalists and wise women.[29]

It is not surprising, therefore, that many people still relied on healing practices that were lodged in religious concepts and practices—for example, in relics, icons, pilgrimages, blessings, amulets, consecrations, sacraments, and the intercessory power of miracles and prayers. In the wake of the Scientific

Revolution, many of these were abandoned, as were the principles of Galenic and medieval medicine.

*   *   *

The contemporary revival of interest in alternative healing did not arise from either the Greco-Roman medicine or from the healing practices embedded in Western religious traditions, but from Eastern religions and from scientific investigations of mind-body procedures such as meditation. As a consequence, there has been a transformation in what the medical community considers to be the type of healing activity from earlier times that has relevance to contemporary medicine. The ancient and medieval therapeutic practices described in histories of medicine are of no clinical use today,[30] but the medical research community is deeply involved in the investigation of mind-body relationships that distantly recall miraculous cures, that is, interventions in which a subject apparently inspired by beliefs alone was able to trigger the body's resources into reversing a potentially threatening condition; as did a woman called Innocentia, of whom Augustine speaks in *The City of God* (22.8), whose breast cancer went into remission after she prayed at the shrine of St. Stephen in Carthage.

Also, it would appear that the rise of scientific medicine was not the cause, or at least not the principal cause, of the decline of meditative healing in premodern Europe. If this had been the case, there should have been a confrontation, or at least a conversation, between these approaches to healing. Scientific medicine and meditative spirituality were in fact rarely in contact after the translation of the corpus of Aristotle's writings, which began in the late twelfth century. Early medical science saw Aristotelian and Galenic natural philosophy as its intellectual predecessors, not ancient or medieval mind-body procedures. Finally, the rise of scientific medicine does seem to have played a significant role in the post-sixteenth-century decline of types of spirituality involving textual or visual meditation. This appears to have taken place within religion itself and affected both post-Reformation Protestantism and Catholicism.

As a result of these historical developments, it is clear that the source of a change that eventually affected medical science cannot be sought in the documented history of the science itself. It is not in earlier medical practices that we should look for the predecessors for contemporary applications for meditation, but in the complex history of Western meditation itself in both its early philosophical phase and its later religious configurations. One of the important chapters in this history concerns the transformation of meditation that took place in the late Hellenistic period and remained an influential force in thinking about meditation down to the seventeenth century, when the modern history of medicine began. During these centuries firm connections were established between the disciplines of meditation and reading. These included reading aloud, which was the dominant form of reading in these centuries, and silent reading, practiced by increasing numbers of people after the fourteenth century. This was a change that pertained to meditation on texts as well as images, since early in its development it was observed by Gregory the Great that religious images were like texts for those who could not read.[31]

The association of healing words and images with the reading process was both an advantage and a disadvantage for the history of meditation as it is later employed in medicine. The advantage arose from the continuity of reading practices during the Middle Ages, especially in monastic communities, which provided an institutional context for spiritual exercises like meditation and visualization, developing their techniques in ways unprecedented in antiquity. The disadvantage arose when those practices were abandoned in the early modern period, especially after the Reformation. Later education, whether secular or religious, did not give as large a role to the meditative aspects of reading as did the late ancient world or the Middle Ages, except within religious communities. Because meditation was thoroughly embedded in the reading process during this lengthy stretch of time, its disappearance was not noticed during the rise of the modern outlook, even though other changes in the reading and interpretation of sacred writings attracted considerable attention.

One possible reason for the lack of interest was that there was no single force at work, as there was, for example, in the challenge to the inherited view on the laws of bodies in motion by Galileo, thereby bringing about a fundamental change in mentality. The abandonment of meditative reading was not a direct consequence of the change from oral to silent reading, since one can read silently and meditatively, as did Anselm in his meditative prayers in the late eleventh century. Nor was it an automatic result of the new methods of book production that intervened three centuries later, as discussed by Elizabeth Eisenstein, Roger Chartier, Robert Darnton, and Adrian Johns,[32] since changes in book formats that preceded the age of print were at work as early as the twelfth and thirteenth centuries, when meditative monastic reading was widespread. Deeper causes have to be sought in education, theology, and social history to account for the fact that the religious and therapeutic effects of meditative reading that were found in ancient and medieval settings were

reduced, or restricted to special communities, by 1600. This transformation
appears to have taken place in spite of the wave of post-Reformation piety that
swept through Protestant and Catholic populations and created the first mass
readership for the Bible.

With the exception of the Devotio Moderna, the followers of Ignatius of
Loyola, and scattered Protestant groups, early modern people read less meditatively than their medieval predecessors, and read more often in order to get
at information that was contained in books. The intimacy of the manuscript
codex, which was often written for a single person or group of persons, offered no advantages for this kind of reading; this was also true of the images
in such books, which, like those illustrating *The St. Albans Psalter*, were created principally with one viewer in mind, in this case Christina of Markyate.[33]
In the age of print texts were standardized, and images became more repre-
sentational and rhetorically persuasive, as in Bernini's controversial Santa
Teresa in ecstasy, which offended contemporary viewers because it was thought
that an interior conversion had been presented as an exterior drama. Hugh of
St. Victor, who wrote the first modern treatise on reading in the 1140s, and
Petrarch, who was a self-conscious reader in the 1340s, stood at opposite ends
of a frontier that separated two ways of looking at the purposes of reading.[34]
One of these directed the reader's energies inward toward the self: its goal
was self-scrutiny and self-improvement within an institutionalized scheme;
the other, although it could be personal as well, was chiefly channeled outward to a reading audience.

Spirituality

These are some of the reasons why the mind-body dimension of healing has
been called the forgotten factor in modern medicine.[35] In the popular literature on the subject, this omission is usually traced to the medical consequences
of the Scientific Revolution. The thinker most often singled out for scrutiny, as
noted, is Descartes, who is thought to have established philosophical dualism
as the norm in medical thinking about the mind and body.[36] This is of course
an oversimplification of his views, which based on his *Meditations* of 1641
rather than later writings, such as *The Passions of the Soul*, published in 1650. In
his mature reflections on the subject, Descartes abandons strict dualism and
adopts a notion of the self in which mind and body are integrated.

Also, from a historical point of view, it is questionable whether an elitist discipline such as philosophy can be held responsible for the then prevailing attitudes in the field. Mistrust of mind-body methods for healing has much broader roots in Western medical thinking. As noted, resistance can be traced to Greco-Roman and Islamic traditions of medicine, which consistently favored the physical explanation of illnesses, as well as to the intellectual changes that preceded the Reformation, which discredited many healing practices embedded in magic, superstition, and popular religion, some of which involved connections between mind and body. Among the models that were abandoned during this period were the theory of the four humors, which accounted for illnesses through the disequilibrium of the emotions, and the concept of macrocosm and microcosm, in which it was thought that the same pattern of forces promoting physical harmony was reproduced at all levels of the universe, from the largest to the smallest. While one still finds pseudo-scientific schemes of this kind on the fringes of theories about healing, they have no relevance to serious research in mind-body relationships, which is based on experimentation.

It would be more accurate to say that, to the degree that mind-body procedures have Western roots in medicine, they fall into a branch of learning that historians of religion broadly call "spirituality." The term and the discipline it represents are largely modern in conceptualization. The noun "spirituality" is not found in English before 1500, and its Latin predecessor, *spiritualitas*, is a relatively late invention in the ancient world, which is first used by Pelagius in the early fifth century.[37] Later usage depended largely on context; for instance, in the phrase "spiritual healing," which is often used by Christian authors to refer to the acts of anointing or the laying on of hands.

During the Middle Ages and afterward, the word was frequently employed in a manner that suggested a close connection with reading and meditative practices. One of the important figures in this tradition was Ignatius of Loyola, whose *Spiritual Exercises* recommended a combination of sensory impressions, creations of the imagination, theological studies, and the exertion of the will as a way of conquering the passions and seeking a pathway to the interior life and to God. In keeping with this tradition, the term "spiritual" is sometimes employed in the literature on mind-body medicine as a synonym for "'internal."

This is a style of spirituality that goes back to the ancient literature on the subject, in which Latin authors sometimes see *spiritualis* as a translation of the Greek *pneumatikon*, referring to breathing; the usage survives in Tertullian and Augustine, and is based on the translation and interpretation of phrases concerning *pneuma* in the Pauline epistles.[38] Anyone who enters the field of Western spirituality is bound to be struck by the frequency with which the mind-body theme reappears over the centuries. From antiquity to the present, people at all levels of society have had a continuing interest in this dimension of the meditative or contemplative life. In the Latin West, heresies, schisms, charismatic movements, and theological schools come and go with regularity, but an interest in the fundamentals of the spiritual life is reasserted in every period.

This thinking has ancient roots in the history of asceticism. Isocrates said that the training or exercise that pertains to philosophy (*philosophias askesis*) is for the soul what medical attention is for the body.[39] Xenophon compared the disciplined methods of *hoi asketai*, the war-hardened soldiers, with the amateur approach of *hoi idiotai*, the inexperienced in battle.[40] Plato, followed by the Sophists, used *askesis* as a synonym for *melete*,[41] which was (sometimes) translated into Latin by *meditatio*. Stoics, Cynics, and Epicureans situated ascetic exercises within the practices of their respective schools: to pursue mind-body equilibrium, as a preparation for the pursuit of wisdom, was to become a member of this type of "textual community," that is, a group of people from diverse backgrounds who altered significant details of behavior in response to a scenario, a plan of living, or a set of principles.

Contributions to ascetic and spiritual thinking subsequently came from a number of different directions. It was through a Jewish thinker writing in Greek, namely Philo of Alexandria, that the Christian church fathers acquired a vocabulary for describing self-improvement by means of disciplined meditative exercises that involved the reading of scripture. In *De Vita Contemplativa*, Philo wrote an account of an ideal community, the Essenes, in which the Christian use of such exercises is anticipated, even though his writings on the subject do not appear to have influenced early Christian monasticism. Among Latin authors, *exercitium* or *exercitatio* was gradually adopted as a translation of Greek *askesis*, as a way of speaking about this dimension of mind-body relations, although neither term occurs frequently in the Septuagint, Old Latin, or Vulgate translations. In philosophy, Seneca and Marcus Aurelius utilized readings as spiritual exercises for changing long-standing habits and correcting emotions. Seneca recommended the compilation of pithy statements that could be carried about, memorized, and rehearsed as a kind of "medicine" for the soul. Among Christian readers, the routines of asceticism became familiar through such works as the *Historia Monachorum*, where reference is made to *monachorum exercitia, exercitia spiritualia,* and *spiritualis vitae exercitia* in the context of fasts and vigils.[42] Cassian spoke of *exercitia virtutum*; others used such terms as *studium, exercitium, spiritualia studia, virtutum studia,* and *salutaria studia.* Isidore of Seville quoted Servius's maxim: "Exercitium est meditatio"[43] (Exercise is meditation or reflective thought). During the medieval revival of spiritual thinking, many monastic authors shared the opinion of Peter the Venerable, who quoted 1 Timothy 4:7–8 to support the view that prayer, reading, and psalmody had greater value in preparing for salvation than exercises involving the body.

Judaism played an important if sometimes unacknowledged role in the formation of medieval Christian methods of meditation.[44] In contrast to ancient philosophy, in which the link between reading, meditation, and ethics was a late development, the Jewish tradition incorporated the relationship from the beginning. In the Hebrew Bible, the idea of meditation is expressed by terms derived from the root *haga,* as mentioned in Chapter 1, meaning to murmur in a low voice; this was translated into Greek by *meletan/melete* and into Latin by *meditari/meditatio.*[45] The auditory or corporeal element in meditation was associated with a spiritual or mental constituent, for example in Joshua 1:8: "Let the scroll of this law always be on your lips: meditate on it day and night in order to be ready to act in accord with what is written." Meditation led the believer to govern his or her life by means of the law, including rules relating to health. The same sense of rigorous adherence is found in Psalm 1:2, frequently quoted by Christian writers: "Happy . . . is he who murmurs/meditates the law of the Lord day and night." The translation of the Hebrew term by *meditari* expanded the range of meaning of the original. In a comparable manner, the Greek verb *meletan* meant to take care of, to watch over, or to take to heart. The notion of an exercise involving routine physical activity and reiterated mental activity reappeared in the *Benedictine Rule,* as noted, in which reference is made to students and monks who are engaged in the exercise of reciting the Psalms (c. 8.3). The term was frequently used to refer to the devotional life of the community as a whole (c. 58.5), which differed from its ancient predecessors in that its foundational writings were explicit and accessible to all members.

* * *

Earlier in this volume I noted that the history of spirituality after Augustine, Benedict, and Gregory the Great is commonly divided into two types of reading, *lectio divina* and *lectio spiritualis.* By way of conclusion, I would now

like to extend the discussion into a later period of time and to say a little
about the therapeutic implications of these styles of reading. In addition to
these categories, it is also possible to speak in this context of a phenomenon
called *lectio saecularis*: this refers to writings on the subject composed by lay
persons, dealing with religious topics, as well as the nonreligious contemplative practices accompanying the premodern reflective study of literature.

As I have mentioned, these lay and religious styles of reading have much
in common in the late medieval and early modern periods, and their chronological boundaries frequently overlap. *Lectio divina* has been practiced without
interruption from the patristic period to the present. The early stages of *lectio
spiritualis* are found in such authors as Augustine, Evagrius Ponticus, and John
Cassian, who prepare the way for the full development of this technique of
reading in the twelfth century. In the fourteenth century a formal distinction
is made between *lectio divina* and *lectio spiritualis*. However, during the thirteenth century traditions in *lectio spiritualis* are already popular in the mendicant orders, for example, figures like the Franciscan David of Augsburg and
the Dominican Humbert of Romans, who died respectively in 1272 and 1277.

For ancient authors, *clara lectio* (reading aloud) was a type of physical
exercise, like walking or running, which was recommended as a treatment for
illnesses by Cornelius Celsus as early as 30 A.D.[46] In adapting oral reading to
the needs of monastic communities, Benedict of Nursia added the psychological
benefit of reflective silence, however, chiefly in order to prevent disturbances
during periods of oral reading.[47] Building on this heritage, later monastic authors deepened the notion of silence in a manner in which it no longer referred
to the absence of noise but rather to the presence of an inner spiritual quality
that was allied with the meditative experience of *lectio divina* and *lectio spiritualis*.

The two processes, reading and meditation, functioned together. Reading
proceeded from the outside, through the sense of hearing, into the interior of
the mind, while meditation, originating in the mind, proceeded toward outer
expression in prayer, liturgy, or oral reading. Under the influence of medieval
liturgical and devotional practices, the periods of silence associated with
meditation and the interior life of the mind increased in length in many religious
communities, such as the Cluniacs and Cistercians, and these were linked in
turn to the benefits of solitude and the exploration of subjective states of mind.
As this type of reading and meditation evolved, the ancient Socratic program
of questions and answers, which had, before Augustine, been devoted to the
exploration of philosophical questions, became, partly under Augustinian
influence, a series of inquiries into relations between mind and body.

By contrast with this type of meditation, *lectio spiritualis* typically relied on a combination of reading, writing, and mental images. The synthesis of these elements is well represented by the practices of the Brethren of the Common Life, who lived together as a confraternity near the monastery of the regular Augustinian canons at Windersheim and started a school at Deventer, where Erasmus studied between 1475 and 1484. Johann Huizinga sums up their interest in education and spirituality by noting that it

> was rather a matter of sentiment and practice than of definite
> doctrine. . . . Sincerity and modesty, simplicity, industry, and above
> all constant ardour of religious emotion and thought, were its
> objects. Its energies were devoted to tending the sick and other
> works of charity, but especially to instruction in the art of writing.
> [The brethren] exerted their crowning activities in the seclusion of
> the schoolroom and the silence of the writing cell.[48]

This was a new style of meditation, in which there was a union of the activities of reading and writing, since the writing that emerged was the by-product of devotional reading, with which it was inseparably conjoined in the subject's mind. Also, the *mentis exercitatio*, as Gerard Groote called it, utilized, in addition to reading, a combination of internal words and images. These consisted in the mental recreation of the narrative of Christ's life; this was the subject of the students' devotions, along with the lives of the saints and selected writings of the church fathers.

Groote wrote at the end of a development of some two centuries that witnessed a great increase in the use of images in the religious life based on physical exemplars, that is, on paintings, sculptures, and manuscript illustrations; accompanying this was a revival of the ancient habit of recreating visual imagery from verbal descriptions, which became popular after the Fourth Lateran Council of 1215. Transferred to a largely unlettered public through mendicant preaching, biblical writings were thus recreated as a set of instructive narratives without first passing through the reading process. Physical images were often employed as an aid to preaching, the combination resulting in the creation of secondary mental images, based on both former words and images, in the minds of the listeners. Through Latin and vernacular preaching, biblical narratives and hagiographical cycles were thus incorporated into local liturgies, with the result that healing images, some of them taking as subject Christ's miracles, became accessible to large numbers of people. The emphasis on internal images in popular religious culture may have been one of the sources of opposition to the emotional qualities of external religious images that reappeared with Protestantism.

Between the twelfth and fourteenth centuries, a number of tendencies developed within the practice of *lectio spiritualis*. First of all, there was a literary development, which produced a recognizable set of genres and distinctive commentaries, as well as a gradual intellectualization of the process of reading and meditation, in which emphasis was placed on mental activity involving *rationes*, *imagines*, and internal narratives, as well as an on interest in the subjective, personal, or autobiographical element of the author's life, which became, under Augustinian influence, a point of departure for therapeutic meditation. There was also a process of synthesis and systematization, as reflected in treatises on meditation and manuals of meditative technique, and through them, a transformation of institutional affiliations, such as those in monasticism, permitting authors of meditative works to speak not as members of a group but with individual voices. Their numbers included religious, as well as lay persons and many women; as a result, spirituality was given a gendered context.[49] Furthermore, within such reading communities, a distinction was increasingly made between *lectio divina* and *lectio spiritualis* as interrelated approaches to spiritual healing: the one was built on the relationship between sound and silence, the other on the internal coherence of words, images, and narratives, leading in time to the appearance of *lectio saecularis*.

Finally, let us recall that in the early modern period meditative and nonmeditative readers approached the text in different ways. If the goal was meditation, then reading was considered to be a means to an end, and if ethical questions arose during the reading process, the answers were to be sought during a period of post-reading meditation, not during the reading itself. On the other hand, if the goal was the understanding of the text, then the reading was an end in itself; there was no post-reading, cognitive experience, except that which pertained to the explication of the text. If ethical questions arose, the answers had to grow out of the acquaintance and re-acquaintance with the text; through its rereading, and from the search for meaning within a philological framework, which could of course continue after the text was put down. These differing configurations of the reading process, the one subjective, the other largely objective, were conceptualized at a time when reading was ceasing to be a mind-body exercise and beginning to become a philological discipline. In order to establish empirical, observational, and philologically defensible standards in interpretation, humanist readers, following the suggestions of Petrarch, had to assume that reading was an independent activity. Humanists were no less concerned with the care of the soul than the ancient and medieval thinkers who preceded them. But it was difficult for them to combine the two objectives in the same activity, since one was clearly a part of a philological agenda, while the other was not. As a consequence, the certainty of the premodern reader, who knew that the solution to ethical problems lay outside the reading process, was replaced by the uncertainty of the early modern reader, who was committed to finding ethical values within the autonomous world of reading and interpretation.

Clinical Narrative

One of the most instructive ways to understand the medical dimension of these developments is through narrative and its associations in the premodern age. A useful point of departure for such an inquiry is Thomas Merton's observation that "meditation has no point and no reality unless it is firmly rooted in *life*."[50]

At a practical level, mind-body treatments involving meditation that arise in a literary context, such as writing a diary, a journal, or a record of treatment for disease, frequently explore the themes of rootedness, authenticity, and spiritual values through the concept of a healing journey. This process, sometimes called "journaling," attempts to create a personal awareness of the ways in which specific events can be used to present a harmonious narrative view of life as a whole. Alastair Cunningham divides this journey into three stages: (1) "taking control," which means "learning what can be done to have some control over the way in which we react, mentally and physically, to our environment"; (2) "getting connected," which implies that "the process of self-understanding has now become of value in and for itself"; and (3) the "search for meaning," which "seems to evolve naturally from a growing realization that we are not separate entities, but are part of a larger social, natural, and spiritual world."[51]

An interesting feature of this type of self-reporting is that historians are able to put rough chronological dates around its appearance, development, and even its application to early mind-body therapy. Unlike some treatments in alternative medicine, such as yoga, *quigong*, therapeutic touch, and music therapy, which have little connection with reading, writing, or other literary pursuits, the therapeutic uses of confessional, autobiographical, and self-reflective literature can be situated historically in late antiquity. They emerged at the time when meditation was becoming an aspect of sacred reading practices: personal accounts of healing experiences were, so to speak, one of the literary by-products of this connection. The appearance of a specific autobiographical genre is associated with Augustine's *Confessions*, written between 397 and 400 A.D., but the broader relationship between healing and personal spiritual development is touched upon by a variety of Christian writers, who gradually evolved a distinctive approach within late ancient theories of healing.

In such writing an alternative is proposed to the purely naturalistic interpretation of disease; this consists in distinguishing between the *cause* of an illness and its *meaning*.[52] The cause is considered to be natural, but the meaning is cultural and perhaps religious, if one believes, like many ancient Christians, that disease is associated with sin. The cause of a disease can be understood through the analysis of material or physical conditions, but the meaning, however it is conceived, has to be taken up by means of thought and language. In Christianity, this understanding begins with the healing framework for human thought, namely the Word of God. There are numerous discussions of the connection between the classical "therapy of the word" and the Christian dispensation of the Word.

It was here that narrative played a role. This began with Jesus' miracles, which were invariably related as episodes in his life story. It was through the different versions of this story, each embellished with the transcriber's interpretation of his healing powers, that the figure of *Christus medicus* emerged in patristic literature and was passed to later generations of believers.[53] For most Christians in late antiquity, the establishing of a narrative tradition meant that in the end it was not Jesus' words that healed but his words as they were transmitted by a composite work of literature, namely the synoptic Gospels. The entire narrative was considered to be a source of "health" (*salus*), or, as Clement of Alexandria put it, "gentle medicine."

The words of the literary interpretation, which were frequently spoken aloud to interested parties, were thus connected with the notion of healing through the actually spoken words of Christ. The two formed a single hermeneutic program within the healing experience. This could be transmitted to other lives, for example, to those of saints, pious religious, and holy healers, provided that they illustrated the same type of relationship between healing and meaning as the original. A tradition was built up in which the connection between mind and body could be thought about as a literary and conceptual matter, even though questions of health and disease might be taken up concurrently in naturalistic terms, as they were in Hellenistic and late ancient physical medicine. The authoritative narrative of Christ's life and its associated commentaries became the central subject of both religious healing and religious meditation in the centuries that followed. If the accounts of witnesses are to be trusted, healing in this context was brought about by a combination of extrinsic and intrinsic means, that is, through outward forms of worship and through inner expressions of spirituality, the latter comprised chiefly of meditation and visualization.[54]

Philosophy was only a minor influence on such thinking during the apostolic age but grew considerably during the patristic period, as authors like Gregory of Nyssa, Origen, and Augustine attempted to write defenses of Christian teachings on the spiritual aspects of health and disease. A good example of this combination of healing, religion, and literary themes in Christian writing is found in Gregory of Nazianzus's conception of the Christian as priest and physician, which is presented in *Orations* 1, 3, and 6. The notion of healing likewise entered theology: an example is Jerome's translation of Exodus 15:26, in which God speaks of himself as *sanator*, healer, rather than as a Greek or Latin physician, *medicus*.

Christian authors adopted guided visual imagery as a mind-body treatment for disease under the influence of images that were found in the Hebrew Bible. External images were rejected in Judaism, as a form of idolatry, but internal images are found throughout the Bible, particularly in the prophetic books that were read carefully by the Christian fathers for the light that they might shed on the divinely inspired foreshadowing of the incarnation. The vivid images in these writings were frequently recommended by patristic writers as an internal focus of attention for their readers, who might thereby initiate meditation on Christian themes and even bring about a reaffirmation of their faith through conversion, which was itself viewed as a healing activity.

Old Testament images were freely reinterpreted in this process, for example, in Ambrose's extravagant allegories on the book of Genesis, which were heard by the enthusiastic Augustine in Milan in the spring of 386. If the spiritual sense of Ambrose's sermons was to be made a part of a personal healing journey, as Augustine observed at *Confessions* 6.4.6, this freedom of interpretation had to be understood as a stage of spiritual therapy, and as a response to what was interpreted as purely physical imagery in Manichaeism. Through such adaptations of Jewish themes, the Christian concept of meaning in illness came to imply that there was a literary, narrative, and metaphorical context for the notion of healing that combined God's transcendent power with the immanent force of meditative visualization. These diverse approaches to the problem of meaning in narratives of health and disease inevitably gave rise to conflicting opinions about what healing meant. Christian writers assumed that it was Christ who healed, but this led to the pagan retort that Christianity was an inferior religion designed for only the sick and infirm—an idea that had a long life, turning up, little modified, in Nietzsche. Yet, behind Christian rhetoric about the advantages of spiritual healing, and the need for mercy and humility in dealing with suffering, there was a reliance both on miraculous interventions and on skillful mediation between healers and the communities they served, in which the gap between naturalistic and spiritualistic medicine was frequently a subject of negotiation, as were, in another context, the canonical procedures for sainthood.[55]

As illustrations of this point, I offer two brief examples, one pagan, the other Christian. The first is taken from the life of Proclus (d. 485 A.D.) by his student, Marinus of Samaria.[56] Marinus gives evidence of being acquainted with Christian hagiographical writing; accordingly, Proclus is portrayed as an ascetic, who, along the lines of St. Antony, renounces wealth and seeks spiritual values within a quasi-religious way of life. He was allegedly converted to the practice of philosophy in a series of dreams. In the first, Athena appeared before him, inspiring him to a life of celibacy, contemplation, and the cult of the gods. He was subsequently visited in sleep by Telesphorus, the child god associated with the cult of Asclepius, who cured him of illness by touching his forehead. The philosopher afterward enjoyed some seventy-five years of uninterrupted health.

When he was expelled from Athens for a year by the zealous Christians who had taken control of the city (c. 15), he responded in a manner which they would have recognized as being close to their own traditions. This consisted in fasts, singing of hymns, recitations of devotional prayers, and extended periods of silent meditation. Through the continual practice of spiritual exercises (cc. 21, 24), Marinus notes, he acquired the habit of focusing his attention uniquely on the state of his mind or soul, which, thus nourished, progressed, despite being imprisoned in his body. He gave a dramatic demonstration of his healing powers in restoring the health of a young girl, Asklepigenia, who had been pronounced untreatable by her physicians, by praying continually at the temple of Asclepius, which Christians had fortunately not destroyed (c. 29). In a significant addendum to this event, Marinus notes that prayer likewise prevented Proclus from later contracting arthritis, which had crippled his father (c. 31). This may be the first account of the reversal of a hereditary disease by means of a mind-body technique.

The other example of mind-body arbitrage that I wish to bring forward is from the life of Theodore of Sykeon, who died in 613 A.D.[57] One would be tempted to say that Theodore came to spiritual healing by an indirect route, since his mother was an innkeeper, who earned extra cash by entertaining the guests, and his father a circus acrobat, whose specialty was performing riding tricks on camels. He was destined for the imperial service by his mother but was dissuaded from entering by St. George, who spoke to him in a dream. The family fortunes were subsequently improved by his mother, who hired a pious elderly cook called Stephen. Owing to the superior quality of the food, the inn at Sykeon made enough money for her to give up hostelry and procure a wealthy husband.

Despite his culinary expertise, Stephen advised the young Theodore not to profit from gastronomy, but instead to practice fasting and abstinence. Accordingly, Theodore entered the church and after ordination became a radical ascetic who lived for lengthy periods in a metal cage suspended above his cave at Arkea, a few kilometers from Sykeon, clad in a belt, collar, handcuffs, and breastplate of cast iron. He was renowned for his lengthy fasts, continual prayers, and miraculous cures, including the healing of the emperor's son, who was then suffering from elephantiasis. In his official *Life*, it is reported that he advised those suffering from illnesses to avoid doctors and to put their faith instead in prayers and blessings;[6] but he also prescribed medical remedies and, where necessary, recommended surgery, sometimes choosing the appropriate doctor himself. His career is thus one in which science is aided, but not superseded, by complementary medicine.

Numerous other biographies in late antiquity likewise anticipate uses for narrative that are found in contemporary mind-body medicine. A frequently mentioned topic, which has turned up in experiments in psychoneuroimmunology, is the progressive education of the emotions, particularly through internal narrative. Another is the sharing of feelings by means of the creation of a support community, a theme that is widely reflected in contemporary programs for coping with the symptoms of cancer and the effects of chemotherapy. Ancient hagiographers spoke about the role of improper stories in generating negative emotions, which is a persistent theme in Buddhism as well as in contemporary research in psychology. The emphasis on the behavioral consequences of narratives has permitted medical researchers to link certain types of emotion, for example, random hostility, with the onset of specific conditions, in this case cardiovascular disease. Still another type of narrative in ancient and medieval biographies deals with the emotional support that individuals can receive from fictional, imagined, or deceased communities. Experiments have shown that the body responds to the intense emotions created

by these communities of mind and memory as if they were living. There is also
the reshaping of personal narrative. Take a patient who suffers from mi-
graine. When the symptoms appear, he feels helpless because he thinks he is
soon to be incapacitated. His stress creates changes in blood flow that make
his symptoms worse than they otherwise might be. Can such a patient rewrite
this internal narrative? It would seem so, at least to some degree, by means of
guided visual imagery. In a comparable experiment, potential cardiac patients
who experienced high levels of hostility presented their feelings in personal
narratives, and their measurable output of adrenalin and cortisol was considerably reduced.

In the late ancient and medieval periods the source of this interest in the
interior, imagined, and fictional qualities of healing narratives was not medical but religious. Guibert of Nogent, a twelfth-century critic of the irrespon-
sible trust in miracles and relics, summed up the view of many earlier thinkers
when he connected successful spiritual healing to a combination of authenticated beliefs and disciplined inwardness. His statement was part of a widespread revival of interest in the interior life in which, in Giles Constable's
words, "there was a tendency . . . to interiorize and spiritualize all aspects of
monastic life and morality."[58] In this revival the notion of healing crept into
numerous literary genres, for example, secular allegory. The habit of writing
healing allegories was taken over during the Middle Ages from later ancient
Neoplatonic writers like Prudentius, Apuleius, and Boethius, in whom it already had a strongly psychological orientation. This was adapted to different
ends during the Middle Ages by making the central characters personifications of both positive and negative passions. In the *De Planctu Naturae* and
the *Anticlaudianus*, two learned but widely studied works in this tradition,
Alan of Lille dramatized virtues, vices, and emotions in a manner that permits the reader to visualize thoughts and to follow them step by step as they
develop toward good or bad intentions. In contemporary mind-body healing,
a comparable method is employed in meditative journaling and narrative writing, in which diseases like cancer are pictured, in order to distance patients
from symptoms and thereby to visualize physical changes that may bring about
improvement.

*   *   *

What can we conclude? First of all, if the evidence of late antiquity and the
Middle Ages is taken into consideration, it would appear that the received

interpretation of historical relations between spiritual and naturalistic healing over the centuries is in need of revision. These relations are often presented
as conflictual, but by and large they are cooperative.

Second, we must take into account in evaluating the mind-body field that
the major tradition of medicine in the West since Hippocrates has been naturalistic. It is only minor traditions that have been concerned with mind-body
factors in disease. Even before the rise of biological medicine, there was no
period in which mind-body healing was preferred to standard medical practices.
On the other hand, it also has to be observed that the triumph of biological
medicine was not as swift or thorough as has been imagined. Mind-body factors
continued to be taken seriously as late as 1871, when Sir Thomas Watson
observed that "mental stress [was] influential in hastening the development
of cancerous disease in persons already predisposed."[59] What is new in contemporary mind-body medicine is the unwillingness to accept such statements
uncritically, without experimental corroboration.

The fact that spiritual and naturalistic medicine enjoyed a mutually beneficial relationship in the past is a clue to another distinctive feature of the
Western handling of mind-body issues. In contrast to Eastern religions, where
purely contemplative traditions are not unusual, the typical ancient and medieval situation in the West is an alternation of contemplative and noncontem-
plative traditions (or, as some would prefer, nonrationalistic and rationalistic).
In later ancient and medieval thought in the West, mysticism and rationalism
are pictured as rivals: however, in the fields of healing and religion, they were
often good neighbors. In the past, as nowadays, mind-body healing can be
divided into two parts. In the one, healing is concerned with specific illnesses;
in the other, it has to do with a general philosophy of life. The philosophical
inquiries form part of a lengthy discussion, which has been undergoing development since antiquity. In my view, this conversation will continue well after
the scientific questions are settled because the inspiration for this part of the
debate is not scientific, and because the answers to the questions that are being
raised are not scientific either. They are cultural and religious.

We have an accepted method for testing the scientific results in the mind-
body medical field. But we do not have a method for examining the ethical
dimension of the subject, as ancient and medieval thinkers did, through
contemplative practice itself. With the abandonment of meditation in early
modern sacred reading, it became difficult, if not impossible, to make ethical decisions as the ancients did, and, in the present climate in literary studies, it is doubtful that those methods will soon enter curricula again. As long as

reading practices incorporated meditation, they were in contact with a spiritual exercise by which philosophers and theologians for centuries related mind and body. These exercises demanded an ascetic commitment, not an intellectual orientation: the individual seeking an answer to questions concerning a philosophy of life engaged in a series of tasks that were designed to separate himself or herself from the material, the sensorial, and the circumstantial, as a first step in attaining the detachment that was necessary for achieving valid self-knowledge. By contrast, in analytical reading this possibility was greatly reduced in scope. One could advance with some degree of certainty toward the meaning of the text, but one could not advance at the same time or by the same methods toward knowledge about oneself. Literary studies, which had been strongly associated with ethics in the ancient and medieval periods, gradually abandoned the view that ethics and literature could be meaningfully connected through inquiries involving the individual's inner spiritual life. In view of this situation, it is not at all surprising that patients in clinics and hospitals are discovering the spiritual dimension of their lives quite outside the traditional study of literature, theology, or academic religion.

Finally, in comparison with ancient attitudes on this subject, the contemporary experience is different in at least one respect. This concerns the time of life at which the fundamental questions are asked. In mind-body medicine, spiritual questions are only posed at a moment of grave crisis. The assumption in mind-body clinics that utilize meditation is that the patient arrives, so to speak, spiritually bankrupt: he or she is thought to have no resources to fall back upon; these have to be generated from within the clinical environment. By contrast, in the ancient view, whether among pagans, Jews, or Christians, the journey of life was conceived to be a preparation for the moment when such resources were needed: these were like a small capital sum that had been put aside for a period of economic turbulence, which, if unused, might continue to accrue interest. If that capital is missing, mind-body medicine can only supply it in the short term. Our society has not yet relearned what the ancients knew, namely, that the time to prepare oneself for a crisis is not the moment when the crisis takes place: then it may be too late.

NOTES

INTRODUCTION

1. See Christopher Gill, *The Structured Self in Hellenistic and Roman Thought* (Oxford: Oxford University Press, 2006), 3–73.

2. Heinrich von Staden, "Body, Soul, and Nerves: Epicurus, Herophilus, Erasistratus, the Stoics, and Galen," in *Psyche and Soma: Physicians and Metaphysicians on the Mind-Body Problem from Antiquity to the Enlightenment*, ed. John P. Wright and Paul Potter (Oxford: Clarendon, 2000), 116.

3. See A. A. Long, "Socrates in Hellenistic Philosophy," in Long, *Stoic Studies* (Cambridge: Cambridge University Press, 1996), 1–34; Long, "The Socratic Legacy," in *The Cambridge History of Hellenistic Philosophy*, ed. Keimpe A. Algra, Jonathan Barnes, Jaap Mansfeld, and Malcolm Schofield (Cambridge: Cambridge University Press, 1999), 617–41; also Long, *Epictetus: A Stoic and Socratic Guide to Life* (Oxford: Oxford University Press, 2002). For a detailed study, see Francesca Alesse, *La Stoa e la tradizione socratica*, Elenchos, Collana di testi e studi sul pensiero antico 30 (Naples: Bibliopolis, 2000).

4. Gill, *The Structured Self*, xix.

5. On Augustine's opposition to tenets of Epicureanism; see *Conf.*, 6.16.26 (the soul); *De Civitate Dei* 5.20 (pleasure); 8.5 (atomism); 11.5 (cosmology); 14.2 (ethics); 8.7 (epistemology). His chief source of the school's doctrines is Varro, *De Civ.Dei* 6.5. The problem of Stoic influences on Augustine's philosophical education is more difficult to resolve; see Gérard Verbeke, "Augustin et le stoicisme," *Recherches Augustiniennes* 1 (1958): 67–89; Charles Baguette, "Une période stoicienne dans la formation de saint Augustin," *Revue des Études Augustiniennes* 16 (1970): 47–77; and Michel Spanneut, "Le stoicisme et saint Augustin," in *Forma futuri: Studi in onore del cardinale Michele Pellegrino* (Turin: Bottega d'Erasmo, 1975), 796–805.

6. On this topic, see G. R. Boys-Stones, *Post-Hellenic Philosophy: A Study of Its Development from the Stoics to Origen* (Oxford: Oxford University Press, 2001).

7. *Conf.*, 7.9.13; on the scholarly questions raised by this collection, see Goulven Madec, *Saint Augustin et la philosophie* (Paris: Institut d'Études Augustiniennes, 1996), 37–44.

8. *De Civitate Dei* 11.1.

9. *Conf.*, 9.10.23–26.

10. Charles Taylor, *Sources of the Self: The Making of the Modern Identity* (Cambridge, Mass.: Harvard University Press, 1989); also in the analytical tradition see Sydney Shoemaker, *Self-Knowledge and Self-Identity* (Ithaca, N.Y.: Cornell University Press, 1963), Marya Schechtman, *The Constitution of Selves* (Ithaca, N.Y.: Cornell University Press, 1996), and Richard Swinburne, "How to determine which is the true theory of personal identity," in

Personal Identity: Complex or Simple?, ed. Georg Gasser and Mattias Stefan (Cambridge: Cambridge University Press, 2012), 105–22.

11. I say elusive because there is no Greek or Latin term for the self; for an introduction to this subject as well as broader questions concerning the self in ancient thought, see the authoritative statement of Richard Sorabji, *Self: Ancient and Modern Insights About Individuality, Life, and Death* (Oxford: Clarendon, 2006), 17–22, 30–31, and 48–53; on the notion of the self in Stoic and Epicurean sources, see the thoughtful remarks of Gill, *The Structured Self*, xiv–xx, 326–407; on Augustine's relationship to this tradition, a useful early synthesis is Max Zepf, "Augustinus und das philosophische Selbstbewusstsein der Antike," *Zeitschrift für Religions- und Geistesgeschichte* 11, 2 (1959): 105–32. On the widely acknowledged contribution to his thinking about the self by Plotinus, see Paulina Remes, *Plotinus on Self: The Philosophy of the "We"* (Cambridge: Cambridge University Press, 2007), 1–20.

12. These have been the subject of numerous studies, among which are the classic essay of M.-D. Chenu, "La nature et l'homme: La renaissance du XIIe siècle," in *La théologie au douzième siècle* (Paris: J. Vrin, 1957), 19–51. Later syntheses include Colin Morris, *The Discovery of the Individual* (London: SPCK, 1972) and Robert W. Hanning, *The Individual in Twelfth-Century Romance* (New Haven, Conn.: Yale University Press, 1977). No attempt can be made here to recapitulate the now abundant literature in the field. Among review essays see John F. Benton, "Consciousness of Self and Perceptions of Individuality," in *Renaissance and Renewal in the Twelfth Century*, ed. Robert L. Benson and Giles Constable (Cambridge, Mass.: Harvard University Press, 1982), 263–95, and Caroline Walker Bynum, "Did the Twelfth Century Discover the Individual," in *Jesus as Mother: Studies in the Spirituality of the High Middle Ages* (Berkeley: University of California Press, 1982), 83–109. On relations between self and textual experience, see Sarah Spence, *Texts and the Self in the Twelfth Century* (Cambridge: Cambridge University Press, 2006); on theological approaches, see the innovative study of Susan R. Kramer, *Sin, Interiority, and Selfhood in the Twelfth-Century West* (Toronto: Pontifical Institute of Mediaeval Studies, 2015).

13. See Christopher Gill, *Personality in Greek Epic, Tragedy, and Philosophy: The Self in Dialogue* (Oxford: Oxford University Press, 1996).

14. Ernst Robert Curtius, *European Literature and the Latin Middle Ages*, trans. Willard R. Trask, Bollinger Series 36 (New York: Pantheon, 1953), 64–78.

15. For a review of the issues in a post-ancient context, see William Robins, "The Study of Medieval Italian Textual Culture," in Robins, ed., *The Textual Culture of Italy* (Toronto: University of Toronto Press, 2011), 11–49.

16. See the classic essay "Sermo Humilis" in Erich Auerbach, *Literary Language and Its Public in Late Latin Antiquity and in the Middle Ages*, trans. Ralph Manheim, Bollingen Series 74 (Princeton, N.J.: Princeton University Press, 1965), 25–81.

17. For an introduction, see Pierre Hadot, "Spiritual Exercises," in *Philosophy as a Way of Life*, ed. and intro. Arnold I. Davidson (Oxford: Blackwell, 1995), 82–125.

18. Jerome, *Ep.* 112; Augustine, *Epp.* 28, 71, and 72.

19. See Pierre Hadot, "Les *Libri Platonicorum*," in *Marius Victorinus: Recherches sur sa vie et ses oeuvres* (Paris: Études Augustiniennes, 1971), 201–10; Madec, *Saint Augustin et la philosophie*, 37–44.

20. *Conf.*, 1.14.23. The difficulty may have arisen in part from the fact that Augustine was already bilingual; he was presumably able to speak Punic with his mother, who was Berber in origin, as well as Latin with his father, who was Roman.

21. There are indications that Augustine had some knowledge of Seneca, for example, at *De Civitate Dei* 6.11, where he reports Seneca's negative observations on the Jews of Rome; see Romano Penna, "The Jews of Rome in the Time of the Apostle Paul," in *Paul the Apostle: Jew and Greek Alike: A Theological and Exegetical Study*, trans. Thomas P. Wahl (Collegeville, Minn.: Liturgical Press, 1996), 23 and note 13. However, there are no direct quotations from Seneca in Augustine's statements on reading, writing, and the self. This suggests that Augustine cannot be linked by means of precise Latin sources to the lengthy discussion of 'the scripted self' in Hellenistic thought to which attention was drawn by Michel Foucault in 1983; see "L'écriture de soi," *Corps Écrit* 5 (1983): 3–23, *Histoire de la sexualité*, vol. 3 (Paris: Gallimard, 1984), and *L'herméneutique du sujet: Cours au Collège de France (1982–1983)* (Paris: Gallimard, 2001). On the subsequent discussion of this theme in Seneca's writings, see the essays of Christopher Gill, Brad Inwood, and Anthony Long in *Seneca and the Self*, ed., Shadi Bartsch and David Wray (Cambridge: Cambridge University Press, 2009); James Bernauer and Michael Mahon, "The Ethics of Michel Foucault," in *The Cambridge Companion to Michel Foucault*, ed., Gary Gutting (Cambridge: Cambridge University Press, 1994), 141–58; and Arnold Davidson, "Ethics as Ascetics," ibid., 115–40.

22. For a specific example, see Margaret R. Graver, "Honeybee Reading and Self-Scripting: *Epistulae Morales* 84," in *Seneca Philosophus*, ed. Jula Wildberger and Marcia L. Colish (Berlin: de Gruyter, 2104), 269–93, in which a distinction is made between the ethical notion of selfhood in the letters and Seneca's fictional presentation of himself.

23. For a development of this theme, see Jula Wildberger, "The Epicurus Trope and the Construction of the 'Letter Writer' in Seneca's *Epistulae Morales*," in *Seneca Philosphus*, 432–65.

24. David Konstan, "The Active Reader in Classical Antiquity," *Argos* 30 (2006): 10.

25. On this topic, see Ilsetraut Hadot, "The Spiritual Guide," in *Classical Mediterranean Spirituality: Egyptian, Greek, and Roman*, ed. A. H. Armstrong (London: SCM Press, 1986), 436–59.

26. See H.-I. Marrou, *Saint Augustin et la fin de la culture antique*, 4th ed. (Paris: Boccard, 1958), 297–337.

27. Plutarch appears convinced that the speech of Lysias in *Phaedrus* 230e ff. was genuine and not a discourse concocted by Plato; however, that assumption does not greatly weaken his argument, since the point he is making is about Nicander's recreation of a speech, not whether it is the speaker's own words.

28. *Epistulae Morales* 8.6.

29. *Convivio*, 1.2.12–13.

30. *De Brevitate Vitae* 10.2–6.

31. Sorabji, *Self: Ancient and Modern Insights About Individuality, Life and Death*, 172. On Epicurus, see Diogenes Laertius, *Vitae Philosophorum*, 10.22.

32. *De Brevitate Vitae* 10.2.

33. *Epistulae Morales*. 58. 22–23; trans. Oldfather (Loeb).

34. *Epp.* 4.1–2.

35. *Epp.* 1.1–3.

36. *Epp.* 4.9.

37. See Montaigne, "De la solitude," *Les essais*, livre 1, c. 39, ed. Pierre Villey (Paris: Presses Universitaires de France, 1965), 241.

38. *Conf.*, 11.27.35–38; on spiritual exercises in ancient philosophy, see the excellent introduction of Pierre Hadot, *Philosophy as a Way of Life*, 79–144.

39. As recognized by Paul Ricoeur, *Time and Narrative*, trans. David Pellauer (Chicago: University of Chicago Press, 1984), vol. 1, chap. 1.

40. For experimental evidence, see Raymond A. Mar, "The Neural Basis of Social Cognition and Story Comprehension," *Annual Review of Psychology* 62 (2011): 103–34.

41. *Ep.*, 80, *Patrologia Latina*, vol. 33, col. 274; my trans.

42. *Conf.*, 11.27.34–36.

43. Cf. Frederic Bartlett, *Remembering: A Study in Experimental and Social Psychology* (Cambridge: Cambridge University Press, 1932), 197; Mary Carruthers, *The Book of Memory: A Study in Medieval Culture* (Cambridge: Cambridge University Press, 1990).

44. The term is used by both Seneca and Quintilian; for a discussion of its hermeneutic expansion in Augustine, see Michael Fiedorowicz, "Enarrationes in Psalmos: B. Theologische Aspekte," in *Augustinus-Lexikon*, ed. C. Mayer et al., vol. 2 (Basel: Schwabe, 1996–2002), cols. 838–58.

45. David Hume, *A Treatise of Human Nature*, 1.4.6; ed. L. A. Selby-Riggs (Oxford: Oxford University Press, 1988), 252.

CHAPTER 1. READING WITH THE WHOLE SELF

1. E.g., *De Civ. Dei* 10.5–8.

2. E.g., *Contra Academicos* 3.13.37.

3. *Conf.*, 8.1.1; 8.3.6; 8.5.11, and especially 8.6.14–15, which describes the monastic communities founded by Ambrose of Milan.

4. On the general topic of sacred reading, or *lectio divina*, a good introduction and bibliography are found in Duncan Robertson, *Lectio Divina: The Medieval Experience of Reading* (Collegeville, Minn.: Liturgical Press, 2011); on the Augustinian tradition, see Franklin T. Harkins, *Reading and the Work of Restoration: History and Scripture in the Theology of Hugh of St. Victor* (Toronto: Pontifical Institute of Mediaeval Studies, 2009). An excellent overview is provided by Mary Carruthers, *The Craft of Thought: Meditation, Rhetoric, and the Making of Images, 400–1200* (Cambridge: Cambridge University Press, 1998). The earlier literature on sacred reading is reviewed in Jacques Rousse, "La *lectio divina*," in Rousse, "*Lectio divina* et lecture spirituelle," *Dictionnaire de spiritualité*, vol. 9 (1976), col. 470–87. Among foundational studies are Ursmer Berlière, *L'ascèse bénédictine des origines à la fin du 12e siècle* (Paris: de Brouwer, 1927); Henri de Lubac, *Exégèse médiévale: Les quatre sens de l'Écriture*, première partie, tome 2 (Paris: Aubier, 1959), 571–86 (Exégèse monastique); Jean Leclercq, *The Love of Learning and the Desire for God: A Study of Monastic Culture*, trans. Catharine Misrahi (New York: Mentor Omega Books, 1962); and Leclercq, *Aux sources de la spiritualité occidentale: Étapes et constants* (Paris: Éditions du Cerf, 1964). A more recent study of reading in relation to early Christian monastic life in both Eastern and Western communities with an appreciation of contemporary developments in criticism is Elizabeth A. Clark, *Reading Renunciation: Asceticism and Scripture in Early Christianity* (Princeton, N.J.: Princeton University Press, 1999), chaps. 3–6, pp. 45–152. For an outline of Augustine's views on the ascetic life, an excellent brief introduction is Henry Chadwick, "The Ascetic Ideal in the History of the Church," in *Monks, Hermits and the Ascetic Tradition*, ed. W. J. Shields (Oxford: Blackwell for the Ecclesiastical History Society, 1985), 1–23.

5. For an introduction, see Adalbert de Vogüé, *The Rule of Saint Benedict: A Doctrinal and Spiritual Commentary*, trans. J. B. Hasbrouk (Kalamazoo, Mich.: Cistercian Publications, 1983), 239–50.

6. Cuthbert Butler, *Benedictine Monachism: Studies in Benedictine Life and Rule* (London: Longmans, Green: 1919), 13. For a precise description of these traditions and their origins, see Antoine Guillaumont, "Monachisme et éthique judéo-chrétienne," in *Aux origines du monachisme chrétien*, Spiritualité Orientale 30, Bégrolle en Mauges (Maine et Loire: Abbaye de Bellefontaine, 1979), 201–18.

7. Owen Chadwick, *John Cassian*, 2nd ed. (Cambridge: Cambridge University Press, 1968), 14.

8. Cf. Chadwick, *John Cassian*, 85. For an introduction to the thought of Evagrius, see Antoine Guillaumont, "Un philosophe du desert: Evagre le Pontique," in *Aux origines du monachisme chrétien*, 185–212.

9. Jacques Rousse, "Lectio divina et lecture spirituelle," 470–71.

10. On which, let us note, the blessed Isaac is said to have discoursed at greater length (*copiosa*) than is reproduced in Cassian's *compte-rendu*; Jean Cassien, *Conférences*, ed. and trans. Dom E. Pichery, SC 42 (1955); here *Conlatio* 9.1, p. 40. I use this edition, including vol. 54 (1958), and 64 (1959). On the role of meditation in these prayers, see Antoine Guillaumont, "La Prière de Jésus chez les moines d'Égypte," in *Aux origines du monachisme chrétien*, 130–34.

11. *Coll* 9.2, vol. 54, p. 40: "Omnis monachi finis cordisque perfectio ad iugem atque indisruptam orationis perseuerantiam tendit."

12. 9.2, p. 40: "Et est inter alterutrum reciproca quaedam inseparabilisque coniunctio."

13. Cf. Lk. 14:28.

14. This is a rare, early monastic example of the rhetorical technique of *enargeia* (vivid description), which is discussed in Chapter 2.

15. *Coll.*, 9.3, p. 42, referring, respectively, to 1 Thess. 5:17 and 1 Tim. 2:8.

16. *Coll.*, 9.4, p. 43: "Etenim qualitas animae non inepte subtilissimae plumae seu pennae leuuissimae comparatur." The idea is elaborated in 9.5, pp. 43–45.

17. *Coll.*, 9.6, p. 45.

18. *Coll.*, 9.8, p. 48: "Secundum mensuram namque puritatis, in quam mens unaquaeque proficit et qualitatem status in quo uel ex accedentibus inclinatur uel per suam renouatur industriam, ipsae quoque momentis singulis reformantur."

19. Summarizing *Coll.*, 9.8, p. 49.

20. *Coll.*, 9.12, p. 50–51.

21. *Coll.*, 9.17, pp. 53–55.

22. *Coll.*, 9.26, p. 62: "Nonnumquam etenim psalmi cuiusque uersiculi occasionem orationis ignitae decantantibus nobis praebuit. Interdum canora fraternae uocis modulatio ad intentam supplicationem stupentium animos excitauit. Nouimus quoque distinctionem grauitatemque psallentis etiam adstantibus plurimum contulisse feruoris."

23. *Coll.*, 9.36, p. 72. The monks were not required to recite the psalter once a week, as instructed in the *Rule* of St. Benedict. The lack of this requirement accounts for the spontaneity of the numerous statements on the reading of the Psalms in the *Conferences*.

24. *Coll.*, 9.35, p. 71: "ut intrantes in cubiculum nostrum clauso ostio nostro oremus patrem nostrum" (Mt. 6:6).

25. *Coll.*, 9.35, p. 71: "Clauso oremus ostio, cum strictis labiis omnique silentio supplicamus non uocum sed cordium scrutatori."

26. *Coll.*, 9.35, p. 71 quoting Mt. 7:5: "Put no trust in a neighbour. . . ."

27. *De Institutis Coenobiorum de Incarnatione contra Nestorium* 2.10, 11; ed. Michael Petschenig and Gottfried Kreuz (CSEL 17, Vienna, 2004), 25–26.

28. *Coll.*, 10.8, vol. 54 (1958), 83: "ut primum nouerimus qua meditatione teneatur uel cogitetur deus."

29. *Coll.*, 10.11, p. 90: "Istam, istam mens indesinenter formulam teneat, donec usu eius incessabili et iugi meditatione firmata cunctarum cogitationum diuitias amplasque substantias abiciat et refutet."

30. Chadwick, *John Cassian*, 102.

31. *Coll.*, 10.11, p. 91: "Et ita quis per istiusmodi paupertatem egregius pauper exsistens illud propheticum inplebit eloquium."

32. *Coll.*, 10.11, p. 92: "Quorum iugi pascuo uegetatus omnes quoque psalmorum adfectus in se recipiens ita incipiet decantare, ut eos non tamquam a propheta conpositos, sed uelut a se editos quasi orationem propriam profunda cordis conpunctione depromat uel certe ad suam personam aestimet eos fuisse directos, eorumque sententias non nunc tantammodo per prophetam aut in propheta fuisse conpletas, sed in se cotidie geri inplerique cognoscat."

33. *Coll.*, 10.14, p. 95.

34. *Coll.*, 10.14, p. 96: "Constat igitur neminem prorsus ob inperitiam litterarum a perfectione cordis exclude nec rusticitatem obese ad capessendam cordis atque animae puritatem."

35. Cf. *Regula* 11.10: perlegere.

36. *Reg.* 38.7: "Si quid tamen opus fuerit, sonitu cuiuscumque signi potius petatur quam voce."

37. Is this because the *hospes*, if a layman, is assumed to be ignorant or illiterate?

38. E.g., Prov. 4:10; 4:20.

39. On the ear of the heart, see Augustine, *De Continentia* 1.1, CSEL 41.141.3–4.

40. Prol., 9–12; 33; e.g., Rev. 2:7; Ps. 34:12; Jn. 12:35.

41. Leclercq, *The Love of Learning and the Desire for God*, 24–25.

42. E.g., *Gorgias* 447a–449a.

43. *Coll.*, 1.2 and 1.4, vol. 1, p. 79.

44. *Coll.*, 1.17, vol. 1, pp. 99–110.

45. Leclercq, *The Love of Learning*, 25.

46. *Coll.*, 1.17, p. 99.

47. *Coll.*, 7.6, p. 253.

48. *Coll.*, 7.4, p. 248.

49. Ibid.

50. Ibid., p. 249.

51. *Coll.*, 7.5, p. 249; cf. 2 Cor. 10:4.

52. *Coll.*, 7.6, p. 253.

53. Prov. 28:19; cf. Prov. 14:23; 16:26.

54. *Coll.*, 7.21, p. 262.

55. Non perfectio sed perfectionis instrumenta sunt, p. 85.

56. *Coll.*, 9.2, vol. 2, pp. 40–41.

57. Ibid., p.40: "Ob quam omnem tam laborem corporis quam contritionem spiritus indefessa et iugiter exercemus."

CHAPTER 2. THE CONTEMPLATIVE IMAGINATION

1. *Orator*, 1.1, quoted in the edition of H. M. Hubbell, in Cicero, *Brutus Orator*, Loeb Classical Library (London: Heinemann, 1939): ". . . et suscipere tantam rem, quantam non modo facultate consequi difficile esset sed etiam cogitatione complecti."

2. *Orator*, 2.7; my trans.

3. *Orator*, 2.8: "Sed ego sic statuo, nihil esse in ullo genere tam pulchrum, quo non pulchrius id sit unde illud ut ex ore aliquo quasi imago exprimatur."

4. *Orator*, 3.9: "Ut igitur in formis et figuris est aliquid perfectum et excellens, cuius ad cogitatam speciem imitando referuntur ea quae sub oculos ipsa non cadunt . . . ."

5. *Institutio Oratoria* 6.1.7: "Necessarios tamen adfectus fatebuntur, si aliter obtineri vera et iusta et in commune profutura non possint."

6. The following summary is based on 6.2.8–6.2.18.

7. Quintilian adds that, for some, *pathos* is temporary, while *ethos* is continuous; however, some situations require *pathos* as an ongoing state of mind; 6.2.10.

8. *Inst. Orat.* 6.2.26: "Summa enim, quantum ego quidem sentio, circa movendos adfectus in hoc posita est, ut moveamur ipsi."

9. *Inst. Orat.*, 6.2.27: "Quare in iis, quae esse verisimilia volemus, simus ipsi similes eorum qui vere patiuntur adfectibus, et a tali animo proficiscatur oratio qualem facere iudicem volet."

10. *Inst. Orat.*, 6.2.28: "Primum igitur, ut apud nos valeant ea quae valere apud iudicem volumus, adficiamurque antequam adficere conemur."

11. *Inst. Orat.*, 6.2.29: "At quomodo fiet, ut adficiamur? Neque enim sunt motus in nostra potestate."

12. *Inst. Orat.*, 6.2.29–30: "Quas φαντασίας Graeci vocant, nos sane visiones appellemus, per quas imagines rerum absentium ita repraesentantur animo, ut eas cernere oculis ac praesentes habere videamur. Has quisquis bene conceperit, is erit in adfectibus potentissimus."

13. *Inst. Orat.*, 6.2.30: ". . . qui sibi res, voces, actus secundum verum optime finget."

14. *Inst. Orat.*, 6.2.32: "Insequitur ἐνάργεια quae a Cicerone illustratio et evidentia nominatur, quae non tam dicere videtur quam ostendere; et adfectus non aliter, quam si rebus ipsis inersimus, sequentur."

15. He is perhaps referring here to *Inst. Orat.*, 4.2.63–65, where *enargeia* forms part of the discussion of *narratio* and refers to the clarification of facts in a case. As later at 6.2.32, the chief influence is Cicero.

16. *Inst. Orat.*, 8.3.61: "Eius primi sunt gradus in eo quod velis concipiendo et exprimendo, tertius, qui haec nitidiora faciat, quod proprie dixeris cultum."

17. Two examples are given: Virgil, *Aeneid* 5.426 and Cicero, *Verrine Orations* 5.33.86.

18. *Phantasia in Classical Thought* (Galway: Galway University Press, 1988), 69.

19. *Inst. Orat.*, 12.1.

20. Henry Chadwick, *Saint Augustine. Confessions*, trans. with Intro. and notes (Oxford: Oxford University Press, 1991), 36n3.

21. Trans. Chadwick with minor modifications.

22. *Conf.*, 3.2.4; trans. Chadwick.

23. Pierre Courcelle, *Recherches sur les Confessions de saint Augustin*, 2nd ed. (Paris: E. de Boccard, 1950).

24. E.g., Courcelle, *Recherches*, 2nd ed., 47.

25. *Conf.*, 8.6.13: "Agebam solita crescente anxitudine. . . ."

26. For a comparable but more detailed account of this development, see my study, *Ethics Through Literature: Ascetic and Aesthetic Reading in Western Culture* (Hanover, N.H.: University Press of New England, 2007), 47–85.

27. *Conf.*, 5.1.1, 8–11: "Non cessat nec tacet laudes tuas universa creatura tua, nec spiritus omnis per os conuersum ad te nec animalia nec corporalia per os considerantium . . . ." trans. Chadwick.

28. Cf. Plotinus, *Enneads* 3.2.11.10 ff.

29. Plato, *Sophist* 260d–e.

30. Watson, *Phantasia*, xi.

31. Plotinus, *Enneads* 3.4.8, trans. Armstrong, slightly modified.

32. *Plotinus*, vol. 3, pp. 368–69, n. 1.

33. *Ep.* 3.3: "Certe sensibilis mundus nescio cuius intelligibilis imago esse dicitur."

34. As Augustine acknowledges, *Ep.* 4.1, written in 387. Augustine's notion of *phantasia* in his early letters and elsewhere has been the subject of several previous studies, each developing a particular aspect of the theme. Two good general introductions to the theme of the imagination in his writings are O'Daly, *Augustine's Philosophy of Mind* (1987) and Watson, *Phantasia in Classical Thought* (1989); more specialized studies include two books by J. R. O'Connell, *Imagination and Metaphysics in St. Augustine* (Milwaukee: Marquette University Press, 1986) and *Soundings in Augustine's Imagination* (New York: Fordham University Press, 1994). An excellent analysis of *Ep.* 7 is found in Giovanna Ceresola, *Fantasia e illusione in S. Agostino dai "Soliloquia" al "De Mendacio"* (Genoa: il Melangolo, 2001), 70–91.

35. *Ep.* 4.1: "quid in sensibilis atque intellegibilis naturae discernentia profecerimus."

36. *Ep.* 6.2: "Cur, quaeso te, non a se potius quam a sensu phantasiam habere omnes imagines dicimus?"

37. *Ep.* 6.1: "Nam aut uerba intellectui cogitationibusque nostris adiunximus, quae uerba sine tempora non sunt et ad sensum uel phantasiam pertinent, aut tale aliquid noster intellectus cogitatione passa est, quod in animo phantastico memoriam facere potuisset."

38. *Ep.* 7.1: "Memoria tibi uidetur nulla esse posse sine imaginibus uel imaginariis uisis, quae phantasiarum nomine appellare uoluisti."

39. *Ep.* 7.1: "In utroque tamen horum generum praeteritum tempus memoria tenet. Nam et illum hominem et istam urbem ex eo, quod uidi, non ex eo, quod uideo, memini."

40. E.g., *Conf.*, 1.6.8; 1.8.13.

41. Cf. *Ep.*, 120 (to Consentius, ca. 410), in which Augustine refers to three classes of things which are "seen": material objects, images of objects, and noncorporeal things, e.g., wisdom.

42. *De Genesi ad Litteram* 12.1.1; *Patrologia Latina*, vol. 34, cols. 453–54: "*Scio hominem in Christo ante annos quatuordecim, sive in corpore nescio, sive extra corpus nescio, Deus scit, raptum ejusmodi usque in tertium caelum: et scio ejusmodi hominem sive in corpore sive extra corpus nescio, Deus scit, quia raptum est in paradisum, et audivit ineffabilia verba, quae non licet homini loqui.*" 2 Cor. 12:2–4.

43. The point is illustrated by the familiar example of the cities of Carthage, which he knows, and Alexandria, which he knows only from report.

44. *De Genesi* 12.6.18; PL 34.460: "Dicitur spiritus et ipsa mens rationalis, ubi est quidam tanquam oculus animae, ad quem pertinet imago et agnitio Dei."

45. Cf. *De Doctrina Christiana* 2.1.1.

46. *De Genesi* 12.11.22: "Jam quidem superius exemplum proposuimus, quo in una sententia omnia tria videntur genera." At *Conf.* 11.27.35 the reading of a single line of an Ambrosian hymn, *Deus creator omnium*, is Augustine's means of measuring time.

47. *De Gen.*, 12.11.22: "Corporaliter littera videntur, spiritualiter proximus cogitatur, intellectualiter dilectio conspicitur." Augustine proceeds directly from *litterae* which are seen rather than voiced, suggesting that the movement from text to thought is silent, as contrasted with *Conf.* 11.27.35, where the reading is oral, because measurement takes place through the meter.

48. *De Gen.*, 12.11.22: "Sed et litterae absentes possunt spiritualiter cogitari, et proximus praesens potest corporaliter videri."

49. *De Gen.*, 12.11.22: "nec per imaginem corporis similem spiritu cogitari, sed sola mente, id est, intellectu, cognosci et percipi."

50. *De Gen.*, 12.11.22.

51. *De Gen.*, 12.11.22: "aut intelligatur continuo quid significet, aut quaeritur; quoniam nec intelligi nec requiri nisi officio menti potest."

52. *De Gen.*, 12.16.33: "His existit quiddam mirabile, ut cum prior sit corpore spiritus, et posterior corporis imago quam corpus, tamen quia illud quod tempore posterius est, fit in eo quod natura prius est, praestantior sit imago corporis in spiritu, quam ipsum corpus in substantia sua."

53. *De Gen.*, 12.16.33: "Quos unique non tenet; nisi imaginaliter a se factos in se."

54. *De Gen.*, 12.16.33: "Ipsarum etiam futurarum motionum imagines praeveniunt fines actuum nostrorum." Cf. 12.23.49.

55. *De Trinitate* 11.2.2; CSEL 50a, pp. 334–36.

56. Cf. Virgil, *Aeneid* 8.202; 6.289.

57. *De Trin.*, 8.4.6: "Sed dilectione standum est ad illud et inhaerendum illi ut praesente perfruamur a quo sumus, quo absente nec esse possemus."

58. *De Trin.*, 8.4.6: "Amatur ergo et quod ignoratur sed tamen creditur."

59. *De Trin.*, 8.6.9: "Quid enim tam intime scitur seque ipsum esse sentit quam id quo etiam cetera sentiuntur, id est ipse animus?"

60. *De Trin.*, 8.6.9: "Animum igitur cuiuslibet ex nostro nouimus et ex nostro credimus quem non nouimus."

61. *De Trin.*, 8.6.9: "Non enim alibi hoc inuenio cum quaero ut hoc eloquar nisi apud me ipsum; et si interrogem alium quid sit iustus, apud se ipsum quaerit quid respondeat."

CHAPTER 3. THE PHILOSOPHICAL SOLILOQUY

1. See my study, *Augustine's Inner Dialogue: The Philosophical Soliloquy in Late Antiquity* (Cambridge: Cambridge University Press, 2010).

2. Catherine Lefort, "Soliloques d'Augustin: Introduction, texte, critique, traduction, et notes complémentaires," dissertation, Université de Paris IV, 2010.

3. For a review of pertinent themes on this topic, see the collection of essays in *Literarische Formen der Philosophie*, ed. Gottfried Gabriel and Christiane Schildknecht (Stuttgart: Metzlersche Verlagsbuchhandlung, 1990). On the dialogue as a literary and philosophical form in Plato, see above all Charles H. Kahn, *Plato and the Socratic Dialogue: The Philosophical Use of a Literary Form* (Cambridge: Cambridge University Press, 1996); also Andrea Wilson Nightingale, *Genres in Dialogue: Plato and the Construct of Philosophy* (Cambridge: Cambridge University Press, 1995). On the historical origins of the Socratic dialogue, see Gabriele Giannantoni, *Socratis et Socratorum Reliquiae*, 4 vols. (Naples: Bibliopolis, 1990). For a more general overview on the development of the Western dialogue and its literary landscape, see Vittorio Hösle, *The Philosophical Dialogue: A Poetics and a Hermeneutics*, trans. Steven Rendell (Notre Dame, Ind.: University of Notre Dame Press, 2012).

4. *Soliloquia*, 2.7.14; *Retractationes*, 1.4.1; the term is employed only in the plural. Ancient Greek has no equivalent; however, modern Greek expresses the notion by means of μονόλογος.

5. E.g., *Iliad* 4.43; *Odyssey* 20.18. On drama, see Friedrich Leo, *Der Monolog im Drama*, Abhandlung der Göttingen Gesellschaft der Wissenschaften, phil.-hist. Kl. N.F. X, 5 (Berlin, 1908); Wolfgang Schadewaldt, *Monolog und Selbstgespräch. Untersuchungen zur Formgeschichte der griechischen Tragödie*, 2nd ed. (Berlin: Weidemann, 1966 [1926], 38–262); cf. John Dean Bickford, "Soliloquy in Ancient Comedy" (dissertation, Princeton, N.J.: Princeton University Press, 1922).

6. Attention is drawn to these by Epictetus, *Discourses* III.x.2, with the suggestion that they be "kept on hand"; cf. *Disc.*, IV.vi.12.

7. The evidence is succinctly summarized by R. B. Rutherford, *The Meditations of Marcus Aurelius: A Study* (Oxford: Clarendon, 1989), 15.

8. *Sophist* 228c–d; *Theaetetus* 189c–190a; *Philebus* 38c–39a; cf. *Crito* 50b ff., where the laws speak internally to Socrates, and *Hippias Major* 287a ff., where an internal dialogue takes place within the open dialogue between Socrates and Hippias. For anecdotal evidence of their use by Pyrrho of Elis, see Diogenes Laertius, *Vitae Philosophorum*, 9.4.6.

9. On the roots of this transformation, see Harold Cherniss, "Ancient Forms of Philosophic Discourse," in *Selected Papers*, ed. Leonardo A. Tarán (Leiden: Brill, 1977), 14–35.

10. Cicero, *Tusc. Disp.*, 5.117: "Etenim qui secum loqui poterit, sermonem alterius non requiret;" on Horace, see *Sat.*, 1.4.137–39.

11. See A. A. Long, "Socrates in Hellenistic Philosophy," in *Stoic Studies*, 1–34, and *Epictetus*, 67–96.

12. See David Sedley, "Plato's *Auctoritas* and the Rebirth of the Commentary Tradition," in *Philosophia Togata II*, ed. Miriam Griffin and Jonathan Barnes (Oxford: Oxford University Press, 1997), 111–29.

13. See Seneca, *Epistulae Morales*, ed. L. D. Reynolds (Oxford: Clarendon, 1965), 95.1–3, where the method is briefly described. For a general account of the period's educational techniques in philosophy and other disciplines, see H.-I. Marrou, *A History of Education in Antiquity*, trans. George Lamb (New York: Sheed and Ward, 1956), 282–308; on the philosophical implications of this type of instruction, see Pierre Hadot, "Forms of Life and Forms of Discourse in Ancient Philosophy," in *Philosophy as a Way of Life*, trans. Michael Chase, ed. and intro. Arnold I. Davidson (Oxford: Blackwell, 1995), 50–70; on the broader intellectual context, see G. R. Boys-Stones, *Post-Hellenic Philosophy: A Study of Its Development from the Stoics to Origen*, and on the methods utilized see Pier Luigi Donini, "Testi e commenti, manuali e insegnamento. La forma sistematica e i metodi della filosofia in età posthellenica," *Aufstieg und Niedergang der Römischen Welt* II, 36, 7 (1989): cols. 5027–5100. The classic account of Augustine's use of such means of instruction remains Aimé Solignac, "Doxographies et manuels dans la formation philosophique de S. Augustin," *Recherches Augustiniennes* 1 (1958): 113–48.

14. On the role of silent reading in this evolution, see in general Paul Saenger, *Space Between Words: The Origins of Silent Reading* (Stanford, Calif.: Stanford University Press, 1997), 18–82; Guglielmo Cavallo, "Between *Volumen* and Codex: Reading in the Roman World," in *A History of Reading in the West*, ed. Guglielmo Cavallo and Roger Chartier, trans. Lydia G. Cochrane (Amherst: University of Massachusetts Press, 1999), 64–89; and M. B. Parkes, "Reading, Copying and Interpreting a Text in the Early Middle Ages," ibid., 90–102.

15. See Josef Balogh, "*Voces paginarum*: Beiträge zur Geschichte des lauten Lesens und Schreibens," *Philologus* 82 (1927): 84–109, 202–40.

16. Plutarch, *Quomodo adolescens poetas audire debeat* 16e, in Plutarch, *Moralia*, vol. 1, with an English translation by Frank Cole Babbit, Loeb Classical Library (Cambridge, Mass.:

Harvard University Press, 2009 [1927]), 84; for a discussion, see David Konstan, "The Active Reader in Classical Antiquity," *Argos* 30 (2006): 10.

17. *De Ordine*, 1.3.8.

18. For a review of issues in this field, see Sadi Bartsch and David Wray, eds., *Seneca and the Self*, especially the essays of A. A. Long and Brad Inwood on the heritage of Michel Foucault.

19. On the use of the term "eclectic" to describe this expansion of sources, see Ilsetraut Hadot, *Arts libéraux et philosophie dans la pensée antique: Contribution à l'histoire de l'éducation et de la culture dans l'Antiquité*, 2nd ed. (Paris: Vrin, 2005), 483–94.

20. *De Ira* 3.36.1–3, in Seneca, *Moral Essays*, vol. 1, ed. and trans. John W. Basore, Loeb Classical Library (Cambridge Mass.: Harvard University Press, 2003), 338, 340; my trans.

21. *Ep. Mor.*, 28.10, ed. L. D. Reynolds, vol. 1, p. 81, 3–7, where a maxim of Epicurus is the point of departure: "'Initium est salutis notitia peccati.' Egregie mihi hoc dixisse videtur Epicurus; nam qui peccare se nescit corrigi non vult; deprehendas te oportet antequam emendas . . . . Ideo quantum potes te ipse coargue, inquire in te; accusatoris primum partibus fungere, deinde iudicis, novissime deprecatoris."

22. Hadot, "Forms of Life and Forms of Discourse," 49–70 and "Spiritual Exercises," in *Philosophy as a Way of Life*, 81–125. The literature on the subject is extensive; for a bibliography, see Stock, *Augustine's Inner Dialogue*, 23–24n18. Anglo-American philosophy has evolved a different vocabulary for treating the issues; see Rutherford, *The Meditations of Marcus Aurelius*, ch. 1, and Long, *Epictetus*, chs. 3–4.

23. Ilsetraut Hadot, *Seneca und die griechische-römische Tradition der Seelenleitung* (Berlin: de Gruyter, 1969), 105; cf. Robert J. Newman, "*Cotidie meditare*: Theory and Practice of the *meditatio* in Imperial Stoicism," *Aufstieg und Niedergang der Römischen Welt* II, 36, 3 (1989): 1480.

24. Quoting Marcus Agrippa, *Ep. Mor.* 94.48.

25. *De Vita Beata* 2, ed. John W. Basore, Loeb Classical Library (London: Heinemann, 1932), 102.

26. On this topic see Ilsetraut Hadot, "The Spiritual Guide," in *Classical Mediterranean Spirituality: Egyptian, Greek, Roman*, ed. A. H. Armstrong, 445–55.

27. As suggested by the presence of numerous mock internal dialogues: e.g., *De Ira* 1.1.3, 1.1.6, 1.8.4, 1.11.1, etc. These views are paralleled by statements (often paraphrased in Seneca's words) from Plato, Aristotle, Stoics, Epicureans, and others. The work thereby advances by means of a double internal dialogue, which is based on texts that Seneca has read and on his own views, both of which are expressed in dialogue form.

28. Miriam T. Griffin, *Seneca: A Philosopher in Politics* (Oxford: Clarendon, 1992 [1976]), Appendix B 2, pp. 413–14.

29. *De Tran. An.* 1.14, trans. Basore.

30. In which the other voice is sometimes portrayed as that of his brother, Gallio, to whom the treatise is dedicated; e.g., 6.1–2, p. 114.

31. E.g., *De Vita Beata* 4.1–2, p. 109.

32. Ibid., 4.4, p. 110.

33. Ibid., 4.2–3, p. 108.

34. Ibid., 16.1–3, p. 140.

35. Ibid., 8.3, p. 118: "Incorruptus vir sit externis et insuperabilis miratorque tantum sui, fidens animo atque in utrumque paratus, artifex vitae." Cf. 16.3, p. 140: "Quid extrinsecus opus est, qui omnia sua in se colligit?"

36. On this dimension of self-address, see Rutherford, *The Meditations of Marcus Aurelius*, 18–19.

37. *De Tran. An.*, 1.2–3, ed. Basore (1932), 202.

38. Ibid., 1.1.

39. Ibid., 2.1, p. 212.

40. Ibid., 5.2, p. 234.

41. Ibid., 2.4, p. 214.

42. For a review of the literature on the *Epistulae*, see Giancarlo Mazzoli, "Le '*Epistulae Morales ad Lucilium*' di Seneca. Valore letterario et filosofico," *Aufstieg und Niedergang der Römischen Welt* II 36, 3 (1989): 1823–77; for an introduction to major themes, see Brad Inwood, *Seneca: Selected Philosophical Letters*, trans. with an Introduction and Commentary (Toronto: Oxford University Press, 2007), xi–xxi, and Inwood, "The Importance of Form in Seneca's Philosophical Letters," in *Ancient Letters: Classical and Late Antique Epistolography*, ed. Ruth Morello and A. D. Morrison (Oxford: Oxford University Press, 2007), 133–48. For a brief statement on the use of reading in the early letters, see Stock, "Éthique et humanités: quelques leçons de l'expérience historique," in *Bibliothèques intérieures*, trans. Philippe Blanc and Christophe Carraud (Grenoble: Jérôme Millon, 2005), 73–76, and Stock, *Augustine's Inner Dialogue*, 69–71.

43. On this type of self-construal and its potential relationship to Renaissance writers, see Catherine Edwards, "Self-Scrutiny and Self-Transformation in Seneca's Letters," *Greece and Rome* 44, 1 (1997): 23–38.

44. E.g., *Ep. Mor.*, 95; on this topic see Inwood, *Reading Seneca: Stoic Philosophy in Rome* (Oxford: Clarendon, 2005); and Inwood, *Seneca: Selected Philosophical Letters*.

45. On the first type, examples include *Ep. Mor.* 1, 2, 3, 7, 8, 9; on the second, see *Epp.* 5, 6, 10, 12, 13, and 14.

46. It is tempting to ascribe a larger role to the reader in the *Epistulae*, but it must be remembered that for Seneca reading is a rational activity, parallel to the dialogue, as well as a form of spiritual direction. A fully autonomous function for reading is not envisaged. For a different view, see Dieter Teichert, "Der Philosoph as Briefschreiber: Zur Bedeutung der literarischen Form von Senecas Briefen an Lucilius," in *Literarische Formen der Philosophie*, 64–69.

47. See *Discourses* I.x.1–9, ed. W. A. Oldfather, *Epictetus: The Discourses as Reported by Arrian, the Manual, and Fragments*, 2 vols., Loeb Classical Library (London: Heinemann, 1925), vol. 1, 76–77; this edition is quoted throughout along with Oldfather's translation, except where noted. On the possibility that Arrian revised the text, see T. Wirth, "Arrians Errinerungen an Epiktet," *Museum Helveticum* 24 (1967): 149–89, 197–216. Yet even in revision Arrian may have captured the authentic flavor of Epictetus's teaching; for a positive assessment, see A. A. Long, "Epictetus and Marcus Aurelius," in *Ancient Writers*, ed. T. J. Luce (New York: Scribner, 1982), 989–90.

48. See P. A. Brunt, "From Epictetus to Arrian," *Athenaeum* N.S. 55 (1977): 21–30.

49. The enthusiasm can partly be attributed to Arrian; see Jean-Baptiste Gourinat, "Le Socrate d'Épictète," *Philosophie Antique* 1 (2001): 137–38. On the "Socratic Paradigm" in the *Discourses*, see Long, *Epictetus*, chap. 3; cf. Epictetus, *Discourses* I.viii.11, vol. 1, p. 62; however, Socrates's teaching is frequently represented by Xenophon's paraphrase and by allusions, comparisons, or loose summaries. For a list of citations, see K. Döring, "Sokrates bei Epiktet," in *Studia Platonica: Festschrift für Hermann Gündert zu seinem 65. Geburtstag . . .*, ed. W. Kullmann (Amsterdam: Grüner, 1974), 195–226; on the image of Socrates more generally, see A. A. Long, "Socrates in Hellenistic Philosophy." Among Epictetus's borrowings from Plato are *Disc.*, I.xxv.29–30; vol. 1, p. 164; I.xxvi.8; vol. 1, p. 170 (cf. Plato, *Apology*, 38a); I.xxix.16; vol. 1,

p. 187 (cf. *Apology*, 30c); II.i.15; vol. 1, p. 216; II.i.32; vol. 1, p. 222; II.ii.8–9 et seq. (cf. *Apology* 2f.); II.iv.8; vol. 1, p. 236 (referring possibly to the *Symposium*); II.xii.5; vol. 1, p. 290 (cf. *Gorgias* 474a); II.xviii.22; vol. 1, p. 354 (cf. *Symposium* 218D); III.i.19; vol. 2, p 10. Among other moral heroes are the Cynics, Heracles, and Diogenes; see B. L. Hijmans, Jr., *"ΑΣΚΗΣΙΣ.' Notes on Epictetus's Educational System* (Assen: Van Gorcum, 1959), 72–77.

50. As Arrian claims in his prefatory letter to Lucius Gellius; *Discourses*, ed. Oldfather, vol. 1, p. 4.

51. E.g., Long, *Epictetus*, ix, 2.

52. Possibly in illustration of the Stoic principle of teaching ethics by means of specific case histories; however, a notable exception to this suggestion is Epictetus's lengthy discussion of freedom; *Disc.*, 4.1; vol. 2, pp. 245–305.

53. Long, *Epictetus*, 3.

54. Cf., on Cynicism, M. Billerbeck, *Der Kyniker Demetrius: Ein Beitrag zur Geschichte der frühkaiserzeitlichen Popularphilosophie* (Leiden: Brill, 1979), 3–43.

55. E.g., *Disc.*, I.xi; vol. 1, pp. 78ff.

56. E.g., *Disc.*, I.x.2–6; vol. 1, p. 74; I.xxiii (with Epicurus); vol. 1, 148f; II.ii.15–20 (with Socrates and Heraclitus); vol. 1, pp. 228, 230.

57. E.g., *Disc.*, I.xii.6–9; vol. 1, p. 90; I.xiii; vol. 1, pp. 98f.; I.xvii.1–12, vol. 1, pp. 112ff.; I.xxv.11–13; vol. 1, p. 160; I.xxvii.1–6; vol. 1, pp. 170, 172; I.xxx; vol. 1, p. 204, 206; II.vi.6–10; vol. 1, p. 248; II.xiii.15–22; vol. 1, pp. 302, 304; II.xviii.15–18; vol. 1, pp. 352, 354.

58. *Disc.*, III.i.19 ff.; vol. 2, pp. 10 ff; III.xii.15; vol. 2, p. 84, 86; IV.iv.29–30; vol. 2, p. 324.

59. *Disc.*, I.xx.2–5; vol. 1, p. 136.

60. *Disc.*, I.i.4; vol. 1, p. 8; I.xvi.2–3; vol. 1, p. 108; cf. Augustine, *De Ord.*, II.11.30, where a comparable distinction is made between *ratio* as *mentis motio*, and what is *rationale* or *rationabile*, as *quod ratione uteretur vel ut posset*. In Augustine this is followed by an inner dialogue in which the speaker is Reason, whereas Epictetus employs a fictive dialogue with Zeus, possibly drawing on Homer, *Odyssey* X, 21, and by a soliloquy, presumably in Zeus' presence, on what is and is not truly within his jurisdiction; *Disc.*, I. i. 21–25; vol. 1, p. 12.

61. E.g., *Disc.*, I.xii.12–21; vol. pp. 92, 94. It is also possible—although the suggestion must be made with caution—that in Epictetus inner dialogues give expression to personal freedom at a time when political options were limited; e.g., the soliloquy at II.1.21–24; vol. 1, p. 220.

62. *Disc.*, I.xvii.14; vol. 1, p. 116: ". . . *autos dia seatou parakoloutheis?*"

63. E.g., *Disc.*, II.xxi.9–10; vol. p. 386; III.xxii.30; vol. 2, p. 144. The fullest outline is at III.xxiv.105–14; vol. 2, pp. 216, 218, 220.

64. *Disc.*, III.xiv.1–3; vol. 2, p. 96; on the limitations of open conversation as contrasted with solitude and talking to oneself, see III.xvi; vol. 2, 104, 106, 108.

65. E.g., *Disc.*, III.xxi.23; vol. 2, p. 130. The reader's soliloquy, as practiced by Seneca, is rare in Epictetus; but see *Disc.*, III.xxiii.21–23; vol. 2, p. 176.

66. *Disc.*, III.xxiv.103; vol. 2, p. 216.

67. *Disc.*, IV.1.128–40, a passage on self-consciousness, possibly unique in the period's writings in philosophy, discussing the potential thoughts of a student during a course of lectures.

68. E.g., *Disc.*, IV.1.6–10; vol. 2, p. 246, where dialogue and soliloquy are indistinguishable.

69. *Disc.*, I.xviii.15–20; vol. 1, pp. 116, 118.

70. *Disc.*, II.vi.6–10; vol. 1, p. 248. These include proverbial expressions which one says to oneself; see II.xv.13–19; vol. 1, pp. 318, 320; on occasion such inner speeches contain literary references; e.g., II.xix.5–11; vol. 1, pp. 360, 362.

71. *Disc.*, III.i.34, vol. 2, p. 16. On the topos of attractiveness in young men entering the field, see IV.xi.25–30; vol. 2, p. 418.

72. As well as in other creatures, e.g., dogs and horses, thereby endowing them with a form of self-consciousness. Cf. *Hippias Major*, 286c–d, where Socrates asks a similar question.

73. *Disc.*, III.i.8–9, vol. 2, pp. 6, 8; cf. III.i. 15, pp. 8, 10. In Epictetus's view, this means making oneself beautiful in the sight of god; II.xviii.19–20; vol. 1, p. 354.

74. *Disc.*, III.i.25; vol. 2, p. 14.

75. *Disc.*, III.i.10–13; vol. 2, p. 8, trans. Oldfather with modifications.

76. On the Aristotelian roots, see Robert Dobbin, "Προαίρεσις in Epictetus," *Ancient Philosophy* 11 (1991): 111–16 and the bibliography therein.

77. Adolf Bonhöffer, *Epiktet und die Stoa* (Stuttgart: Ferdinand Enke, 1890), 259–60.

78. *Disc.*, II.xxii.1–19; vol. 1, pp. 404, 406, 408.

79. *Disc.*, II.xxiii.10–19; vol. 1, pp. 408, 410; II.xxiii.28; vol. 1, p. 414.

80. A.A. Long, *Epictetus*, 227.

81. *Disc.*, I.xxii.9–10; vol. 1, p. 144; my trans.

82. *Disc.*, I.xxv.1; vol. 1, p. 156.

83. *Disc.*, I.xxii.9; vol. 1, p. 144.

84. *Disc.*, I.xxiv; vol. 1, p. 150 ff.

85. *Disc.*, I.xxv.6, vol. 1, p. 158.

86. *Disc.*, I.xxii.17–18; vol. 1, p. 146; my trans.

87. *Disc.*, I.xxv.11; vol. 1, p. 158, 160.

88. See above all Adolf Bonhöffer, *Epiktet und das Neue Testament* (Giessen: Alfred Töpelmann, 1911). For a review of the issues, see Amand Jagu, "La morale d'Épictète et le christianisme," *Aufstieg und Niedergang der römischen Welt* II, 36, 3 (1989): 2164–99; in greater detail, see Michel Spanneut, *Le stoïcisme des Pères de l'Église*, Patristica Sorbonensia 1 (Paris: Le Seuil, 1957). On the question of the teaching methods of Socrates and Christ, see the thoughtful essay of Paul W. Gooch, *Reflections on Jesus and Socrates: Word and Silence* (New Haven, Conn.: Yale University Press, 1996), 1–18, 47–107; on the use of Epictetus's *Manual* by Christian writers, see Gerard Boter, *The "Encheiridion" of Epictetus and Its Three Christian Adaptations* (Leiden: Brill, 1999).

89. *Disc.*, III.xxiv.2–4; vol. 2, p. 184; in general, see Keimpe Algra, "Epictetus and Stoic Theology," in *The Philosophy of Epictetus*, ed. Theodore Scaltsas and Andrew S. Mason (Oxford: Oxford University Press, 2007), 32–33.

90. See Bonhöffer, *Epiktet und die Stoa*, 80.

91. E.g., *Disc.*, I.iii.1–2; vol. 1, p. 24; cf. Epictetus, *Encheiridion*, c. 26. On the superiority of divine to human will, see *Disc.*, IV.vii.20; vol. 2, p. 366.

92. *Disc.*, I.vi.1–7; vol. 1, p. 40; cf. I.xiii.1–5; vol. 1, p. 98. One of the purposes of inner dialogue is the contemplation of these functions; I.vi.37 ff; vol. 1, pp. 48 ff.

93. *Disc.*, III.xxvi.29; vol. 2, p. 230; my paraphrase; cf. IV.1.103; vol. 2, p. 278.

94. On these and other theological topics, see the summary of Algra, "Epictetus and Stoic Theology," 42–47.

95. *Disc.*, III.i.36; vol. 2, p. 18; III.xiii.11–12; vol. 2, p. 90.

96. On the justification for hymns of praise to god, see *Disc.*, I.xvi.15–21; vol. 1, p. 112.

97. *Disc.*, II.xiv.11; vol. 1, p. 308.

98. *Disc.*, III.xxiv.3; vol. 2, p. 184.

99. *Disc.*, I.xxv.2–6; vol. 1, pp. 156, 158; trans. Oldfather with modifications.

100. *Disc.*, I.xxv.27–28; vol. 1, pp. 162, 164.

101. *Disc.*, I.xxvi.13–15; vol. 1, p. 166.

102. See *Disc.*, I.xxix.59; vol. 1, p. 198

103. *Disc.*, I.xxix.41–47; 4.7.13; *Handbook*, 17.

104. *Disc.*, 3.xxii.4–8; I.xxix.41–47; 4.vii.13.

105. *Self: Ancient and Modern Insights About Individuality, Life, and Death*, 161; on *pro-hairesis* and self, see pp. 11–185.

106. *Disc.*, II.viii.12–14; vol. 1, pp. 260, 262; my paraphrase.

107. *Disc.*, II.x.1; vol. 1, p. 274.

108. *Disc.*, II.xvii.1–3; vol. 1. p. 336; my paraphrase.

109. *Disc.*, II.xvii.5–13; 29–33; vol. 1, pp. 336 ff.

110. *Disc.*, II.xviii.2; vol. 1, pp. 348, 350; my paraphrase.

111. *Disc.*, IV.1.63; vol. 2, p. 264; trans. Oldfather slightly modified.

112. *Disc.*, II.xviii.4; vol. 1, p. 350.

113. *Disc.*, II.xviii.5–8; vol. 1, p. 350.

114. *Disc.*, I.xx.7; vol. 1, p. 138.

115. *Disc.*, II.xviii.20; vol. 1, p. 354 (cf. Plato, *Laws* IX, 854b and for the following example *Symposium* 218d ff.).

116. *Disc.*, II.xviii.27; vol. 1, p. 356.

117. *Disc.*, III.viii.1; vol. 2, p. 60; my paraphrase.

118. *Disc.*, I. iv. 5ff. III.i.; vol. 2, pp. 4 ff.

119. *Disc.*, I.iv.18; vol. 1, p. 32.

120. *Disc.*, II.xix.11; vol.1, p. 362.

121. *Disc.*, II.ix.13; vol. 1, p. 270.

122. *Disc.*, IV.iv.29–30; vol. 2, p. 324.

123. *Disc.*, II.xix.20; vol. 1, p. 366.

124. *Disc.*, II.ii.21–26; vol. 1, p. 230; cf. II.xiv.15, p. 310.

125. *Disc.*, II.xxi.8–10; vol. 1. pp. 384, 386; my paraphrase.

126. The term "meditations," referring to internal reflections of a moral or philosophical nature, is derived from a late ancient and medieval rather than ancient meaning for *meditatio*; an early example is found in Jerome's translation of Genesis XXIV, 24: "Et egressus fuerat [Abraham] ad meditandum in agro."

127. Rutherford, *The Meditations of Marcus Aurelius*, xvii, 45–47.

128. Rutherford, *The Meditations of Marcus Aurelius*, 8–9; 13–14; cf. Pierre Hadot, *The Inner Citadel: The "Meditations" of Marcus Aurelius*, trans. Michael Chase (Cambridge, Mass.: Harvard University Press, 1998), 34.

129. *Med.*, I.9; see Hadot, *Inner Citadel*, 59–69. References to the *Meditations* in this section are taken from *The Communings with Himself of Marcus Aurelius Antoninus, Emperor of Rome, Together with his Speeches and Sayings*, ed. C. R. Haines, Loeb Classical Library (London: Heinemann, 1916); translation unless otherwise stated from *The "Meditations" of Marcus Aurelius Antoninus*, trans. A. S. L. Farquharson (Oxford: Clarendon, 1944), and *A Selection from the Letters of Marcus and Fronto*, trans. with Intro. and Notes by R. B. Rutherford (Oxford: Oxford University Press, 1998). In addition to Epictetus, Marcus was influenced by Democritus, Heraclitus, Pythagoras, and Socrates; see the Index to Haines, *The Communings . . .* , *sub nominibus*.

130. The presentation is the philosophical equivalent of what is called, in literary criticism, "a stream of consciousness."

131. But see *Med.*, V.16, where Marcus argues that the soul acquires its coloring, i.e., its disposition for virtue, from the succession of our thoughts.

132. *Med.*, I.7. On this theme, see the important observations of Hadot, *Inner Citadel*, 30–34.

133. *Med.*, III.14; Epictetus, *Disc.*, I.7.

134. He complains about the lack of leisure for reading, *Med.*, III.14; the evidence is thoughtfully summed up by Rutherford, *The Meditations of Marcus Aurelius*, 28–29.

135. See Hadot, *Inner Citadel*, 48–51.

136. It is not clear that he intended to record them; however, against this view, see *Disc.*, II.1.32, vol. 1, p. 222, where he speaks of the extensive "writings" of Socrates. What is possibly meant is private notes not intended for publication but circulated to a small number of students; cf. II.1.34–35, vol. 1, p. 222, where he refers to writings of his own. Notes are scattered throughout the *Discourses* on the ways reading and writing prepare students for leading a philosophical life. As noted, writing is viewed as a model skill, permitting individuals to adapt to a variety of spoken sounds, just as trained Stoics adapt to different challenges in life; II.ii.21–26; vol. 1, p. 230; cf. II.xiv, 15–16; and vol. 1, p. 310, on writing in relation to other techniques. Similarly, reading is viewed as a preparation for living; IV.iv.11; vol. 2, 316.

137. Arrian, *Letter to Lucius Gellius*, in Epictetus, *Disc.*, vol. 1, pp. 4, 6; for a different view, see Wirth, "Arrians Errinerungen."

138. In this respect his method resembles that of Christian exegetes to whom he was fervently opposed; see P. A. Brunt, "Marcus Aurelius and the Christians," in *Studies in Latin Literature and Roman History*, ed. Carl Derous, vol. 1 (*Latomus*, vol. 164, Brussels, 1979), 483–518.

139. E.g., *Med.*, I.14; for a review, see Hadot, *Inner Citadel*, 2–20.

140. See Rutherford, *The Meditations of Marcus Aurelius*, 126–37.

141. E.g., *Med.*, III.4.

142. For a convincing analysis, see Rutherford, *The Meditations of Marcus Aurelius*, 126–77 and Hadot, *Inner Citadel*, 257–60.

143. Although he hints at his method at *Med.*, VI.26, where he compares the enumeration of life's duties to reading the letters of a name, one by one; cf. VI.30, describing Antoninus's habit of close scrutinization before reaching decisions; cf. VIII.11; VIII.22.

144. Cf. Hadot, *Inner Citadel*, 34.

145. Matthew Arnold, "Marcus Aurelius," in *Essays in Criticism: First Series* (London: Macmillan, 1865), 279. For a reassessment of this view, see Rutherford, *The Meditations of Marcus Aurelius*, chap. 4, and Hadot, *Inner Citadel*, 257–63. Some of the infelicities in style are those one would expect from a Latin speaker who is writing Greek.

146. E.g., *Med.*, II.1–2; on this theme and its evolution between Epictetus and Marcus, see the important observations of Hadot, *Inner Citadel*, esp. pp. 105–25.

147. *Med.*, VIII.48; ed. Haines, p. 222.

148. *Med.*, VI.1; ed. Haines, p. 130.

149. *Med.*, VI.3; ed. Haines, p. 130; cf. III.11, where Marcus advises us to make a mental outline of an object as it appears in our minds in order to see its essence distinctly; similarly, at VI.31, on dreams and waking images.

150. *Med.*, IV.1, 2; trans. Farquharson, modified.

151. *Med.*, IV.4; ed. Haines, p. 70.

152. *Med.*, XI.12; ed. Haines, p. 302.

153. *Med.*, XII.19; ed. Haines, p. 339; trans. Farquharson, modified.

154. *Med.*, VI.11; ed. Haines, p. 132.

155. *Med.*, IX.15; ed. Haines, p. 242; trans. Farquharson, modified.

156. *Med.*, VII.68; ed. Haines, pp. 192, 194.

157. *Med.*, I.7, trans. Farquharson , modified.

158. *Med.*, V.1; ed. Haines, p. 98; my trans.

159. *Med.*, V.11; ed. Haines, p. 112; trans. Farquharson, modified.

160. *Med.*, VIII.2; ed. Haines, p. 200; my trans.

161. *Med.*, VIII.29; ed. Haines, p. 210; cf. VII.15; VIII.36; IX.7.

162. *Med.*, X.1; ed. Haines, p. 260; my paraphrase.

163. *Med.*, XI.16; ed. Haines, p. 304; my paraphrase.

164. *Med.*, III.1; ed. Haines, p. 44, 46; my paraphrase; cf. IV.20–21; V.23, 33; VI.4, 15, 25. On Plutarch, see *On the E at Delphi*, 392C-E; on Seneca, *Epistulae Morales* 24.19–21 and 58.22–23.

165. *De Ord.*, I.3.6: "Sed nocte quadam, cum evigilassem de more mecum ipse tacitus agitarem; *Sol.*, I.1.1: "volventi mihi multa ac varia mecum diu ac per multos dies sedulo quaerenti memetipsum."

166. For an outline, see Stock, *Augustine's Inner Dialogue*, 18–120. On the philosophical background of Augustine's approach to the liberal arts, see above all Ilsetraut Hadot, *Arts libéraux et philosophie dans la pensée antique*, 101–36 (on *De Ord.*, book 2) and 377–90 (on Augustine's education); cf. Philip Burton, *Language in the "Confessions" of Saint Augustine* (Oxford: Oxford University Press, 2007). The influence of Manichaean exegetical traditions on the early phase of Augustine's development as a commentator cannot be ruled out; on the background, see Michel Tardieu, "Principes de l'exégèse manichéenne du Nouveau Testament," in *Les règles de l'interprétation*, ed. Michel Tardieu (Paris: Éditions du Cerf, 1987), 123–46.

167. Respectively at *Conf.*, VIII.10.23–11.25, *Sol.*, II.1.1, and *Conf.*, XI.14.17.

168. E.g., *De Mag.*, XI.36; see Goulven Madec, "Analyse du *De magistro*," *Revue des Études Augustiniennes* 21 (1975), 63–71, and, on the use of language, Myles Burnyeat, "Wittgenstein and Augustine *De Magistro*," *Proceedings of the Aristotelian Society*, Supplement 61 (1987): 1–24 and Stock, *Augustine's Inner Dialogue*, 196–211.

169. Saint Augustine, *Confessions*, trans. Henry Chadwick with an Introduction and Notes (Oxford: Oxford University Press, 1991), 230–31; slightly modified.

170. See Porphyry, *Vita Plotini* 3–6, ed. and trans. A. H. Armstrong, *Plotinus*, vol. 1: *Porphyry on the Life of Plotinus and the Order of His Books: Enneads I.1–9*, Loeb Classical Library (Cambridge, Mass.: Harvard University Press, 1989), 6–24.

171. *Vita Plotini* 8; ed. and trans. Armstrong, vol. 1, pp. 29, 31.

172. Although it cannot be proven, we must admit the possibility that Plotinus's unusual form of composition arose in part because he was dyslexic.

173. Plotinus, *Enn.*, 4.8.1, trans. Armstrong, vol. 4, 397; cf. *Enn.*, 6.9.11.24; 6.9.11.45–51; also, Augustine, *De Quant. An.*, 15.25; cf. *Ep.*, 4.2, 4.9, and 148.38. For a review of the issues, see Goulven Madec, *Saint Augustin et la philosophie*, 15–29.

174. On the background, see H. R. Schwyzer, " 'Bewusst' und 'Unbewusst' bei Plotin," in *Les sources de Plotin*, Entretiens sur l'Antiquité tardive 5 (Vandœuvres-Genève: Fondation Hardt, 1957), 344–90; cf. E. R. Dodds, "Tradition and Personal Achievement in the Philosophy of Plotinus," reprinted in Dodds, *The Ancient Concept of Progress and Other Essays on Greek Literature and Belief* (Oxford: Clarendon, 1973), 135–36. Dodds's claim that Plotinus invented the Western notion of the self is now considered an overstatement; see Richard Sorabji, *Self: Ancient and Modern Insights About Individuality, Life, and Death* (Oxford: Clarendon, 2006), 119.

175. See the discussion of time and personal identity in James Wetzel, *Augustine and the Limits of Virtue* (Cambridge: Cambridge University Press, 1992), 26–37.

176. On this topic see the survey of Peter Brown, *The Body and Society: Men, Women and Sexual Renunciation in Early Christianity* (New York: Columbia University Press, 1988), 387–427; on soliloquy, autobiography, and the incarnation, see Stock, "Self, Soliloquy, and Spiritual Exercises in Augustine and Some Later Authors," *Journal of Religion* 91, 1 (2011): 8–13.

177. See Pierre Hadot, "Platon et Plotin dans trois sermons de saint Ambroise," *Revue des Études Latines* 34 (1956): 202–20.

178. On this topic, see Goulven Madec, " 'Verus philosophus est amator Dei': S. Ambroise, S. Augustin, et la philosophie," *Revue des Sciences Philosophiques et Théologiques* 61 (1977): 549–66.

179. See Pierre Courcelle, *Recherches sur les "Confessions" de saint Augustin*, 93–138; cf. Courcelle, "Nouveaux aspects du platonisme chez saint Ambroise" *Revue des Études Latines* 34 (1956): 225–39. It is possible that the sermon also drew the attention of Augustine to this text when he came to write *De Genesi*, book 12.

180. For a line by line comparison of sources, see André Mandouze, "L'extase d'Ostie: Possibilités et limites de la méthode des parallèles textuels," in *Augustinus Magister* (Paris: Études Augustiniennes, 1954), vol. 1, 67–84. See also Jean Pépin, "Primitiae spiritus: Remarques sur une citation paulinienne des 'Confessions' de saint Augustin," reprinted in *"Ex Platonicorum Persona": Études sur les lectures philosophiques de saint Augustin* (Amsterdam: Hakkert, 1977), 133–80; more generally, Paul Henry, *La vision d'Ostie: Sa place dans la Vie et l'Œuvre de saint Augustin* (Paris: Vrin, 1938), 15–26, and Aimé Solignac in *Les Confessions, livres I–VII*, Œuvres de saint Augustin, *BA*, vol. 14 (Paris: Desclée de Brouwer, 1962), 191–97.

181. For an example of a text citing Plotinus and Paul that was probably known to Augustine see Ambrose, *On Isaac or the Soul* 4.1; *CSEL*, vol. 32 (Vienna, 1897), p. 650, 15–651, 7.

182. See *De Trin.*, XV.11.20.

183. See above all Isabelle Bochet, *"Le firmament de l'Écriture": L'herméneutique augustinienne* (Paris: Institut d'Études Augustiniennes, 2004), 157–325.

184. E.g., Marcus Aurelius, *Med.*, II.14; II.17; III.1, and especially VIII.36, where he advises his readers not to be confused by the mental image created by an entire life; for the philosophical justification, see V.23.

185. On this topic and its contemporary echo, see Isabelle Bochet, *Augustin dans la pensée de Paul Ricoeur* (Paris: Éditions des Facultés Jésuites, 2004).

186. *Disc.*, I.xxviii.12; vol. 1, p. 180; cf. I.xxviii.31; vol. 1, p. 186, for a similarly negative view of the plays of Euripides and Sophocles.

187. For an alternative approach, see Sabine MacCormack, *The Shadow of Poetry: Vergil in the Mind of Augustine* (Berkeley: University of California Press, 1998).

188. *De Civ. Dei* XI.18, where he speaks of a rhetoric of facts rather than words.

189. Philostratus, *Life of Apollonius*, VI.19.

190. On the distinction to which Augustine refers often see *De Musica*. VI.11.32 and chapter 5; for a recent discussion of the background, see Emmanuel Bermon, "Un échange entre Augustin et Nebridius sur la *phantasia* (Lettres 6–7)," *Archives de Philosophie* 72 (2009): 199–222.

191. See Jerome Bruner, "The Narrative Creation of Self," in *Making Stories: Law, Literature, Life* (Cambridge, Mass.: Harvard University Press, 2002), 63–87.

192. See James Olney, *Memory and Narrative: The Weave of Life-Writing* (Chicago: University of Chicago Press, 1998), 1–83.

193. On Boethius's literary orientation, a good introduction is Seth Lerer, *Boethius and Dialogue: Literary Method in "The Consolation of Philosophy"* (Princeton, N.J.: Princeton

University Press, 1985), 46–56, 69–93. On the method of alternating prose and verse, see John Magee, "Boethius' Anapestic Dimiters (Acatalectic), with Regard to the Structure and Argument of the *Consolatio*," in *Boèce ou la chaîne des savoirs*, ed. Alain Galonnier (Louvain-La-Neuve: Éditions de l'Institut Supérieur de Philosophie, 2003), 147–69, with a useful bibliography on the *prosimetrum*, 147, n.1.

194. Henry Chadwick, *Boethius: The Consolations of Music, Logic, Theology, and Philosophy* (Oxford: Clarendon, 1981), 223. For an excellent introduction to the thought of Boethius, see John Magee, "Boethius," in *The Cambridge History of Philosophy in Late Antiquity*, ed. L. P. Gerson (Cambridge: Cambridge University Press, 2010). 798–810. A recent commentary is Joachim Gruber, *Kommentar zu Boethius, De consolatione philosophiae*, 2nd ed. (Berlin: de Gruyter, 2010).

195. On this theme see the eloquent statement of John Magee, "Boethius' *Consolatio* and the Theme of Roman Liberty," *Phoenix* 59 (2005): 348–64.

196. On Boethius's Greek and Latin sources, see Joachim Gruber, *Kommentare zu Boethius De Consolatione Philosophiae*, 2nd ed.

197. Cf. Friedrich Klingner, *De Boethii consolatione philosophiae*, 3rd ed. (Hildesheim: Weidmann, 2005 [1921]), 9–12, 17, 20, 22.

198. Examples include Servius Sulpicius in Cicero, *Letters to his Friends*, IV.5; Horace, *Odes* I.xxiv; and Seneca, *Consolations* to Marcia, Helvia, and Polybius. Cicero's *consolatio* on the death of his daughter, Tullia, has not survived. The themes of the *consolatio* enter the tradition of the philosophical soliloquy in the *Meditations* of Marcus Aurelius, where they draw attention to the inevitability of death, no matter what one's station in life; e.g., III.3, IV.32, 33, 48, 50; VI.27, 47; VII.49; VIII.5, 25, etc.

199. Examples include Plato's *Apology* and *Euthydemus* and Cicero's (lost) *Hortensius*, which converted Augustine to the study of philosophy at age nineteen; *Conf.* III.2.4. Important studies on the subject include Ingemar Düring, *Aristotle's Protrepticus: An Attempt at Reconstruction* (Götheborg: Acta Universitatis Gotoburgensis, 1961); A. J. Festugière, *Les trois "protreptiques" de Platon: "Euthydemus," "Phédon," "Epinomis"* (Paris: Vrin, 1973); Cicero, *Hortensius*, ed. Alberto Grilli (Milan: Istituto Editoriale Cisalpino, 1962). On the difficulty of defining the genre, see Mark D. Jordan, "Ancient Philosophic Protreptic and the Problem of Persuasive Genres," *Rhetorica* 4, 4 (1986): 309–33.

200. Cf. Pierre Courcelle, *La Consolation de Philosophie dans la tradition littéraire* (Paris: Études Augustiniennes, 1967), 18.

201. Boethius, *De Consolatione Philosophiae* I, prose 2, ed. Ludwig Bieler, rev. ed. (CCSL 94): "Sui paulisper oblitus est; recordabitur facile, si quidem nos ante cognouerit."

202. On this topic, see Pedro Laín Entralgo, *The Therapy of the Word in Classical Antiquity*, trans. and ed. L. J. Rather and J. M. Sharp (New Haven, Conn.: Yale University Press, 1970).

203. *De Cons. Phil.*, I, pr. 3.

204. *De Cons. Phil.*, I, pr. 5: "Sed tu quam procul a patria non quidem pulsus es sed aberrasti; ac si te pulsum existimari mauis, te potius ipse pepulisti."

205. *De Cons. Phil.*, I, pr. 5, trans. P. G. Walsh, *Boethius: The Consolation of Philosophy* (Oxford: Oxford University Press, 1999), 15. On Boethius's conception of a private library, see Michael Lapidge, *The Anglo-Saxon Library* (Oxford: Oxford University Press, 2006), 11–12.

206. *Crito* 44b–c, trans. G. M. A. Grube in *Plato: Complete Works*, ed. with Intro. and Notes by John M. Cooper and D. S. Hutchinson (Indianapolis: Hackett, 1997), 39. The references to this passage, which has been drawn to my attention by John Magee, may have been

based on the Latin translation of Calcidius; see *Timaeus a Calcidio translatus commentarioque instructus*, ed. J. H. Waszink, Plato Latinus, vol. 4 (London: Warburg Institute, 1962), 263, 7–8: "Uisa est mihi quaedam, inquit [Plato, *Crito* 44a], mulier eximia uenustate, etiam candida ueste."

207. *De Cons. Phil.*, I, pr. 6 ff. One might add that the source behind this source is very probably Cicero's lost *Hortensius*; on the background see Goulven Madec and Isabelle Bochet, "Augustin et l'*Hortensius* de Cicéron: Notes de lectures," in *Augustin philosophe et prédicateur: Hommage à Goulven Madec*, ed. Isabelle Bochet (Paris: Institut d'Études Augustiniennes, 2012), 197–294.

208. For an enduring analysis of the sources of Boethius's views including *Crito*, see Klingner, *De Boethii consolatione philosphiae*, 112–18.

209. *Sol.*, 2.1.1.

210. *De Cons. Phil.*, I, pr. 6.

211. *De Cons. Phil.*, I, pr. 6, trans. P. G Walsh, pp. 16–17.

212. The texts differ but the argument is comparable (my italics):

Augustine,	Boethius,
Sol., 2.1.1:	*De Con. Phil.*, I, pr. 6, 14–17:
Ratio: Tu qui vis te nosse, *scis esse te*?	Phil: Sed hoc quoque respondeas
Aug.: Scio.	uelim: hominemne te esse
Ratio: Unde scis?	meministi?
Aug: Nescio.	Boe.: Quidne, inquam, meminerim?
Ratio: Simplicem te sentis anne	Phil.: Quid igitur homo sit poterisne
multiplicem?	proferre?
Aug.: Nescio.	Boe.: Hocine interrogas, an *esse me*
Ratio: Moveri te scis?	*sciam* rationale animal atque
Aug.: Nescio	mortale? *Scio*, et id me esse
Ratio: Cogitare te scis?	confiteor.
Aug.: *Scio*.	Phil.: Et illa: Nihilne aliud te esse
Ratio: Ergo verum est cogitare te.	nouisti?
Aug.: Verum.	Boe.: Nihil.
Ratio: Immortalem te esse scie	
Aug.: Nescio	
Ratio: Horum omnium, quae te	
nescire dixisti,	
quid sit scire prius mavis?	
Aug.: Utrum immortalis sim.	

213. Courcelle argued that Augustine was not one of Boethius's major philosophical sources; *La Consolation de Philosophie dans la tradition littéraire*, 24; however, Klingner points out that Boethius echoes Augustine on such questions as the good and free will; *De Boethii consolatione philosophiae*, pp. 43 and 72 (the good) and pp. 103–4 (free will). To the list of Augustinian works mentioned in Klingner's Index, namely *De Civ. Dei*, *Conf.*, *De Lib. Arbit.*, and *Enn. in Psalmos*, should be added *Sol.* (at *Cons. Phil.*, I pr. 6) and *De Mag.* (at III, pr. 12) as well, perhaps, as *De Beata Vita* in both.

214. E.g., *Apology* 21b, ff.

215. *De Cons. Phil.*, III, pr. 12: "'Ludisne,' inquam, "me inextricabilem labyrinthum rationibus texens." Cf. Augustine, *Sol.*, I2.7.13–14; *De Mag.*, 10.31.

216. Plato, *Theaetetus* 189–90a; trans. M. J. Levett, rev. Myles Burnyeat, in *Plato: Complete Works*, ed. Cooper and Hutchinson, 210.

CHAPTER 4. SELF AND SOUL

1. Trans. G. M. A. Grube in *Plato: Complete Works*, ed. Cooper and Hutchinson, 97–98.

2. For a critical review of publications in the field, see Goulven Madec, *Saint Augustin et la philosophie*, 15–52.

3. See Christopher Gill, *Personality in Greek Epic, Tragedy and Philosophy: The Self in Dialogue*, 2nd ed. (Oxford: Oxford University Press, 1996 [1969]).

4. *Conf.*, 1.14.23. Another reason, as noted, may have been his bicultural family, in which it is assumed both Punic and Latin were used. Greek was not his second language but his third.

5. On this theme, see the reflections of Sabine McCormack, *The Shadows of Poetry: Vergil in the Mind of Augustine.*

6. The most thorough study of this question is Maurice Testard, *Saint Augustin et Cicéron*, 2 vols. (Paris: Institut des Études Augustiniennes, 1968).

7. *Conf.*, 10.16.25.

8. For a review of the subject and a full bibliography, see Gerald G. P. O'Daly, "Anima, animus," *Augustinus-Lexikon*, vol. 1, 315–40.

9. O'Daly, 315–16.

10. *De Trin.* 14.26.

11. *De Genesi ad Litteram*, 7.21.28; my trans.

12. *De Immortalitate Animae* 1.1; PL 32.1021: "Si alicubi est disciplina, nec esse nisi in eo quod vivit potest, et semper est."

13. *De Imm. An.*, 3.4; 1023: "Hinc jam colligimus, posse esse quiddam quod cum movet mutabilia, non mutatur."

14. *De Imm. An.*, 3.4: 1023: "Non igitur si qua mutatio corporum movente animo fit, quamvis in eam sit intentus, hinc eum necessario mutari, et ob hoc etiam mori arbitrandum est."

15. *De Imm. An.*, 6.10: 1025–26, "Ergo incumbendum omnibus rationcinandi viribus video, ut ratio quid sit, et quoties definiri possit sciatur, ut secundum omnes modos et de animae immortalitate constet."

16. *De Imm. An.*, 6.10.1026: "Ratio est aspectus animi, quo per seipsum, non per corpus . . . , aut ipsa vera contemplatio . . . aut ipsum verum quod contemplator."

17. *De Imm. An.*, 6.10.1026: "Nam omne quod contemplamur, sive cogitatione capimus, aut sensu aut intellectu capimus. Sed ea quae sensu capiuntur, extra etiam nos esse sentiuntur, et locis continentur; unde nec percipi quidem posse afirmantur. Ea vero quae intelliguntur, non quasi alibi posita intelliguntur, quam ipse qui intelligit animus: simul enim etiam intelliguntur non contineri loco."

18. *De Quantitate Animae* 33.70 (CSEL, vol. 79): "In primis tamen tibi amputem latissimam quandam et infinitam exspectationem, ne me de omni anima dicturum putes, sed tantum de humana, quam solam curare debemus, si nobismetipsis curae sumus."

19. *De Quant. An.* 33.71: "Ubi evidentior manifestiorque vita intelligitur."

20. *De Quant. An.*, 33.71: "Removet se ab his sensibus certo intervallo temporum et eorum motus quas per quasdam ferias reparans imagines rerum, quas per eos hausit, secum catervatim et multipliciter versat; et hoc totum est somnus et somnia."

21. *De Quan. An.*, 33.71: "Pro copulatione sexus agit quod potest atque in duplici natura societate atque amore molitur unum."

22. *De Quant. An.*, 33.71: "Rebus inter quas corpus agit, et quibus corpus sustentat, consuetudine sese innectit, et ab eis quasi membris aegre separatur: quae consuetudinis vis etiam seiunctione rerum ipsarum atque intervallo temporis non discissa memoria vocatur." In my rendering of the first clause I read *corpus* as subject of *agit* but object of *sustentat*.

23. *De Quant. An.*, 33.73, reading *si quam universi partem agit* as an "even if" clause in relation to *sed ipsi*, etc., which follows in a lengthy series of clauses. Augustine is suggesting that the soul, as an aspect of world-soul, always acts on behalf of a part of the whole order (*universi partem*) and in reaching level four acts on behalf of the whole order (*sed ipsi universe corpori audit praeponere*).

24. Matt. 28: 9; Jn. 20: 11 ff.

25. *De Beata Vita* 4.34, citing Jn. 14: 6.

26. *Confessions*, 3.4.8.

27. Mk. 8: 34–38, trans. *The New English Bible: New Testament* (Oxford: Oxford University Press, 1961), 70.

28. Vincent Taylor, *The Gospel According to St. Mark* (London: Macmillan, 1952), 381.

29. Cf. Mk. 4: 10, where both are mentioned.

30. However, see Mk. 8: 34; 9: 38; 10: 21, etc.

31. *Vita Antonii*, c. 2; Matt. 19: 21.

32. *Conf.*, 8.12.29, trans. Chadwick.

33. Gal. 3:27; Colos. 3:12; cf. 1 Thess. 5:8.

34. E.g., *De Trinitate* 8.6.9, where we find Augustine's favorite examples of these two types of memory images, i.e., Carthage, which he has seen, and Alexandria, which he has not seen.

35. Pierre Courcelle, *Recherches sur les Confessions de saint Augustin*, 175–202. The ensuing literature on the veracity of the garden scene is summarized by H.-I. Marrou, "La quelle autour du 'Tolle, lege,'" *Revue d'Histoire Ecclésiastique* 53 (1958): 47–57. For a judicious review of the issues, see Henry Chadwick, "History and Symbolism in the Garden at Milan," in *From Augustine to Eriugena: Essays in Neoplatonism and Christianity in Honor of John O'Meara*, ed. Francis X. Martin and John A. Richmond (Washington, D.C.: Catholic University of America Press, 1991), 42–55.

CHAPTER 5. RHYTHMS OF TIME

1. *Ep.* 166, c. 5.13; *Patrologia Latina* 34, col. 726; trans. Sister Wilfrid Parsons, S.N.D., *Saint Augustine: Letters*, vol. 4 (New York: Fathers of the Church, 1955), 18–19; slightly modified.

2. A. A. Long, "The Harmonics of Stoic Virtue," in *Stoic Studies*, 202.

3. This is of course a formal rather than substantive source; on Augustine's general knowledge of Plato, see the excellent review of Goulven Madec, *Saint Augustin et la philosophie*, 1–52.

4. Trans. G. M. A. Grube in *Plato: Complete Works*, ed. Cooper and Hutchinson, 880. For a discussion, see Gregory Vlastos, "*Anamnesis* in the *Meno*," *Dialogue* 4 (1965–66): 143–67.

5. *De Magistro* 13.43; cf. Goulven Madec, "Analyse du *De magistro*," *Revue des Études Augustiniennes* 21 (1975), 69.

6. For a review, see O'Daly, *Augustine's Philosophy of Mind*, 70–75.

7. William Wordsworth, *The Lyrical Ballads 1798–1805*, ed. George Sampson (London: Methuen, 1961), 33.

8. *De Imm. An.*, 4.6.

9. For a brief account of other features of Augustine's theory of memory, see my study, *Augustine's Inner Dialogue: The Philosophical Soliloquy in Late Antiquity*, 211–21; on his place in the subject's lengthier history, see Mary Carruthers, *The Book of Memory: A Study* and Janet Coleman, *Ancient and Medieval Memories: Studies in the Reconstruction of the Past* (Cambridge: Cambridge University Press, 1992).

10. *Conf.*, 10.27.38.

11. My translation is based on the version of Maria Boulding, O.S.B., *The Confessions: Saint Augustine*, trans. and intro. R. S. Pine-Coffin (New York: Vintage, 1997), 222, however with modifications.

12. *Conf.*, 1.1.1.

13. Trans. Chadwick.

14. Plotinus, *Enneads* 1.6.8, trans. A. H. Armstrong, *Plotinus*, vol. 1, revised ed. (Cambridge, Mass.: Harvard University Press, 1989), 255, 257; for other examples, see Armstrong, 255, n. 5.

15. On this theme see the enduring study of E. R. Curtius, *European Literature and the Latin Middle Ages*, chap. 10.

16. This retrospective text is more complicated than it first appears, since Augustine intermingles the reading of Psalm 4, which he was studying and reading aloud at the time, with his memory of the reading of other texts after 387, for example Ps. 18:7, 30:7–8, 138:21, and 142:10, as well as his reading of Paul, Eph. 1:20, Rom. 8:34, 1 Cor. 15:54, 2 Cor. 4:18, and other New Testament texts, e.g., Jn. 14:16 ff., Matt. 3:6. The overall schema of his reading of Psalm 4 is typological.

17. See *De Musica* 6.9.23; 6.13.39.

18. See Leo Ferrari, "The Theme of the Prodigal Son in Augustine's *Confessions*," *Recherches Augustiniennes* 12 (1979): 105–18 and James J. O'Donnell, ed., *Confessions*, vol. 2 (Oxford: Clarendon, 1992), 95–98.

19. Cf. *Conf.*, 2.5.10, on types of beauty, on which Augustine had apparently spoken in *De Pulchro et Apto* (380–81).

20. *Retractationes.*, 1.6; cf. *Ep.*, 101.3, to Memorius in 405.

21. *De Grammatica* was known to Cassiodorus and may have survived as the *Ars Breviata*. The number of surviving texts rises to three if *De Dial.* is included. *De Mus.* was to have six books *quae rhythmus vocatur*, i.e., on rhythm (*Retr.*, 1.6) and six books *de melo*, i.e., on harmonics (*Ep.*, 101). H.-I. Marrou, *S. Augustin et la fin de la culture antique*, 4th ed. (Paris: E. de Boccard, 1958), 580–83, suggested 408–9 as a *terminus ad quem* for book 6, but internal evidence suggests a much earlier date for at least a provisional revision of books 1–5, which I cite in this chapter from *De Musica libri sex*, ed. G. Finaert and F.-J. Thonnard, *Bibliothèque Augustinienne*, 1 ser., vol. 4 (Paris: Institut des Études Augustiniennes, 1947). This text reproduces with minor corrections *Patrologia Latina* 32.1081–1194 from the Maurist edition of 1836, and has occasionally been checked against two early manuscripts, B.N. lat 13375 and B.N. lat. 7200. I quote book 6 in the edition of Martin Jacobsson, Aurelius Augustinus, *De musica liber VI: A*

Critical Edition with a Translation and an Introduction, Acta Universitatis Stockholmiensis, Studia Latina Stockholmiensia 47 (Stockholm: Almqvist & Wiksell, 2002). This edition contains a useful review of issues concerned with the dating and interpretation of *De Mus.*, pp. ix–xxvii, concluding, with Marrou, that book 6 was in some form emended, as Augustine wrote to Memorius in 408 or 409 (*Ep.*, 101.3–4); also that "there exists . . . only one version of the sixth book" (p. xxvii).

22. *Ep.* 101.3.

23. *Retr.*, 1.6: "sed haberi ab aliquibus existimo."

24. Ilsetraut Hadot, *Ars libéraux et philosophie dans la pensée antique*, 101.

25. In his enthusiasm, Alypius overlooks the fact that there are two principles of organization, language and number.

26. *De Ordine.*, 2.20.53–54; cf. Claudius Mamertus, *De Stat. An.*, 2.8, noting Varro's remark that in music, arithmetic, geometry, and philosophy, one moves from the corporeal to the incorporeal.

27. Books 2–5 are largely concerned with technical matters pertaining to versification, i.e., types of feet (book 2), aspects of rhythm and harmony (books 3–4), and verse forms (book 5).

28. The transition is paralleled in *De Libero Arbitrio*, in which books 1 and 2 contain no quotations from Scripture, whereas in book 3, written after Augustine's ordination, they are numerous.

29. Cf. Ragnar Holte, *Béatitude et sagesse: Saint Augustin et le problème de la fin de l'homme dans la philosophie ancienne* (Paris: Institut d'Études Augustiniennes, 1962), 46–47. Augustine's reverence for Pythagoras echoes Cicero, *Tusculanae Disputationes*. 1.17.38–39; 4.1.2.

30. Cf. Marrou, *Saint Augustin*, 200; and, on *scientia*, 561–62. In what follows, I have normally rendered *scientia* as "knowledge," except where the context specifically demands another translation. Augustine's use of *musica* is more difficult to translate by a single term. The usual translation, "music," based on Varro and Cicero, is too restricted. Within *De Mus.*, Augustine has in mind something closer to the Greek μουσική, which includes music, dance, metrical poetry, and the playing of instruments.

31. *Laws* 668d; trans. Trevor J. Saunders in *Plato: Complete Works*, ed. Cooper and Hutchinson, 1358.

32. I am indebted here to the valuable synthesis of Phillip de Lacey, "Stoic Views of Poetry," *American Journal of Philology* 69 (1948): 241–71.

33. *De Civ. Dei*, 10.14, quoting Matt. 6:28 ff., in the light of Plotinus, *Enn.*, 3.2.13.

34. The student is unidentified in the extant manuscript; cf. Evodius in *De Lib. Arbit.* Some believe that Augustine's partner in *De Mus.* is Licentius, since the person in question is knowledgeable about the technical aspects of classical poetry; e.g., *De Mus.*, 3.1.1: "qui uersus te semper cum uoluptate audisse confessus sis." The evidence for this view is summarized and discussed by G. Finaert, *Bibliothèque Augustinienne*, vol. 4, n. 1, pp. 483–84; however, Finaert points out that Licentius appears to have no knowledge of the dialogue at the time of writing *Ep.*, 26, where he notes: "si mihi morem / Gesseris et libros in lenta recumbit / Musica tradideris, nam ferveo in illis." Yet, at *De Mus.*, 1.12.23, speaking of proportion (*analogia*), the master refers to *illa unitas, quam te amare dixisti, in rebus ordinatis*, which recalls Licentius's speech at *De Ord.*, 1.5.14: "Quis neget, deus magne, . . . te cuncta ordine administrare? Quam se omnia tenent! quam ratis successionibus in nodos suos urgentur! " The last of these exclamations speaks of proportion in the mathematical context in which the problem is raised in

De Mus. Another possibility for the student, although remote, is Adeodatus, who was clever enough to follow the technical discussion of meter, just as he appears to have assimilated ancient teachings on language for his role in *De Mag.* When distinguishing between *phantasiae* and *phantasma* at 6.11.32, Augustine states that he knew his father but not his grandfather; he also uses the example *parens* at 2.8.15. The force of these references would have been enhanced if the student had been his son. Also, at 6.5.9, there may be an echo of the discussion of *De Mag.*, when the master enlists the student's aid in helping him explain what happens when something is heard: "[Magister]: Cito dicam quid sentio: tu vero aut sequere, aut etiam praecede, si valebis, ubi me cunctari et haesitare animadverteris." Augustine spoke of the difficulty at *Ep.*, 101.3: "Difficillime quippe intelliguntur in eo quinque libri, si non adsit qui non solum disputantium possit separare personas."

35. Cf. *De Beata Vita* 4.33, on achieving wisdom through virtue (*moderatio animi*): "Modus animi, hoc est quo sese animus librat, ut neque excurrat in nimium neque infra quam plenum est coartetur."

36. Cf. *De Civ. Dei*, 8.17, on *pathos* as an irrational movement of the soul, which can affect even the wise man; cf. 9.4; cf. Cicero, *Tusc. Disp.*, 4.6.11; for Quintilian, see Chapter 2. Augustine cites Aulus Gellius, and through him Epictetus, in support of his doctrine of involuntary *affectus*, *passiones*, and *perturbationes animi*, which nowadays might be called "emotional disturbances." For the Stoics, these are "advantageous" or "disadvantageous" depending on the circumstances; for Christians, they are training for the soul to be used in the pursuit of justice; 9.5.

37. *De Civ. Dei*, 11.18: "Ita quadam non uerborum, sed rerum eloquentia contrariorum oppositione saeculi pulchritudo componitur." Cf. ibid., 11.23, where the same principle is applied to painting.

38. Cf. *De Mus.*, 6.13.41–42, where Augustine notes that *numeri examinatores* can be called *sensuales*, since it is by means of *sensibilia signa* that souls act on each other.

39. *De Mus.*, 1.1.1: "A grammaticis haec audire soleo, et ibi ea didici; sed utrum hoc ejusdem artis sit proprium, an aliunde usurpatum, nescio."

40. He will subsequently adopt the view that both grammar and numerical harmony are involved; e.g., 2.1.1; 6.1.1.

41. Cf. *De Mus.*, 1.13.27, where this point is important in establishing the role of the senses *in scientia modulandi*. Cf. Cicero, *Tusc. Disp.*, 2.16.37, who notes that the marching meter of the Roman troops was the anapest.

42. *De Mus.*, 1.1.1: "An per teipsum istos pulsus didicisti, sed nomen quod imponeres, a grammatico audieras?" The master will modify this view in the prefaces to books 2 and 5, where the correctness of grammatical instruction is affirmed through both authority and reason.

43. *De Mus.*, 1.1.1: "quidquid in hujusmodi sit vocibus numerosum artificiosumque." The name of the discipline arises from its connection with the Muses, who were traditionally responsible for musical expression; for a less sanguine view of their powers, see *De Doct. Christ.*, 2.17.27

44. Reiterated in *Ep.*, 166, 5.13.

45. This view is modified in *De Mus.*, 1.3–5, through the notion of implicit knowledge.

46. *De Mus.*, 1.2.2: "Numquidnam hoc verbum quod modulari dicitur, aut numquam audisti, aut uspiam nisi in eo quod ad cantandum saltandumve pertineret?" This is the first of a number of negative remarks concerning actors, singers, and comedians, doubtless inspired by the low reputation of stage performers in the late empire; cf. *Soliloquia*, 2.10.18; *Conf.*, 3.2.2. Augustine nonetheless develops a commentary on popular versus learned conceptions of music in book 1 that grants an important role for the implicit knowledge of the discipline among

uneducated performers and their equally unsophisticated audiences. When he remarks at 1.2.2 that the pair have not entered into a dialogue just to talk about what any singer or actor knows, he refers to the baser aspects of popular entertainment but looks forward to the role of the senses, judgment, and memory at 1.5.10–1.6.11. The innate knowledge of harmony in performers is recognized as early as 1.2.3; and at 1.4.5 he proposes that educated persons, when they relax, engage in a nontheoretical appreciation of music. Performers who engage in imitation nonetheless employ art, which implies the presence of reason.

47. Cf. *De Mus.*, 1.13.27, where the argument is reiterated without the example.

48. Augustine's sense is close to Cicero, *De Oratore*, 3.48.185–86 and *Orator*, 43.178 and 58.198, the last utilizing the adjective *numerosus*; on the source and meaning of Cicero's statement, which is applied to poetry in *De Mus.* and to prose in *De Doctrina Christiana*, book 4, see the judicious note of G.B. Pighi, " 'Impressio' e 'percussio' in Cic. De Orat. 2,185–86," *L'Antiquité Classique* 28 (1959): 214–22. Cf. Victorinus, *Ars Grammatica*, in H. Keil, *Grammatici Latini*, vol. 6 (Leipzig: Teubner, 1874), 188, under the topic *De lectione*: "Partes lectionis quot sunt? Quattuor. Quae sunt? Accentus, discretio, pronuntiatio, modulatio . . . . Modulatio quid est? Continuati sermonis in iucundiorem dicendi rationem artificialis flexus in delectabilem auditus formam conversus asperitatis vitandae gratia."

49. Cf. *De Mus.*, 1.2.3–1.3.4.

50. Cf. *De Ord.*, 2.19.49: Ratio: "Non ergo numerosa faciendo sed numeros cognoscendo melior sum."

51. A neologism, from *numerosus*; cf. *De Doct. Christ.*, 4.20.40–41, where the topic is prose clausula. Cf. Cicero, *Orat.*, 166, 188.

52. *De Mus.*, 1.2.3: "Non enim possumus dicere bene moveri aliquid, si modum non servat."

53. Ibid.: "Numquidnam ergo ipse motus propter se appetitur, et non propter id quod vult esse tornatum?"

54. Ibid., 1.4.5 ff. One is tempted to compare these levels to the three types of existence in *De Libero Arbitrio*, namely *esse*, *vivere*, and *intellegere*, but there is no type of artistic harmony in *De Mus.* that corresponds to the inanimate in this work. What the two triads have in common is a contrast between animals and humans based on the latter's possession of reason.

55. Cf. *De Mag.*, 1.1, where birds' and humans' popular songs are similarly discussed as types of music that provide only pleasure.

56. Cf. *De Mag.*, 1.1 [Aug.]: "Aliud est loqui aliud cantare; nam et tibiis et cithara cantatur, et aues cantant, et nos interdum sine uerbis musicum aliquid sonamus, qui sonus cantus dici potest, locutio non potest."

57. Augustine will offer a solution to this problem at *De Civ. Dei* 11.29, where he distinguishes between a knowledge of an art and the knowledge of the works in that art. On his earlier distinction, cf. *usus* and *natura* in *De Dialectica*, 10, ed. Jan Pinborg and B. Darrell Jackson (Boston: Reidel, 1975), 114, 38–44.

58. Even teaching (*docere*), since teachers often propose themselves as models *ad imitandum*. Augustine does not consider his other examples, namely popular music and dance, in this part of the discussion. The role of imitation here is comparable to that of gesture when an infant learns to speak; *Conf.*, 1.8.13.

59. *De Mus.*, 1.4.6: "Ex quo jam colligi potest, omnem qui imitando assequitur aliquid, arte uti; etiamsi forte non omnis qui arte utitur, imitando eam perceperit. At si omnis imitatio ars est, et ars omnis ratio; omnis imitatio ratio: ratione autem non utitur irrationale animal; non igitur habet artem: habet autem imitationem; non est igitur ars imitatio."

60. *De Mus.*, 1.4.7: "Istam enim hoc volvimus quaestionem, ut intelligamus, si possumus, quam recte sit scientia in illa definitione musicae posita."

61. Ibid., 1.4.8: "Animo puto esse tribuendam. Non enim si per sensus percipimus aliquid quod memoriae commendamus, ideo in corpore memoria esse putanda est." The master postpones a further discussion of this question until book 6.

62. Ibid., 1.4.9: "quia difficile nobis est; scientia potius quam usu et sedula imitatione ac meditatione fieri putemus."

63. Ibid., 1.5.10: "Illud restat, ut opinor, ut inveniamus, si possumus, has ipsas artes quae nobis per manus placent ut illius usus potentes essent, non continuo scientiam, sed sensum ac memoriam secutas."

64. Ibid.: "Numquidnam id a vulgo per artem musicam fieri credendum est?"

65. Ibid.: "Natura id fieri puto, quae omnibus dedit sensum audiendi, quo ista judicantur." Augustine will refine his notion of aesthetic judgment in book 6.

66. There is also a change in the nature of the dialogue. The student, who has actively participated to this point, increasingly limits himself to asking questions that merely demand further explanation on the master's part. In this respect, book 1 of *De Mus.* and book 1 of *De Lib. Arbit.* are comparable in relation to the rest of their respective discussions.

67. Cf. *Conf.*, 11.14.19–11.16.21; 11.16.33. The numerical relations outlined by Augustine in this section of *De Mus.* have been the subject of commentary by Marrou, *Saint Augustin*, 251–62. This is in my view a rather too negative a view of Augustine's achievement, which is elementary in number theory but sophisticated in its application of harmony and proportion to aesthetics.

68. Cf. *Sol.*, 2.6.11, which provides a classification of things that resemble each other by being either equal or inferior, paralleled here by the rational and irrational. In his discussion of numerical relations, Augustine distantly echoes the Pythagorean and Platonic view that emphasizes the importance of the primal numbers, one, two, three, and four, which, as suggested in *De Mus.*, provide the connection between the abstract harmony of mathematics and the harmony of the empirical world.

69. *Sesque* is not descended from *se absque*; see Finaert, *Bibliothèque Augustinienne*, vol. 4, n. 19, 494–95.

70. *De Mus.*, 1.12.22: "Ergo haec duo principia numerorum sibimet copulata, totum numerum faciunt atque perfectum." The relationship is lucidly described by Marrou, *Saint Augustin*, 260.

71. Ibid., 1.12.23: "Quae quantum valeat, eo jam assuesce cognoscere, quod illa unitas quam te amare dixisti, in rebus ordinatis hac una effici potest, cujus graecum nomen ἀναλογία est." At *De Utilitate Credendi*, 5.4–9, written shortly after his ordination, Augustine refers to *analogia* in an interpretive context as one of the four senses of scripture; 5.1–4. Cf. *De Gen. ad Litt. Imper.*, 2.5, and, for a discussion of Augustine's usage, H. de Lubac, *Exégèse médiévale*, vol. 1 (Paris: Aubier, 1959), 177–87, which, unfortunately, does not take account of the statement on *analogia* in *De Mus.*

72. *De Mus.*, 1.13.27.

73. Cf. *De Mus.*, 1.1, where the master, giving this example, remarked, "Post ista videbimus."

74. Ibid., 2.1.1: "An vero sive ista noris sive ignores, malis ut ita quaeramus, quasi omnino rudes harum rerum simus, ut ad omnia nos ratio potius perducat, quam inveterata consuetudo, aut praejudicata cogat auctoritas."

75. Ibid.: "Atqui scias velim totam illam scientiam, quae grammatica graece, latine autem litteratura nominatur, historiae custodiam profiteri, vel solam, ut subtilior docet ratio, vel maxime, ut etiam pinguia corda concedunt."

76. Ibid.: "Grammaticus . . . jubet emendari . . . secundum majorum, ut dictum est, auctoritatem, quorum scripta custodit." Cf. *De Mag.*, 2.3 and the interesting appendix of John Rist, *Augustine* (Cambridge: Cambridge University Press, 1994), 314–16, arguing for Porphyry as source.

77. Ibid., 2.1.1: "Tempora enim vocum ea pervenere ad aures, quae illi numero debita fuerunt."

78. Cf. *Ep.*, 101.4; Marrou, *Saint Augustin*, 580–83.

79. Ibid., 6.1.1: "Illos igitur libros qui leget inueniet nos cum grammaticis et poeticis animis non habitandi electione sed itinerandi necessitate uersatos."

80. Marrou, *Saint Augustin*, 270, notes four metrical uses for silence: to justify the indifference of the final syllable, to complete this syllable, to begin a meter or verse, and to facilitate scansion. This emphasis is new in Augustine, as contrasted with his sources on meter, and may have resulted from his conception of reading, in which was natural to speak of periods of sound and silence, even when reading aloud.

81. Ambrose, *Hymni* 1.2.1; quoted at *De Mus.*, 6.2.2, 6.9.23, and 6.17.57. For other occurrences in Augustine's writings, see James J. O'Donnell, ed., *Augustine. Confessions*, vol. 3 (Oxford: Oxford University Press, 1992), 142–43. Augustine's approach is partly anticipated by Aristoxenus, *Elementa Rhythmica*, 1.8–10 and in particular 2.38–39, where it is argued that the comprehension of a melody requires that the hearer register a succession of sounds by means of the ears and the mind. This is achieved through sense perception and memory, since, in order to appreciate a musical composition, it is necessary to perceive the sound that is present and to remember the sound that has passed. Against the possibility of direct (or, as is probable, indirect) influence, it should be noted that Aristoxenus does not discuss the implications for the conception of time. His anti-Platonic attitude contrasts with that of Augustine, who, as noted, derives his notions of time directly or indirectly from Plato.

82. A sentiment expressed in numerous ways in the early writings, e.g., *De Genesi ad Manichaeos*, 1.21.32: "Totus enim ille sermo non de singulis syllabis aut litteris, sed de omnibus pulcher est."

83. Cf. *De Mag.*, 12.39.

84. Cf. *De Lib. Arbit.*, 2.8.20–23.

85. Marrou, *Saint Augustin*, 580–83, suggested that the preface was sent to Memorius in order to make book 6 appear to be a unit in itself; however, the statement in the letter applies to the transition between books 1–5 and book 6. The former were not sent; therefore, it is an introduction to the whole treatise, admittedly written as an afterthought.

86. *De Mus.*, 6.1.1: "Nam turba cetera de scholis linguarum tumultuantium, et adplaudentium strepitu uulgari leuitate laetantium, si forte inruit in has litteras [i.e., librum sextum], aut contemnet omnes aut illos quinque libros sufficere sibi arbitrabitur. Istum vero in quo fructum illorum est, uel abiciet quasi non necessarium, uel differet quasi post necessarium." The *adplaudentium strepitus* is a negative reference to the reproduction of poetic meters by clapping, striking an instrument, or other physical means; cf. 1.13.27.

87. Ibid., 6.1.1: "cuncta puerilia transvolauerunt, . . . uolando se posse etiam ignorata transire."

88. Ibid.: [qui] . . . puluerem huius itineris euadant ."

89. Ibid. The *retia* may refer to Manichaeans or Academics; cf. 6.4.7, whereas Augustine speaks of his readers as "holy and better persons," who understand the inner meaning of Christ's death and resurrection.

90. *De Mus.*, 6.2.2: "Responde, si uidetur, cum istum uersum pronuntiamus, *Deus creator omnium*, istos quatuor iambos quibus constat, et tempora duodecim, ubinam esse arbitreris, id est, in sono tantum qui auditur, an etiam in sensu audientis qui ad aures pertinet, an in actu etiam pronuntiantis an, quia notus uersus est, in memoria quoque nostra hos numeros esse fatendum est?" It is assumed that one of the twelve intervals of time occurs at the beginning and the other at the end when the line is read.

91. Ibid.: Disc.: "In his omnibus puto." It is interesting, although perhaps accidental, that this involves a transformation of the primary sequence of books 1 and 2, namely 1, 2, 3, 4; cf. 1.12.23–24. Augustine's fascination with numerical relations is an aspect of his several commentaries on Wisd. 11:21: "You have ordered all things in measure, number, and weight"; e.g., *De Civ. Dei*, 11.30.

92. Ibid., 6.2.2: "ut in aliquo loco aliquis sonus existat huiuscemodi morulis et dimensionibus uerberans aerem uel stillicidio uel aliquo alio pulsu corporum, ubi nullus adsit auditor."

93. Ibid., 6.2.3: "Non enim et cum silentium est, nihil a surdis differunt."

94. Ibid.: "Siquidem aliud est habere numeros, aliud posse sentire numerosum sonum."

95. Ibid.: "Idipsum ergo quidquid est, quo aut adnuimus aut abhorremus, non ratione sed natura, cum aliquid sonat, ipsius sensus numerum uoco." This statement returns to the problem of nature and reason discussed in another context at 1.4.5 ff.

96. E.g., 1.5.10; 1.6.12; 1.13.27.

97. Cf. 1.7.13–1.8.14; 2.2.2.

98. Ibid., 6.2.3: "Adfectio ergo haec aurium cum tanguntur sono, nullo modo talis est ac si non tangantur." It is assumed that *tangere* refers both to the sound and to the beating of the metrical rhythm.

99. Ibid.: "Similis est enim uestigio in aqua impresso."

100. Ibid.: "non in silentio."

101. Ibid., 6.3.4: "Adtende igitur hoc tertium genus, quod est in ipso nisu et operatione pronuntiantis."

102. Ibid.: "Nam et taciti apud nosmet ipsos possumus aliquos numeros cogitandi peragere ea mora temporis qua etiam uoce peragerentur." This would be the musical equivalent of the *dicibile*, the word that is thought but not said; *De Dial.*, 5.

103. Ibid.: "Hos in quadam operatione animi esse manifestum est, quae quoniam nullum edit sonum nihilque passionis infert auribus."

104. If we then direct our thoughts elsewhere, these recollections recede again into the regions of our minds in which they were located when we are not thinking about them; ibid., 6.3.4: "Nam si eos recordatione depromimus, et cum in alias cogitationes deferimur, hos rursum relinquimus uelut in suis secretis reconditos."

105. Ibid., 6.4.5: "quintum genus, quod est in ipso naturali iudicio sentiendi, cum delectamur parilitate numerorum, uel cum in eis peccatur, offendimur."

106. Ibid., 6.4.6: "Quia uideo ibi diuturniores esse numeros quam cum sonant, uel cum audiuntur, uel cum aguntur."

107. Ibid., 6.4.6; reiterating the example from 1.13.27.

108. Does this analogy hold? Not precisely: the student has in mind the same genus, i.e., a line of verse read at different speeds (or configured in the mind as if it were read), whereas the

master is speaking of two different species within a single genus, i.e., health/illness or reading/ writing.

109. *De Mus.*, 6.4.6: "Ita numeri, qui sunt in memoria, etiamsi diutius manent quam illi, a quibus inprimuntur, non eos tamen anteponere oportet eis, quos agimus non in corpore sed in anima. Vtrique enim praetereunt, alii cessatione, alii obliuione."

110. Ibid., 6.4.6: "Non sentitur ista diminutio."

111. Ibid.: "Vnde intelligi datur ab illo tempore quo inhaeret memoriae, incipere labi. Hinc est illud, quod plerumque dicimus, 'tenuiter memini,' . . . . Quapropter utrumque hoc numerorum genus mortale est."

112. Ibid., 6.4.7: "Hos enim sentimus audientes, et cum hos sentimus, hos patimur. Hi ergo faciunt eos qui sunt in aurium passione cum audimus. Hi autem rursus quos sentiendo habemus, faciunt alios in memoria, quibus a se factis recte praeferuntur."

113. Ibid.: "Illud me conturbat, quomodo sonantes numeri, qui certe corporei sunt uel quoquo modo in corpore, magis laudandi sint quam illi, qui, cum sentimus, in anima esse reperiuntur."

114. Ibid.: "Sed rursus conturbat, quomodo non magis laudandi sint, cum hi faciant, illi ab his fiant."

115. On the conceptions of *numerositas* and *convenientia* in this section, see Nello Cipriani, "Lo schema dei *tria vizia (uoluptas, superbia, curiositas* nel *De uera religione*. Antropologia sogiacente e fonti," *Augustinianum* 38 (1998), 162–68.

116. Ibid., 6.4.7: "Hoc enim esse fortasse non posset, si non peccato primo corpus illud quod nulla molestia et summa facilitate <anima> animabat et gubernabat, in deterius commutatum conruptioni subiceretur et morti; quod tamen habet sui generis pulchritudinem et eo ipso dignitatem animae satis commendat, cujus nec plaga nec moribus sine honore alicujus decoris meruit esse."

117. Ibid.: "Ergo animam in carne mortali operantem passionem corporum sentire non mirum est. Nec, quia ipsa est corpore melior, melius putandum est omne quod in ea fit, quam omne quod fit in corpore."

118. Ibid., 6.5.13: "Conuersa ergo a domino suo ad seruum suum necessario deficit: conuersa item a seruo suo ad dominum suum necessario proficit."

119. See Martine Dulaey, *Le rêve dans la vie et la pensée de saint Augustin* (Paris: Institut d'Études Augustiniennes, 1973), 102–5.

120. *De Mus.*, 6.4.7: "At ejus forma in anima fit, hujus autem, quam nunc uidemus, in corpore facta est."

121. Ibid.: "Quare cum et uerum falso et anima corpore melior sit, uerum in corpore melius est quam falsum in anima."

122. Augustine's example of impropriety is a man dressed in a woman's clothing; but this is improper by convention, not reality, since the clothes, although inappropriate, are recognized to be what they are. This example parallels other situations in which the senses are fooled by appearances.

123. *De Mus.*, 6.4.7: "Quid numeros numeris, et facientes factis, non corpus animae praeponimus."

124. Ibid.: "Anima uero istis quae per corpus accipit, carendo fit melior, cum sese auertit a carnalibus sensibus, et diuinis Sapientiae numeris reformatur." The argument is extended at *De Civ. Dei*, 14.23 in the discussion of human sexuality, where it is proposed that when the soul is in opposition to itself, it can, so to speak, be conquered by itself.

125. Augustine comments at length on this statement in *De Lib. Arbit.*, and at *De Gen. ad Litt.*, 1.21.32 and 1.22.38, where the notion of the parts and the whole is put in a hermeneutic context.

126. *De Mus.*, 6.5.8: "Diligenter considerandum est utrum reuera nihil sit aliud quod dicitur audire, nisi aliquid a corpore in anima fieri."

127. The student, possibly mindful of the conclusion reached at 1.13.28, is now unclear on the relation between the body's and the soul's rhythms, and for this reason asks what takes place when something is heard.

128. On the translation of *facientis*, earlier views are summarized in Jacobsson, p. 27n12, including the alternative translation "in the intention of the creator" suggested by F.-J. Thonnard, *De Musica, Bibliothèque Augustinienne*, vol. 7 p. 517n 78; cf., Sofia Vanni Rovighi, "La fenomenologia della sensazione in Sant'Agostino," *Rivista di Filosofia Neo-Scolastica* 54 (1962), 24n 9. Although the translation of *faciens* as "doer" or "agent" is correct, there is a relationship between the desire of the soul to ascend toward God and the desire of God for the soul to move upward, which is suggested in the next sentence by the phrase *tamquam subiecto diuinitus dominationi suae*. Augustine's thinking about this relationship is better expressed in *De Lib. Arbit.*, books 1 and 3.

129. *De Mus.*, 6.5.9: "Corporalia ergo, quaecumque huic corpori ingeruntur aut obiciuntur extrinsecus, non in anima, sed in ipso corpore aliquid faciunt, quod operi ejus aut aduersetur aut congruat."

130. Summarizing 6.5.9. In the final sentences, Augustine speaks of the soul's needs, so to speak, its hunger or thirst, as at *De Beata Vita*, 2.7–8, as well as illness brought on by excess.

131. *De Mus.*, 6.5.10: "Uidetur mihi anima, cum sentit in corpore, non ab illo aliquid pati sed in eius passionibus adtentius agere, et has actiones, siue faciles propter conuenientiam siue difficiles propter inconuenientiam, non eam latere, et hoc totum est quod sentire dicitur."

132. Ibid., 6.5.10.

133. Ibid., 6.5.11: "Animam illam, quae ante istum sonum uitali motu in silentio corpus aurium uegetabat."

134. Ibid., 6.5.12: "Cum autem ab eisdem suis operationibus aliquid patitur, a se ipsa patitur, non a corpore, sed plane cum se adcommodat corpori, et ideo apud se ipsam minus est, quia corpus semper minus quam ipsa est."

135. Ibid., 6.6.16: "Vegetabat quomodo eos ab illis discernis, quos in actu esse animaduertimus, etiam cum in silentio non recordans agit aliquid anima per temporalia spatia numerosum." The student adds that rhythms that exist in silence seem to be freer than those associated with the soul's movement toward the body or those that arise in the body's passions, but he does not say why. The answer may lie in the notion of *otium liberum intrinsecum* (6.5.14).

136. Cf. *occursio*, which means "encountering" or "meeting" in medieval Latin; R. E. Latham, *Revised Medieval Latin Word-List from British and Irish Sources* (London: British Academy, 1965).

137. The terms *progressor* and *occursor* seem to have been coined by Augustine respectively from the verbs *progredior* (to advance) and *occursare* (to meet).

138. *De Mus.*, 6.4.5. In the second scheme the bottom and top levels thus remain the same, as does the role of memory, while variants are introduced at the intermediary levels, which, in the later scheme, give greater weight to what might be called the sending and receiving of

signals (i.e., *progressores* and *occursores numeri*). This change is consistent with Augustine's shift in interest from the text to the reader/recipient.

139. *De Mus.*, 6.7.17: "Et dic mihi, quinam istorum inmortales tibi uideantur. An omnes suis temporibus labi atque occidere aestimas."

140. I take as an example the second in the list of meters at 2.8.15.

141. *De Mus.*, 6.7.17: "Dic ergo, cum aliquanto conreptius siue productius, dum seruiam temporum legi qua simplo ad duplum pedes conueniunt, uersum pronuntio, num offendo ulla fraude iudicium sensus tui?" The problem is introduced at 2.2.2.

142. *De Mus.*, 6.7.17: "Adparet hos igitur mora temporum, qui iudicando praesident, non teneri."

143. Ibid., 6.7.17–18, where the example used by the master to illustrate the point is to think of the two different readings of iambic feet along the lines of two people walking, one at double the pace of the other. The two walkers are presumably walking in single and double rhythm respectively, beginning at a single point in time that is arbitrarily chosen, like the starting point of a race. One has to imagine a reader reciting a single syllable while the two are in motion at speeds whose ratio is $A = 1$, $B = 2 \times 1$. The discussion recalls the suggestion of beating out the time at 1.1.1 and anticipates *Conf.*, 11.27–28, offering, in fact, connections that are omitted from this account.

144. Ibid., 6.7.19: " nisi quia unicuique animanti in genere proprio, proportione uniuersatis, sensus locorum temporumque tributus est."

145. Ibid.: "Sic habendo omnia magnus est hic mundus, qui saepe in scripturis divinis caeli et terrae nomine nuncupatur ." The phrase *magnus est . . .* anticipates *Conf.*, 1.1.1, "Magnus es, domine," both possibly drawing on Ps. 47:2, 95: 4, and here especially 144:3: "Magnus Dominus, et laudabilis nimis; et magnitudinis ejus non est finis," etc.

146. *De Mus.*, 6.7.19–6.8.20: "Quapropter, si humanae naturae ad carnalis uitae actiones talis sensus tributus est, quo maiora spatia temporum iudicare non possit, quam interualla postulant ad talia uitae usum pertinentia, quoniam talis hominis natura mortalis est, etiam talem sensum mortalem puto . . . . Sed quoquo modo sese habeant hi numeri iudiciales, eo certe praestant, quod dubitamus, uel difficile peruesitigamus utrum mortales sint."

147. Ibid., 6.7.19. The neologism, *affabricata*, presumably from *affaber* or *adfaber*, incorporates the notion of ingenious, contrived, or artificial fabrication into the concept of habit—a novel term for a novel idea.

148. This negative conception of habit contrasts with the positive view, concerning the playing of an instrument, at *De Mus.*, 1.4.8.

149. *De Mus.*, 6.8.20: "Nam et illi progressores, cum aliquam in corpore numerosam operationem adpetunt, latente istorum nutu modificantur."

150. Ibid., 6.8.21: "Numerus namque iste interuallis temporum constat et, nisi adiuuemur in eo memoria, iudicari a nobis nullo pacto potest."

151. An apt description of Trygetius, as observed by Monica, at *De Beata Vita*, 2.7, as well as, perhaps, an echo of the problem of anamnesis.

152. *De Mus.*, 6.8.21: "sed quia intentione in aliud subinde exstinguitur motionis inpetus, qui si maneret, in memoria utique maneret, ut nos et inueniremus et sentiremus audisse."

153. The experiment is repeated at *Conf.*, 11.27.35–36 using two lines of verse.

154. *De Mus.*, 6.8.21: "Quapropter iudiciales illi numeri, qui numeros in intervallis temporum sitos—exceptis progressoribus quibus etiam ipsum progressum modificant—iudicare non possunt, nisi quos eis tamquam ministra memoria obtulerit."

155. Ibid., 6.8.22: "Quid enim aliud agimus, cum reuocamus nos in memoriam, nisi quodam modo quod reposuimus quaerimus? Recurrit autem in cogitationem occasione similium motus animi non exstinctus, et haec est, quae dicitur recordatio."

156. Another reason that Augustine advances concerns the freshness of the memories in question. When we recall something, he argues, we feel that the motion taking place in our minds arose at some moment in the past. It is this pastness, as present in our thoughts, that is the subject of recognition. In comparing the present and the past, our more recent motions will be more familiar than those that are deep-seated.

157. *De Mus.*, 6.9.23. I have added the *numeri sonores*, which are understood here but not specifically mentioned until 6.9.24: "quibus cum addideris corporales illos quos sonantes uocauimus." In the end, the master states, our judgment is influenced, if not reinforced, by other, more hidden harmonies, which he does not specify. This recalls aspects of the *quintum genus*, 6.4.5–6.

158. Ibid., 6.9.23, referring to 6.8.22 on memory.

159. Ibid., 6.9.24: "Nos ergo in istis generibus numerandis et distinguendis unius naturae, id est animae motus adfectionesque dispicimus."

160. The master repeats what the student has already said; 1.3.4: "Amo quidem rixas verborum praeterire atque contemnere." Cf. 1.12.26.

161. Ibid., 6.9.24: "Recte etiam uideri potest ratio, quae huic delectationi superinponitur, nullo modo sine quibusdam numeris uiuacioribus de numeris quos infra se habet posse iudicare." The principle by which that which judges is superior to that which is judged is mentioned *inter alia* at *De Vera Religione*, 29.53, ff., and *De Lib. Arbit.*, 2.3.7–8. Cf. Plotinus, *Enn.*, 1.4.2.23.

162. I.e., *numeri sonantes*; 6.4.7.

163. Cf. *De Mag.*, 11 ff., where the view that language communicates through sound is rejected in favor of instruction from within.

164. Ibid., 6.10.27: "Cur in silentiorum interuallis nulla fraude sensus offenditur, nisi quia eidem iuri aequalitis, etiamsi non sono, spatio tamen temporis, quod debetur, exsoluitur?"

165. Ibid., 6.11.30: "Quoniam si quis, uerbi gratia, in amplissimarum pulcherrimarumque aedium uno aliquo angulo tamquam statua conlocetur, pulchritudinem illius fabricae sentire non poterit, cuius et ipse pars erit."

166. Ibid.: "Et in quolibet poemate si quanto spatio syllabae sonant, tanto uiuerent atque sentirent, nullo modo illa numerositas et contexti operis pulchritudo eis placeret, quam totam perspicere atque adprobare non possent, cum de ipsis singulis praetereuntibus fabricata esset atque perfecta."

167. Ibid., 6.11.31: "quos omnes inpetus suos eadem anima excipiens, quasi multiplicat in se ipsa et recordabiles facit, quae uis eius memoria dicitur, magnum quoddam adiutorium in huius uitae negotiosissimis actibus."

168. Ibid., 6.11.32: "quas [phantasias] pro cognitis habere atque pro pro certis opinationis est, constituta ipso erroris introitu."

169. Ibid.: "Horum primum phantasia est, alterum phantasma. Illud in memoria inuenio, hoc in motu animi qui ex iis ortus est quos habet memoria."

170. As noted, Augustine's normal example of *phantasia* and *phantasma* is the mental picture that he has of two cities, Carthage and Alexandria, since he has seen the former but not the latter; cf. *De Trin.*, 8.6. Here the example is his father, whom he has seen, and his grandfather,

whom he has never seen; 6.11.32. The phrase *imagines imaginum* is paralleled in *De Mag.*, 4.7 by signs that are shown on behalf of signs (*signa signis monstrari*).

171. *De Mus.*, 6.11.32: "Quod autem ex eo quod uidi facio, memoria facio, et tamen aliud est in memoria inuenire phantasiam, aliud de memoria facere phantasma."

172. Ibid., 6.11.32: "Quae omnia uis animae potest. Sed uero etiam phantasmata habere pro cognitis summus error est."

173. Ibid., 6.11.33: "Talis enim delectatio uehementer infigit memoriae quod trahit a lubricis sensibus . . . . Sed in spiritalia mente suspensa atque ibi fixa et manente, etiam huius impetus consuetudinis frangitur et paulatim repressus exstinguitur."

174. Ibid., 6.12.35: "Consentiendum est ergo ab aliquibus manentibus numeris praetereuntes aliquos fabricari?"

175. Ibid.: "Quid? si eum quisquam interrogando conmemoret remigrare ad eum putas illos numeros ab eo ipso, qui interrogat; an illum intrinsecus apud mentem suam movere se ad aliquid, unde sibi quod amiserat redhibeatur?" The statement recalls classical reminiscence, as well as teaching from within as described at the end of *De Mag.*

176. Augustine doubtless has in mind the contrast between the grammatical and mathematical understanding of meter at 2.1.1, 3.1.1, and especially 5.1.1.

177. Ibid., 6.12.35: "Quo igitur se etiam istum moturum putas, ut menti eius inprimantur hi numeri, et illam faciant adfectionem, quae ars dicitur?"

178. Ibid.: "Eo modo etiam istum arbitror apud semet ipsum agere, ut ea quae interrogatur, uera esse intellegat atque respondeat."

179. Cf. *De Lib. Arbit.*, 2.8.21.

180. *De Mus.*, 6.12.36: "Vnde ergo credendum est animae tribui quod aeternum est et incommutabile, nisi ab uno aeterno et incommutabili Deo?"

181. Ibid.: "Illud nonne manifestum est eum qui alio interrogante sese intus ad Deum mouet, ut uerum incommutabile intellegat, nisi eundem motum suum memoria teneat, non posse ad intuendum illud uerum, nullo extrinsecus admonente reuocari?"

182. The master proposes that the mind could only turn in three directions, toward something equal, superior, or inferior. But, as there is nothing equal or superior to eternal laws, the third option must be correct.

183. Ibid., 6.13.39: "Amor igitur agendi aduersus succedentes passiones corporis sui, auertit animam a contemplatione aeternorum, sensibilis uoluptatis cura eius auocans intentionem."

184. Ibid. It is interesting to note that, from the perspective of the soul, it is *numeri occursores* that commence reception, whereas, when speaking of the senses earlier in book 6, Augustine begins with the *numeri sonantes*, which are here transformed into *numeri sensuales*. He later notes that it is accurate to call them *sensuales*, since it is by means of *sensibilia signa* that souls act on each other; 6.13.41–42.

185. Ibid., 6.13.40: "Generalis uero amor actionis, quae auertit a uero, a superbia proficiscitur, quo uitio Deum imitari quam Deo seruire maluit anima." The master supports his statement with two quotations from Ecclesiasticus, 10:14–15 and 10: 9–10. The order in which these quotations appear is reversed, and in each case only a part of the original is presented. This results in a single strong statement on the consequences of pride for the soul's equilibrium, which can be translated as follows: "Justly it is written in the holy books," "The beginning of human pride is to desert the Lord " and "The beginning of every sin is pride." And the nature of pride could not be better demonstrated than in the accompanying statement, "How else can one take pride in earth and ashes . . . , but by living a life in which [the soul] projects

outwards its inmost being." The implied subject of "quoniam in vita sua proiecit intima sua" is *rex insipiens* (10:3), which Augustine replaces silently with *anima* from the previous sentence in 6.13.40, omitting the rest of Eccli. 10:10. The emphasis is thereby placed on self-mastery.

CHAPTER 6. LOSS AND RECOVERY

1. The popularity of nonbiological medicine rose considerably in the 1990s; see David M. Eisenberg et al., "Unconventional Medicine in the United States," *New England Journal of Medicine* 328 (1993): 246–52.

2. For a brilliant account of the possibilities of mind-body practices, see Jon Kabat-Zinn, *Wherever You Go, There You Are: Mindfulness Meditation in Everyday Life* (New York: Hyperion, 1994); for a recent review of the scientific literature in one area, see Richard J. Davidson with Sharon Begley, *The Emotional Life of Your Brain* (New York: Hudson Street Press, 2012).

3. For a strong criticism of these dualisms, see Antonio Damasio, *Descartes's Error: Emotion, Reason, and the Human Brain* (New York: Putnam, 1994).

4. On this topic in ancient philosophy, see Pierre Hadot, *Philosophy as a Way of Life*, 49–125.

5. Often noted; see Frederic M. Luskin et al., "A Review of Mind-Body Therapies in the Treatment of Cardiovascular Disease," *Alternative Therapies* (1998): 4, 46.

6. See Herbert Benson, M.D., with Miriam Z. Klipper, *The Relaxation Response* (New York: William Morrow, 1975), esp. chap. 5.

7. Especially in cancer research; see A. J. Cunningham et al., "A Randomized Controlled Trial of the Effects of Group Psychological Therapy on Survival in Women with Metastatic Breast Cancer," *Psycho-Oncology* 7, 6 (1998): 508–17.

8. For a recent review, see Victoria Menzies and Ann Gill Taylor, "The Idea of Imagination: An Analysis of 'Imagery,'" *Advances* 20, 4 (2004); an earlier, more specialized account is Elizabeth A. Brett and Robert Ostroff, "Imagery and Posttraumatic Stress Disorder: An Overview," *American Journal of Psychiatry* 142, 4 (1985): 417–24.

9. See Dean Ornish et al., "Intensive Lifestyle Changes for Reversal of Coronary Heart Disease," *Journal of the American Medical Association* 280 (1998): 2001–7; on more general applications for Buddhist mindfulness meditation, see Jon Kabat-Zinn, *Full Catastrophe Living: Using the Wisdom of Your Body and Mind to Face Stress, Pain, and Illness* (New York: Delta, 1991) and *Wherever You Go, There You Are.*

10. See Kevin J. Tracey, "The Inflammatory Reflex," *Nature* 420 (2002): 853–89.

11. See Jerome Sarris, "Mind-Body Medicine for Schizophrenia and Psychotic Disorders. A Review of the Evidence," *Clinical Schizophrenia and Related Psychoses* 7, 3 (2013): 138–48.

12. See Therese Schroeder-Sheker, *Transitus: A Blessed Death in the Modern World* (Missoula, Mont.: St. Dunstan's Press, 2001).

13. See Daniel Goleman, *Emotional Intelligence* (New York: Bantam, 1995).

14. Among numerous contributions see Sundar Ramaswami and Anees A. Sheikh, "Meditation East and West," and Anees A. Sheikh, Robert G. Kunzendorf, and Katharina S. Sheikh, "Healing Images: From Ancient Wisdom to Modern Science," in *Eastern and Western Approaches to Healing: Ancient Wisdom and Modern Knowledge*, ed. Anees A. Sheikh and Katharina S. Sheikh (New York: Wiley, 1998), respectively 427–69 and 470–515.

15. An early and authoritative article on the subject is Henry K. Beecher, "The Powerful Placebo," *Journal of the American Medical Association* 159 (1955): 1594–1602.

16. See Matthew D. Liberman et al., "The Neural Correlates of Placebo Effects: A Disruption Account," *NeuroImage* 22 (2004): 447–55.

17. On this topic, see the enduring contribution of Pedro Laín Entralgo, *Doctor and Patient*, trans. F. Parridge (New York: McGraw-Hill, 1969).

18. A point emphasized in a number of historical surveys; see, for instance, *The Church and Healing*, ed. W. J. Shiel (Oxford: Blackwell, 1982); Pedro Laín Entralgo, *Mind and Body: A Short History of the Evolution of Medical Thought* (New York: Kennedy, 1956).

19. Heinrich von Staden, "'In a pure and holy way': Personal and Professional Conduct in the Hippocratic Oath?" *Journal of the History of Medicine and Allied Sciences* 51 (1996): 412; cf. 416–17; cf. von Staden, "Character and Competence: Personal and Professional Conduct in Greek Medicine," in *Médecine et moral dans l'antiquité*, ed. Hellmut Flashar and J. Jouanna, Entretiens sur l'Antiquité Classque 43 (Vandœuvres-Génève, 1997), 157–95.

20. von Staden, "In a pure and holy way," 431–32. On the possible debt of the *Oath* to Pythagoreanism, see Ludwig Edelstein, "The Hippocratic Oath: Text, Translation, and Interpretation," in *Ancient Medicine: Selected Papers of Ludwig Edelstein*, ed. Oswei Temkin and C. Lilian Temkin, trans. C. Lilian Temkin (Baltimore: Johns Hopkins University Press, 1967), 17–49; 58–61; cf. Edelstein, "The Relation of Ancient Philosophy to Medicine," in *Ancient Medicine*, 349–66.

21. On these questions, see Edelstein, "The Hippocratic Physician," in *Ancient Medicine*, 87–110.

22. See Edelstein, "The History of Anatomy in Antiquity," in *Ancient Medicine*, 271–73, 294–96.

23. L. D. Hankoff, "Religious Healing in First-Century Christianity," *Journal of Psychohistory* 19, 4 (1992): 388; see also R. Hengel and M. Hengel, "Die Heilungen Jesu und medizinisches Denken," in *Der Wunderbegriff im neuen Testament*, ed. A. Suhl (Darmstadt: Wissenschaftliche Buchgesellschaft, 1980), 338–73.

24. See Darrel W. Amundsen and Gary B. Ferngren, "The Perception of Disease and Disease Causality in the New Testament," *Aufstieg und Niedergang der Römischen Welt* II, 37, 3 (1996): 2934–56.

25. On this topic, see, for example, in general, Jürgen Helm, "Sickness in Early Christian Healing Narratives: Medical, Religious, and Social Aspects," in *From Athens to Jerusalem: Medicine in Hellenized Jewish Lore and Early Christian Literature*, ed. Samuel Kottek, Manfred Horstmanshoff, and Gerhard Baader (Rotterdam: Erasmus. 2000), 241–58; Stephen d'Irsay, "Christian Medicine and Science in the Third Century," *Journal of Religion* 10 (1930): 515–44; Michael Dörnemann, *Krankheit und Heilung in der Theologie der frühen Kirchenvater*, Studien und Texte zu Antike und Christentum 20 (Tübingen: Mohr Siebeck, 2003); and for a general review, see Darrel W. Amundsen, *Medicine, Society, and Faith in the Ancient and Medieval Worlds* (Baltimore: Johns Hopkins University Press, 1996), 127–57. Specific studies include G. Rialdi, *La medicina nella dottrina Tertulliano*, Scientia Veterum 126 (Pisa: Casa Editrice Giardini, 1968); J. Courtès, "Augustin et la médecine," in *Augustinus Magister* (Paris: Institut d'Études Augustiniennes, 1954–55), I, 43–51.

26. See H. J. Magoulis, "The Lives of the Saints as Sources of Data for the History of Byzantine Medicine in the Sixth and Seventh Centuries," *Byzantinische Zeitschrift* 57 (1964): 127–50; Peregrine Horden, "Saints and Doctors in the Early Byzantine Empire: The Case of

Theodore of Sykeon," in *The Church and Healing*, ed. W. J. Shiels, Ecclesiastical History Society (Oxford: Blackwell, 1982), 1–13; and Susan Ashbrook Harvey, "Physicians and Ascetics in John of Ephesus: An Expedient Alliance," in *Symposium on Byzantine Medicine*, ed. John Scarborough, Dumbarton Oaks Paper 38 (1984), 87–93.

27. See Oleg Voskoboynikov, "Thérapie du corps et thérapie de l'âme à la cour frédéricienne," in *Terapie et guarigioni*, ed. Agostino Paravicini Bagliani, Edizione Nazionale "La Scuola Medica Salernitana" (Florence: Sismel: Edizione del Galluzzo, 2010), 272–81.

28. This was a legacy dating from the early Christian period; for a recent review, see Gary B. Ferngren, *Medicine and Health Care in Early Christianity* (Baltimore: Johns Hopkins University Press, 2009); on religion and healing, chap. 4, 64–85.

29. Keith Thomas, *Religion and the Decline of Magic* (Harmondsworth: Penguin, 1973), 16–17.

30. With the exception of pharmacology; see Nicholas Everett, *The Alphabet of Galen: Pharmacy from Antiquity to the Middle Ages* (Toronto: University of Toronto Press, 2012).

31. Gregory the Great, *Ep.* 9; *CCSL*, vol. 140a, p. 768; cf. *Ep.* 11; 140a, pp. 873 ff.

32. Bibliography is collected in Adrian Johns, *The Nature of the Book: Print and Knowledge in the Making* (Chicago: University of Chicago Press, 1998).

33. See Jane Geddes, *The St Albans Psalter: A Book for Christina of Markyate* (London: British Library, 2005), 93–104.

34. On Hugh, see Franklin T. Harkins, *Reading and the Work of Restoration: History and Scripture in the Theology of Hugh of St. Victor*; on Petrarch, see my Jerusalem Lectures, *Ethics Through Literature: Ascetic and Aesthetic Reading in Western Culture*, 93–139, and on a related theme Gur Zak, *Writing from Exile: Petrarch's Humanism and the Ethics of Care of the Self* (Cambridge: Cambridge University Press, 2008).

35. See Dale A. Matthews, "Religion and Spirituality in Primary Care," *Mind/Body Medicine* 2 (1997), 9; see also D. B. Larson and S. S. Larson, *The Forgotten Factor in Physical and Mental Health: What Does the Research Show?* (Rockland, Md.: National Institute for Healthcare Research, 1994).

36. On this thesis, see Antonio Damasio, *Descartes' Error: Emotion, Reason, and the Human Brain*.

37. Jean Leclercq, "Spiritualitas," *Studi medievali* 3 (1962): 280.

38. See, for instance, Rom 7:14, Gal. 6:1, I Cor. 2:15; also Tertullian, *Adversus Marcionem* 4.20; *CCSL*, vol. 1 (Turnhout: Brepols, 1954), 594–97.

39. Isocrates, *Busiris*, c. 24; for text and translation see *Isocrates*, trans. Larue van Hook, vol. 3 (Cambridge, Mass.: Harvard University Press, 1954), 115.

40. Xenophon, *Cyropaedia*, 1.5.11; for text and translation see Walter Miller, trans., *Xenophon*, vol. 5 (Cambridge, Mass.: Harvard University Press), 83.

41. Examples from Plato include *Phaedo* 269d, *Republic* 374b, and *Meno* 70a.

42. See *Historia Monachorum*, ed. Eva Schulz-Flügel (Berlin: de Gruyter, 1990), Index, *s.u. exercitium*.

43. Isidore of Seville, *Etymologiae*, 15.2.30; *Patrologia Latina* 82.539A; cf. Servius, *In Virgilii Aeneidos lib.IV commentarii*, verse 171; ed. G. Thilo (Leipzig: Teubner, 1881), 494–95.

44. On this topic, see Gerald Epstein, "Hebraic Medicine," *Advances* 4 (1987): 56–66.

45. Jean Leclercq, *The Love of Learning and the Desire for God*, 24–26.

46. Celsus, *De Medicina*, 1.2.6; for text and translation, see W. G. Spence, trans. *Celsus*, vol. 1 (Cambridge, Mass.: Harvard University Press), 46; cf. *De Medicina*, 1.7.1, 1.8.1.

47. *Regula Benedictina*, c. 52.2; *Patrologia Latina*, 66.747–48.

48. Johann Huizinga, *Erasmus and the Age of the Reformation* (New York: Harper, 1957), 3–4.

49. The classic account of this subject is Caroline Walker Bynum, *Holy Feast and Holy Fast: The Religious Significance of Food to Medieval Women* (Berkeley: University of California Press, 1987).

50. Thomas Merton, *Contemplative Prayer* (New York: Herder and Herder, 1969), 39.

51. Alastair J. Cunningham, *The Healing Journey: Overcoming the Crisis of Cancer* (Toronto: Key Porter, 1992). On this topic, see also Cheryl Mattingly, *Healing Dramas and Clinical Plots: The Narrative Structure of Experience* (Cambridge: Cambridge University Press, 1998).

52. On this topic, an early discussion of value is Pedro Laín Entralgo, *Mind and Body: Psychosomatic Pathology* (New York: Kennedy, 1956), 64, 70.

53. See Wolf von Siebenthal, *Krankheit als Folge der Sünde: eine medezin-historische Untersuchung* (Hanover: Schmorl and Von Seefeld, 1950). It is worth noting that the miracles, which form an important part of the narrative in the Gospels of Matthew and Mark, are deemphasized in Luke.

54. For a review of the contemporary use of these methods, see Dale A. Matthews, "Religion and Spirituality in Primary Care," *Mind/Body Medicine* 2 (1997): 13.

55. See Aviad M. Kleinberg, *Prophets in Their Own Country: Living Saints and the Making of Sainthood in the Later Middle Ages* (Chicago: University of Chicago Press, 1992).

56. *Vita Procli*, trans. K. S. Guthrie, ed. D. R. Fideler (Grand Rapids, Mich.: Phanes, 1986).

57. For the Greek text, see André-Jean Festugière, *Vie de Théodore de Sykéôn* (Brussels: Société des Bollandistes, 1970); on the life, see Horden, "Saints and Doctors in the Early Byzantine Empire: The Case of Theodore of Sykeon," in *The Church and Healing*, vol. 1, 1–13.

58. Giles Constable, *The Reformation of the Twelfth Century* (Cambridge: Cambridge University Press, 1996), 266.

59. Quoted in Lawrence J. LeShan, *Cancer as a Turning-Point: A Handbook for People with Cancer, Their Families, and Health Professionals* (New York: Dutton, 1989), 10.

ACKNOWLEDGMENTS

During the period in which the essays in this volume were written a number of colleagues and friends have kindly offered me their advice on the material in the individual papers as well as on the organization of the book as a whole. I should like to thank Isabelle Bochet, the late Ralph Cohen, Édouard Jeauneau, Ilsetraut Hadot, the late Pierre Hadot, Brad Inwood, Maruja Jackman, Aviad Kleinberg, the late Goulven Madec, John Magee, Carlo Ossola, Willemien Otten, James C. Paupst, M.D., and Harald Weinrich.

I wish to express my gratitude to the Collège de France, the Fondation Maison des Sciences de l'Homme, Paris, the Institut d'Études Avancées de Paris, and the Institut d'Études Augustiniennes for the support of my research over many years. I owe a special debt to the Maison Suger, FMSH, Paris, and to its director, Jean-Luc Lory, as well as to his capable associates, especially Mme. Nadia Cheniour. I have been assisted by the technical staff at Victoria College, University of Toronto, the Reference and Research Unit, Gerstein Science and Information Centre, University of Toronto Libraries, and Manda Vrkljan in the John Kelly Library, St. Michael's College, University of Toronto. I have for many years profited from the the bibliographical skills of William Edwards in the library of the Pontifical Institute of Mediaeval Studies, Toronto. Two other institutions whose support I acknowledge are the American Academy in Rome, whose hospitality I have enjoyed on more than one occasion, and the Accademia Nazionale dei Lincei, Rome, without whose financial support neither this volume nor its predecessor, *Augustine's Inner Dialogue*, could have been completed.

Some of the material in this book has appeared in an earlier form in the following publications and lectures:

"Vers un pluralisme interprétatif: Histoire littéraire et histoire de la lecture," in *La pluralité interprétative: Fondements historiques et cognitifs de la notion de point de vue*, ed. Alain Berthoz, Carlo Ossola, and Brian Stock, Conférences du Collège de France (Paris: Collège de France, 2010), 9–25; published in English as "Toward Interpretive Pluralism: Literary History and the History of Reading," *New Literary History* 39 (2008): 389–413.

"The Soliloquy: Transformations of an Ancient Philosophical Technique," in *Augustin philosophe et prédicateur: Hommage à Goulven Madec*, Actes du Colloque International Organisé à Paris les 8 et 9 septembre 2011, ed. Isabelle Bochet, Collection des Études Augustiniennes, Série Antiquité 195 (Paris: Études Augustiniennes, 2012), 315–47; published in French as "Le soliloque: Transformations d'une technique philosophique antique," *Conférence* 39 (2014): 371–472.

"Self, Soliloquy, and Spiritual Exercises in Augustine and Some Later Authors," in the *The Augustinian Moment*, ed. Willemien Otten, *Journal of Religion* 91 (2011): 3–23.

"La cultura letteraria italiana e l'identità europea," in *La cultura letteraria italiana e l'identità europea*, Accademia Nazionale dei Lincei, Atti dei Convegni Lincei 170 (Rome: Accademia Nazionale dei Lincei, 2001), 15–27; published in French as "Le Moyen Âge et l'identité européenne," *Conférence* 15 (2002): 237–55.

"Il dilemma del lettore: Lettura ascetica e lettura estetica nella cultura occidentale," in Accademia Nazionale dei Lincei, Fondo Antonio Feltrinellei, Adunanze Straodinarie per il Conferimento dei Premi A. Feltrinelli, vol. 4, fasc. 7 (Rome: Accademia Nazionale dei Lincei, 2008), 183–95.

"De la réminiscence philosophique à la réminiscence littéraire: *Sero te amavi, pulchritudo* (Augustin, *Conf.*, 10.27.38–10.29.40)," in *Poésie, mémoire, et oubli: Colloque de la Fondation Hugot du Collège de France*, ed. Yves Bonnefoy and Odile Bombarde, La conscience de soi de la poésie, Colloque de 1997 (Turin: Nino Aragno Editore, 2005), 105–20.

"Minds, Bodies, Readers," The A. S. W. Rosenbach Lectures, University of Pennsylvania, 1999," *New Literary History* 37 (2006): 489–501; published in French as "Le corps, l'esprit, et la lecture," *Conférence* 13 (2001): 223–83.

"In Search of a Secular Spirituality," lecture, Conference on Contemplative Practice in Higher Education, Amherst College, 9–11 May 2003.

"Contemplative Traditions in the Humanities and Medicine," lecture, Alpert Medical School and Department of Religion, Brown University, 17 March 2011.

"Western Contemplative Traditions and Higher Education," Master Lecture, Mind and Life Institute. International Symposia for Contemplative Studies, Denver, Colorado, 26–29 April 2012.

Lightning Source UK Ltd.
Milton Keynes UK
UKOW03n2159201216

290484UK00002B/29/P